Developments in Business Law and Policy

By Marc I. Steinberg
Radford Professor of Law
Southern Methodist University

cognella
San Diego, CA

Bassim Hamadeh, Publisher
Christopher Foster, Vice President
Michael Simpson, Vice President of Acquisitions
Jessica Knott, Managing Editor
Stephen Milano, Creative Director
Kevin Fahey, Cognella Marketing Program Manager
Rose Tawy, Acquisitions Editor
Jamie Giganti, Project Editor
Brian Fahey, Licensing Associate

First published in the United States of America in 2012 by University Readers, Inc.

16 15 14 13 12   1 2 3 4 5

Printed in the United States of America

ISBN: 978-1-60927-782-6

cognella™

www.cognella.com 800.200.3908

CONTENTS

ACKNOWLEDGMENTS

THIS HAS BEEN a very enjoyable project for me. This is largely due to my excellent administrative assistant Ms. Jan Spann and to my research assistants. I wish to thank my research assistants—Seth Brown, Lorelee Dodge, Honey Gandhi, Isabela Garcia, Hayden Hooper, Merissa Lowenstein, and Jared Pace—for their input.

This project was supported by the award of a summer research grant from the SMU Dedman School of Law, funded in part by the John C. Biggers Faculty Research Fund. I express my appreciation to the John C. Biggers Faculty Research Fund. Also, I wish to thank our Law School's outstanding Dean, Dean John B. Attanasio, for his strong support.

This book is dedicated with all my love to my wonderful family—my wife Laurie, our children Alex, Avi, and Phillip (Bear)—and our two lively dogs, Popeye and Patsi.

INTRODUCTION

LET'S SUPPOSE YOUR client is an entrepreneur or an investor. She decides to go into business—perhaps by herself, with her brother, or a group of acquaintances. She may do so for many reasons, such as to earn a livelihood, to supplement her main income received from another job, to receive a decent return on her investment, or as a lark because the idea sounds like it will be fun and interesting. Her concept may include any type of business—consulting, home improvements, retail clothing, sporting goods, or the refining of raw materials.

Clearly, she wants to make a good profit. But she also knows that business is filled with risks. If the business goes under, its participants will lose the amount they contributed to the enterprise. What is even more frightening is that their personal assets—such as their individual bank accounts, automobiles and homes—also may be at risk. Understanding these risks from a legal standpoint is key.

Let's review some scenarios to set the stage:

What about the type of business enterprise? Do you advise that your client form a corporation, limited liability company (LLC), or a partnership? If a partnership, should it be general or limited? If a corporation, to what extent are shareholder agreements needed? Or, do you recommend the increasingly popular LLC structure? The answers to these questions are significant. Most importantly, they impact the extent of one's liability and tax exposure.

We will also see that, regardless of the business form chosen, additional steps often should be taken. These include partnership and shareholder agreements, stock transfer restrictions, and participant buy-out provisions. Formal procedures, although seemingly technical, should be followed. The holding of board of director and shareholder meetings, for example, may be crucial to establish that the corporate action was in fact authorized legitimately and is now enforceable against an outside party.

Note that as partners in a partnership, shareholders in a small corporation, or when serving on a governing board, such as the board of directors, the participants may be viewed as fiduciaries, owing one another and the enterprise duties of care and loyalty. These duties at times are vague. But they certainly encompass such notions as care, candor and loyalty. The extent of these duties and their applications will be addressed herein. Given today's litigious climate, a basic understanding of these concepts is necessary for attorneys, entrepreneurs and other business participants. The application of these concepts in the publicly-held corporation setting also will be explored.

As a general matter, at least at the outset of the venture, hopefully the prospective business participants trust one another. Certainly, if suspicion prevails, they should think long and hard about entering into the venture. But even if there is trust at the outset, there still are difficulties. For example, assume that one participant Henry wants to sell his interest in the business to Victor. The other business owners (whether they be partners or stockholders) have problems with Victor. They think he is incompetent. Can they keep Victor out of the business? The answer perhaps is "yes," especially if this contingency was taken care of by agreement among the participants when the business was set up. Of course, without an agreement prior to the controversy arising, risk of hostility and stalemate increases.

Now, let's "put the shoe on the other foot." Your client Ignacio wishes to sell his interest and has found a bona fide purchaser at an attractive price. But his fellow co-owner Sylvia says "no" to the proposed sale. Can Ignacio nonetheless make the transfer? What are his options? As we will see, without an agreement among the participants, the answer to this situation may well depend on the type of business enterprise (e.g., partnership or corporation) formed. And, needless to say, rancor and litigation may ensue.

A last example should suffice for introductory purposes. Suppose that your client earns a comfortable livelihood by working as the manager at the enterprise's clothing boutique. There are two other participants in the venture. Each owns one-third of the business. When your client shows up for work one day, her two co-participants tell her that she is fired, to take a hike, and that she no longer may actively participate in the business (such as by serving as a director or officer). Needless to say, this would not be "good news." Unfortunately, episodes such as this occur frequently. Although bringing a law suit is an alternative, it may be costly and time consuming. Once again, there is need for an agreement at the outset when the parties are getting along—in this case, an employment contract (among other agreements) would have been prudent.

The bottom line is that trusting one's co-participants is vital when embarking on a business venture. Hopefully, the relationship will remain stable and amicable. But it may not. One needs to anticipate this risk and protect his or her assets by written agreement at the very beginning.

The chapters that follow will treat each of the points raised in this preliminary discussion in greater detail. Other issues also will be raised, focusing on such timely subjects as corporate governance, insider trading, shareholder litigation, and government enforcement.

Chapter 1

Focus on "Agency" Principles

Agency is defined as "the fiduciary relationship that arises when one person [a "principal"] manifests assent to another person [an "agent"] that the agent shall act on the principal's behalf and subject to the principal's control, and the agent manifests assent or otherwise consents so to act."[1] Whether an agency relationship arises for a particular transaction depends on the facts and circumstances.[2] Nonetheless, as a general proposition, an agency relationship exists between an employer and an employee, a corporate executive officer and a corporation, a general partner and a partnership, or a lawyer and a client.

For example, professional baseball players are typically considered employees and agents of their respective teams.[3] As such, baseball players, like all other agents, must "act solely for the benefit of the principal in all matters connected with [their] agency."[4] This presented a conundrum for Boston Red Sox first basemen, Doug Mientkiewicz, following the 2004 World Series. As soon as the Red Sox won the Series, Mientkiewicz personally kept the baseball used in the final out of the game.[5] The organization argued that as an agent of the Red Sox, Mientkiewicz was duty-bound to account for all profits arising out of employment which meant returning the keepsake to the team.[6] Mientkiewicz, on the other hand, believed himself to be the rightful owner of the ball (much to the chagrin of "Red Sox Nation" fans and Boston executives) as it was league custom for players to keep balls after games.[7] Nonetheless, after an awkward 18 months of controversy, the ball was given to the Baseball Hall of Fame where it now resides.[8] This case illustrates how the existence of an agency relationship affects rights and duties of both the principal and the agent to one another.

Note moreover that, in many instances, third parties have rights with respect to either the principal or the agent, or both. Issues relating to third parties often focus on whether an agent had the requisite authority to act on behalf of the principal.

An agent must have the requisite authority to bind the principal. Such authority may be implied or express actual authority. If an agent purports to bind its principal without the requisite authority, then the principal is generally not bound by the agent's acts. Nonetheless, an agent's acts may still bind the principal, regardless of a lack of actual authority, if concepts such as apparent authority, estoppel, laches, or ratification apply.[9] Moreover, an agent who exceeds the scope of her actual authority may be subject to liability to her principal as well as to the third party who reasonably relied on the agent's purported authority.[10]

Actual Authority

Actual authority entitles an agent to act on behalf of a principal and to legally bind the principal.[11] The source of actual authority rests in *manifestations* which may be in the form of "written or spoken words or *other conduct*" from the principal to the agent.[12] Based on the principal's manifestations to the agent, the agent must reasonably believe that he is acting in accordance with the principal's directive. An agent's actual authority may be express or implied.[13] For example, an agent is clearly given express actual authority when the principal tells the agent, with written or spoken words, precisely what the agent must accomplish and how to accomplish it on behalf of the principal.[14] On the other hand, an agent's actual authority may be implied from the principal's conduct, the nature of the relationship between the principal and the agent, and the objective to be achieved.[15] Accordingly, based on "manifestations" from the principal to the agent, actual authority entitles an agent to act on its principal's behalf in a manner that the agent reasonably believes the principal desires the agent to act.[16]

The relationship between an officer and a corporation is often characterized as an agency relationship.[17] As such, an officer binds the corporation when she acts with the requisite authority. But, when an officer acts without such authority, a corporation's legal obligations remain unaffected by the officer's acts (assuming the corporation is not otherwise bound due to the presence of apparent authority, estoppel, laches, or ratification).[18] Therefore, it is crucial to ensure that a corporate agent acts with actual authority. A written resolution authorized by the board of directors is the preferable way to bestow actual authority on corporate officers. Directives in writing greatly enhance the enforceability of contracts in determining after-the-fact whether an agent acted with actual authority.[19]

Thus, when acting with actual authority, an agent binds the principal as if the principal had committed the act itself.[20]

APPARENT AUTHORITY

Apparent authority is the agent's power to bind the principal because the principal has caused a third party to reasonably believe that the agent has the requisite authority.[21] Apparent authority is, therefore, derived from a principal's manifestations to a third party rather than (in the case of actual authority) the principal's manifestations to the agent.[22] In fact, an agency relationship need not exist in order for one to act with apparent authority so long as it reasonably appears to a third party based on the principal's manifestations to the third party that an agency relationship does indeed exist. Thus, apparent authority is wrongfully exercised by an agent who exceeds the scope of his actual authority. Or, apparent authority may be wrongfully exercised by one who is not an agent at all, but who reasonably appears to the third party to be an agent.[23] Regardless, one acting with apparent authority binds the principal as if the authority was actual. The rationale lies in the fact that apparent authority focuses on the principal's own manifestations which causes the third party to reasonably believe that the agent has the requisite authority.[24]

Unlike actual authority, apparent authority is exercised wrongfully as to the principal when an agent (or purported agent) exceeds the scope of her actual authority. A principal would still be bound to the third party by the agent's conduct; however, the principal would then have a cause of action against the agent individually.[25] Indeed, depending on the underlying circumstances, an employee who acts with apparent authority may bind the employer even as to the employee's fraudulent, unauthorized acts.[26]

INHERENT AGENCY POWER

Inherent agency power focuses on the *relationship* between the agent and the principal rather than on the principal's manifestations.[27] For example, an executive officer (such as the chief executive officer) of a corporation may bind the corporation to ordinary transactions when acting within the normal course of business even when such officer lacks actual authority.[28] Thus, inherent agency power is generated from the status of the agent.[29] Generally, such authority is limited to those agents considered to customarily have the authority to bind their principals, *e.g.*, chief executive offers, presidents, and other executive officers of corporations.[30]

Estoppel, Laches, and Ratification

A principal may be bound by the conduct of an agent even when the agent acts without either actual or apparent authority. Under some circumstances, a principal may be estopped from asserting that an agent did not act with the requisite authority. Or, the principal may unjustifiably delay objecting to the validity of the transaction while enjoying the benefits therefrom. In other situations, a principal may choose to treat conduct of an agent as if the agent indeed possessed the requisite authority when in fact the agent did not act with actual or apparent authority.[31] Estoppel, laches, and ratification have the effect of binding the principal as if the agent had acted with actual authority.[32]

Estoppel

A principal will be estopped from denying the actions of an agent when it is held responsible for inducing a third party to detrimentally rely on the agent's ostensible authority. Unlike actual or apparent authority, estoppel does not depend on the principal's manifestations. A principal generally must use reasonable care to prevent circumstances that foreseeably could cause a third party to erroneously believe that an agent has the requisite authority, and to correct such a belief once on notice of it.[33] Otherwise, the principal may be estopped from denying the enforceability of the agent's actions.[34]

In addition to the foregoing, estoppel further requires that a third party detrimentally change its position in response to the principal's behavior. Detrimental change signifies that the third party suffer some harm, such as an expenditure of money or suffering of financial loss.[35] In this regard, application of estoppel will be enhanced when the principal retains the benefits of the agent's conduct.[36]

LACHES

The doctrine of laches may be viewed as a specific type of estoppel.[37] Quite plainly, laches is an unreasonable delay that "works to the disadvantage of another party."[38] The doctrine has application beyond agency law, but in practice, laches may preclude a principal from denying the validity of a transaction after too much time has passed.[39] Determining whether such a delay is unreasonable rests on the underlying facts and circumstances.[40] Moreover, "prejudice to the [third party] resulting from delay is an essential element of laches."[41] As an equitable remedy, whether to apply the doctrine of laches is within the sound discretion of the court.[42]

RATIFICATION

Ratification occurs when a principal chooses to treat the conduct of an agent as binding on the principal even though the agent lacked the requisite authority to bind the principal at the time that the agent acted.[43] Adequate disclosure of material facts must be provided to the principal in order for the ratification to be effective.[44] Once properly ratified, the ratification relates back in time as if the agent had acted with actual authority. Hence, ratification has the effect of binding the principal as if the agent had acted with actual authority at the time the agent acted.[45]

Generally, an attorney may act as his client's agent (irrespective of whether the client is an individual or business enterprise).[46] For example, legal counsel may bind a corporate client if the lawyer's acts are authorized, or if such acts are ratified, either implicitly or expressly, by the corporation. In one such case, an attorney entered into a settlement agreement on behalf of his client, a corporation, purporting to settle the products liability claims of scores of plaintiffs.[47] The attorney in fact lacked the requisite authority to bind the corporation to such an agreement.[48] Nonetheless, the court held that the corporation had subsequently ratified the settlement agreement, stating that "when an act is performed for the benefit of another by a person without authority, or by an authorized agent in excess of his authority, the person for whose benefit the act was done may ratify the act."[49] Significantly, ratification may be implied: "Ratification need not be express; it may be inferred from surrounding circumstances, including long-term acquiescence, after notice, to the benefits of an allegedly unauthorized transaction."[50] The court held that the corporate client had ratified the settlement agreement entered into by the attorney because it distributed funds for 128 claims in accordance with the agreement for several months after the corporation acquired notice of the agreement.[51] The court noted that such implied ratification based on long-term acquiescence and the retention of benefits is closely tied to the theory of estoppel.[52] Thus, the corporation's ratification of the settlement agreement also operated to estop it from denying the attorney's authority to enter into the agreement.[53]

RESPONDEAT SUPERIOR

The doctrine of respondeat superior concerns the specific agency relationship between an employer and an employee. Respondeat superior holds that "an employer is vicariously liable for the [misconduct] of an agent or employee acting within the scope of his or her agency or employment, although the principal or employer has not personally committed a wrong."[54] Two issues often arise under respondeat superior: (1) whether an employer/employee relationship existed; and (2) whether the employee acted within the scope of his employment. Regarding the former, "as a general rule, an employer is not responsible for torts committed by its employee when the employee exercises an independent business and is not subject to the immediate direction and control of the employer."[55] Thus, courts must decide if a particular tortfeasor was an employee at the time of the tort or an independent contractor. In this inquiry, courts consider a number of factors but a key criterion "is whether the employer retains the right to control the time, manner and method of executing the work."[56] If so, then the actor is ordinarily deemed an employee, thereby potentially subjecting the employer to liability for the actor's tortious conduct.

However, employers are not vicariously liable for every wrongful act of their employees. Rather, an employee must also be acting within the scope of her employment at the time of the tortious conduct in order for an employer to be liable.[57] In other words, "the injurious act must be incidental to the conduct authorized or it must, to an appreciable extent, further the employer's business."[58] As stated by one court, "the employer is liable for the negligent, willful, malicious or criminal acts of its employees when such acts are committed during the course of employment and in furtherance of the business of the employer; but when the act is committed solely for the benefit of the employee, the employer is not liable to the injured third party."[59] In this respect, some courts interpret "scope of employment" broadly so as to encompass even those acts that violate the employer's direct orders so long as the employee has not departed "from his duties for purely personal reasons."[60] The result of such broad interpretations is the imposition of liability on employers for a wide array of their employee's wrongful acts. This may seem overly harsh. However, the modern rationale justifying respondeat superior is that it is:

> a rule of policy, a deliberate allocation of a risk. The losses caused by the torts of employees, which as a practical matter are sure to occur in the conduct of the employer's enterprise, are placed upon that enterprise itself, as a required cost of doing business. They are placed upon the employer because, having engaged in an enterprise which will, on the basis of all past experience, involve harm to others through the torts of employees, and sought to profit by it, it is just that [the employer], rather than the innocent injured plaintiff, should bear [such costs]; and because [the employer] is better able to absorb them, and to distribute them, through prices, rates or liability insurance, to the public, and so to shift them to society, to the community at large. Added to this is the makeweight argument that an employer who is held strictly liable is under the greatest incentive to be careful in the selection, instruction and supervision of [its] servants, and to take every precaution to see that the enterprise is conducted safely.[61]

Under this rationale, society chooses, via the doctrine of respondeat superior, to hold employers liable for the wrongful acts of their employees committed within the scope of their business because employers should foreseeably expect such wrongful acts to be committed from time to time and are in a better position to distribute the losses caused by those wrongful acts through price adjustments and obtaining liability insurance. Imposing liability based on respondeat superior, therefore, places on employers another cost of doing business.[62]

CONCLUSION

Agency law affects business relationships in various manners. Because an agency relationship defines the relationship of officers and corporations, general partners and partnerships, attorneys and their corporate clients, and employees and their employers, agency law plays an important role in the business arena. The enforceability of day-to-day transactions often depends on whether an agency relationship exists and whether an agent acts with the requisite authority to bind the principal.

NOTES

1. American Law Institute, Restatement (Third) of Agency § 1.01 (2006).
2. See *State ex rel. Medlin v. Little*, 703 N.W.2d 593, 597 (Neb. 2005) ("Whether an agency relationship exists depends on the facts underlying the relationship of the parties irrespective of the words or terminology used by the parties to characterize or describe their relationship.").
3. See Tierney, *A Fielder's Choice: How Agency Law Decides the True Owner of the 2004 Red Sox Final-Out Baseball*, 3 Williamette Sports L. J. 1, 14–15 (2006), *available at* http://www.willamette.edu/wucl/pdf/sportslaw/spring06/tierney.pdf.
4. *Id.* at 15 (quoting Restatement (Second) of Agency § 387).
5. See Tierney, *supra* note 3, at 1.
6. See *id.* at 15–16.
7. See *id.* at 21.
8. See Ulman, *Mientkiewicz Raps Lucchino over 2004 World Series Ball*, available at http://www.usatoday.com/sports/baseball/al/2006-07-18-mientkiewicz-lucchino_x.htm. (July 18, 2006).
9. Restatement (Third) of Agency § 1.01 cmt. c.
10. See *New England Whalers Hockey Club v. Nair*, 474 A.2d 810, 813 (Conn. App. 1984) ("An agent who does an act which his principal could not or did not authorize acts on his own responsibility and may be liable to third persons.").
11. See *Highland Capital Management LP v. Schneider*, 607 F.3d 322, 327 (2d Cir. 2010) ("An agent must have authority, whether apparent, actual or implied, to bind his principal.").
12. Restatement (Third) of Agency § 1.03 (emphasis added).
13. *Id.* at § 2.02.
14. See *In re Harnischfeger Industries, Inc.*, 294 B.R. 47, 55 (Bankr. D. Del. 2003) ("An agent's express actual authority will be found in the contract between the principal and the agent.").
15. See *id.* ("Implied actual authority results when the agent, and not a third party, reasonably believes he has authority based on the principal's actions.").
16. See *Highland Capital Management LP*, 607 F.3d at 327 ("Actual authority is created by direct manifestations from the principal to the agent, and the extent of the agent's actual authority is interpreted in the light of all circumstances attending those manifestations, including the customs of business, the subject matter, any formal agreement between the parties, and the facts of which both parties are aware.").
17. See *Godina v. Resinall International, Inc.*, 677 F. Supp. 2d 560, 570 (D. Conn. 2009) ("Beyond the board of directors, the corporation may validly act through its ... officers as authorized corporate agents. In general, an officer's powers stem from the organic law of the corporation, or a board delegation of authority which may be express or implied."). See also S. Williston, *A Treatise on the Law of Contracts* § 35.69 (R. Lord ed. 4th ed. 2010) ("Whenever, in the usual course of the business of

a corporation, an officer or other agent is held out by the corporation or has been permitted to act for it or manage its affairs in such a way as to justify third persons who deal with him in inferring or assuming that the agent is doing an act or making a contract within the scope of his authority, the corporation is bound, even though such officer or agent does not have actual authority from the corporation to do such an act or make such a contract.").

18. See *Schmidt v. Farm Credit Serv.*, 977 F.2d 511, 514 (10th Cir. 1992) ("The relationship between a corporation and its president is that of principal and agent ... An agent may bind its principal as to a third party when the agent acts under actual authority or when the actions of the principal lead the third party to reasonably believe that such authority exists.").
19. See *Dunham v. Anderson-Dunham, Inc.*, 466 So.2d 1317, 1320–1321 (1st Cir. 1985) ("Actual, express authority of corporate officers stems from statute, articles of incorporation, by-laws, or resolutions of the board of directors.").
20. See *id.* at 1321 (holding that representative of the corporation had the actual authority to bind the corporation based upon a board of director resolution conferring such authority).
21. See *Goldston v. Bandwith Tech. Corp.*, 859 N.Y.S. 2d 651, 654–656 (Sup. Ct. 2008).
22. See *Highland Capital Management LP*, 607 F.3d at 328 ("Where an agent lacks actual authority, he may nonetheless bind his principal to a contract if the principal has created the appearance of authority, leading the other contracting party to reasonably believe that actual authority exists.").
23. See Restatement (Third) of Agency § 2.03 cmt. a.
24. *Id.* at § 2.03 cmt. c.
25. *Id.* at § 8.09 cmt. b.
26. See *Westinghouse Credit Corp. v. Green*, 384 F.2d 298 (10th Cir. 1967) (holding that, under the circumstances of the case, a lender was bound even to the unauthorized, fraudulent acts of its employee).
27. See *Gallant Ins. Co. v. Isaac*, 751 N.E.2d 672, 675 (Ind. 2001) ("[Inherent authority also referred to as inherent agency power] is grounded in neither the principal's conduct toward the agent nor the principal's representation to a third party, but rather in the very status of the agent.").
28. See *American Heritage Banco, Inc. v. Cranston*, 928 N.E.2d 239, 249 n.9 (Ind. App. 2010).
29. See *Gallant Ins. Co.*, 751 N.E.2d at 675.
30. *Id.*
31. Restatement (Third) of Agency § 4.01.
32. See *Frontier Leasing Corp. v. Links Engineering, LLC*, 781 N.W.2d 772, 777 (Iowa 2010) (holding that a principal may be liable for the acts of an agent regardless of whether the agent possessed authority to bind the principal under the doctrine of estoppel or the principle of ratification).
33. See Restatement (Third) of Agency § 2.05 cmt. c.
34. See *id.*
35. *Id.* at § 2.05 cmt. b.

36. See *In re Westec Corp.*, 434 F.2d 195, 200 (5th Cir. 1970) (noting that a principal may be "estopped to assert [an agent's] lack of authority because it continues to enjoy the benefits of the contract").
37. S. Williston, *supra* note 17, at § 79.11 ("Laches is an equitable defense, independent of the statute of limitations, and when any delay becomes inequitable, it may operate as an estoppel against the assertion of a right.").
38. *Schmidt*, 977 F.2d at 516.
39. See *id.* (stating that a principal's assertion against a third party that an agent lacked authority to bind the principal to a particular transaction may be precluded by the doctrine of laches depending "on the circumstances of the particular case").
40. *Id.*
41. *Anderson v. First National Bank of Pine City*, 228 N.W.2d 257, 260 (Minn. 1975) (holding that laches did not establish an agency relationship between husband and wife where, without husband's knowledge, wife entered into a mortgage with a bank and bank "did not alter its position in reliance on its mortgage between the time that [the husband] learned of his wife's conduct and the time of the commencement of the action").
42. See *Wyler Summit Partnership v. Turner Broadcasting System, Inc.*, 235 F.3d 1184, 1193 (9th Cir. 2000) ("Under California law, laches is available as a defense only to claims sounding in equity, not to claims at law.").
43. See *Maxitrol Co. v. Lupke Rice Insurance Agency, Inc.*, 924 N.E.2d 179, 183 (Ind. App. 2010) ("Ratification is the adoption of that which was done for and in the name of another without authority. It is in the nature of a cure for a lack of authorization." [citations omitted]).
44. See *id.* at 184 ("Whenever a principal is sought to be held liable on the ground of ratification, either express or implied, it must be shown that the principal ratified upon full knowledge of all material facts, or that he was willfully ignorant, or purposely refrained from seeking information.").
45. See *id.* at 183 ("When ratification takes place, the transaction stands as an authorized one, and the transaction is good from the beginning.").
46. See *Kulchawik v. Durable Manufacturing Co.*, 864 N.E.2d 744 (Ill. App. 2007).
47. *Id.* at 747.
48. *Id.* at 749.
49. *Id.* at 750.
50. *Id.*
51. *Id.*
52. *Id.* at 751.
53. *Id.*
54. *Baptist Memorial Hosp. Sys. v. Sampson*, 969 S.W.2d 945, 947 (Tex. 1998).
55. *Lopez v. El Palmar Taxi, Inc.*, 676 S.E.2d 460, 463 (Ga. App. 2009).
56. *Id.* at 464.
57. *Barnett v. Clark*, 889 N.E.2d 281, 283 (Ind. 2008).
58. *Id.*

59. *Bremen State Bank v. Harford Acc. & Indem. Co.*, 427 F.2d 425, 428 (7th Cir. 1970).

60. *Wilson v. Drake*, 87 F.3d 1073, 1076–1077 (9th Cir. 1996).

61. *Jennings v. Davis*, 476 F.2d 1271, 1274–1275 (8th Cir. 1973) (quoting W. Prosser, Law of Torts 458-459 (4th ed. 1971)).

62. See *United States v. Romitti*, 363 F.2d 662, 665 (9th Cir. 1966) ("The principal justification for the application of the doctrine of respondeat superior in any case is the fact that the employer may spread the risk through insurance and carry the cost thereof as part of [its] costs of doing business.") (quoting Johnston v. Long, 181 P.2d 645, 651 (Cal. 1947) (per Traynor, CJ).

PRINCIPLES OF AGENCY law continue to arise with regularity. The following two cases—the first decided in 2010 by the United States Court of Appeals for the Second Circuit and the second by the Delaware Supreme Court in 2006—provide good illustrations.

HIGHLAND CAPITAL MANAGEMENT L.P. V. SCHNEIDER
UNITED STATES COURT OF APPEALS
607 F. 3D 322 (SECOND CIRCUIT 2010)

Leval, Circuit Judge:

Defendants Leonard Schneider ("Schneider") and his children, Leslie, Scott, and Susan Schneider (collectively, "Defendants" or "the Schneiders") appeal from the judgment of the United States District Court for the Southern District of New York, which held them liable for damages to Plaintiff Highland Capital Management LP ("Highland") and Counter-Claimant RBC Dominion Securities Corp. ("RBC") (jointly, "Appellees"), pursuant to a jury verdict after trial, in the amount of approximately $40 million for breach of an alleged contract for the sale of promissory notes. Highland claimed to be the third-party beneficiary of an alleged contract by which the *Schneiders, acting through an agent, Glen Rauch Securities ("GRS")*, agreed to sell promissory notes of the McNaughton Apparel Group, Inc. ("McNaughton") at fifty-one percent of their face value to RBC. Appellees contend that, after several weeks of negotiation between Glen Rauch of GRS, acting for the Schneiders, and RBC, they concluded the alleged contract in an unrecorded telephone conversation on March 14, 2001. The Schneiders argue, among other contentions, that there could be no contract because their agent, GRS, had neither actual nor apparent authority to make the alleged contract on their behalf. We agree with the Schneiders that the evidence cannot support a finding that Rauch had either actual or apparent authority to make the contract. ... We therefore remand to the district court with instructions to set aside the verdict and enter judgment in favor of the Schneiders.

Background

This case turns on the events of … March 14. Rauch and Ambrecht [of RBC] had two recorded phone calls that day. Approximately ten minutes after the second recorded call, RBC called Rauch back, in an effort to "pin Mr. Rauch down." This call, unlike the others, was not recorded. … Appellees contend that during the unrecorded call, RBC and Rauch, on behalf of the Schneiders, formed a contract for the sale of the notes at fifty-one [percent of their face value.] … [T]he trial evidence was insufficient to sustain a finding, by a preponderance of the evidence, that Rauch had received authorization from the Schneiders to make the sale, that RBC could have reasonably believed that Rauch had received authorization from the Schneiders to conclude the trade, or that, under the circumstances, RBC could have reasonably interpreted Rauch's words as expressing agreement to sell the notes at fifty-one.

Rauch learned soon after the unrecorded call that the Schneiders had lost interest in selling the notes. On the night of March 14, the Schneiders' attorney, Jim Alterbaum, left a message for Rauch telling him that Alterbaum was "not sure [the] Schneiders want [Rauch] to proceed with phone calls" to RBC and advising Rauch not to "spin his wheel." The Schneiders then told Rauch they had decided to put on hold any sale of the notes. On March 20, Rauch told Ambrecht, "nothing is going happen with the bonds probably for five weeks."

The Schneiders never sold the notes. On April 16, 2001, Jones Apparel Group announced that it would buy McNaughton. On June 19, the notes were paid in full.

This litigation followed, involving claims by RBC and Highland that, during the unrecorded March 14 call between Rauch and RBC's representatives, the Schneiders contracted to sell their McNaughton notes at fifty-one and that they subsequently breached the contract. The Schneiders denied that Rauch had actual authority to make such a sale, that apparent authority for the transaction was ever communicated to the buyers, or that Rauch ever agreed to sell the notes. … The jury found against the Schneiders and awarded damages for breach of contract totaling approximately $40 million to RBC and Highland. The district court denied the Schneiders' motion for judgment as a matter of law ("JMOL") or a new trial, and this appeal followed.

Discussion

Appellees' claims rely on [an alleged] contract between the Schneiders and RBC, which they contend Rauch agreed to on the Schneiders' behalf during the unrecorded phone call of March 14. The evidence would support a finding of such a contract only if it allowed for a reasonable finding that Rauch had actual authority to make the agreement or if RBC relied on his apparent authority to do so. *Merrill Lynch Interfunding, Inc. v. Argenti, 155 F. 3d 113, 122 (2d Cir. 1998)* ("[A]n agent must have authority, whether apparent, actual or implied, to bind his principal."). We conclude that the record contains insufficient evidence to support either finding, or indeed even a finding that Rauch purported to enter a contract without authorization.

I. Actual Authority

Under New York law, an agent has actual authority if the principal has granted the agent the power to enter into contracts on the principal's behalf, subject to whatever limitations the principal places on this power, either explicitly or implicitly. As we have explained:

> Actual authority is created by direct manifestations from the principal to the agent, and the extent of the agent's actual authority is interpreted in the light of all circumstances attending those manifestations, including the customs of business, the subject matter, any formal agreement between the parties, and the facts of which both parties are aware.

...

To conclude that Rauch had actual authority to enter a contract to sell the notes at fifty-one, a jury would have to find that the Schneiders authorized a sale of the notes at that price or that they had authorized Rauch to exercise discretion as to the terms of the sale. Leonard Schneider and Rauch, of course, expressly denied that the Schneiders authorized the sale of the notes at fifty-one, and nothing in the record supports a finding that the Schneiders gave Rauch such authorization. At the time of the last recorded call on March 14, ten minutes prior to the unrecorded call, they had not done so, and Appellees put forward no evidence that the Schneiders gave Rauch any further authorization in the ten intervening minutes. Indeed, it is virtually inconceivable that they would have done so after learning that McNaughton was likely to be acquired and then to pay the notes at their face amount.

Nor does the record contain evidence that Rauch had actual authority to conclude a contract without obtaining the Schneiders' agreement to the terms. The Letter Agreement [between Rauch and RBC that outlined the terms of the negotiations] unequivocally states that "the consummation of any transaction remains in the sole discretion and satisfaction of" the Schneiders and RBC. All the evidence of the behavior of the parties during the course of the negotiations further confirmed that the Schneiders withheld authorization from Rauch to conclude a contract on their behalf without their consent to the terms. Rauch presented firm offers to RBC only after obtaining the Schneiders' permission to do so, and he presented RBC's offers to the Schneiders before responding to [RBC]. There was, therefore, no basis upon which a jury could conclude that Rauch had received actual authorization to enter into a contract without the Schneiders' express agreement to its terms, which he never received.

II. Apparent Authority

Appellees also contend that Rauch had apparent authority to bind the Schneiders to a contract for the sale of the notes at fifty-one. Where an agent lacks actual authority, he may nonetheless bind his principal to a contract if the principal has created the appearance of authority, leading the other contracting party to reasonably believe that actual authority exists. "Apparent authority exists when a principal, either intentionally or by lack of ordinary care, induces [a third party] to believe that an individual has been authorized to act on its behalf." ... A party cannot claim that an agent acted with apparent authority when it "knew, or should have known, that [the agent] was exceeding the scope of its authority." ...

To conclude that Rauch had apparent authority to make the contract, a jury would need to find that the Schneiders induced the reasonable belief by RBC that Rauch made the contract having received the authorization of the Schneiders to do so. No evidence suggests that the Schneiders did anything to induce RBC to believe that Rauch was authorized to enter an agreement without their specific assent to its terms. ...

We conclude that the Schneiders were entitled to judgment as a matter of law. We therefore reverse the judgment in favor of Highland and RBC and remand for entry of judgment in favor of the Schneiders.

IN RE THE WALT DISNEY COMPANY DERIVATIVE LITIGATION
SUPREME COURT OF DELAWARE
906 A.2D 27 (2006)

[This litigation focused on the severance payment of approximately $130 million paid to Disney's President Michael Ovitz pursuant to his employment contract which called for such payment upon termination of Ovitz' employment "without cause." The case raises duty of care and loyalty issues, including that of unduly excessive officer compensation. There is another key issue involved in this case—namely, whether Disney's chief executive officer (CEO) Michael Eisner had the authority to unilaterally terminate Ovitz' employment "without cause," thereby triggering the generous severance package. The following excerpt of the case addresses whether Eisner (as Disney's CEO), under principles of agency law, had the authority to make this significant decision of unilaterally terminating Ovitz' employment without Disney board of director approval. Note that the Delaware Supreme Court held that Eisner had such authority. The court also ruled that there was no breach of duty regarding Ovitz' severance package.]

[At trial,] the Chancellor [who was the judge] determined that although the [Disney] board as constituted upon Ovitz' termination (the "new board") had the authority to terminate Ovitz, neither that board nor the compensation committee was required to act, because Eisner [as CEO of Disney] also had, and properly exercised, that authority. The new board, the Chancellor found, was not required to terminate Ovitz under the company's internal documents. Without such a duty to act, the new board's failure to vote on the termination could not give rise to a breach of the duty of care or the duty to act in good faith. Because those are conclusions of law that rest upon the Chancellor's legal construction of Disney's governing instruments, our review of them is plenary.

Article Tenth of the [Disney] Company's certificate of incorporation in effect at the termination plainly states that:

> The officers of the Corporation shall be chosen in such a manner, shall hold their offices for such terms and shall carry out such duties as are determined solely by the Board of Directors, subject to the right of the Board of Directors to remove any officer or officers at any time with or without cause.

Article IV of Disney's bylaws provided that the Board Chairman/CEO "shall, subject to the provisions of the Bylaws and to the control of the Board of Directors, have general and active management, direction, and supervision over the business of the Corporation and over its officers. ..."

...

The issue is whether the Chancellor's interpretations of these instruments, as giving the [Disney] board [of directors] and the Chairman/CEO concurrent power to terminate a lesser officer, is legally permissible. In two hypothetical cases there would be a clear answer. If the certificate of incorporation vested the power of removal exclusively in the board, then absent an express delegation of authority from the board, the presiding officer would not have a concurrent removal power. If, on the other hand, the governing instruments expressly placed the power of removal in both the board and specified officers, then there would be concurrent removal power. This case does not fall within either hypothetical fact pattern, because Disney's governing instruments do not vest the removal power exclusively in the board, nor do they expressly give the Board Chairman/CEO a concurrent power to remove officers. Read together, the governing instruments do not yield a single, indisputably clear answer, and could reasonably be interpreted either way. For that reason, with respect to this specific issue, the governing instruments are ambiguous.

Where corporate governing instruments are ambiguous, our case law permits a court to determine their meaning by resorting to well-established legal rules of construction, which include the rules governing the interpretation of contracts. One such rule is that where a contract is ambiguous, the court must look to extrinsic evidence to determine which of the reasonable readings the parties intended.

Here, the extrinsic evidence clearly supports the conclusion that the board and Eisner understood that Eisner, as Board Chairman/CEO had concurrent power with the board to terminate Ovitz as President. In that regard, the Chancellor credited the testimony of new board members that Eisner, as Chairman and CEO, was empowered to terminate Ovitz without board approval or intervention; and also [Disney's General Counsel] Litvack's testimony that during his tenure as general counsel, many Company officers were terminated and the board never once took action in connection with their terminations. Because Eisner possessed, and exercised, the power to terminate Ovitz unilaterally, we find that the Chancellor correctly concluded that the new board was not required to act in connection with that termination, and, therefore, the board did not violate any fiduciary duty to act with due care or in good faith.

A Critique of Disney—Disney Goes Goofy

In a coauthored article (with Mathew D. Bivona, *Disney Goes Goofy: Agency, Delegation, and Corporate Governance*, 60 Univ. of California, Hastings Law Journal 201 (2008) (reprinted with permission; all rights reserved)), this author offered the following critique regarding the "agency law aspect" of the Delaware Supreme Court's decision in *Disney*. As will be seen, the court's analysis is disappointing. The excerpt of the article (omitting citations) follows.

> Plaintiffs in the Disney case brought a multitude of claims against the company and its fiduciaries. For the purposes of this [discussion], the foregoing analysis will focus on only one of those claims: Whether Eisner, alone and without Disney board of directors approval, was authorized to terminate Ovitz. The Delaware Supreme Court dedicated only two pages of its forty-eight-page opinion to discussion of this subject,[1] despite the fact that this issue was critical when considering not only plaintiffs' claims, but also the wider implications impacting Delaware corporate governance.

---

1 Brehm v. Eisner (*In re* the Walt Disney Co. Derivative Litig.), 906 A.2d 27, 68–70 (Del. 2006).

Creative Artists and Agency

This brings the analysis to perhaps its most important point: agency. Indeed, having examined the language of Disney's governing documents and the principles of Delaware corporation law, there remains the critical task of discerning Eisner's authority as chief executive officer under the scope of agency law. Remarkably, this issue was never addressed by the Delaware Supreme Court. Under the law of agency, in construing the enforceability of contracts entered into by the corporation at the direction of a high-level corporate officer such as the CEO, numerous courts have relied on principles of actual authority and inherent agency power.[2]

The Restatement (Third) of Agency [§ 201] describes actual authority as "when, at the time of taking action that has legal consequences for the principal, the agent reasonably believes, in accordance with the principal's manifestations to the agent, that the principal wishes the agent so to act."[3] The key examination for actual authority thus rests with the principal's manifestations to the agent. Actual authority may be either "express" or "implied." Generally, "express authority" refers to actual authority that a principal has expressed in a detailed or specific manner.[4] [As set forth in § 2.02 of the Restatement (Third) of Agency,] implied authority generally includes the agent's authority "to take action designated or implied in the principal's manifestations to the agent and acts necessary or incidental to achieving the principal's objectives, as the agent reasonably understands the principal's

---

2 See, e.g., Gumpert v. Bon Ami Co., 251 F.2d 735, 738–739 n.1 (2d Cir. 1958) (questioning whether hiring another corporate officer absent express board delegation is incident to corporate officer's power); Liberty Mut. Ins. Co. v. Enjay Chem. Co. (Now Exxon Corp.), 316 A.2d 219, 222 (Del. Super. Ct. 1974) (identifying three types of authority: express, implied, and apparent); Menard, Inc. v. Dage-MTI, Inc., 726 N.E.2d 1206, 1211 (Ind. 2000) (finding that a company was bound to a contract by the inherent authority of its president); Newberry v. Barth, Inc., 252 N.W.2d 711, 714 (Iowa 1977) (finding that a corporate agent lacked express, implied, apparent, and inherent power to bind the corporation to a real estate transaction).

3 RESTATEMENT (THIRD) OF AGENCY § 2.01 [hereinafter AGENCY THIRD]; *see generally* 3 Am. Jur. 2d *Agency* § 70.

4 AM. JUR. 2D *Agency* § 70; AGENCY THIRD, *supra* note 3, § 2.01 cmt. b; see generally Billops v. Magness Constr. Co., 391 A.2d 196, 197 (Del. 1978).

manifestations and objectives when the agent determines how to act."[5] In both express and implied actual authority, the authority is derived from the relationship between the principal and the agent, based on either manifestations or statements from the principal to the agent.

Query whether Eisner acted with actual authority when terminating Ovitz. In order to have actual authority, the "principal must make a manifestation ... that expresses this willingness" to allow another party to act as its agent.[6] Such authority could come from the certificate of incorporation or the bylaws; however, ... the certificate of incorporation and bylaws [were inconclusive] in conferring concurrent removal power on both Eisner and the board of directors.[7] Thus, Eisner may well have lacked the actual authority to unilaterally fire the president of Disney. If Eisner lacked actual authority, then analysis must focus on whether Eisner possessed any other form of agency power.

In contrast to actual authority, apparent authority involves the reasonable belief held by a third party. Apparent authority has been defined [under § 2.03 of the Restatement (Third) of Agency] as "the power held by an agent or other actor to affect a principal's legal relations with third parties when a third party reasonably believes the actor has authority to act on behalf of the principal and that belief is traceable to the principal's manifestations."[8] Thus, the power of an agent under apparent authority may be determined based upon the manifestations between the principal and the third party. This is because the third party must have a reasonable belief that is "traceable to the principal's manifestations." Apparent authority, therefore, does not require manifestations between the principal and the agent, just

---

5 Agency Third, *supra* note 3, § 2.02; *see generally* Guyer v. Haveg Corp., 205 A.2d 176, 180 (Del. Super. Ct. 1964).

6 Agency Third, *supra* note 3, § 3.01 cmt. b.

7 Assuming the certificate of incorporation properly authorized the CEO to terminate officers unilaterally, the question then arises whether such delegation would be valid as a matter of law. Such an inquiry becomes a matter of *delegation* and *abdication*, rather than a matter of agency. Under Delaware law, the operative inquiry would be whether such delegation removes from the board its duty of oversight so as to violate section 141(a) of the Delaware General Corporation Law. This question is distinct from whether a transaction is "extraordinary" for the purposes of agency power.

8 *Id.* § 2.03; see Billops, 391 A.2d at 198; 3 Am. Jur. 2d *Agency* § 76.

"expressive conduct" between the principal and the third party. [*Id.* at 3.03 cmt. b][9] Indeed, an agent acting solely with apparent authority lacks actual authority.[10] [*Id.* at § 2.03 cmt. b]

Inherent authority is a concept that is somewhat related to apparent authority. The Restatement (Third) of Agency declines to use the term "inherent authority" because it considers such authority to be covered by other doctrines (such as respondeat superior).[11] Despite the Restatement (Third)'s perspective, the doctrine of inherent authority has been analyzed for decades, if not centuries, in U.S. case law.[12] Accordingly, this [discussion] will examine inherent authority as articulated by the Restatement (Second) and the courts. Under [§ 8A of] the Restatement (Second) of Agency, inherent authority refers to the "power of an agent which is derived not from authority, apparent authority or estoppel, but solely from the agency relation and exists for the protection of persons harmed by or dealing with a servant or other agent."[13]

Inherent authority and apparent authority are therefore related concepts. Indeed, inherent authority and apparent authority seem so similar that courts have had difficulty drawing a distinction between the two concepts.[14] This difficulty in application of those two broad principles of agency is one (of the many) reasons why the Restatement (Third) elects to abolish the use of the term "inherent" authority.[15]

---

9 AGENCY THIRD, *supra* note 3, § 3.03 cmt. b; *see generally* Finnegan Constr. Co. v. Robino-Ladd Co., 354 A.2d 142, 144-45 (Del. Super. Ct. 1976).

10 *See* 3 AM. JUR. 2D *Agency* § 75; AGENCY THIRD, *supra* note 3, § 2.03 cmt. b; *see also In re* Mulco Prods., Inc., 123 A.2d 95, 103 (Del. Super. Ct. 1956).

11 See Gregory S. Crespi, *The Proposed Abolition of Inherent Agency Authority by the Restatement (Third) of Agency: An Incomplete Solution*, 45 SANTA CLARA L. REV. 337 (2005); AGENCY THIRD, *supra* note 3, § 2.01 introductory note.

12 *See, e.g., Gumpert*, 251 F.2d at 738-39; Roscoe Co. v. Lewis Univ., Coll. of Law, 398 N.E.2d 1083, 1086 (Ill. App. Ct. 1979) (identifying inherent authority as one of the three ways a principal may be bound by his agent); *Newberry*, 252 N.W.2d at 714; Fidelity & Cas. Co. of N.Y. v. Carroll, 117 N.E. 858 (Ind. 1917) (discussing the agency inherent in certain corporate offices).

13 RESTATEMENT (SECOND) OF AGENCY § 8A (1958); *see also* Menard, Inc. v. Dage-MTI, Inc., 726 N.E.2d 1206, 1211 (Ind. 2000).

14 Crespi, *supra* note 11, at 354.

15 *See id.*; *see also* AGENCY THIRD, *supra* note 3, §§ 1.03, 2.01 introductory note.

Because of the difficulty in separating these two concepts, they will be considered together.

Inherent authority has been found to provide broad powers to an agent based upon the customary authority of the agent. In *Menard, Inc. v. Dage-MTI, Inc.*,[16] [726 N.E. 2d 1206, 1212 (Ind. 2000),] for example, the Indiana Supreme Court found that inherent authority bound a corporation to a contract executed by its president. In *Menard*, the court held that an agent acts with inherent authority when engaging in transactions that usually accompany or are incidental to transactions which that agent is authorized to conduct, provided the third party reasonably believes that the agent is authorized and has no notice to the contrary.[17] In reaching this decision, the court recognized that the president of a corporation is one of the officers through which the corporation normally acts. As a result, the court found that the president's actions were those that "usually accompany or are incidental to transactions [in which he was] authorized to conduct."[18] [*Id.* at 1214]

Generally, the prevailing view is that the "president of a corporation is empowered to transact, without special authorization from the board of directors, all acts of an ordinary nature which are incident to the office by usage or necessity and to thus bind the corporation."[19] [2 A. Fletcher, *Laws of Corporations* § 559 (2001)] Stated conversely, acts which are extraordinary in nature are outside the bounds of an executive's inherent authority. Of course, when courts and treatises refer to the "president" of a corporation, they merely refer to the chief executive, whether that officer is referred to as "president" or "CEO."[20] References to the "president," for the purposes of this discussion, therefore, will not be intended to refer to Ovitz, but rather Eisner, as the CEO of Disney.

---

16 *Menard, Inc. v. Dage-MTI, Inc.*, 726 N.E.2d 1206 (Ind. 2000).

17 *Id.* at 1212.

18 *Id.* (citations and quotations omitted).

19 FLETCHER CYCLOPEDIA OF THE LAW OF CORPORATIONS § 559 (2007). Thus, "the president of a corporation has no apparent authority to bind the corporation to an unusual, extraordinary, or unreasonable contract." *Id.* § 592.

20 *See* 19 C.J.S. Corporations § 553 (2007) ("The president is frequently the chief executive officer of the company and invested with broad general powers of management, and accordingly has many implied powers.")

Under Delaware law, a chief executive officer of a corporation may engage in ordinary[21] acts which are incident to his office, and "by virtue of his office he may enter into a contract and bind his corporation in matters arising from and concerning the usual course of the corporation's business."[22] [156 A. 2d 350, 352 (Del. Sup. Ct. 1931)] These powers inhere to the chief executive as a result of her position as such. [T]hese powers of the chief executive are not without limit under Delaware law.[23] Implicit in this analysis, therefore, is the concept that an agent's authority may not exceed the "legitimate scope" of what is necessary to perform the agent's delegated duties.[24]

The "Incredibles" of the Transaction: What Is Extraordinary?

Transactions authorized under the inherent or implied authority of a chief executive officer must, therefore, be ordinary.[25] ["Extraordinary" transactions normally require board of director approval.] The next

---

21 It is "reasonable to assume that the general manager of a corporation may make contracts in the ordinary course of business." Canister Co. v. Nat'l Can Corp., 63 F. Supp. 361, 367 (D. Del. 1945).

22 Joseph Greenspon's Sons Iron & Steel Co. v. Pecos Valley Gas Co., 156 A. 350, 352 (Del. Super. Ct. 1931); *see also* Italo-Petroleum Corp. v. Hannigan, 14 A.2d 401, 406 (Del. 1940).

23 For example, the president of a corporation "has no implied or presumed authority" to bind the corporation by a contract of guaranty, in which the corporation does not have an interest. Atl. Ref. Co. v. Ingalls & Co., 185 A. 885, 886 (Del. Super. Ct. 1936). In addition, a corporate president has "no implied or inherent power" to consent to the appointment of a receiver to wind-up the corporation's affairs. Bruch v. Nat'l Guar. Credit Corp., 116 A. 738, 740 (Del. Ch. 1922). Also, execution of a contract which completely divests a corporation of all its assets "is, in the absence of corporate authorization or ratification, beyond the power of the president of a corporation to make." Andrew Jergens Co. v. Woodbury, Inc., 273 F. 952, 962 (D. Del. 1921).

24 Kolcum v. Bd. of Educ., 335 A.2d 618, 623 (Del. Super. Ct. 1975); *see generally* Amtower v. Hercules Inc., C.A. No. 97C-09-018 WTQ, 1999 Del. Super. LEXIS 107, at *31 (Feb. 26, 1999).

25 Even "if an officer is also a general manager ... [with powers] which are markedly broader than the inherent powers of a president or other officer," those powers still have limits. Folk, Delware General Corporation Law, at § 142.6. Although general managers are considered to possess broad powers, they still have "no

step in the analysis of Eisner's authority to unilaterally terminate Ovitz from Disney's presidency thus rests with the nature of the transaction: was this an unusual or extraordinary transaction? Such questions regarding the ordinary or extraordinary nature of a transaction are usually questions of fact.[26]

In one of his several opinions in the Disney case, Chancellor Chandler described the "corporate board's *extraordinary* decision to award a $140 million severance package" to Ovitz.[27] [731 A. 2d at 350 (emphasis added)] It is interesting that the chancellor refers to the Disney board's decision as "extraordinary," when the decision to award this severance package was, in fact, made by CEO Eisner. Also, in this casual reference to the payment, the chancellor chooses to use the word "extraordinary" to describe the determination. Of course, such casual language does not characterize the transaction as "extraordinary" as a matter of law. Nonetheless, the chancellor's use of this term is indicative that Ovitz' termination, thereby triggering the $130 million severance package, was no ordinary matter.

With respect to the economics of the transaction, for the fiscal year ending September 29, 2007, Disney reported $35.51 billion in revenues and $4.687 billion in net income.[28] These financial figures reflect the fact that Disney is a huge corporation. In 2007, Disney ranked sixty-fourth on the Fortune 500 list.[29] When faced with these financial numbers, a severance payment of over $130 million may appear rather insignificant. Indeed, in the chancery court opinion, Chancellor Chandler addresses the fact that, relative to the size of the corporation, the terms of Ovitz's employment and termination seem small.[30] However, as is well recognized, quantitative magnitude is not the only factor to consider when analyzing the importance of a transaction; one

implied authority to enter into this unusual and extraordinary contract." Colish v. Brandywine Raceway Ass'n, 119 A.2d 887, 891 (Del. Super. Ct. 1955).

26 Lee v. Jenkins Bros., 268 F.2d 357, 370 (2d Cir. 1959); *see also* Mgmt. Techs. v. Morris, 961 F. Supp. 640, 648 (S.D.N.Y. 1997); DELAWARE CORPORATION LAW AND PRACTICE § 14.02 (2006).

27 *In re* Walt Disney Co. Derivative Litig., 731 A.2d 342, 350 (Del. Ch. 1998), *aff'd in part, rev'd in part sub nom.* Brehm v. Eisner, 746 A.2d 244 (Del. 2000) (emphasis added).

28 The Walt Disney Co., Annual Report (Form 10-K), at 31–32 (Sept. 29, 2007).

29 *Largest U.S. Corporations*, FORTUNE, Apr. 20, 2007, at 210.

30 907 A.2d at 768, n.533.

must also consider the qualitative impact of the transaction to assess its overall magnitude.[31] Significantly, although Chancellor Chandler recognizes the overall size of the corporation relative to the payment, he still describes the severance package as "extraordinary."[32]

The qualitative features of a transaction cannot be ignored during analysis. For example, in the context of assessing qualitative materiality of a misrepresentation in a financial statement, the staff of the Securities and Exchange Commission (SEC) has promulgated Staff Accounting Bulletin 99 (SAB 99).[33] Under SAB 99, the SEC staff advised that both the "quantitative" and the "qualitative" aspects of an item must be evaluated.[34] Also, as observed by the Ninth Circuit Court of Appeals, in ascertaining whether a transaction is extraordinary, "a payment made by a company that would otherwise be unremarkable may be rendered extraordinary by unusual circumstances."[35] [401 F. 3d 1031, 1045 (9th Cir. 2005)] Admittedly, materiality, at times, is distinct from extraordinariness, but overlap between the two concepts provides a useful tool for analysis. Furthermore, when determining whether authority was delegated to a chief executive officer, the "likelihood that a board intends to delegate authority for a particular matter usually will be related inversely to the significance of the action

---

31 See, e.g., Staff Accounting Bulletin 99, 17 C.F.R. pt. 211 subpt. B, 64 Fed. Reg. 45,150 (Aug. 19, 1999); Ganino v. Citizens Utils. Co., 228 F.3d 154, 163 (2d Cir. 2000) (evaluating the materiality of a transaction according to both quantitative and qualitative factors).

32 731 A.2d at 350.

33 Staff Accounting Bulletin 99, 64 Fed. Reg. at 45,150. *See generally In re Dearlove*, SEC Initial Decision Release No. 315, 2006 SEC LEXIS 1684, at *143 (July 27, 2006) (recognizing that SAB 99 expresses the SEC's view that financial misstatements are not immaterial merely because they fall below a numerical threshold).

34 Staff Accounting Bulletin 99, 64 Fed. Reg. at 45,151; *see Ganino*, 228 F.3d at 163 (finding SAB 99 "persuasive guidance" for evaluating materiality according on both quantitative and qualitative factors); *see also In re* Huntington Bancshares, Inc., Securities Act Release No. 8579, Exchange Act Release No. 51,781 (June 2, 2005) (noting that materiality analysis for financial misstatements under SAB 99 requires an analysis of both quantitative and qualitative factors).

35 Sec. & Exch. Comm'n v. Gemstar-TV Guide Int'l, Inc., 401 F.3d 1031, 1045 (9th Cir. 2005), *cert. denied sub nom.* Yuen v. Sec. & Exch. Comm'n, 546 U.S. 933 (2005); *see also Ganino*, 228 F.3d at 163-64.

for the corporation."[36] [961 F. Supp. at 648] Also of relevance is the Ninth Circuit's inclusion of the circumstances surrounding the transaction and the purpose of the transaction (in addition to the size of the transaction) in its list of "context-specific" factors for determining extraordinariness under the Sarbanes-Oxley Act.[37] Such an analysis clearly embraces the qualitative aspects, and not solely the quantitative size, of the transaction.

At first glance, Ovitz' no-fault termination payment appears to be a nonevent, constituting less than 1% of Disney's assets and income.[38] Chancellor Chandler reflected on this small percentage.[39] Under a qualitative measure, however, a different rationale comes into play. Exorbitant termination severance payments to the president of a Fortune 100 company[40] may potentially cause havoc to a company's market following, particularly institutional shareholders who are concerned with vibrant corporate governance standards.[41] To thus point solely to quantitative dollar amounts ignores the economic reality underlying such conduct. Under standards of modern corporate governance, the termination and severance payments to Ovitz were of a material nature, deserving of board of director consideration.

...

---

36 Mgmt. Techs., Inc. v. Morris, 961 F. Supp. 640, 648 (S.D.N.Y. 1997) (discussing whether a CEO, whose position was never created in the company bylaws, had the authority to act in insolvency proceedings in the United Kingdom).

37 *Gemstar-TV Guide Int'l, Inc.*, 401 F.3d at 1045. For literature on the Sarbanes-Oxley Act, see, e.g., J.W. Bostelman, The Sarbanes-Oxley Deskbook (2005); Marc I. Steinberg, Attorney Liability after Sarbanes-Oxley (2011); Joseph Morrissey, *Catching the Culprits: Is Sarbanes-Oxley Enough?*, 2003 Colum. Bus. L. Rev. 801 (2003).

38 Disney reported assets of almost $61 billion in 2007 and net income of $4.687 billion. The Walt Disney Co., Annual Report (Form 10-K), at 31-32 (Sept. 29, 2007)

39 907 A.2d at 768 n.533

40 In 2007, Disney ranked 64 on the Fortune 500. See *Largest U.S. Corporations*, Fortune, Apr. 20, 2007, at 210.

41 *See* Paul Farhi, *Disney's Dizzying Bonus Approved for CEO Eisner: Dissenters Protest 'Lucrative' Package at Shareholder Meeting*, Wash. Post, Feb. 26, 1997, at C11; *A Vote Against Disney*, N.Y. Times, Feb. 25, 1997, at B7; Bruce Orwall & Joann S. Lublin, *Entertainment: The Rich Rewards of a Hollywood Exit*, Wall St. J., Dec. 16, 1996, at B1.

Ratification by the House of Mouse

Finally, the doctrines of ratification and estoppel provide alternatives to actual and apparent authority under agency law. [As set forth in § 401 of the Restatement (Third) of Agency,] ratification refers to the "affirmance of a prior act done by another, whereby the act is given effect as if done by an agent acting with actual authority."[42] Ratification thus serves to confirm the legitimacy of a prior act on behalf of the principal. In a related matter, estoppel refers to situations in which an actor's manifestations "induce[d] the third party to make a detrimental change in position."[43] [*Id.* at § 4.08] When these manifestations have induced such detrimental reliance, the actor making the manifestations may be "estopped" from denying the transaction's validity.[44]

The timing of the ratification is an important element of confirming authority.[45] A critical distinction must be drawn, however, between ratification in the past for previous actions and ratification for a present action. Several Disney officers in the past had been fired without any action from the board of directors.[46] "Implied authority of the president of a corporation cannot be inferred from the fact that in other instances the president's previously *unauthorized* acts have been ratified by the board of directors."[47] [18B Am. Jur. 2d *Corporations* § 1337 (2004)] In other words, the concepts of ratification and implied authority must not be conflated when determining a chief executive's authority to bind the corporation. Thus, when considering whether Eisner possessed the authority to terminate Ovitz independent of the board of directors, manifestations that may be deemed "ratifications" for past unauthorized terminations of other Disney officers cannot be

---

42 AGENCY THIRD, *supra* note 3, § 4.01(1); *see also* Lewis v. Vogelstein, 699 A.2d 327, 334 (Del. Ch. 1997); Hannigan v. Italo Petroleum Corp., 47 A.2d 169, 173 (Del. 1945).

43 AGENCY THIRD, *supra* note 3, § 4.08; *see also* McCabe v. Williams, 45 A.2d 503, 505 (Del. 1944).

44 3 AM. JUR. 2D *Agency* § 79; AGENCY THIRD, *supra* note 3, § 4.08; see generally Guyer v. Haveg Corp., 205 A.2d 176, 181 (Del. Super. Ct. 1964).

45 AGENCY THIRD, *supra* note 3, § 4.05; *see generally* 3 Am. Jur. 2d Agency § 177.

46 *See* Brehm v. Eisner (*In re* the Walt Disney Co. Derivative Litig.), 906 A.2d 27, 69 (Del. 2006).

47 18B AM. JUR. 2D *Corporations* § 1337 (2007) (emphasis added) (citing Stoneman v. Fox Film Corp., 4 N.E.2d 63 (Mass. 1936)).

considered a source for Eisner's present inherent or implied authority to unilaterally fire Ovitz.

Furthermore, by implication, other officers may well have been lower-level officers, but Ovitz was president. Thus, even if previous acts in fact were authorized or ratified, Ovitz' termination and severance are of an entirely different category. The firing of the number-two executive in the corporate hierarchy should be treated differently than the dismissal of lower level officers such as corporate vice presidents.

Nonetheless, even if Eisner originally lacked the authority to unilaterally terminate Ovitz from Disney's presidency, thereby triggering the severance payment, the board of directors ratified the transaction. Ratification of a transaction may occur by virtue of the principal's "failing to object to it or to repudiate it." [Restatement (Third) of Agency § 4.01 cmf. f][48] Because the Disney board of directors declined to object to Ovitz's termination, the board, in all practicality, ratified the transaction.

SCENARIO

Ben, Damian and Lewis fulfill their childhood "dream" by opening a baseball card and memorabilia shop, named "Home Run Cards." The business is a general partnership. Ben, Damian and Lewis each is a general partner and full-time employee of the general partnership. The "prize" card of the business is a 1952 Topps Mickey Mantle "Rookie" card graded in "excellent" condition, valued at approximately $15,000. The Card is a drawing "magnet" for junior and seasoned card collectors who frequent the shop and who are eager to view the Mantle card. Because of the popularity of the Mantle card and its positive impact on the business, Ben, Damian and Lewis agree that the Mantle card is not to be sold at any price that may be offered. They also agree that they will reverse this decision only if all three of them agree that the card should be sold.

---

48 3 AM. JUR. 2D *Agency* § 193; AGENCY THIRD, *supra* note 3, § 4.01 cmt. f; Law v. Cross, 66 U.S. 533, 539 (1861).

On a "quiet" Tuesday afternoon, Damian is working at Home Run Cards when George, an avid collector of vintage baseball cards, visits. George has shopped at the shop since its opening ten months ago and has purchased roughly $3,000 worth of cards at the shop. Seeing the tantalizing Mantle card, George tells Damian that he has just sold some Apple Computer stock that he had purchased many years earlier and wants to buy the Mantle card. Before Damian responds that the card is not for sale, George offers $20,000 for the card. Knowing that this is a terrific "over-market" price for the card and believing that his partners Ben and Lewis will be delighted, Damian accepts the offer. George takes out his VISA card (having a limit of $35,000) and purchases the card.

After George leaves the shop, Damian has "second" thoughts about the sale of the Mantle card. Will his co-partners Ben and Lewis be okay with the sale or upset? Damian decides to keep the sale of the Mantle card to himself for as long as practicable.

Ten days later, Home Run Cards receives a deposit in its bank account of $19,600 ($20,000 less the 2% VISA transaction fee). Damian thereupon informs Ben and Lewis of the sale of the Mantle card to George. Ben and Lewis are very upset. Ben and Lewis immediately contact George to return the card and tell him that he will receive a full $20,000 refund upon the card's return. George refuses to do so and the 1952 Topps Mantle card is currently in his personal collection.

Three weeks later, Home Run Cards sues George seeking return of the Mantle card, arguing that Damian did not have authority to sell the card to George. In addition, Ben and Lewis sue Damian for breach of his agency authority. What result and why?

Chapter 2

Types of Business Forms

YOUR CLIENT DECIDES to go into business. It may be by herself or with others. If with others, they may be people she intimately trusts, such as a brother, or they may be simply individuals she believes have good business acumen and whom she trusts. Either way, there are many questions that should be answered.

Let's first generally discuss the types of business organizations that are available.

Sole Proprietorships

First, if one will be the sole owner of the business, a sole "proprietorship" is an option. There are no steps or formalities that are required to form a proprietorship. Simply by starting the business—whether it be by hanging the shingle, entering into contracts (such as a lease), or opening up bank accounts, a sole proprietorship comes into existence. There are no written documents or filings with the applicable state authority (such as the Ohio Secretary of State when one does business in Cleveland).

What is the effect of a sole proprietorship? As to any losses, they are attributed to the owner personally—in other words, the sole proprietor has personal and unlimited liability. That is not a good thing. For example, if the sole proprietorship enters into a one-year lease for $30,000 ($2,500 per month), the landlord can look not only to the proprietorship for payment but also to the owner's personal assets. Of course, the sole proprietor can try to convince the landlord when she enters into the lease to put in a clause in the agreement that only the proprietorship can be liable on the lease. But it is unlikely that the landlord will accept such a modification, if he/she has any business "smarts."

What about tax consequences? Generally, profits and losses from the proprietorship flow to the owner personally. The proprietorship is not a taxable entity. Therefore, in Schedule C of the sole proprietor's federal income tax form, she would reflect the profits (or losses) of the business, deduct business expenses incurred, and take other suitable allowances. For example, let's assume that she has 2011 income of $60,000 not connected with the proprietorship (for instance, from her job as manager of a home improvements store). Assume that the net income of the proprietorship (after allowing for business expenses and the like) is $30,000. Therefore, her personal income for 2011 tax purposes is $90,000 ($60,000 plus $30,000). On the other hand, if the proprietorship lost $30,000 in 2011, her taxable income is $30,000 ($60,000 less $30,000).

As you can see, a very good benefit of a sole proprietorship is the tax treatment, especially if there are losses. We will explore this issue in more depth a little later. But it should be emphasized that there are numerous ways an entrepreneur can structure the business for tax purposes.

For ease of operation, the sole proprietorship is quite simple. There are no filing requirements with the government for starting up the enterprise. Nor are there any formalities that must be followed, such as holding annual meetings. Nonetheless, accurate record keeping is important to show, for example, that valid contracts have been entered into and that the business expenses incurred are legitimate.

As we will read below, many of the principles that apply to sole proprietorships also are true for general partnerships.

General Partnerships

Let's next assume that Dustin wants to go into business with two others, Julia and Neil. The business is a dating service for professional singles called "LHC Professional Singles" (which we'll simply call "LHC"). For $700 per year, a client can sign up for as many dates with "quality" persons as he or she chooses. As part of the service, each client has a video taken of him or herself and fills out a comprehensive questionnaire on his or her background, desires, and goals.

Upon commencing the business with these objectives, Dustin, Julia, and Neil have formed a general partnership. Like a sole proprietorship, there are no formalities that must be done, such as filing a document with the State. Indeed, there is not even a requirement that there be an express agreement; the understanding among the partners may be implicit, based on their conduct.

To better understand this idea, let's look at the definition of a general partnership: As set forth in Section 202(a) of the Revised Uniform Partnership Act, a general partnership is "the association of two or more persons to carry on as co-owners a business for profit." Without getting too detailed, the first point is that the business be ongoing, not simply an isolated incident. For example, the buying of one piece of real estate for investment likely would be a "joint venture." Nonetheless, many of the same rules that apply to partnerships also extend to joint ventures.[1] For our scenario, LHC clearly involves the carrying on of a business and this will practically always be the case when individuals go into business.

What is meant by the phrase "two or more persons?" Can only individuals be partners? The answer is that corporations, other partnerships, and other inanimate or "soul-less" entities can be partners.[2] The importance of this point is discussed below.

The term "for profit" means that the business is formed for the purpose or expectation of making a profit. That a business in fact loses money in no way takes away from the fact that a partnership exists. Indeed, even when businesses are formed with a purpose to generate losses in the short-term that may be passed onto the individual partners for tax benefits, there still remains an ultimate profit motive.

Last, what does the term "co-owner" mean? This is very significant: A co-owner has ultimate control. This means that a general partner can vote on matters affecting the partnership.[3] He or she also can bind the partnership in many business dealings, even when that partner does not in fact have the actual authority to engage in a particular transaction.[4] In other words, if the matter is fairly ordinary and if it is reasonable for the creditor to believe that the partner has been given authority to act by the partnership, then the partnership ordinarily is bound by the contract.[5]

This is a scary situation. Like a sole proprietorship, the general partners have personal and unlimited liability. In forming a general partnership, the partners put their personal assets at risk. Going back to the LHC situation, let's provide an example. Suppose that the general partnership is renting its premises from Abner Square Properties ("Abner") for an amount of $24,000 for a one-year lease ($2,000 per month). All checks to pay the rent are signed by Neil (who is one of the partners). Being an innovative sort, Neil contacts Abner, offering to renegotiate the lease on the partnership's behalf. Thereupon, Neil enters into a five-year lease for a total amount of $108,000 ($1,800 per month). It may be the case that Abner reasonably believed that Neil had authority to engage in this transaction. If so, the partnership likely will be stuck for the $108,000 lease, even if Neil in fact did not have the actual authority to enter into the transaction.[6] If LHC goes out of business two years from now and is bankrupt, the individual partners—Dustin, Julia, and Neil—remain personally liable on the amount owed.[7] In other words, Dustin's Porsche may no longer belong to him. Although Dustin and Julia may sue Neil for exceeding his partnership authority and recover the damages he caused them,[8] Neil unfortunately may be broke.

This scenario illustrates why partners must trust each other. This is true in any business situation but it particularly strikes home in the general partnership context. The fear of personal and unlimited liability is an ever-present threat that should induce individuals to select their partners carefully and to watch over their conduct.

This last point should be explored. In any type of business, when feasible, co-owners should seek to watch over or monitor their colleagues. One need not be obnoxious about it so as to generate ill will and hostility. But a co-owner should not have his "head in the sand" like an ostrich. Those who act like an ostrich all too often get their feathers clipped. And again, this point takes on even more meaning in a general partnership. In this regard, one thing is clear: if a prospective participant lives in another city or has such a demanding schedule that she cannot actively take part in the business and watch over her partners, she should not become a general partner.

Let's talk about other key issues: first, whether a general partner is entitled to sell his/her interest; and second, assuming a buyer is not found, whether a general partner has the power to "walk" (exit the partnership) and be bought out ("buyout"). In these situations, both the partnership statutes and the partnership agreement entered into by all of the partners are important. Generally, the statutes that apply to partnership law set forth basic rules. With certain few exceptions, these rules can be modified by the execution of a partnership agreement.[9] As we will see, in some situations, the partners may prefer to leave the basic rules in place while in other contexts they will want the partnership agreement to change these rules.

For example, under Section 401(i) of the Revised Uniform Partnership Act, in order for a person to become a general partner, all partners must agree. Even one partner can veto the entry of a general partner. For example, if Dustin wishes to sell his interest to Susan, all of his partners must give their consent in order for Susan to become a general partner. If they do not, Dustin still may transfer his interest to Susan but she would not become a general partner. She would be entitled to profits and other distributions but would have no right to exercise any control over the business[10] (not even the right to inspect the partnership's books and records when she desired).[11] On the plus side, since she would not be a general partner, the extent of her liability is limited—in other words, limited to the amount she paid Dustin for his interest. Would Susan agree to such an arrangement? Probably not, unless she is thrilled with the profits generated by the business or the entrepreneurial skills of the key partners. In most situations, Susan would say "no" to putting up a financial stake in a venture in which she would have absolutely no "say" in the business.

The end result is that under the basic rules a general partner, for all practical purposes, cannot sell his interest and have his transferee become a general partner without receiving the partners' unanimous consent. At first glance, this seems unfairly to lock a partner into the business, particularly when consent is unreasonably withheld. Before deciding to modify this rule in the partnership agreement, look at the other side. Business is loaded with risks. In a general partnership, it is even more so—given that there is unlimited liability and that a general partner can bind his or her co-partners. Therefore, as a general proposition, partners desire to choose wisely and not have a partner who is a jerk thrust upon them by a departing partner.

Let's also illustrate this situation in another context. In the LHC scenario, Dustin has selected his co-partners, Julia and Neil, because he trusts them. But let's suppose that Julia wants to transfer her general partnership status to her son Leon. Or let's suppose that Neil dies and wills his general partnership status to his wife Enid. Dustin may want nothing to do with Enid or Leon. He may think they're nice but the last thing he wants is to be in business with either of them. That's because Dustin believes that Enid (or Leon) is incompetent or untrustworthy. In other words, Dustin has good reason for keeping them out of the business. As the partnership rules are written, he is entitled to exercise his veto and prevent either of them from becoming his partner.[12]

In a related scenario, let's assume that Dustin is a general partner in LHC and needs to get out of the partnership in order to have access to cash. Or, alternatively, he is moving from Portland, Maine to Portland, Oregon and certainly does not want to be a general partner 3,000 miles away from the business. Also, he needs the cash to use for his new business in Oregon. Dustin has tried to find a buyer for his partnership interest but has not been successful. His co-partners have refused to buy him out at a fair price. What are his options? Is he stuck with being a general partner in the Maine partnership?

The answer is no—that Dustin can get out. The general rule is that, unless the partners agree otherwise, a partnership can be ended at any time by any partner.[13] Once the partnership terminates and its debts have been paid (or there is sufficient cash remaining for creditors to be paid), the partners generally are entitled to receive (if there are sufficient funds), the return of their contribution (such as the $50,000 each partner put in at the beginning) and their respective share of the profits.[14] If Dustin is the partner leaving, this is good news for Dustin. For the partners staying in the business, this can be far from good.

In other words, assume that a struggling partnership has to pay $50,000 to the departing partner. It clearly needs much of this cash to continue as a healthy enterprise. Where is it going to find it? Perhaps the cash may come from a bank loan, by the entry of a new general partner, or other source, such as the winnings from a lucky state lottery ticket. But the reality is that the business faces a significant hurdle. It must find needed funds on a basis that it can tolerate. In an economy suffering a short credit supply or high interest rates, this can present insurmountable difficulties. At worst, the partnership will have to sell certain assets of its business or, worse yet, have a liquidation or "fire" sale ("going out of business" sale) to cover its debts.[15]

Another way of looking at this situation—when any partner can leave the partnership at any time and receive the amount owed—is that it gives any partner, practically speaking, a veto power. Going back to the LHC scenario, look at it this way: A major decision is to be made by LHC, namely, whether to hire two new employees. Julia and Neil are in favor of this expenditure, believing that LHC's success will increase with the input of new personnel. Dustin disagrees, believing that hiring these prospective employees would be a poor use of LHC's resources. Even though majority vote technically controls (presume there is no provision in the partnership agreement requiring unanimity),[16] Dustin threatens to terminate the partnership if the others insist on hiring the two prospective employees. If the other partners perceive that Dustin is not bluffing and if a good amount of cash is owed to him that is hard to replace from other sources (such as a bank on acceptable terms), it is likely that Dustin will get his way. The bottom line is that Dustin's departure would cause an intolerable financial drain on the partnership and may result in the failure of the business. Given this outcome, Julia and Neil likely will back down, giving effect to Dustin's de-facto veto.

Needless to say, this situation does not induce harmonious relations. It may also cause a tyranny by the minority upon the majority and stagnation of the business. There is no guarantee that the minority will exercise its de-facto veto power wisely. Indeed, the minority's excessive use of its veto power will result in the partnership losing business opportunities. Competitors may take advantage of the situation. In sum, the partnership will stop growing, its business will go flat, and it will stagnate. At worst, the partnership will cease being profitable and become insolvent.

Based on the above discussion, the partners probably do not want to permit any partner to walk at any time and be entitled to be bought out. Instead, the partners may want to put a provision in the partnership agreement stating that the partnership will be of a certain length of time or will terminate only upon certain specified conditions.[17] For example, the partnership agreement may provide that "this partnership shall terminate on October 1, 2021." If a specified time period is not the goal, then an alternative may read as follows: "The partnership shall terminate upon the consent of all of the partners."[18]

The above provisions certainly do not solve all problems. For example, under the first scenario, the partners will have to work out a new agreement in 2021 or the partnership will terminate on October 1st of that year. Under the second scenario, a partner can withhold consent to end the partnership (when the agreement provides unanimous consent to terminate the partnership) and prevent the other partners from recouping their investment in a timely fashion. It should be pointed out that in both of these situations an unhappy partner, even in violation of the agreement, may still leave the partnership and demand the amount owed but, in so doing, will be subject to damages to the other partners for the harm inflicted by his breach of the agreement.[19]

A subject that will be explored in greater depth later is that the partners owe one another certain duties, commonly called fiduciary duties, based on the relationship of trust that is supposed to be present in a partnership-like situation.[20] Historically, partners owe one another the utmost duties of care and loyalty. They are to treat each other fairly.[21] Of course, this does not always happen. When a partner feels that he is being victimized or "ripped-off," a law suit for breach of fiduciary duty is an option.[22] Moreover, under modern partnership statutes, these duties have become more lax whereby, for example, a partner's duty of care is simply to refrain from engaging in what may be viewed as egregious conduct (namely, not to act with gross negligence or reckless or intentional misconduct).[23] Moreover, today these duties can be further limited or modified in the written partnership agreement.[24]

In sum, there are many questions that must be faced in forming a partnership. Some of these questions are discussed above. But several others remain. The key point here is that a written partnership agreement among all partners normally is essential. In Chapter 3, we will focus on the types of questions that should be addressed by the parties when signing such a written agreement.

Tax consequences are the last point to be raised for general partnerships. Basically, partnerships are treated like sole proprietorships for tax purposes. For tax purposes, a general partnership is not a separate legal entity (although it must file an informational return). The partnership's gains, losses, and deductions are allocated among the individual partners pursuant to the partnership agreement and reported on each partner's individual tax return.[25]

In the absence of a partnership agreement, the provisions of the applicable State's general partnership law will control the allocation of gains, losses, and deductions.[26] Because such allocation frequently would not reflect the partners' intent, the partners should cover this subject in a written partnership agreement. For example, in the absence of an agreement, all partners under the partnership law share equally in the profits of the business.[27] Dissatisfied with this arrangement, a partner who contributes more cash to the business than the other partners may be able to successfully negotiate for receipt of a greater percentage of profits.

Let's return to the LHC scenario for a simple tax illustration. Assume that Julia has contributed 25% of the cash, Neil 25%, and Dustin 50%. Pursuant to the partnership agreement, Dustin is to receive 50% of all profits and his share of the losses is allocated at 50%. During 2011, the partnership shows a net income of $100,000. Under this example, Dustin's personal taxable income will increase by $50,000. If his non-partnership income is $60,000, then his total taxable income would be $110,000 ($60,000 plus $50,000). On the other hand, if the partnership loses $60,000, his allocated share of the loss on his individual tax return would be $30,000 and his total taxable income would be $30,000 ($60,000 less $30,000).

We will next turn to limited partnerships. It may be helpful at this point to simply point out that general and limited partnerships are treated the same for tax purposes. Therefore, the above tax illustration also holds true for limited partnerships.

LIMITED PARTNERSHIPS

The benefits of limited partnerships generally are related to liability and tax considerations. As seen above, limited partnerships are not taxed separately (although an informational filing must be made). Rather, the gains, losses, and deductions flow-through to the individual partners. This can result in beneficial tax treatment to all concerned.

Unlike a general partnership, the limited partners in a limited partnership have only limited liability.[28] This means that limited partners generally are liable only to the extent of their investment in the business. For example, if a limited partner's contribution to purchase a partnership unit is $40,000, that is the extent of financial risk. No other property or asset of the limited partner is at risk. Of course, if a limited partner in addition co-signs as a personal guarantor for a loan extended to the partnership, she will become personally liable—though not as a partner but as a personal guarantor of the loan's repayment.

Here we have the key benefits of being a limited partner—limited liability and preferential tax treatment. By comparison, general partners in a limited partnership are treated very much like general partners in a general partnership. Among other things, they still have personal and unlimited liability.

There is a very significant trade-off for a limited partner to incur only limited liability: Unlike general partners, a limited partner cannot participate in the control of the business. If he does, personal liability (to those creditors who reasonably believe based on such "partner's conduct that the limited partner is a general partner") may be the consequence.[29] But what does "participating in the control of the business" mean? The term certainly is vague. Generally, under state partnership law, limited partners can still have significant input in the business without being subject to personal liability. For example, a limited partner can engage in the following for the partnership and still be considered a limited partner: be an employee, serve as an agent, serve as an officer or director of a corporation that is the general partner of the limited partnership, render advice, and vote on matters designated in the limited partnership agreement, such as the removal and replacement of the general partner or a change in the partnership's type of business (for example, the partnership changing from a catering business to that of operating restaurants).[30]

Nonetheless, this is an area where limited partners should be careful. If they make significant decisions for the partnership, personally take on managerial responsibilities or exercise veto powers, there is a risk that a limited partner will incur personal and unlimited liability, just like a general partner. In such event, the limited partner would incur personal liability only to those creditors who reasonably believe, "based upon the limited partner's conduct, that the limited partner is a general partner."[31]

This is a good point to talk about business planning and limiting one's liability exposure. Let's assume that the prospective co-partners do not want to take on the liability risks of general partners. Moreover, each participant wants to take part in the control of the business—they all seek to be active entrepreneurs, not passive investors. There seems to be a major problem: All want to exert control without risking their personal assets. Sounds like the best of human nature, if we can make it work—all gain, and no pain.

Happily, there is a solution here. As seen later, the co-participants may form a limited liability partnership, a limited liability company, or a corporation. Even if they elect to form a limited partnership, the dilemma may be solved. Here's how: Let's return to the LHC scenario. The co-partners can form a separate corporation which they name LHC Corporation and make that corporation the general partner of the limited partnership. The co-partners can be the sole shareholders, officers and directors of the corporate general partner, LHC Corporation. In their individual capacities, the co-partners can be the limited partners of the limited partnership. This way, because shareholders of a corporation generally have only limited liability, there is no individual who has personal and unlimited liability when a corporation is set up as the only general partner.[32]

Of course, the participants must make sure that the limited partnership is controlled by the corporate general partner, LHC Corporation. Decisions have to be made by the corporate general partner (and not by the limited partners in their limited partner role) through appropriate board of director resolutions and the like.

If the individual limited partners in their role as limited partners make these decisions, they will be deemed to be exercising control, rendering them personally liable to creditors who reasonably believe that they in fact are general partners.[33] The limited partners therefore have to be careful to ensure that LHC Corporation, the corporate general partner, adopts appropriate and timely resolutions to meet the managerial needs of the limited partnership. This may be time-consuming and easy to neglect. Yet, it is crucial to insulate the limited partners from personal liability.

What about formalities? Unlike a general partnership which can be an informal arrangement and requires no filing with the State, a limited partnership comes into existence only where there is a certificate filed with the applicable State (for example, filing with the Illinois Secretary of State for a limited partnership that will conduct its business in the Chicago metropolitan area).[34] This is key. Failure to file the certificate may result in the enterprise being labeled as a general partnership even if the partners thought they had formed a limited partnership. If so, personal liability may ensue.[35] Another situation is where the enterprise transacts business, such as entering into contracts, before filing the limited partnership certificate with the State. Again, the risk is that the partners will be subject to unlimited liability.[36] The better route simply is to wait until the limited partnership certificate is filed before doing business.

As with a general partnership, a written limited partnership agreement is necessary. The same concerns arise, such as the ability to sell or transfer one's interest and to demand the return of one's investment. Also, like in a general partnership, fiduciary duties are owed. These duties especially are implicated in the way that the general partners treat the limited partners. There is always the prospect that those in control, namely the general partners, will enhance their financial return by exploiting (i.e. ripping-off) the limited partners. This is called "self-dealing" and raises duty of loyalty concerns. Nonetheless, to an increasing degree, under modern limited partnership law, general partners are allowed to significantly reduce these fiduciary duties pursuant to the limited partnership agreement.[37] For example, the limited partnership agreement, by its terms, may entitle the general partner to take business opportunities that otherwise would belong to the limited partnership or to be subject to liability for reckless (rather than negligent) conduct.[38]

Regarding a general partner's duties and rights in a limited partnership, they are generally the same as in a general partnership. For instance, general partners can bind the limited partnership and exercise control in a multitude of ways. The same issues with a problematic general partner in a general partnership also may surface in the limited partnership context.[39]

What about being able to sell or transfer one's interest? Generally, although the applicable limited partnership statute covers this situation, the written limited partnership agreement may modify the statutory provisions.[40] Because limited partners do not exercise control and often do not play a significant role in the business, most agreements permit a limited partner to transfer her limited partnership status. Practically speaking, however, selling one's limited partnership interests will be difficult at best as the market for these interests normally is abysmal. On the other hand, the limited partners should be concerned when the proposed agreement gives the general partner on its own the right to designate additional general partners. Because general partners have control over the enterprise, limited partners ought to be wary of cavalierly permitting the entry of additional general partners.

Limited partnership agreements may provide that the partnership will last for a specified period of time, such as ten years. At that time, the partnership will end and the net proceeds will be distributed to the partners.[41] Such a clause may be advisable to induce limited partners to part with their money. Such a provision, however, has its costs. If the business is to be dissolved and then restarted, replacement funds will have to be found, a task that can be difficult if the business is marginal or economic conditions are poor. The bottom line is that, if the limited partners are principally investors, a specified time period for return of the amount owed may have to be included in the limited partnership agreement. On the other hand, if the limited partners mainly perceive themselves as entrepreneurs who intend to be somewhat active in the business, such a provision may not be needed to induce these individuals to part with their money. Another provision, such as that the limited partnership shall terminate upon the written consent of 75% of the general and limited partners, may be inserted into the agreement.[42]

The limited partnership agreement, like a general partnership agreement or a shareholder agreement in a corporation, is a product of negotiation among the participants. Those who have the resources that the enterprise needs, whether it be cash, entrepreneurial skills, or expertise in a needed area (such as a master chef for a restaurant), have leverage and should be able to bargain effectively for their own interests. This, of course, assumes that these individuals can intelligently perceive their strengths, can communicate effectively, and that the other potential co-partners are flexible. This is by no means something that should be taken for granted. Indeed, deals have been scuttled by the parties being unable to reach mutually acceptable terms. And persons, who enter into business agreements without watching out for themselves, all too often become disenchanted once they see the consequences of their poor bargaining. The point here is that going into business with others calls for one to be vigilant in protecting his/her financial interests. In so doing, the investor/entrepreneur should ascertain what variables are important and effectively bargain for them.

LIMITED LIABILITY PARTNERSHIPS

A relatively recent development is the recognition of the limited liability partnership (LLP). A general partnership or a limited partnership may form a LLP. Under many LLP statutes, a general partner is not subject to personal liability unless she personally guarantees a debt of the partnership, engages in misconduct herself (whether by negligence or malfeasance), supervises another (such as a partner who supervises an associate in a law firm) who commits the impropriety, or learns of the misconduct and fails to take reasonably corrective action. Depending on the applicable State's statute, the LLP limited liability protection may or may not extend to the partnership's contractual obligations (such as a loan obtained by the LLP from a bank). A filing with the applicable State is required to form a LLP, to be renewed annually. A fee (such as $200) per partner must be paid annually to the State as well as the escrowing of a specific monetary amount or, alternatively, the procurement of insurance (such as $1 million in coverage) to enable a claimant to access at least some funds that provide compensation for the loss incurred.[43]

The LLP is "good news" for an individual who serves as a general partner in either a general partnership or limited partnership. With a properly formed LLP, the general partner no longer is subject to personal liability unless one of the exceptions set forth in the above paragraph arises (for example, the partner herself acts improperly). Individuals who are general partners should take advantage of the LLP umbrella. Indeed, professional firms, such as law firms, are becoming LLPs with regularity. Note that the LLP is attractive primarily for individuals who are general partners. Where a limited liability enterprise (such as a corporation or limited liability company) serves as a general partner, there is no need to seek LLP status as the enterprise already has limited liability exposure.

CORPORATIONS

The corporation form is a popular way of doing business. Its key advantages are limited liability and the right of the equity holders (called shareholders or stockholders) to exercise control. Except in the case of "close" corporations (which will be discussed shortly), one's control status is affected by serving on the board of directors or as an executive officer of the corporation. These benefits are important and should not be underestimated. The comfort of limited liability means a lot, especially when one also can be in control of the business.

Of course, a prospective creditor for the corporate contract to be signed can try to have the shareholders personally guarantee payment of the services or products that will be delivered. But this simply involves negotiation as is true with all contracts. And importantly, such negotiation on the creditor's part is successful only if the creditor has the sophistication to raise the matter and the bargaining leverage to persuade the shareholders that they can receive the desired goods or services only by relinquishing their limited liability. Otherwise, the status quo operates and that means that the shareholders ordinarily can only be liable to the extent that they have invested in (or contributed to) the business.[44]

Let's return to the LHC scenario and assume that LHC is a corporation. Julia, Neil and Dustin own one-third of the business represented by the ownership by each of 100 shares for which each has paid $200 per share. That means that Julia, Neil and Dustin each have contributed or invested $20,000. If the business then goes under, that is the extent of their liability. Or, stated another way, unless a creditor successfully bargains ahead of time to hold the shareholders personally liable on the contract, the creditor normally can look only to the assets of the business for payment. This is a huge benefit of being a shareholder in a corporation.

A corporation, however, does not simply "spring" into existence. Rather, a certificate of incorporation must be filed with the State.[45] Also, in any other State that the corporation will be doing business, the enterprise must become qualified as a "foreign" corporation and designate to whom and where it can be "served" in that State.[46] These acts of incorporating in the State (as well as becoming qualified to do business in any other States) cost money, probably in the range of hundreds (if not thousands) of dollars (not counting any attorney's fees).

As mentioned above, a corporation comes into existence when a certificate of incorporation is filed with the State. The certificate is not a complicated document but it is essential that it be filed before the enterprise engages in business. Otherwise, contracts entered into and debts incurred prior to filing may result in the individuals involved being held personally liable. That is why the certificate of incorporation should be filed with the State before engaging in any business transaction. The process is easy and can even be completed within a single day.[47]

The corporation is viewed by the law as a separate entity. Because of this, it acts through its designated body, namely, the board of directors which in turn appoints the officers. The board is elected by the shareholders.[48] For our purposes here, the point is that the law requires that certain corporate actions must be taken at duly called board of director and shareholder meetings (or pursuant to written consents executed by directors or shareholders as set forth in State statutes). These formalities should not be neglected. Failure to comply with requirements to have board of director or shareholder approval in some cases may invalidate the action taken.[49] Neglect of formalities also may help persuade a court upon the request of creditors to ignore the limited liability of the shareholders and hold them personally liable.[50] This is colorfully called "piercing the corporate veil" which is covered in Chapter 4.

Note, however, like limited partnerships and limited liability companies in many States, franchise fees (also called a margin tax) must be paid to the State where the corporation is incorporated.[51] This can amount to a significant sum for a small business. Also, fees are required to be paid to States where the corporation is not incorporated but seeks to be qualified to do business in such States.[52]

Note that the task of complying with corporate formalities has been made much easier by the passage of laws authorizing the use of written consent for the actions taken in lieu of actually holding a board of director or shareholder meeting.[53] For example, rather than holding a "formal" board of director meeting to approve the opening of certain corporate bank accounts or to authorize the undertaking of certain contracts, such action may simply be taken by all of the directors agreeing in writing. This certainly simplifies the formalities and can be used so long as everyone agrees. Moreover, with respect to shareholder written consents, rather than mandating unanimity, an increasing number of States require only that the consent be signed by the number of shares needed to authorize the action as if a physical meeting were held.[54] Notice must be provided to the non-consenting shareholders of the action taken.[55]

Let's next look at the situation where a shareholder wants to sell his stock. As you may remember, in both general and limited partnerships, partners cannot sell their interests and designate their buyers as partners unless the partnership agreement allows or the partners at the time of the sale unanimously give their approval.[56] A corporation is very different: The shares of a corporation are freely transferable. A shareholder can sell his stock to whomever he pleases and may give or will the stock to grouchy and incorrigible relatives.

This may sound good to the shareholder who is selling or "gifting" his stock. It is far from good for participants who still are shareholders and are active in the business. Let's return to the LHC venture to highlight this situation: Julia, Neil and Dustin all work in the business and get along pretty well. Julia, however, decides that she has had enough of disgruntled clients complaining about the quality of their dates. She sells her stock to Alfred who by consensus is both incompetent and a "know-it-all," a very bad combination indeed—a "double zero." Can Neil or Dustin veto Julia's sale of her stock to Alfred? The answer is no unless there are in place what are called "stock transfer restrictions." We'll discuss the details of these provisions in Chapter 3. Suffice it to say here that appropriate stock transfer restrictions are necessary in an enterprise consisting of few participants.

There is another side of the coin to these stock transfer restrictions, one type of which is called a buy-sell agreement. Unlike partnerships, corporations have perpetual life. No shareholder has the power to terminate the business. This is both good and bad: Good if one wishes to stay in the business for the foreseeable future, with a son or daughter ready to take one's place upon retirement. But lousy if one is a minority shareholder and wants out in the fairly near future. Remember we are dealing with shares having only a minority interest in an illiquid corporation with no ready resale market. To solve or at least make the situation bearable, a buy-sell agreement may be the answer. For example, upon Neil reaching the age of 65 years, the corporation agrees to buy and Neil agrees to sell all of his shares at a designated price. The details of such provisions can be complicated and raise difficult judgment calls (which are further discussed in Chapter 3).

Mention should briefly be made that fiduciary duties—the duty of care and the duty of loyalty—arise in the corporate setting. As we will see in greater detail in Chapter 6, fiduciaries like directors and officers owe the corporation and its shareholders the duties of care and loyalty.[57] Those who control the corporation ("controlling persons"), such as one who owns over 50% of the stock, generally have the same obligations.[58] The duty of care means that one must act with more or less reasonable prudence. Perfection is not required; rather, one must not be too negligent or more blameworthy, such as acting with reckless or intentional misconduct.[59] The duty of loyalty basically means that the fiduciary must seek to act in the corporation's best interest and should not "fill his pockets" at the expense of the corporation's and shareholders' well being. Any contract that an officer or director enters into with the corporation must be fair to the corporation. In other words, the fiduciary should not profit at the corporation's expense.[60] As we will see, these duties often are more flexible than they seem in theory, permitting fiduciaries to maneuver somewhat for their own advantage.

Let's next move on to a very important aspect—tax considerations. The ordinary corporation that is set up is called a "C Corporation" under the federal tax laws. Under this structure, the corporation is taxed separately.[61] Unlike a partnership, the profits and losses of a C Corporation do not flow-through directly to the shareholders. This means that if LHC Corporation earns $50,000 for 2011, it will be obligated as a taxpayer on that $50,000. State taxes also will be due. On the other hand, if LHC Corporation loses $35,000 for 2011, its taxable income will be zero. This is a great disadvantage for a C Corporation—its losses cannot be passed through to the individual shareholders so that they can deduct their pro rata share on their individual tax returns. Contrast the C Corporation with a partnership or with a Subchapter S or Limited Liability Company (both of which will be discussed shortly). Unlike the C Corporation, these enterprises permit the flow-through of income and losses to its members.

Another problem with a C Corporation is what has been coined as "double taxation." This means that the corporation is taxed on its income and, when these profits are distributed to the shareholders as dividends, the shareholders separately are taxed on these amounts.[62] Stating the obvious, the term "double taxation" is a double whammy. There are fortunately three basic strategies that can be used to curb Uncle Sam's appetite. First, instead of using large amounts of stock as a vehicle for equity financing, the corporation can sell (or "issue") debt instruments, like bonds or notes, to its members. The benefit of this strategy is that the payment of interest on the debt (such as a bond), unlike the payment of dividends on stock, is a deductible business expense for the corporation. Second, where shareholders are employed by the corporation, the payment of generous yet reasonable salaries is also a deductible business expense for the corporation. And, third, instead of declaring large dividends, the corporation can retain a good percentage of its earnings to be used for business improvements, expansion, and research and development.[63] But, with respect to these strategies to lessen tax liability, the Internal Revenue Service

(IRS) may seek to challenge the validity of any deduction or other action taken. If the deduction taken is deemed excessive, unwarranted or fraudulent, the deduction will not be allowed and penalties may be levied.[64] Needless to say, before engaging in these tax strategies, a competent tax advisor should be consulted.

Nonetheless, there is another strategy that can be used that will lessen tax liability to the federal government and that (believe it or not) has the blessing of the IRS. This is the "Subchapter S" corporation. Basically, a Subchapter S corporation is taxed like a partnership. The profits and losses of the corporation therefore flow through directly to the shareholders on a pro rata basis. For example, if a shareholder owns 25% of the stock, then 25% of the corporation's losses can be deducted on her individual tax return. Similarly, the shareholder would be individually taxed on 25% of the corporation's earnings. In other words, the Subchapter S corporation receives tax treatment very much like a partnership.[65]

Many states also have their version of Subchapter S. The problem of double taxation goes "bye-bye." Some requirements, however, apply for an enterprise to be Subchapter S. For example, the corporation can have no more than 75 shareholders. For most privately-held businesses, this should not pose any difficulty. Second, while individuals are eligible shareholders of a Subchapter S corporation, corporations in certain circumstances are ineligible to be shareholders. For instance, if ABC Corporation owns 60% of XYZ Corporation's stock, XYZ cannot be a Subchapter S corporation. A third key requirement is that a Subchapter S corporation can have (with certain exceptions) only one class of stock and is restricted on the types of debt instruments, such as bonds or notes, that it can use.[66] This last requirement may be a significant one since it may hinder the shareholders' ability to flexibly structure the enterprise so as to meet both their individual needs and the monetary needs of the corporation.

It must be stressed that Subchapter S is a creature of only the tax laws. It has nothing to do with the state corporation statutes. This means that if Subchapter S treatment is elected for the enterprise, a certificate of incorporation must still be filed with the appropriate State. Failing to file the certificate may result in the participants being held personally liable.[67] In sum, the certificate of incorporation must be filed with the State and then the corporation may elect Subchapter S treatment under the federal and state tax laws.

STATUTORY CLOSE CORPORATIONS

In several states, there is an alternative for small business and the entrepreneur/investor—to incorporate as a "statutory close corporation." A statutory close corporation is every bit a corporation as any other corporation. Like a regular corporation, a certificate of incorporation for a statutory close corporation must be filed with the State.[68]

As in a partnership and a limited liability corporation, an important document in a statutory close corporation is the written shareholder agreement. This shareholder agreement, like a partnership agreement, spells out the relations among the shareholders (and between shareholders and the corporation).[69] As one can imagine, negotiations may be difficult as unanimity may be hard to attain.

Going back to the LHC situation, assume that Julia, Neil, and Dustin agree to incorporate the venture as a "statutory close corporation." Without a shareholder agreement, the general rules of corporation law apply. But the three may want greater flexibility. For example, they may want to do away with a board of directors and simply have all decisions, no matter how trivial or important, made by the three of them informally. Or Neil and Dustin may be solely investors, relying on Julia's business acumen. If that is the case, the shareholder agreement can designate Julia as being the decisionmaker for the company. Other types of provisions may be included in the shareholder agreement, such as employment contracts, mandatory dividend declarations if the business shows a profit, and stock transfer restrictions such as right of first refusal and buy-sell agreements. The virtue of a statutory close corporation is its flexibility so that shareholders can tailor the shareholder agreement to meet their needs.[70]

Surprisingly, however, statutory close corporations are rarely chosen by entrepreneurs. This is mainly because the more flexible provisions contained in the statutory close corporation statutes today also may be used by a regular corporation. As discussed in Chapter 3, the participants in a regular corporation, by executing separate employment contracts and stock transfer restrictions, can achieve comparable benefits. Today, a unanimous stockholder agreement may be entered into in the regular corporation context dispensing with the board of directors, designating managers of the enterprise, and providing for declaration of permissible dividends.[71] Moreover, as discussed above, shareholders and directors can conduct business by signing consents rather than holding formal meetings.[72] The informality now allowed in a regular corporation makes a statutory close corporation far less attractive.

LIMITED LIABILITY COMPANIES

Limited liability companies, also called LLCs, have become increasingly popular, particularly for businesses that have relatively few participants. Remember that LLCs are not corporations. The major benefits are that members of a LLC have limited liability just like a corporation and that tax treatment is similar to a partnership. Except for the franchise (or margin) tax, an LLC is not taxed as a separate enterprise (unless the LLC affirmatively elects to be taxed like a corporation). Like a partnership, the income or losses of the business "flow-through" to the individual participants and are reflected on their individual tax returns.[73]

To form a limited liability company, a filing with the State is required.[74] Normally, the LLC is governed by the terms contained in the operating agreement entered into by its members. The LLC operating agreement sets forth how decisions are to be made—whether by a group called the board of managers (similar to a board of directors in a corporation) or by the members themselves.[75] Such other matters as dividend policy, employment provisions, stock transfer restrictions, and voting rights also may be included.[76] When the operating agreement does not address a particular situation or when certain obligations cannot be eliminated as a matter of public policy (such as eliminating the duty of loyalty owed by the board of managers to the LLC's members), the LLC statute acts by default as the governing standard.[77] The simplest way to look at these agreements is to analogize them to the partnership agreement in a general or limited partnership or to the shareholder agreement in a corporation.

In a way, limited liability companies (LLCs) are treated the same as corporations that choose Subchapter S tax status. In both situations, the individual receives both the benefits of limited liability and partnership-like tax treatment. The advantage of the LLC is that it is not saddled with some of the confining requirements that apply to Subchapter S. For example, to qualify for Subchapter S, with certain exceptions, a corporation must have only one class of stock that it can issue.[78] These restrictions may prevent the shareholders from structuring the enterprise in the best way.

To illustrate this, let's return to the LHC Corporation scenario. Assume that Neil plans to contribute twice as much cash to the business as Julia or Dustin and understandably wants certain assurances. For example, Neil may want to elect two of the four directors, desire 50% of the profits, and, if dividends are declared, receive twice the amount than either Julia or Dustin. One possible way to meet Neil's demands is for the business to issue to Neil a separate class of stock that has these attributes. Neil, for instance, can be issued "Class B

Stock" that, as provided in the corporation's articles of incorporation, has the power to elect one-half of the directors and be entitled to 50% of the profits and dividends declared. Structuring the classes of stock in this manner would make LHC ineligible for Subchapter S status.

Unlike Subchapter S, this flexibility is available to limited liability companies. The LLC form thus provides for limited liability, partnership-like tax treatment, and flexibility in structuring the enterprise. Due to these benefits, the LLC is becoming the business form of choice for many entrepreneurs.

Notes

1. See W. Klein, J. Coffee and F. Partnoy, *Business Organizations and Finance* 53 (11th ed. 2010).
2. See § 101(10) of the Revised Uniform Partnership Act (RUPA).
3. RUPA § 401(f), (j).
4. *Id.* § 301(1).
5. *Id.* See *RNR Investments Limited Partnership v. Peoples First Community Bank,* 812 So. 2d 561 (Fla. Ct. App. 2002).
6. See RUPA §§ 301(1), 305.
7. *Id.* § 306(a).
8. *Id.* § 405. See *Rouse v. Pollard,* 21 A.2d 801 (N.J. 1941).
9. See RUPA § 103(a).
10. *Id.* § 503(a)(3), (b)(1).
11. *Id.* § 503(a)(3).
12. *Id.* § 401(i).
13. *Id.* §§ 601(1), 801(1).
14. *Id.* § 807(a), (b).
15. *Id.* § 807(a).
16. *Id.* § 401(j).
17. *Id.* § 801(2), (3).
18. *Id.* § 801(2)(ii).
19. *Id.* §§ 601(1), 701.
20. See Chapter 6 of this book.
21. See, e.g., *Meinhard v. Salmon,* 164 N.E. 545 (N.Y. 1928).
22. See, e.g., *Bane v. Ferguson,* 890 F. 2d 11 (7th Cir. 1989).
23. See RUPA § 404(c) (setting forth that "[a] partner's duty of care to the partnership and the other partners ... is limited to refraining from engaging in grossly negligent or reckless conduct, intentional misconduct, or a knowing violation of law").
24. *Id.* § 103(b)(3), (b)(4).

25. See J. Bauman, A. Palmiter and F. Partnoy, *Corporations—Law and Policy* 143 (6th ed. 2007).
26. See RUPA § 401(b).
27. *Id.* (stating that "[e]ach partner is entitled to an equal share of the partnership profits").
28. See § 303(a) of the Revised Uniform Limited Partnership Act (1985) (RULPA).
29. *Id.*
30. *Id.* § 303(b).
31. *Id.* § 303(a).
32. *Id.* § 303(b)(1). See *Zeiger v. Wilf,* 755 A.2d 608 (N.J. Super. Ct. 2000).
33. See RUPA § 303(a).
34. *Id.* § 201.
35. *Id.* § 304.
36. *Id.* Cf. *Cranson v. International Business Machines Corp.,* 200 A.2d 33 (Md. 1904).
37. RUPA § 403. See RUPA §§ 103(b)(3), (b)(4), 404(a)–(d).
38. *Id.* § 103(b)(3), (b)(4), (b)(5). See *Singer v. Singer,* 634 P.2d 766 (Okla. App. 1981). Cf. *McConnell v. Hunt Sports Enterprises,* 725 N.E. 2d 1193 (Ohio App. 1999).
39. See *RNR Investments Limited Partnership v. Peoples First Community Bank,* 812 So. 2d 561 (Fla. App. 2002).
40. See RULPA §§ 702, 704.
41. *Id.* §§ 801(1), 804.
42. *Id.* § 801(3).
43. See §§ 152.801–152.805 of the Texas Business Organizations Code.
44. See § 6.22 of the Revised Model Business Corporation Act (MBCA); *Brunswick Corp. v. Waxman,* 599 F. 2d 34 (2d Cir. 1979).
45. See MBCA § 2.03.
46. See Klein, Coffee and Partnoy, *supra* note 1, at 151.
47. See D. Branson, J. Heminway, M. Lowenstein, M. Steinberg and M. Warren, *Business Enterprises: Legal Structures, Governance, and Policy* 145 (2009).
48. See MBCA § 8.03(c).
49. See *Menard, Inc. v. Dage-MTI, Inc.,* 726 N.E. 2d 1206 (Ind. 2000).
50. See *Kinney Shoe Corporation v. Polan,* 939 F. 2d 209 (4th Cir. 1991).
51. See Klein, Coffee and Partnoy, *supra* note 1, at 151.
52. *Id.*
53. See MBCA §§ 7.04, 8.21.
54. See, e.g., § 228(a) of the Delaware General Corporation Law.
55. *Id.* § 228(e).
56. See RUPA § 401(i); RULPA §§ 702, 704.
57. See, e.g., *Smith v. Van Gorkom,* 488 A. 2d 858 (Del. 1995); *Ryan v. Gifford,* 918 A. 2d 341 (Del. Ch. 2007).
58. See *Weinberger v. UOP, Inc.,* 457 A. 2d 701 (Del. 1983).

59. See *Francis v. United Jersey Bank,* 432 A. 2d 814 (N.J. 1981).
60. See *State ex. rel. Hayes Oyster Co. v. Keypoint Oyster Co.*, 391 P. 2d 979 (Wash. 1964).
61. See Bauman, Palmiter and Partnoy, *supra* note 25, at 143.
62. *Id.* at 144.
63. *Id.* at 147.
64. *Id.* See *Smith v. Atlantic Properties, Inc.*, 422 N.E. 2d 798 (Mass. 1981).
65. See Bauman, Palmiter and Partnoy, *supra* note 25, at 146.
66. *Id.*
67. See *Thompson & Green Machinery Co. v. Music City Lumber Co.*, 683 S.W. 2d 340 (Tenn. App. 1984).
68. See § 343 of the Delaware General Corporation Law.
69. *Id.* § 350.
70. *Id.* §§ 350, 351. Under Delaware law, a number of these provisions must be set forth in the corporation's articles of incorporation. *Id.* § 351. When the shareholders take on duties that are normally performed by the board of directors, these fiduciary duties are imposed upon the shareholders rather than the directors. *Id.* § 350.
71. See MCBA § 7.32.
72. *Id.* § 7.04.
73. See 26 U.S.C. § 7701; Bauman, Palmiter and Partnoy, *supra* note 25, at 143–144.
74. See § 202 of the Uniform Limited Liability Company Act (ULLCA).
75. *Id.* §§ 103; § 18-402 of the Delaware Limited Liability Company Act.
76. See ULLCA § 103.
77. *Id.*
78. See Bauman, Palmiter and Partnoy, *supra* note 25, at 146.

THE FOLLOWING CASES discuss issues that arise in the context of business enterprises other than the corporation (which receives extensive coverage throughout this book). The portions excerpted are intended to provide a better understanding of these enterprises.

CREEL V. LILLY
COURT OF APPEALS OF MARYLAND
729 A. 2D 385 (1999)

...

We begin our analysis by reviewing the law of partnership as it pertains to the issues in this case. Maryland enacted the UPA [Uniform Partnership Act] in 1916. Section 9-101(g) [of that Act] defines a partnership as "an association of two or more persons to carry on as co-owners a business for profit." There is no requirement that the partnership be formally established with a writing; so long as this definition is met, a partnership exists whether the parties intend it to or not. However, the "general rule is that the partnership agreement governs the relations among the partners and between the partners and the partnership. The provisions of [the UPA] govern to the extent the partnership agreement does not provide otherwise."...

A partnership is either (1) for a definite term or a particular undertaking or (2) at will, which means the business has no definite term or particular undertaking. An at-will partnership continues indefinitely and can be dissolved by the express will of any partner or automatically by the happening of a specific event as mandated by the UPA, such as the death of a partner. Under the UPA, partners may avoid the automatic dissolution of the business upon the death of a partner by providing for its continuation in their partnership agreement. Sophisticated partnerships virtually always use carefully drafted partnership agreements to protect the various partners' interests by providing for the continuation of the business, the distribution of partnership assets, etc., in the face of various contingencies such as death. Less sophisticated partnerships, however, are often operating under oral terms or a "homemade" agreement that does not contain protections for the partners or the business.

CASE STUDIES

While the death of a partner automatically dissolves the partnership unless there is an agreement stating otherwise, the partnership is not terminated until the winding-up process is complete. *See also* § 9-601 ("On dissolution, the partnership is not terminated, but continues until the winding up of partnership affairs is completed.") Winding up is generally defined as "getting in the assets, settling with [the] debtors and creditors, and appropriating the amount of profit or loss [to the partners]." ... The surviving partners have the right to wind up the partnership or the deceased partner's representative may obtain a winding up through the courts. Section 9-609 [of the Maryland Act] details the winding-up procedures and whether Subsection (a) or (b) applies depends on whether dissolution was caused in contravention of the partnership agreement or not, wrongfully, etc. The winding-up procedure that applies in this case is found in § 9-609(a), which states in pertinent part: "When dissolution is caused in any way ... each partner ... unless otherwise agreed, may have the partnership property applied to discharge its liabilities, and the surplus applied to pay in cash the net amount owing to the respective partners."

Historically, under many courts and commentators' interpretation of the UPA, when a partner died and the partnership automatically dissolved because there was no consent by the estate to continue the business nor was there a written agreement allowing for continuation, the estate had the right to compel liquidation of the partnership assets. ... Reducing all of the partnership assets to cash through a liquidation was seen as the only way to obtain the true value of the business. However, while winding up has often traditionally been regarded as synonymous with liquidation, this "fire sale" of assets has been viewed by many courts and commentators as a harsh and destructive measure. Consequently, to avoid the drastic result of a forced liquidation, many courts have adopted judicial alternatives to this potentially harmful measure ...

Over time, the UPA rule requiring automatic dissolution of the partnership upon the death of a partner, in the absence of consent by the estate to continue the business or an agreement providing for continuation, with the possible result of a forced sale of all partnership assets was viewed as outmoded by many jurisdictions including Maryland. The development and adoption of [the Revised Uniform Partnership Act] RUPA by the National Conference of Commissioners on Uniform State Laws (NCCUSL) mitigated this harsh UPA provision of automatic dissolution and compelled liquidation.

RUPA's underlying philosophy differs radically from the UPA's, thus laying the foundation for many of its innovative measures. RUPA adopts the "entity" theory of partnership as opposed to the "aggregate" theory that the UPA espouses. Under the aggregate theory, a partnership is characterized by the collection of its individual members, with the result being that if one of the partners dies or withdraws, the partnership ceases to exist ... On the other hand, RUPA's entity theory allows for the partnership to continue even with the departure of a member because it views the partnership as "an entity distinct from its partners." ...

This adoption of the entity theory, which permits continuity of the partnership upon changes in partner identity, allows for several significant changes in RUPA. Of particular importance to the instant case is that under RUPA "a partnership no longer automatically dissolves due to a change in its membership, but rather *the existing partnership may be continued if the remaining partners elect to buy out the dissociating partner.*" ... In contrast to the UPA, RUPA's "buy-out" option does not have to be expressly included in a written partnership agreement in order for it to be exercised; however, the surviving partners must still actively choose to exercise the option, as "continuation is not automatic as with a corporation." ... This major RUPA innovation therefore delineates two possible paths for a partnership to follow when a partner dies or withdraws: "[o]ne leads to the winding up and termination of the partnership and the other to continuation of the partnership and purchase of the departing partner's share." ... Critically, under RUPA the estate of the deceased partner no longer has to consent in order for the business to be continued nor does the estate have the right to compel liquidation.

Like the UPA, RUPA is a "gap filler" in that it only governs partnership affairs to the extent not otherwise agreed to by the partners in the partnership agreement. *See* 9A-103(a), which states: "[R]elations among the partners and between the partners and the partnership are governed by the partnership agreement. To the extent the partnership agreement does not otherwise provide, this title governs relations among the partners and between the partners and the partnership." There are certain RUPA provisions, however, that partners cannot waive, such as unreasonably restricting the right of access to partnership books and records, eliminating the duty of loyalty, unreasonably reducing the duty of care, and eliminating the obligation of good faith and fair dealing.

Along with [many] other states, Maryland has adopted the RUPA ... In adopting RUPA, the Maryland legislature was clearly seeking to eliminate some of UPA's harsh provisions, such as the automatic dissolution of a viable partnership upon the death of a partner and the subsequent right of the estate of the deceased partner to compel liquidation. In essence, the NCCUSL drafted RUPA to reflect the emerging trends in partnership law. RUPA is intended as a flexible, modern alternative to the more rigid UPA and its provisions are consistent with the reasonable expectations of commercial parties in today's business world.

Gotham Partners L.P. v. Hallwood Realty Partners, L.P.
Supreme Court of Delaware
817 A. 2d 160 (2002)

[This case focuses on contractual provisions in a limited partnership agreement that modified the statutory default provisions. The Delaware Supreme Court stated:]

... [A] general partner owes the traditional fiduciary duties of loyalty and care to the limited partnership and its partners, but [the Delaware Revised Uniform Limited Partnership Act] DRULPA "expressly authorizes the ... modification, or enhancement of these fiduciary duties in the written agreement governing the limited partnership." Indeed, we have recognized that, by statute, the parties to a Delaware limited partnership have the power and discretion to form and operate a limited partnership "in an environment of private ordering" according to the provisions in the limited partnership agreement. We have noted that DRULPA embodies "the policy of freedom of contract" and "maximum flexibility." DRULPA's "basic approach is to permit partners to have the broadest possible discretion in drafting their partnership agreements and to furnish answers only in situations where the partners have not expressly made provisions in their partnership agreement" or "where the agreement is inconsistent with mandatory statutory provisions." In those situations, a court will "look for guidance from the statutory default rules, traditional notions of fiduciary duties, or other extrinsic evidence." But, if the limited partnership agreement unambiguously provides for [the recognition or limitation of] fiduciary duties, any claim of a breach of a fiduciary duty must be analyzed generally in terms of the partnership agreement. ...

THE NEXT DECISION, authored by Chief Justice Veasey, focuses on the attributes of the limited liability company (LLC).

ELF ATOCHEM NORTH AMERICA, INC. V. JAFFARI
SUPREME COURT OF DELAWARE
727 A. 2D 286 (1999)

The phenomenon of business arrangements using "alternative entities" has been developing rapidly over the past several years. Long gone are the days when business planners were confined to corporate or partnership structures.

Limited partnerships date back to the 19th Century. They became an important and popular vehicle with the adoption of the Uniform Limited Partnership Act in 1916. Sixty years later, in 1976, the National Conference of Commissioners on Uniform State Laws approved and recommended to the states a Revised Uniform Limited Partnership Act ("RULPA"), many provisions of which were modeled after the innovative 1973 Delaware Limited Partnership (LP) Act. Difficulties with the workability of the 1976 RULPA prompted the Commissioners to amend RULPA in 1985.

To date, [several] states have adopted the RULPA in either its 1976 or 1985 form. Delaware adopted the RULPA with innovations designed to improve upon the Commissioners' product. Since 1983, the General Assembly has amended the LP Act eleven times, with a view to continuing Delaware's status as an innovative leader in the field of limited partnerships.

... [By comparison, the limited liability company,] the LLC, is an attractive form of business entity because it combines corporate-type limited liability with partnership-type flexibility and tax advantages. The Act can be characterized as a "flexible statute" because it generally permits members to engage in private ordering with substantial freedom of contract to govern their relationship, provided they do not contravene any mandatory provisions of the Act. Indeed, the LLC has been characterized as the "best of both worlds."

The Delaware [LLC] Act has been modeled on the popular Delaware [limited partnership] LP Act. In fact, its architecture and much of its wording is almost identical to that of the Delaware LP Act. Under the Act, a member of an LLC is treated much like a limited partner under the LP Act. The policy of freedom of contract underlies both the [LLC] Act and the LP Act.

In August 1994, nearly two years after the enactment of the Delaware LLC Act, the Uniform Law Commissioners promulgated the Uniform Limited Liability Company Act (ULLCA). To coordinate with later developments in federal tax guidelines regarding manager-managed LLCs, the Commissioners adopted minor changes in 1995. The Commissioners further amended the ULLCA in 1996. Despite its purpose to promote uniformity and consistency, the ULLCA has not been widely popular. In fact, [relatively few] jurisdictions have adopted the ULLCA since its creation in 1994. ...

The basic approach of the Delaware Act is to provide members with broad discretion in drafting the Agreement and to furnish default provisions when the members' agreement is silent. The Act is replete with fundamental provisions made subject to modification in the Agreement (*e.g.*, "unless otherwise provided in a limited liability company agreement ...").

...

Section 18-1101(b) of the [Delaware LLC] Act, like the essentially identical Section 17-1101(c) of the LP Act, provides that "it is the policy of [the Act] to give the maximum effect to the principle of freedom of contract and to the enforceability of limited liability company agreements." Accordingly, the following observation relating to limited partnerships applies as well to limited liability companies:

The Act's basic approach is to permit partners to have the broadest possible discretion in drafting their partnership agreements and to furnish answers only in situations where the partners have not expressly made provisions in their partnership agreement. Truly, the partnership agreement is the cornerstone of a Delaware limited partnership, and effectively constitutes the entire agreement among the partners with respect to the admission of partners to, and the creation, operation and termination of, the limited partnership. Once partners exercise their contractual freedom in their partnership agreement, the partners have a great deal of certainty that their partnership agreement will be enforced in accordance with its terms.

In general, the commentators observe that only where the agreement is inconsistent with mandatory statutory provisions will the members' agreement be invalidated. Such statutory provisions are likely to be those intended to protect third parties, not necessarily the contracting [LLC] members. ...

...

Whether LLC interests are "securities" under federal and state law is a matter that has not been definitively resolved. The excerpt from the following case (which is covered more extensively in Chapter 8), *Robinson v. Glynn*, 349 F. 3d 166, 173–174 (4th Cir. 2003), discusses in a general fashion certain characteristics of limited liability companies:

The characteristics typically associated with common stock [issued by corporations] are (i) the right to receive dividends contingent upon an apportionment of profits; (ii) negotiability; (iii) the ability to be pledged or hypothecated; (iv) the conferring of voting rights in proportion to the number of shares owned; and (v) the capacity to appreciate in value. [The plaintiff] Robinson's [LLC] membership interest in [the LLC] GeoPhone lacked several of these characteristics.

First, as is common with interests in LLCs, [the LLC] GeoPhone's members did not share in the profits in proportion to the number of their shares. See Larry E. Ribstein, *Form and Substance in the Definition of a "Security": The Case of Limited Liability Companies*, 51 Wash. & Lee L. Rev. 807, 833 (1994) (noting that "LLC statutes usually do not provide for dividend rights"). Pursuant to the [Operating Agreement], Robinson was to receive 100 percent of GeoPhone's net profits up to a certain amount, only after which were funds to be distributed pro rata to the members in proportion to their relative shares.

Second, like interests in LLCs more generally, Robinson's membership interests were not freely negotiable. See *id.* (observing that LLC statutes invariably restrict transferability of management rights"). According to the [Operating Agreement], Robinson could only transfer his interest if he first offered other members the opportunity to purchase his interest on similar terms. Moreover, unlike with stock (except some stock in close corporations), anyone to whom Robinson or other members transferred their interest would not have thereby acquired any of the control or management rights that normally attend a stock transfer. ... Rather, the [Operating Agreement] requires that transferees satisfy several conditions to become members, in addition to receiving the approval of a majority of GeoPhone's managers.

Similarly, Robinson could pledge his interest, but the pledgee would acquire only distribution rights and not control rights. ... As for the appointment of voting rights, the parties dispute whether voting rights were conferred in proportion to members' interest in [the LLC] GeoPhone. ...

The parties have vigorously urged us to rule broadly in this case, asking that we generally classify interests in limited liability companies, or LLCs, as investment contracts (Robinson's view) or non-securities (Glynn's view). LLCs are particularly difficult to categorize under the securities laws, however, because they are hybrid business entities that combine features of corporations, general partnerships, and limited partnerships. As their name indicates, LLCs can limit the liability of their members, which may mean that LLC members are more likely to be passive investors who need the protection of the securities laws. However, LLC members are also able to actively participate in management without piercing the veil of their liability, which would suggest that LLC members are more likely than limited partners or corporate shareholders to be active investors not in need of the securities statutes. ...

Precisely because LLCs lack standardized membership rights or organizational structures, they can assume an almost unlimited variety of forms. ... Certainly the members in a member-managed LLC will often have powers too significant to be considered passive investors. ... And yet even members in a member-managed LLC may be unable as a practical matter to exercise any meaningful control, perhaps because they are too numerous, inexperienced, or geographically disparate. ...

SCENARIO

Louise Lacy, Max Moore, Nancy Nagle, and Stevie Seal, frustrated with their current jobs, decide to combine their resources and start their own business. They have known one another for years and are friends. They anticipate that a wine and food establishment featuring upscale wines and cuisine from such countries as Argentina, Australia, Chile, Israel, South Africa, and Spain will be a huge success.

The written agreement among Lacy, Moore, Nagle, and Seal provides that:

(1) Lacy, Moore, Nagle, and Seal each will own a one-fourth interest.

(2) Lacy, Moore, and Nagle will work actively in the business to be called "Wines Exotics and Culinary Delights" (Wines Exotics) and will earn his/her livelihood earning a salary from working in the business.

(3) Seal will not work in the business and will be relying on dividends for his financial return.

(4) Lacy will be the chief bartender and will be mainly responsible for ordering the wines, Moore will handle the ordering of food and overseeing the chefs, and Nagle will focus on customer relations to ensure that food, wine and service are all superb. And

(5) Lacy, Moore, Nagle and Seal each has veto power over any and all "significant" decisions that involves Wines Exotics (including, for example, a change in the nature of the business, the relocation of the business, and the entry of new participant-owners in the business).

What type of business enterprise do you recommend be formed? What are the reasons supporting your recommendation?

Chapter 3

"PARTNER-SHAREHOLDER" AGREEMENTS

AFTER SELECTING CHOICE of enterprise form (such as a corporation), a key subject to focus on is the entering into agreements that will protect the participants. These agreements relate to such matters as employment, dividends, control in the enterprise, and transfer of ownership interest.

To set the stage, assume that we have four individuals,—Alexandria ("Alex"), Ken, Olivia and Vince—who seek to form a consulting business directed at "etiquette in the workplace." Contracting with businesses that have consumer clientele (such as car dealerships and furniture stores), the enterprise called "Business Etiquette Plus" (BEP) advises sales and service personnel to provide "more professional" client service.

Alex, Ken and Vince intend to earn their livelihoods by working in the business. They each contribute $20,000 and take a 25% ownership interest. Olivia, who is an investor in the venture and who is not working in the business, contributes $50,000 for her 25% interest.

What are important interests for the participants? For example, Alex, Ken, and Vince need employment and wages. Olivia wants dividends if the business shows a profit. They each want to be protected in case of future disagreements with the others. And each may desire an "exit" strategy upon certain events, such as divorce or retirement.

With no agreement, consider if the following occurs: (1) After ten years, Ken has a falling out with Alex, Olivia, and Vince, who terminate his employment; (2) Vince and his wife Sandra get divorced in a "community property" state (e.g., California) and Sandra, who is entitled to 50% of Vince's stock, wants to be active in the business against the wishes of the other participants; (3) In spite of increasing profits, dividends are not declared, leaving Olivia with no returns; and (4) Ken dies, bequeathing his shares to his inept son Bubba.

The above are examples of what can happen in any business. Now, let's turn to ways that one can protect him/herself.

Employment

Many co-owners do not get employment contracts. They either trust their "partners" or don't give it a "second thought." If someone has control and intends to keep it, such an attitude makes sense. If one is a "minority shareholder," however, such trust in one's "partners" may lead to joining the line at the unemployment benefits office.

To a prudent co-owner, such as Alex, who seeks to earn a living from BEP, an employment contract between Alex and BEP is a "must." Rather than being for a set time period, the agreement can be for so long as Alex competently performs her job (or providing that Alex can be fired only "for cause").

Of course, initial remuneration should be agreed upon between Alex and BEP. Alex also may seek additional protection, such as an annual adjustment of her salary to reflect the consumer price index. She also may want her salary to reflect any increase in BEP's profitability. In addition, she may seek a bonus based on BEP's annual net profits, such as 10% — that for every $1,000 in annual net profit earned by BEP, Alex's bonus is increased by $100.

Of course, any employment contract between Alex and BEP will be a product of negotiation. Ken and Vince would want similar, if not identical, agreements. And, for Olivia to go along, she would demand her perceived right to dividends.

Dividends

As used in this setting, dividends means distributing profits to shareholders. More particularly, assume that for 2011, BEP made a net profit (after payment of wages and other expenses) of $40,000. Assuming that there is one class of stock, each 25% shareholder (owning let's assume 25 shares) would receive $10,000 if a dividend of all profits were declared by BEP.

Olivia may be less than thrilled with this scenario. Why? As a passive investor, Olivia must depend on dividends for a return on her investment. In the BEP venture, she contributed $50,000 compared with the three other participants who each contributed $20,000. Because Alex, Ken and Vince also are drawing salaries, sharing of dividends on an equal basis may strike Olivia as unfair.

Let's go a step further. Assume that Alex, Ken and Vince outvote Olivia and refuse to declare any dividends. Rather, all profits are distributed in the form of increased wages (or cash bonuses) to the three "working" co-owners, namely, Alex, Ken and Vince. By dividing the pie into three parts rather than four, Alex, Ken, and Vince get a larger slice. However, Olivia is left with no return.

Of course, Olivia can hire a lawyer, allege minority shareholder "oppression,"[1] and seek a court order requiring that dividends be declared.[2] But such a process takes time and money, with no favorable result guaranteed.

How can Olivia protect herself from the outset? Perhaps the most feasible alternative is to have four classes of stock: Class A—100% owned by Alex, Class B—100% owned by Ken, Class C—100% owned by Vince, and Class D—100% owned by Olivia. As provided in the unanimous shareholder agreement and preferably in BEP's articles of incorporation, Class D stock is entitled to receive annually a dividend of a certain percentage of BEP's profits for that year (let's say 40%). Any other dividends declared, after payment of the Class D dividends, is to be paid equally to the three remaining classes of stock. To ensure that Alex, Ken, and Vince cannot later amend this provision to adversely affect her right to dividends, Olivia should insist that any change to this provision requires unanimous approval.

Because the declaration of dividends traditionally has been under the authority of the corporation's board of directors,[3] the possibility exists that, if challenged, a court may declare a dividend provision, such as that just discussed, invalid.[4] Nonetheless, particularly if this provision is contained in BEP's articles of incorporation, the prevailing standard today upholds the validity of such a dividend provision.[5]

ELECTING DIRECTORS

Assuming that Alex, Ken, Olivia, and Vince each owns 25% of BEP's stock and each desires to exercise some control, it is important for them to serve as directors. It is the board of directors which frequently makes key decisions for the business, such as appointing officers, setting salaries, declaring dividends, and entering into major contracts.

With each co-owner having a 25% interest, how is a directorship for each assured? To illustrate, three ways will be explored. The first is to establish four classes of stock as outlined above with Alex, Ken, Olivia, and Vince each owning 100% of the stock of separate classes (*i.e.*, Alex owns 100% of Class A, Ken owns 100% of Class B, *etc.*). As provided in BEP's articles of incorporation, each class of stock elects one director, allowing, for example, Alex as the 100% stockholder of Class A stock to elect herself as a director.[6]

A second way is to allow for cumulative voting. Under cumulative voting, which applies only to electing directors, a shareholder has voting power which can be divided any way the shareholder so chooses, including voting all shares in favor of one candidate. The number of votes any shareholder has is the number of shares owned multiplied by the number of directors to be elected. Under the BEP scenario, Alex, Ken, Olivia and Vince, all have 100 votes (each owns 25 shares × 4 directors to be elected). By casting all their votes in favor of their own candidacy, each of the four will have sufficient votes to be elected a director.[7]

If the participants elect not to have separate classes of stock or cumulative voting, they can still assure themselves directorships by entering into vote pooling agreements with their fellow participants. For example, Alex can agree to vote for Ken, Olivia, and Vince as directors provided that all three agree to vote for her as a director. Generally, such agreements, if they are not secret, are valid and enforceable.[8]

In any of the foregoing situations, there should be additional protective measures instituted to ensure that each shareholder is assured his/her director position. For example, cumulative voting ordinarily is permitted only if the corporation's articles of incorporation so provide.[9] The BEP shareholders, to be assured of their directorships, may desire to have the number of directors set forth in BEP's articles of incorporation fixed at four and that the articles cannot be amended without the unanimous approval of the shareholders. Such techniques help to assure each shareholder of being elected a director.

Officer Positions

Assume that Alex wants to be President of BEP. As President, she will have significant authority acting as an agent of BEP. For example, unless the BEP Board of Directors directs otherwise, Alex as BEP's president has the authority to enter into ordinary contracts for BEP.[10]

How does Alex assure that she will be President or Ken assure that he will be Treasurer? The clear and valid way is for each to be appointed to their positions by the BEP Board of Directors. Nonetheless, if the Board of Directors becomes disenchanted with Alex's performance as President or Ken's as

Treasurer, the Board has the authority to remove either. This is so even if the removal violates an agreement providing that, for example, Alex shall serve as President for so long as she competently performs or for a specified period of time. It is quite possible that Alex may recover damages for the breach but, nonetheless, generally speaking, she can be fired.[11]

Perhaps the best strategy for Alex to guarantee her officership is to procure an agreement with the individuals who will serve as BEP directors (such as Ken, Olivia, and Vince) to appoint Alex as President so long as she faithfully and competently performs her duties. The agreement also should provide that the remedy for breach of the agreement—dismissal without good cause—is for a court order reappointing Alex as President and that damages alone are not adequate compensation.[12]

A court may or may not enforce such an agreement. The agreement runs afoul of the traditional notions that only the Board of Directors acting as a body can appoint the officers and that the Board retains the authority to fire officers.[13] Nonetheless, an increasing number of courts recognize that informality often reigns in small business enterprises.[14] Moreover, statutes in many states today uphold these types of agreements if they are contained in the corporation's articles of incorporation, bylaws, or in a unanimous shareholder agreement.[15]

But also to the point, why should the other shareholders of BEP agree to Alex's request that dismissal as President be only for good cause? Unless Alex has some irreplaceable skills or other impressive leverage to negotiate, generally they shouldn't. Such an agreement may be against the other shareholders' interests to provide greater flexibility in managerial efficiency. In short, it may make "deadwood" or incompetence harder to eliminate.

SHAREHOLDER AGREEMENTS—VOTING AND CONTROL

Shareholders may wish to join together to help maximize their voting and control interests. We already have looked at one device—the vote pooling agreement. Under a vote pooling agreement, shareholders may join together to vote for one another as directors and to vote their shares as a unit at shareholder meetings.[16]

Another way to enforce such an agreement is for one shareholder to the agreement to provide to the other a proxy to vote the other's shares. A proxy generally is a power of attorney by which the proxy giver (such as Alex) directs the proxy holder (such as Vince) how to vote Alex's shares. Although a proxy normally is revocable,[17] a proxy granted in connection with the carrying out of a vote pooling agreement in many states today is irrevocable and is specifically enforceable.[18]

A more formal arrangement is called a "voting trust." In a voting trust, the voting power actually is separated from other ownership attributes (such as entitlement to dividends). A voting trust certificate is issued pursuant to which shares coming under the agreement's terms are voted as directed by the agreement.[19] Today, the voting trust often is used for the benefit of creditors. For example, as a condition to lending BEP $100,000, a bank may demand that it elect two directors to BEP's Board of Directors until the loan is repaid. To effectuate this objective, a voting trust frequently is an appropriate mechanism.

STOCK TRANSFER RESTRICTIONS

Stock transfer restrictions are key to any business with relatively few participants. The prospect of a partner, shareholder or LLC member thrusting an unwanted entrant upon fellow participants simply is unacceptable. By doing so, as discussed in Chapter 2, liability magnifies and chemistry between the participants deteriorates. To reduce these risks, stock transfer restrictions are necessary. As a generalization, any such restriction to be upheld must be deemed a reasonable restraint on alienation.[20] Moreover, to enforce the stock transfer restriction against a subsequent bona fide purchaser for value, language regarding restrictions on transferability contained on the stock certificate or like instrument must be conspicuous.[21] Types of transfer restrictions follow.

(1) CONSENT BY REMAINING SHAREHOLDERS

The strictest type of transfer restriction prohibits a shareholder from selling his/her stock unless the other shareholders consent. In effect, even if a bona fide purchaser exists, the shareholders may veto the transaction. The result is that the shareholder seeking to sell his/her interest is locked into the investment with no exit available. Because many courts view this type of provision as an unreasonable restraint upon the transferability of ownership interests,[22] there is the distinct possibility that such a provision will not be enforced.

(2) RIGHT OF FIRST REFUSAL

A right of first refusal provides that, once a shareholder finds a bona fide purchaser, the shareholder must offer to sell the shares to the corporation and/or the remaining shareholders at the same price and on the same terms as those offered by the bona fide purchaser. Normally, pursuant to the stock transfer restriction, the shares first must be offered to the corporation. If the corporation declines, the shareholders then have the right to purchase the subject shares generally on a pro rata basis. Only after the corporation and/or the remaining stockholders decline to match the price and terms offered, may the sale be completed to the bona fide purchaser.[23]

Under a right of first refusal, a participant may exit the business by selling his/her interest only if a bona fide purchaser is located. However, if no bona fide purchaser can be found, the participant continues to be locked into the business. Note also that, if a bona fide purchaser emerges, the terms and price of the sale are determined by the deal struck between the departing participant and the bona fide purchaser.[24] An example of a right of first refusal provision is as follows:

Right of First Refusal Provision

> *If at any time during the term of this Agreement, any Stockholder (the "Selling Stockholder") shall desire to Sell all or any part of its Shares pursuant to a bona fide offer from any third party (the "Third Party" or the "Third Party Offer"), it shall give the Corporation and the other Stockholders (the "Non-Selling Stockholders") written notice (the "Notice") of such intention. The Notice shall include an offer (the "Offer") to sell such Shares first to the Corporation and second to the Non-Selling Stockholders, upon the terms and conditions offered by the Third Party.*
>
> *The Corporation shall have 15 days from the date it receives the Notice to accept or reject the Offer in writing. If the Corporation rejects the Offer, the Non-Selling Stockholders shall have 15 days after they receive the Notice that the Corporation has rejected the Offer to accept or reject the Offer in writing on a pro rata basis. In the event the Corporation and the Non-Selling Stockholders fail to agree to purchase all of the Shares subject to the Third Party Offer, the Selling Stockholder shall be released from its obligations under this Agreement as to its Shares subject to the Offer and may sell such Shares to the Third Party.*

(3) *FIRST OPTION*

A first option is identical to a right of first refusal in that, to exit the business and sell his/her interest, the participant must find a bona fide purchaser. And, like a right of first refusal, the corporation and/or the remaining shareholders may exercise their option to purchase the stock. The critical difference is that, unlike a right of first refusal, the terms and price of the sale are determined by the provisions contained in the first option agreement that previously was executed between the affected shareholder and the corporation, or, alternatively, between the shareholders individually.[25]

Let's provide an example. Assume that the first option provides that prior to selling his stock to a bona fide purchaser, Vince must offer the shares to the corporation (BEP) and, if BEP declines to purchase the shares, then to the remaining shareholders (Alex, Ken, and Olivia) at $30 per share on a pro rata basis. Only if BEP, Alex, Ken, and, Olivia decline to purchase the shares can Vince sell his shares to the outsider.

Further assume that the outside party offers Vince $75 per share. If the first option is exercised by BEP or the remaining shareholders, Vince must sell his shares for $30 per share. Needless to say, Vince will cry "foul" when he hears that he is entitled to a fraction of that offered by the bona fide outside party. Nonetheless, unless Vince can prove fraud or other egregious circumstances, courts normally will enforce the contract as it is written.[26]

(4) *BUY-SELL AGREEMENTS*

Buy-sell agreements require that, upon a certain event, the shareholder must sell and the enterprise must buy his/her stock. Buy-sell agreements normally are triggered by such events as retirement and death. In community property states (such as California and Texas), buy-sell agreements also may be triggered on divorce to ensure that the former spouse of a participant in the business does not become an individual shareholder.[27] This scenario was illustrated earlier in this chapter.

As with other types of stock transfer restrictions, funding of the purchase price may be problematic. In the buy-sell scenario, "key-man" life insurance is normally a "must." In this way, upon a shareholder's death, his/her stock interest is redeemed from the proceeds of the life insurance policy. Under such a policy, the deceased shareholder is the insured and the company is named as beneficiary.

Without such a policy in effect, the business may be unable to generate the sum needed to pay off the estate. If that is the case, then loans will have to be procured or certain assets sold off. Indeed, if credit sources and assets are inadequate, the business may have to be liquidated (namely all its assets sold) to generate the requisite cash. In short, a "going out of business" sale will be necessary, resulting in the remaining shareholders being without a job and without significant income.

If the participants do not qualify for life insurance policies or if the premiums are too costly, other funding vehicles should be considered. A good alternative frequently is the installment payout which is discussed later in this chapter. Note also that installment payouts are also used for other situations triggering a buy-sell clause, such as a shareholder's retirement or divorce.

Of course, without a buy-sell agreement, upon a participant's death, the stock will be inherited by relatives and/or friends. Whether these individuals will be welcome as shareholders or active participants is dubious. At worst, havoc and mayhem will prevail.

FUNDING VEHICLES

As a planning technique, funding mechanisms are important and often necessary to generate the cash needed to buy out a participant or his/her estate. Tax consequences may flow from these devices, necessitating specialized legal counsel. For example, three different funding vehicles are:

(1) "KEY-MAN" LIFE INSURANCE

This funding vehicle is discussed above. For each policy, the shareholder is the insured and the business is the beneficiary. Provided that the appropriate coverage is obtained, the amount paid upon the participant's death will enable the business to purchase his/her stock or other ownership interests (such as partnership interests).[28]

(2) INSTALLMENT PAYOUTS

Installment payouts may be used in a variety of circumstances where a business and/or its participants purchase ownership interests (such as stock) from one of its members. Resignation, retirement, and divorce (in order to pay off the former spouse of a shareholder) serve as examples.

If installment payouts are the preferred route, it would be prudent to include this funding vehicle in a written provision. A period of years should be selected, such as five years, during which time a specified percentage of the total amount owed is paid in periodic intervals. Payment of a certain rate of interest until the installments have been completed also should be agreed upon.[29]

Installment payouts normally enable the business to continue without great injury. Financial growth, however, may be stymied, particularly if the installments amount to a significant percentage of the enterprise's assets. Indeed, capital expansion plans may be curtailed and the level of salaries and dividends may take a significant "blow."

In spite of these downsides, installment payouts often may be the best funding alternative for a small business, especially in stock buy-back situations.

(3) DEBT COVENANTS

Lenders normally insist on certain covenants (or commitments) that must be made by the business enterprise. These include, for example: restrictions (or total prohibition) with respect to dividend payouts, limitations on the company taking on more debt, maintenance of the enterprise's property in acceptable condition, limitations (or prohibition) against changes in the nature of the business and voting control, maintenance of the enterprise's financial condition (such as maintaining a specified asset to debt ratio), and the occasional use of sinking funds.[30]

Sinking funds are generally a planning tool by which the business "saves" the funds needed to pay its debts or to purchase participant interests. For example, a specified percentage (e.g., 5%) of the enterprise's profits each year may be set aside in a money market fund to help provide a sufficient cash fund to satisfy contingencies as they arise. Creditors occasionally may demand a sinking fund as a condition to extending a long-term loan to the business. Many creditors, on the other hand, may have sufficient comfort in this respect if personal guarantees are given by company shareholders or if the company maintains an adequate equity cushion (such as a suitable asset to debt ratio). A sinking fund ordinarily is disfavored by a borrower but may have to be implemented as a result of negotiations with the lender. The reason they are disliked by borrowers is clear: Businesses on the brink of failure that need to use revenues to pay salaries and other expenses consider "sinking funds" a luxury they cannot afford.

VALUATION

A huge problem in the buy-sell, first option, and related situations is valuation. If current market value is to be used, how is it determined? Do the participants themselves decide or do they hire an independent expert to ascertain the valuation? If the expert route is chosen, how is the particular expert selected?

A number of valuation formulas may be used. For example, "book value" generally measures the enterprise's worth at its historical cost.[31] If the corporation purchased its building in 1995 for $75,000, book value remains at $75,000 even though the market value today is $265,000. It is possible that "book value" may be adjusted periodically to reflect current value or that a hybrid formula of which "book value" comprises a part of such valuation may be used.

A valuation formula based on "capitalization of earnings" is an alternative. The enterprise's net earnings for a given period of time (e.g., one year) is multiplied by a selected "multiplier" that is appropriate for the industry in which the enterprise conducts its business.[32] For example, if BEP's net earnings for one year is $100,000 and the appropriate multiplier is three, this formula results in a value of $300,000 for BEP ($100,000 multiplied by three). Under a buy-out clause having this provision, Vince owning 25% of BEP would be entitled to $75,000 ($300,000 multiplied by .25).

Alternatively, the shareholders may agree that an "independent" appraiser should be selected periodically or at or near the time of the "buy-out" to determine the "fair value" of the shares (or other interests to be sold). Of course, determining who is to serve as the designated appraiser may prove problematic.

Regardless of the valuation formula used, the participants should have sufficient comfort that the actual formula implemented is acceptable. The "rip-off" potential in the valuation context is real. Often, those remaining in the business wish to pay as little as possible for the departing participant's interest. Even where the participants agree to periodically revise the valuation, the stresses of running a business prevail—frequently resulting in the slighting of this objective. Particularly, where one stockholder is ill or on the verge of retirement, the remaining participants may neglect to modify the valuation formula even though it bears little resemblance to present value.[33]

Unless fraud or other suspicious circumstances are proven, courts generally uphold valuation provisions as agreed to by the participants.[34] In striking a deal when acquiring their ownership interests, participants would be wise to arrive at a mutually acceptable valuation formula that has sufficient detail. Should discord or stagnation later occur, a properly structured valuation technique will help promote certainty and reduce the likelihood of litigation.

MAJORITY VOTE VS. UNANIMITY

In most business contexts, once a quorum is reached,[35] majority vote of the members present determines the outcome.[36] This is not always the case. For example, absent an agreement otherwise, general partners unanimously must agree to amend the general partnership agreement.[37] The subject addressed here is whether the participants should adopt provisions requiring unanimous consent.

Certainly, unanimity protects participants owning minority interests. Each in effect has veto power with respect to each and every action that requires the participants' approval. If sufficiently encompassing language is contained in the necessary provisions, each participant may protect from majority oppression his/her job, salary, dividends, directorships, and managerial positions. Today, most jurisdictions will uphold unanimity provisions contained in the corporation's articles of incorporation, bylaws, or in a unanimous shareholder agreement.[38]

Note that effective use by a minority participant of his/her veto power may be a useful "exit" strategy. In other words, a minority member, who exercises the veto power with frequency and tenacity, may gain sufficient leverage to "persuade" the enterprise or its members to buy his/her ownership at meaningful value. The veto power thus may provide liquidity to one's investment in addition to de facto managerial control.

Needless to say, insertion of a broad veto clause comes at a high price to the enterprise. An obstinate member through unreasonable use of the veto power can impede growth and, at worst, cause the enterprise's stagnation. Without a court order finding that use of the veto power is a breach of such minority shareholder's fiduciary duties,[39] excessive use of this power can induce havoc.

On another front, a stubborn participant who wants out but can find no bona fide purchaser can seek to hold the business "hostage" through his/her tenacious use of the veto power. While such a strategy may further the negotiating leverage of the exiting member, normally it ill serves the best interests of the business and its remaining members.

A possible middle ground is to insert a unanimity provision with respect to fundamental perceived entitlements and characteristics of the business. For example, decreasing the payment of dividends may require the vote of all shareholders. As another example, the participants may desire to change the type of business conducted. Thus, BEP's contemplated change of its operations from business etiquette to retail shoe stores would require unanimity. Nonetheless, to avoid the stagnation and hostage scenarios, the veto power should be included only after due deliberation.

SHAREHOLDER OPPRESSION

As viewed by many courts, shareholders in a closely-held corporation are viewed like partners who traditionally owe the utmost good faith and loyalty to one another.[40] These enterprises—whose characteristics are a small number of shareholders, participation by shareholders in the management of the business, the employment of shareholders in the business as the main source of their income, and lack of liquidity (thereby significantly impacting shareholders who wish to sell their stock)—have been labeled by many as "incorporated partnerships."[41] Going beyond basic duties of due care and loyalty that corporate fiduciaries owe, the oppression doctrine has been embraced by courts and legislatures.[42] Generally, oppression occurs when a minority shareholder's reasonable expectations are denied by the controlling shareholder (or controlling group of shareholders). Such reasonable expectations are those that exist at the commencement of the company, and those that subsequently arise due to a course of dealing agreed to (either expressly or impliedly) by the shareholders.[43] These reasonable expectations may encompass, for example, dividend payouts, employment and salary, and director and officer positions.[44] Nonetheless, not all courts adhere to the oppression doctrine, relying instead on traditional breach of fiduciary duty analysis.[45]

CONCLUSION

Regardless of the enterprise form selected (e.g., partnership vs. corporation), careful decisions must be made between protecting the interests of the individual participants and maximizing the benefits to the enterprise. These interests all too often conflict. Zealous protection of an inept shareholder's job, salary, and directorship, while obviously good for that person, can cause harm to the business. Careful negotiation often is appropriate at the outset of the venture to strike the proper balance between the interests of the individual owners and those of the enterprise as a collective body.

NOTES

1. See *infra* notes 40–45 and accompanying text.
2. See *Galler v. Galler,* 32 Ill. 16, 203 N.E. 2d 577 (1964).
3. See § 170 of the Delaware General Corporation Law; §§ 6.40, 8.25(e) of the Model Business Corporation Act.
4. See *Manson v. Curtis,* 223 N.Y. 313, 119 N.E. 559 (1918).

5. See generally Corporation Law Committee of the Association of the Bar of the City of New York, *The Enforceability and Effectiveness of Typical Shareholders Agreement Provisions*, 65 Bus. Law, 1153 (2010).
6. See *Lehrman v. Cohen,* 222 A. 2d 800 (Del. 1966).
7. See § 7.28(b) of the Model Business Corporation Act.
8. See *Ringling Brothers Barnum & Bailey Combined Shows v. Ringling,* 53 A. 2d 441 (Del. 1947).
9. See § 214 of the Delaware General Corporation Law; § 7.28 of the Model Business Corporation Act.
10. See *Chase v. Consolidated Foods Corp.,*744 F.2d 566 (7th Cir. 1984).
11. See § 8.01(b) of the Model Business Corporation Act.
12. See § 7.32 of the Model Business Corporation Act; *Ramos v. Estrada,* 8 Cal. App. 4th 1070, 10 Cal. Rptr. 2d 833 (1992).
13. See *McQuade v. Stoneham*, 263 N.Y. 323, 189 N.E. 234 (1934).
14. See *Twiggs v. Twiggs,* 413 N.Y.S. 2d 325 (1978).
15. See, e.g., § 21.101 of the Texas Business Organizations Code; § 7.32 of the Model Business Corporations Act.
16. See § 7.31 of the Model Business Corporation Act.
17. See American Law Institute, Restatement (Third) Agency § 310.
18. See §§ 7.22, 7.31 of the Model Business Corporation Act; § 212(e) of the Delaware General Corporation Law.
19. See *Oceanic Exploration Co. v. Grynberg,* 428 A. 2d 1 (Del. 1981).
20. See § 6.27(c) of the Model Business Corporation Act.
21. *Id.* § 6.27(b).
22. See *Rafe v. Hindin,* 288 N.Y.S. 2d 662, *aff'd,* 296 N.Y.S. 2d 955, 244 N.E. 2d 649 (1968). But see § 6.27(d)(3) of the Model Business Corporation Act (approving use of "consent" restraint).
23. See *Groves v. Pickett,* 420 F. 2d 1119 (9th Cir. 1970).
24. *Id.*
25. See *Doss v. Yingling,* 172 N.E. 801 (Ind. App. 1930).
26. See *In re Estate of Mather,* 189 A. 2d 586 (Pa. 1963).
27. See *Lash v. Lash Furniture Company of Barre*, 296 A. 2d 207 (Vt. 1972); § 6.27(d)(2) of the Model Business Corporation Act.
28. See M. Eisenberg, *Corporations and Other Business Organizations,* 423 (9th ed. 2005).
29. See W. Klein, J. Coffee and F. Partnoy, *Business Organizations and Finance* 99 (11th ed. 2010).
30. *Id.* at 255–259.
31. See *Jones v. Harris,* 388 P.2d 539 (Wash. 1964).
32. See D. Branson, J. Heminway, M. Loewenstein, M. Steinberg, and M. Warren, *Business Enterprises: Legal Structures, Governance and Policy* 368 (2009).
33. See W. Hamilton and R. Booth, *Business Basics* 168 (4th ed. 2006).

34. See *In re Estate of Mather,* 189 A. 2d 586 (Pa. 1963). But see *Man O War Restaurants, Inc. v. Martin,* 932 S.W. 2d 366 (Ky. 1996) (invalidating provision requiring terminated employee to sell back his stock to the company at the same price he paid for the stock).
35. A quorum generally is a majority of the authorized and outstanding shares in the shareholder voting context and a majority of the total number of directors in the board of director setting. See §§ 7.25, 8.24 of the Model Business Corporation Act.
36. See §§ 7.25, 8.24 of the Model Business Corporation Act.
37. See § 401(j) of the Revised Uniform Partnership Act.
38. See *Galler v. Galler,* 32 Ill. 2d 16, 203 N.E. 2d 577 (1964).
39. See *Smith v. Atlantic Properties, Inc.,* 422 N.E. 2d 798 (Mass. 1981).
40. See, e.g., *Donahue v. Rodd Electrotype Co.,* 328 N.E. 2d 505 (Mass. 1975).
41. See, e.g., *Hagshenas v. Gaylord,* 557 N. E. 2d 316 (Ill. App. 1990).
42. See e.g., § 1104-a of the New York Business Corporation Law; § 14.30(a)(2) of the Model Business Corporation Act; *Hollis v. Hill,* 232 F. 3d 460 (5th Cir. 2000) (interpreting Nevada law); *In the Matter of Kemp & Beatley, Inc.*, 473 N.E. 2d 1173 (N.Y. 1984); *Meiselman v. Meiselman*, 307 S.E. 2d 551 (N.C. 1983).
43. See, e.g., *Meiselman*, 307 S.E. 2d at 558–559; F. O'Neil, *Close Corporations* § 9.02 (3d ed. 1987).
44. See, e.g., *Meiselman,* 307 S.E. 2d at 558; *Kemp v. Beatley,* 473 N.E. 2d at 1178–1179; *Wilkes v. Springside Nursing Home, Inc.,* 353 N.E. 2d 657 (Mass. 1976). Note that when a minority shareholder exercises his/her veto power improperly, such shareholder may frustrate the reasonable expectations of the majority. See, e.g., *Smith v. Atlantic Properties, Inc.,* 422 N.E. 2d 798 (Mass. 1981).
45. See, e.g., *Nixon v. Blackwell,* 626 A. 2d 1366, 1379–1381 (Del. 1993).

CASE STUDIES

SHAREHOLDER AGREEMENTS—ENFORCEABILITY

As the foregoing discussion explains, unanimous written shareholder agreements are upheld by the overwhelming majority of courts today, even if the agreement sets forth corporate decisions, such as the payment of dividends, that are normally within the province of the board of directors. In fact, statutes enacted in the majority of states deem such unanimous written agreements enforceable when conflicts arise among shareholders who are parties to the agreement (and enforcement against others who become shareholders after the agreement is executed and who have sufficient notice of the agreement).

Are such written shareholder agreements enforceable if they are entered into by less than all the shareholders? Generally, the answer is that this issue is not definitively resolved. The following case illustrates the uncertainty of seeking the enforcement of such agreements.

TRIGGS V. TRIGGS
COURT OF APPEALS OF NEW YORK
413 N.Y.S. 2D 325 (1978)

Jones, J., Opinion of the Court

[The following facts are from the dissenting opinion.]

The bone of contention in this case is control of Triggs Color Printing Corporation, a small firm founded by decedent in 1925. The firm appears to have prospered for some years and, with the passage of time, decedent's three sons became involved in the business to varying degrees. As of 1963, the corporation had issued some 254 shares of voting stock. Of these, decedent personally owned 149 shares and the remainder were distributed equally between his three sons, with each son owning 35 shares. At that time, decedent apparently selected his son Ransford, the plaintiff in this action, as the one he deemed best suited to control the business following decedent's death. To that end, decedent transferred 36 of his shares to plaintiff. Thus, out of the 254 voting shares, decedent owned 113 shares, plaintiff owned 71 shares, and each of the other two sons owned 35 shares.

Shortly thereafter, plaintiff and decedent entered into the written agreement at issue in this case. The two agreed to vote their shares together so as not only to elect both of them as directors, but also to elect decedent chairman of the board at a guaranteed annual salary, and to appoint plaintiff president of the corporation at a guaranteed annual salary. Additionally, the agreement contained the following provision:

> *"It is the present contemplation of Frederick Triggs, Sr. to execute an agreement with the Corporation for the Corporation to repurchase his stock in the event of his death. In the event for any reason that such agreement has not been executed between the said Frederick Triggs, Sr. and the Corporation, then, in that event, the remaining Stockholder, to wit: Ransford D. Triggs, shall have the right and option to purchase the said stock of Frederick Triggs, Sr. for a period of sixty (60) days following the death of Frederick Triggs, Sr."*

A few months later, decedent did enter into a repurchase agreement with the corporation. One year later, in 1964, the repurchase agreement with the corporation was canceled by consent of both decedent and the corporation. During the next few years, plaintiff gradually assumed an ever greater role in corporate affairs, and decedent's influence waned. Eventually the two had a falling out, and decedent appears to have begun to regret his choice of plaintiff as his successor. The corporation experienced some financial difficulties under plaintiff's management, and the salary paid to decedent was decreased, at first with his consent and later over his objections. Finally, in February, 1970, decedent executed a codicil to his will by which he bequeathed his 113 shares of voting stock to his other two sons, and declared the 1963 agreement with plaintiff to be null and void. In April, 1970, decedent died.

Following decedent's death, plaintiff sought to exercise the option to purchase the 113 shares from the estate, but the estate refused to transfer the stock. Some four years later, in September, 1974, plaintiff commenced this action seeking to compel the estate to honor the option. Defendant executor submitted an answer in which he questioned the continuing validity of the option, alleged that even if the option were valid plaintiff was not entitled to specific performance since he had breached that part of the agreement calling for payment of a guaranteed salary to decedent, and counterclaimed for the amount of unpaid salary should the court find that the agreement was valid. Following service of an answer, but some time prior to trial, defendant moved to dismiss the complaint for failure to state a cause of action, alleging for the first time that the agreement was illegal. The court denied that motion on the merits at the beginning of the trial, declaring that the agreement "did not in any way sufficiently stultify the Board of Directors in the operation of this business as to be [illegal]".

At the conclusion of trial, the court ruled in favor of the plaintiff to the extent of granting him specific performance of the option and ordering the estate to transfer the stock to him upon tender of payment. As to the counterclaim, the court held in favor of defendant, awarding the estate judgment for the amount of unpaid salary owed to decedent. [Defendant has appealed this ruling to this Court.] ...

That an agreement between corporate shareholders includes illegal provisions with respect to the election of corporate officers and the fixation of their compensation does not preclude enforcement of the provision for a stock purchase option contained in the same agreement where it has been found that over the seven-year life of their agreement there was in fact no intrusion on the unfettered management of corporate affairs by the board of directors because the parties ignored and made no attempt to enforce the illegal portions of their agreement and the evidence does not show that the parties themselves considered that enforcement of the stock purchase option was contingent on observance of the illegal portions of the agreement.

After a trial without a jury the court granted respondent specific performance of the stock purchase option. A majority at the Appellate Division agreed, and we now affirm. ...

Appellant contends that because the March 19, 1963 agreement *was not executed or approved by all of the corporate shareholders*, its provisions requiring the election of respondent and his father as officers and fixing their compensation constituted an impermissible restriction of the rights and obligations of the board of directors to manage the business of the corporation under the doctrine of *Manson v Curtis* (223 N.Y. 313) and related cases. ... No argument is made that the stock purchase option, standing alone, would be invalid; the assertion is that the agreement must be read as a whole and that it must be invalidated in its entirety. The critical issue is whether, because of the initial inclusion of provisions [entered into by the holders of the majority of shares but less than all] which could have been said to fetter the authority of the board to select corporate officers and to fix their compensation, the stock purchase provision is now unenforceable.

The uncontroverted evidence is that in the years following the signing of the agreement, the assertedly illegal provisions of the agreement were ignored; no attempt was made to observe or enforce them and the management of corporate affairs was in no way restricted in consequence of the 1963 agreement. The evil to which the cited rule of law is addressed was never sought to be achieved nor was it realized. Although Triggs, Sr. and Ransford continued to serve as directors, the record discloses there were also three or four other, independent directors. That Triggs, Sr. continued to be elected chairman of the board (he was also elected corporate treasurer) and Ransford, corporate president, and that for several years their salaries were fixed by the board at the figures stated in the agreement, was in consequence of action freely taken by the entire board of directors and cannot be attributed to the sanction of the March 19, 1963 agreement, of which the other directors, constituting a majority of the board, were wholly unaware. ...

The legal issue here, too, depends on what is now an affirmed factual determination. The claim of illegality, raised for the first time some 13 years after the agreement had been signed, must fail because, as the trial court concluded, the March 19, 1963 agreement "did not in any way sufficiently stultify the Board of Directors in the operations of this business" within the doctrine on which appellant would rely.

Analytically we are presented with an agreement which in a single document deals with two different sets of obligations. On the one hand, the agreement contains the stock purchase option exercisable on the death of the father as to which, standing alone, there is no claim of illegality. On the other, there are the [less than unanimous] provisions with respect to the election of corporate officers and the fixation of their salaries, which are of questionable legality. Any illegality exists, however, only to the extent that the agreement operated to restrict the freedom of the board of directors to manage corporate affairs. There was nothing illegal per se in the election of Triggs, Sr. as chairman of the board or his son Ransford as corporate president or in fixing their annual salaries. ... There would have been illegality only if the election of those officers or the determination of their compensation had been in consequence of the prior agreement and thus in constraint of the freedom of the board of directors to exercise their responsibilities of management. The finding below, however, was that there had been no such stultification. In that circumstance, the fact that the second portion of the 1963 agreement, if it had been enforced, might have involved illegality provides no compulsion not to enforce the other, legal portion of the agreement where, as here, there has been no factual determination that enforcement of the stock purchase option was dependent on enforcement of the terms with respect to corporate management. The fact is that the courts below have enforced only the stock option provisions of the March 19, 1963 agreement.

As to the other issue, on which there was a division at the Appellate Division, there must be an affirmance. Whether the option granted respondent in the agreement dated March 19, 1963 to purchase the shares in Triggs Color Printing Corporation owned by his father on the latter's death survived the execution and subsequent cancellation of the agreement with the corporation for repurchase by the latter of the stock depended on the intention of the parties, father and son, as manifested in their agreement and by their subsequent conduct in its performance. Consistent with the trial court's finding that the stock purchase option did survive is its additional conclusion that when the corporation was experiencing economic difficulty, respondent loaned it $43,000 in the belief "that the operation and control of the business was and would remain in his hands pursuant to the terms of his contract with his father". The issue of survival, an issue of fact or at least a mixed issue of fact and law, having been determined in favor of respondent in the trial court and then affirmed at the Appellate Division, is now beyond the scope of our review.

Accordingly, the order of the Appellate Division should be affirmed, with costs.

Gabrielli, J. (Dissenting):

I respectfully dissent. ... The order appealed from should be reversed since the underlying agreement is unenforceable in that it improperly sought to limit the powers of the board of directors to manage the corporation. Moreover, even were the agreement itself valid, the option was terminated in accord with its own provisions some time prior to decedent's death.

...

It has long been the law in this State that a corporation must be managed by the board of directors who serve as trustees for the benefit of the corporation and all its shareholders. To prevent control of the corporation from being diverted into the hands of individuals or groups who in some cases might not be subject to quite the same fiduciary obligations as are imposed upon directors as a matter of course, the courts have always looked unfavorably towards attempts to circumvent the discretionary authority given the board of directors by law. ... Such matters normally arise in the context of an agreement between shareholders to utilize their shares so as to force the board of directors to take certain actions. Unless in accord with some statutorily approved mechanism for shifting power from the board of directors to other parties ([such as *unanimous shareholder agreements pursuant to* New York] Business Corporation Law, § 620, subd [b]), such agreements have been found valid only where the proponent of the agreement can prove that the violation of the statutory mandate is minimal and, more importantly, that there is no danger of harm either to the general public or to other shareholders (see *Clark v Dodge*, 269 N.Y. 410).

It is, of course, proper for shareholders to combine in order to elect directors whom they believe will manage the corporation in accord with what those shareholders perceive to be the best interests of the corporation. Thus, an agreement between two shareholders to vote for a particular director or directors is not illegal and may be enforceable in an appropriate case. ... If some shareholders seek to go beyond this, however, if they agree to vote their shares so as to impose their decisions upon the board of directors, such an agreement will normally be unenforceable. The agreement sought to be enforced in this case is just such an agreement.

In essence, the agreement between decedent and plaintiff consisted of three fundamental provisions: first, decedent promised to vote his shares so as to ensure the election of plaintiff as a director and his appointment as president for a 10-year period at a given salary; second, plaintiff promised to vote his shares so as to ensure the continuation of decedent as chairman of the board at a given salary for at least 10 years; and, third, decedent gave plaintiff a conditional option to purchase decedent's voting shares after his death. ...

The dispositive consideration must always be the possibility of harm to either the other shareholders or to the general public either prospectively at the time the agreement was entered into or at the time it is sought to be enforced. In those cases *in which the agreement is made by less than all the shareholders*, almost any attempt to reduce the authority granted to the board by law will create a significant potential for harm to other shareholders even if the potential for harm to the general public is minimal. This is so because the effect of such an agreement is to deprive the other shareholders of the benefits and protections which the law perceives to exist when the corporation is managed by an independent board of directors, free to use its own business judgment in the best interest of the corporation.

In the instant case, ... there were and are two other shareholders, not privy to the agreement between plaintiff and decedent. Moreover, the instant agreement for the continuation of plaintiff and decedent in their respective positions is in no way dependent on their performances in those positions. ...

It has been suggested that the option should be severed from the other provisions of the agreement and separately enforced since it alone would not be illegal. The flaw in this argument is that it improperly assumes that decedent would have given plaintiff this option by itself, without the other parts of their agreement. This assumption is one in which we may not indulge. Indeed, it appears that the illegal parts of the agreement were an intrinsic part of the covenant between these parties. While decedent apparently did wish to allow plaintiff to purchase the stock after his death if certain other possibilities did not eventuate, it is quite clear that decedent also wanted to protect his own position within the corporation from any challenge by plaintiff. Thus, the agreement was comprised of several component factors, and was motivated by complex and potentially conflicting objectives. The parties were concerned not only with control of the corporation following decedent's demise, but also with the corporate power structure during the remainder of decedent's life. To conclude that the option alone would have been entered into by the parties would be to engage in untoward speculation. ...

In sum, law and logic both compel the conclusion that the option which plaintiff seeks to enforce was an inseverable part of a basically illegal agreement. As such, it may not be enforced. ...

Accordingly, I vote to reverse the order appealed from and to dismiss the complaint.

Fuchsberg, J. (Dissenting):

My vote too is for reversal. However, the decisional path that I would take differs appreciably not only from that of the majority but from that of my fellow dissenters as well.

Specifically, unlike the other dissenters, I am of the opinion that the parties entered into an enforceable agreement. ... I conclude that we are required to find that the agreement was not ambiguous and that, as a matter of law, it terminated in accordance with its terms during the father's lifetime.

I also take issue with the majority's reasoning that the option was enforceable only because it was separable from an otherwise illegal contract. In my view, the entire agreement is lawful qua agreement, and since it is one entered into between the controlling stockholders of a small, nonpublic corporation, it is not to be scrutinized by a rigid, hypertechnical reading [of the applicable law].

Small, closely held corporations whose operation is dominated, as its stockholders and creditors usually are aware, by a particular individual or small group of individuals, must be distinguished, legally and pragmatically, from large corporations whose stock is traded on a public securities exchange and where the normal stockholders' relationship to those managing the corporation is bound to be impersonal and remote. Obviously, the latter's operations are rarely, if ever, covered by stockholders' agreements, and the Business Corporation Law itself is the sole restriction on their management.

In the close corporation, investors who themselves are not part of the dominant group commonly rely on the identities of the individuals who run the business and on the likelihood of their continuance in power. As a practical matter, these individuals will be expected to exercise a broad discretion and considerable informality in carrying out their management functions; this flexibility may be regarded as one of the strengths of a smaller organization. Indeed, faith in the integrity and ability of the managers is what usually motivates the investment. Looked at realistically, such corporations, often organized solely to obtain the advantage of limited personal liability for their principals, to qualify for a particular tax classification, or for some similar reason, are frequently "little more than charter partnerships". ... Control of such matters as choice of officers and directors, amounts of executive salaries, and options to buy or sell each other's stock—exactly the sort of things with which the agreement before us dealt—is usually mapped out by agreements among stockholders.

In short, so long as an agreement between stockholders relating to the management of the corporation bears no evidence of an intent to defraud other stockholders or creditors, deviations from precise formalities should not automatically call for a slavish enforcement of the statute. For this is the "governing criteri[on]" by which to test "the validity of a stockholders' agreement". ... This would not leave without remedy those minority stockholders in close corporations whose interests may be abused. Available to them and at least equally effective are the equitable remedies by which officers and directors can be made to respond for violations of their trust obligations. ...

Analysis of the agreement and its surrounding circumstances here illustrates the wisdom of this approach. The corporation had for a long time been a one-man business in every sense, the man being Triggs, the father. Until he gave a minority interest to each of his sons, he was the owner of all the voting stock; afterwards, it was all owned by the father and his sons, who were preparing to succeed him. At the time of the agreement, the father, together with the son who was the other party to the disputed writing, held the majority of this stock. Given their service in the business, their stockholding, and their relationship to each other and to the history of the corporation, it was to be expected—and not at all extraordinary—that an arrangement for their continuance in office and their compensation would be executed. There is not the slightest indication that, had the parties gone through the routine of presenting the contract to duly called stockholders' and directors' meetings, it would not have been rubber-stamped as a matter of course. It is significant that no other stockholder challenged the agreement during the father's lifetime and that the dispute since then has gravitated only around the son's insistence that the option to purchase his father's shares had not expired. …

In sum, given that no other shareholder or member of the general public has been harmed, there is no good reason to measure the agreement by the less sophisticated standards of yesteryear. …

As discussed in this chapter, stock transfer restrictions, including buy-sell agreements, are standard fare in close corporations. Absent fraud or illegality, these agreements normally are enforced according to their terms. This is the result even if a wide disparity exists between market value and the formula set forth in the agreement. The following case illustrates this point.

JONES V. HARRIS
SUPREME COURT OF WASHINGTON
388 P. 2D 539 (1964)

Finley, Judge:

This is an action by a minority shareholder in two close corporations to determine the price at which he is contractually bound to sell his shares to the remaining shareholders, and for an accounting by the corporations as to sums allegedly due him.

The parties formed the corporations in question in 1953 to purchase Radio Station KXLY and Television Station KXLY-TV, situated in Spokane, Washington. Joseph Harris and Norman Eisenstein (defendants-appellants) contributed the greater part of the financial backing for the venture and subscribed to ninety per cent of the capital stock of both corporations. Richard E. Jones (plaintiff-respondent) agreed to manage the stations and took the remaining ten percent of the capital stock. At the time the corporations were formed, the parties entered into a written contract respecting the ownership and control of the stations. Among other things, it provided that Jones was to manage the stations until such time as notice of termination was given by either party, sixty days prior to the expiration of any calendar year. In the event that Jones was so terminated, the following sections controlled the disposition of his interest in the corporations:

> "… [T]he parties agree that Jones shall be obligated to sell and Eisenstein and Harris shall be obligated to buy jointly, at book value, the stock of Jones in the Radio Corp. and in the Television Corp. In determining book value *solely for the purposes hereof*, it is agreed that the depreciable assets shall be computed at cost, less eighty (80) percent of the depreciation as the same appears on the books. …

and

> (e) If any part of the purchase price to be paid for either KXLY or KXLY-TV is required to be allocated to good-will, then it is agreed that in arriving at the book value … effect shall be given to the original amount required to be allocated to such good-will without any charge-off or depreciation, even though such charge-off or depreciation may be reflected in the books of said corporations."

In August 1958, the respondent's position as general manager was terminated by notice, effective December 31, 1958. Thereafter, the parties were unable to agree as to the meaning of the contract term "book value," the basic factor in determining the price which the respondent was to receive for his shares. Appellants tendered $36,986.32 in settlement of Jones' claims. This was refused, and the present litigation ensued.

The trial court found that the contract was controlling insofar as it required the sale of the ten per cent stock interest held by Jones, but considered the price setting mechanism (book value plus twenty percent of depreciation taken) ambiguous. Relying, therefore, on the supposed intentions of the parties to pay a fair value for the shares of the respondent, the court, emphasizing equitable considerations, construed the entire provision as setting the price at "market value." When the liabilities were deducted from the appraised value of the corporation, the price of the ten per cent interest was set at $91,919.30. To this was added the admitted salary item of $12,500 owing to the respondent, less certain personal withdrawals made by the respondent from the corporations, and judgment was entered for $95,006.87.

There can be no doubt that a ten per cent interest in the two corporations is worth, in terms of market value, far more than the net worth figure on the corporate balance sheets of December 31, 1958, would indicate. Ten per cent of the December 31, 1958, net worth figure, plus twenty per cent of the depreciation and amortization accounts, totals only $25,936.33. It may be noted that experts set the market value of the corporations at upwards of $2,500,000 at the time of trial, and that by the time of this appeal appellants had sold these same corporations for $3,225,000, cash. It seems quite probably that *at the time the contract was drawn*, considering the way it was drawn, the parties contemplated the price of the shares resulting from "book value," plus twenty per cent of taken depreciation, would continue to represent some reasonable approximation of the fair value. Had the corporations enjoyed a lesser degree of success, the formula might have accomplished the purpose very well, without any problem arising such as that herein involved.

But whether the parties reasonably should have anticipated that book value would not approximate the true value of the corporations, nevertheless, book value was the basic ingredient from its basic of the formula the chose to determine the "buy-out" price. Conceding that the term "book value" can vary from its basic or generally accepted meaning—*i.e.*, according to the purpose for which it is used—the parties here explicitly attempted to limit its meaning and to define book value "solely for the purposes" of the buy-out contract. Because they anticipated a rapid tax write-off in the form of depreciation, they arranged to use only eighty per cent of the amount in calculating the respondent's interest. *The contract cannot be said to have been unfair or inequitable when it was made, and now is too clear to admit of interpretation to include and emphasize equities, nonexistent at the inception of the contract, but which have evolved and now seem persuasive.* Many close corporations have similar buy-out provisions, and the courts would do a disservice to business practice by substituting an "appraisal" or "market value" formula when hindsight shows that "book value," as originally conceived, has become unrealistic with the passing of time.

The courts, of course, are not bound irrevocably to a single definition of "book value." But, when a term that has a generally accepted meaning is used, the parties are hard pressed afterwards to claim their intent was otherwise. "Book value" normally means the value of the corporation as shown on the books of account of that corporation, after subtracting liabilities. In such cases courts should accept the book accounts, when they are kept in accord with accepted accounting practice and not with an eye to the advantageous exercise of the "buy-out" option. If arbitrary valuations appear in the accounts, the court can then substitute amounts determined through correct accounting procedures. …

In the present case the only accounts which the respondent attacks as inconsistent with proper accounting procedure were set up exactly as the organization contract anticipated. Whatever the effect of this might be as to third parties, it is binding on the respondent. He cannot complain that the depreciation accounts were unduly swollen to obtain a rapid tax write-off; the contract anticipated this and provided that he would benefit by twenty per cent of the amount so taken being added in evaluating his shares. Nor can he complain that the absence of a good-will account led to an overevaluation of depreciable assets. Section (e) of the contract specified that good will would be considered in pricing his shares *only* if the Internal Revenue Service later required a reallocation of part of the purchase price to good will. … Respondent's ten per cent interest in the corporations, at book value adjusted in accord with the contract, is as the appellant contends: $25,936.33.

…

The findings of the trial court concerning the accounting are affirmed. The judgment on the price to be paid for the shares belonging to Jones is reversed. The parties shall bear their own costs, and the case is remanded for entry of judgment in accord with the foregoing views and determinations.

CASE STUDIES

SHAREHOLDER "OPPRESSION"

As discussed earlier in this Chapter, the oppression doctrine whereby the majority shareholders are deemed to have frustrated the reasonable expectations of a minority shareholder has been embraced by state courts and legislatures. The following decision from the "pro-business" state of Texas evidences the widespread acceptance of this doctrine. The case also addresses pertinent valuation issues when determining the price at which a minority interest is to be valued in the close corporation context.

RITCHIE V. RUPE
COURT OF APPEALS OF TEXAS
339 S.W. 3D 275 (2011)

Opinion by Justice Moseley

This case involves claims for shareholder oppression filed by a minority shareholder in a closely held corporation, Rupe Investment Corporation ("RIC"). The trial court determined the plaintiff minority shareholder, Ann Caldwell Rupe as trustee for the Dallas Gordon Rupe, III, 1995 Family Trust ("Buddy's Trust"), had been subjected to shareholder oppression by RIC and some of its shareholders and directors ("appellants"). The trial court ordered appellants to cause RIC to redeem Buddy's Trust's stock in RIC (the "Stock") for $7.3 million, which the jury found to be the Stock's fair value.

The evidence is undisputed that appellants told Ann and her representative that they refused to meet with, and refused to allow any RIC management personnel to meet with, any prospective purchasers of the Stock. Based on the evidence and circumstances of this case, we conclude appellants' actions in connections with Ann's efforts to sell Stock to third parties constituted oppressive conduct. We also conclude the trial court did not abuse its discretion in ordering appellants to cause RIC to buy out the Stock as an equitable remedy for this conduct. However, we conclude the trial court erred in ordering the Stock be purchased for a price that did not constitute fair market value. ... Accordingly, we affirm the trial court's judgment in part and reverse in part. ...

Background

A. RIC

RIC was founded by Dallas Gordon Rupe, Jr., a/k/a "Pops," and Robert Ritchie. By the time of the events in this case, all of RIC's common stock was held by their descendants or in trusts for the benefit of their descendants. In 2002, the principal players included: Pops's children, who were Paula Dennard ("Paula") (chairman of RIC's board of directors) and Dallas Gordon Rupe, III ("Buddy") (a director of RIC); Lee Ritchie ("Ritchie") (Robert Ritchie's son, RIC's president, and one of its directors); and Dennis Lutes ("Lutes") (one of RIC's directors and one of its attorneys). In 2002, the relevant voting shareholders of RIC were:

- Paula and Ritchie as co-trustees of the Dallas Gordon Rupe Trust ("Pops's Trust"), who owned 46.6 percent of RIC's voting stock;
- Paula and Ritchie as co-trustees of the Ruby L. Rupe Trust No. One for Grandchildren ("Ruby's Trust"), who owned 7.4 percent of the voting stock;
- Paula and Lutes as co-trustees of the Paula Dennard Management Trust ("Paula's Trust"), who owned 18 percent of the voting stock;
- Ritchie, who personally owned 1.7 percent of the voting stock; and
- Buddy as trustee of Buddy's Trust, who owned the Stock (which comprised 18 percent of the voting stock); Buddy was trustee until his death on September 22, 2002.

After Buddy died, his wife, appellee Ann Caldwell Rupe, succeeded him as trustee of Buddy's Trust.

B. Disputes Among the Parties

The record reflects that several disputes among the individuals in their various capacities came to a head in the months following Buddy's death. For purposes of our discussion, the overriding dispute here concerns Ann's efforts to sell [18% of the Voting] Stock to third parties. *There is no shareholders' or buy-sell agreement, right of first offer, or other restriction on the sale of the Stock to third parties.* Although not required to do so, Ann contacted Ritchie about RIC buying the Stock. After some attempts, they were unable to reach an agreement for the sale of the Stock to RIC. Ann then sought to market the Stock to third parties.

C. Ann's Efforts to Sell the Stock to Others

In 2004, Ann hired a retired capital fund manager, George Stasen, to help sell the Stock to third parties. Stasen met with Ritchie, Paula, and her children and sought their cooperation with his efforts to sell the Stock. Stasen testified that Ritchie told him that neither Ritchie nor any member of RIC's management would meet with any prospective purchasers of the Stock. In addition to Ritchie's own testimony confirming this, the record contains a fax from Ritchie to Ann dated February 1, 2006, stating that "it would be inappropriate for me or any other officer or director of [RIC] to meet with your prospects or otherwise participate in any activities relating to your proposed sale of stock."

Stasen testified that after the meeting, he felt it would be extraordinarily difficult to market the Stock to a third party because any investor would want to meet with RIC's management and RIC's management had made it clear they did not want to meet anyone. He said that interviewing corporate management was a regular part of a prospective investor's due-diligence process for determining whether to invest in a closely held corporation, and that management's refusal to meet with prospective investors made the Stock impossible to sell. Stasen testified that he "got laughed at" by prospective investors when he told them they could not meet with management. Stasen estimated the book value of the Stock at $3.9 million, but he discounted the Stock, pricing it at $3.4 million "[b]ecause I knew it would be incredibly difficult to sell this without offering a discount" because RIC's management refused to meet with prospective buyers. Stasen testified the chance of selling stock in a closely held corporation without affording the prospective purchaser an opportunity to meet with management was "zero." Ultimately, Stasen was unable to sell any of the Stock, "[b]ecause you cannot make a decision on an investment from this limited information without meeting the executives of [RIC] and without meeting the executives of the principal holdings."

D. Ann's Lawsuit

On July 21, 2006, Ann sued Ritchie, Paula, and Lutes in their individual capacities. Ann later added RIC as a defendant. Ann's causes of action included shareholder oppression and breach of fiduciary duty, as well as a demand for access to RIC's books and records. Ann sought an order requiring the defendants to purchase the Stock "at a fair market value" or an order appointing a receiver to liquidate RIC. …

The jury returned a verdict on the issues submitted to it. After conducting a post-trial hearing, the trial court signed a judgment ordering appellants to cause RIC to buy out the Stock for $7.3 million, the "fair value" of the Stock as found by the jury. …

Appellants' Arguments for Reversal

[A]ppellants contend the trial court's judgment should be "reversed and judgment rendered for Appellants." In support of this issue they make several arguments. They assert that the court-ordered buyback of the Stock is not an available remedy for shareholder oppression under Texas law; that their actions do not constitute shareholder oppression as a matter of law; and that the buyout remedy is inappropriate here because it is "unduly harsh" under the circumstances.

A. Standard of Review

Construction of statutes is a question of law for the courts. Whether certain conduct constitutes shareholder oppression is also a question of law. We review questions of law de novo. …

The trial court's order that appellants cause RIC to buy out the Stock was an exercise of its equitable authority. "The expediency, necessity, or propriety of equitable relief is for the trial court, and its ruling is reviewed for an abuse of discretion." …

B. Is a Buyout an Available Remedy for Shareholder Oppression?

Appellants assert that the court-ordered buyback of the Stock is not an available remedy for shareholder oppression under Texas law. They argue the only relief available for shareholder oppression under Texas law is the appointment of a receiver to "rehabilitate" the corporation. Appellants state in their brief: "If the Legislature had intended to create an oppression cause of action for relief other than a receivership, it would have done so clearly and directly." Because we conclude the legislature has in fact done so, we reject appellants' argument.

Texas law expressly authorizes a trial court to appoint a receiver to "rehabilitate" a corporation if, *inter alia*, "the acts of the directors or those in control of the corporation are illegal, oppressive or fraudulent." ... However, this remedy is available "only ... if *all other remedies* available either at law or in equity ... are determined by the court to be inadequate." ... Thus, receivership is a remedy for shareholder oppression, but only as a last resort in the event other, less drastic equitable remedies are inadequate. Rather than barring such lesser equitable remedies, [Texas law] clearly envisions that they are available and, if adequate, preferable to the remedy of appointing a receiver to take over the affairs of the corporation in order to rehabilitate it.

In *Patton v. Nicholas*, 279 S.W.2d 848 (Tex. 1955), the [Texas] Supreme Court addressed the trial court's discretion to fashion equitable relief in shareholder disputes. There the minority-shareholder plaintiffs sued the corporation and the majority shareholder (who was also its president and a director) for fraud and abuse of his controlling position over the corporation. The trial court appointed a receiver to liquidate the company. At that time, no statute authorized the appointment of a receiver (for liquidation or rehabilitation) to remedy such conduct. Although the supreme court reversed the order of liquidation, it held that "under their general equity powers" Texas courts may appoint a receiver for liquidation of a corporation in an extreme case, or for "the less drastic purpose of 'rehabilitation.'" ...

In *Davis v. Sheerin*, 754 S.W.2d 375 (Tex. App. 1988), one of our sister courts recognized that a "buyout" is an available—and sometimes appropriate—remedy for shareholder oppression. There the trial court found the majority-shareholder defendant acted oppressively toward the minority-shareholder plaintiff, appointed a receiver for the corporation, and ordered the majority shareholder and the corporation to buy out the plaintiff's interest in the corporation at the value found by the jury. The court stated that "Texas courts, under their general equity power, may decree a 'buy-out' in an appropriate case where less harsh remedies are inadequate to protect the rights of the parties." In doing so, the court observed that *Patton* had been cited as support for the proposition "that a dissolution statute does not provide the exclusive remedy for injured shareholders, and that courts have equitable powers to fashion appropriate remedies where the majority shareholders have engaged in oppressive conduct." ...

Other courts have followed the holding in *Davis,* and appellants cite no authority rejecting it. ...

...

As the Texas supreme court stated in *Patton*, "[w]isdom would seem to counsel tailoring the remedy to fit the particular case" of shareholder oppression. ... We agree and conclude that Texas law authorizes the trial court, in an appropriate case, to order a buyout of an oppressed minority shareholder as an equitable remedy for shareholder oppression. We reject appellants' argument to the contrary.

C. Was Appellants' Conduct Concerning Ann's Efforts to Sell the Stock Oppressive?

We now arrive at the heart of the case. The trial court concluded that Paula, Ritchie, Lutes, and RIC acted oppressively toward Buddy's Trust by, among other things, refusing to cooperate with Ann's attempts to sell the Stock to a third party. Appellants assert that their alleged conduct was not oppressive.

1. Applicable Law

Statutes ... providing remedies for oppression rarely define the term. The term is expansive and covers a multitude of situations dealing with improper conduct; thus a narrow definition would be inappropriate. Texas courts have generally recognized two non-exclusive definitions for shareholder oppression:

1. majority shareholders' conduct that substantially defeats the minority's expectations that, objectively viewed, were both reasonable under the circumstances and central to the minority shareholder's decision to join the venture; or
2. burdensome, harsh, or wrongful conduct; a lack of probity and fair dealing in the company's affairs to the prejudice of some members; or a visible departure from the standards of fair dealing and a violation of fair play on which each shareholder is entitled to rely.

...

These definitions are not mutually exclusive; depending on the facts of the case, conduct could be oppressive under either or both definitions. ...

The jury determines what acts occurred (assuming those facts are in dispute), but whether those acts constitute shareholder oppression is a question of law for the court. ... And like other questions of law, the trial court's determination of that issue is subject to de novo review.

In deciding whether conduct rises to the level of oppression, courts must exercise caution, balancing the minority shareholder's reasonable expectations against the corporation's need to exercise its business judgment and run its business efficiently. However, ... "Courts take an especially broad view of the application of oppressive conduct to a closely held corporation, where oppression may more easily be found." ...

2. Necessity of Majority Shareholder

Appellants assert the trial court's judgment should be reversed and judgment rendered for them because shareholder oppression can only be committed by a majority shareholder, and it is undisputed that there is no majority shareholder in RIC. ...

[The applicable Texas Statute] authorizes equitable intervention when "the acts of the *directors or those in control of the corporation* are illegal, oppressive or fraudulent." ... This text clearly indicates shareholder oppression claims may be brought against "directors or those in control of the corporation." ... This negates the argument that the absence of a majority shareholder is a bar to such claims.

...

The evidence is undisputed that Paula, Ritchie, and Lutes together control, either through direct ownership or by virtue of their positions as trustees of the shareholder trusts, 73.7 percent of the voting stock. The evidence is undisputed these three persons were also three of RIC's four directors and that Paula's daughter, Gretchen Chrane, has held the fourth seat since 2003. There was also testimony that Paula, Ritchie, and Lutes had never disagreed on any issue at a shareholders meeting or on any action as directors. Thus, the record establishes that appellants are both "directors" and "those in control of the corporation." ... We reject appellants' argument that there can be no shareholder oppression absent a single, majority shareholder.

3. Oppressive Conduct

a. Reasonable Expectations

As noted above, one of the definitions of shareholder oppression is "majority shareholders' conduct that substantially defeats the minority's expectations that, objectively viewed, were both reasonable under the circumstances and central to the minority shareholder's decision to join the venture. ..." Commentators have classified the "reasonable expectations" of shareholders into two broad categories: specific reasonable expectations and general reasonable expectations.[1]

Specific reasonable expectations are those specifically agreed to or expected as part of the transactions forming a particular corporation or that may develop over time among the shareholders of a particular corporation. Thus, specific reasonable expectations require proof of specific facts giving rise to the expectation in a particular case and that the expectation was reasonable under the circumstances and central to the decision to join the venture. *Examples of possible specific reasonable expectations are employment in the corporation or a say in management.*

However, general reasonable expectations are expectations that arise from the mere status of being a shareholder. These expectations belong to all shareholders and thus, absent evidence to the contrary, are both reasonable under the circumstances and central to the decision to invest in the corporation. *Some examples of general reasonable expectations are the right to proportionate participation in earnings, the right to any stock appreciation, the right (with a proper purpose) to inspect corporate records, and the right to vote if the stock has voting rights.*

One of the general reasonable expectations of any property owner-including the owner of stock in a corporation-is the right of free alienation of that property. For this reason, the usual policy of the law opposes restraints on the alienation of personal property, including stock. ... Absent valid restrictions, the general rule applies and unrestricted shares are freely transferable. ...

Thus, one of the general reasonable expectations of a shareholder whose stock contains no restrictions on its alienation, and whose rights are not otherwise limited or qualified by contract, is that she is free to

---

1 See Douglas K. Moll, *Shareholder Oppression & Reasonable Expectations: Of Change, Gifts, and Inheritances in Close Corporation Disputes*, 86 Minn. L. Rev. 717, 765–777 (2002). ...

sell her stock to a party of her choosing at a mutually acceptable price. … This is true even if the stock is that of a closely held corporation.

…

Despite the general reasonable expectation of being able to sell unrestricted shares at a mutually acceptable price, often no ready market exists for the stock in a closely held corporation, especially if it represents a non-controlling, minority interest. In that context, unless the minority shareholder reaches an agreement to sell her stock back to the closely held corporation or to someone already involved in its ownership or management, to sell her stock she must market it to third parties. Because often no ready market exists, to sell her stock to third parties she must market her stock by (1) identifying potential third-party buyers through means such as … networking through brokers and others, and meeting with potential buyers, and then (2) providing to those potential buyers sufficient information about the corporation and its businesses, assets, and management as to allow them to conduct a reasonable investigation as to the proposed transaction. Corporate policies that constructively prohibit the shareholder from performing these activities would substantially defeat the shareholder's general reasonable expectation of being able to market her unrestricted stock.

b. Fair Dealing

The second definition for shareholder oppression is "burdensome, harsh, or wrongful conduct; a lack of probity and fair dealing in the company's affairs to the prejudice of some members; or a visible departure from the standards of fair dealing and a violation of fair play on which each shareholder is entitled to rely." … This definition focuses more on the conduct of the directors or those in control of the corporation than on the reasonable expectations of the minority shareholder. The standards of fair dealing with respect to the owner of unrestricted stock in a corporation would include a requirement that they act fairly and reasonably in connection with a shareholder's efforts to sell that stock to a third party and not adopt policies that unreasonably restrain or prohibit the sale or transfer of the stock or that deprive the owner of its fair market value.

The second definition of shareholder oppression will often overlap the reasonable expectations definition because the standards of fair dealing on which all shareholders are entitled to rely will often include conduct necessary to meet the reasonable expectations of shareholders. Thus, conduct of the directors or those in control of the corporation that substantially defeats the reasonable expectations of a minority shareholder will often constitute conduct that is "burdensome, harsh, or wrongful," or that constitutes "a lack of probity and fair dealing in the company's affairs" or "a visible departure from the standards of fair dealing and a violation of fair play on which each shareholder is entitled to rely." ... Under either definition, oppressive conduct does not require a showing of fraud, illegality, mismanagement, wasting of assets, or deadlock, although these factors are often present.

c. Application

In this case, there are no restrictions on the sale of the Stock to third parties. Thus Ann, even as a minority shareholder in a closely held corporation, had a general reasonable expectation that she could market the Stock to third parties at whatever price the market would bear. Because a holder of unrestricted stock in a closely held corporation has a general reasonable expectation of being able to market her stock to third parties, it is also reasonable to expect that the corporation and its management (as part of the standards of fair dealing on which all shareholders are entitled to rely) will consent to a shareholder's reasonable requests for cooperation with respect to her efforts to sell the stock.

Stasen testified that one of the regular, necessary steps in the due-diligence investigation of any prospective investor in a closely held corporation is a meeting with the corporation's management. As he testified—again, in the context of a closely held corporation—"No investor would ever invest in anything without meeting the management." However, appellants flatly refused to meet with—or allow RIC management to meet with—any prospective purchasers. Ritchie unequivocally told Ann that "it would be inappropriate for me or any other officer or director of [RIC] to meet with your prospects or otherwise participate in any activities relating to your proposed sale of stock." Ritchie testified he refused to speak to potential purchasers of the Stock. Stasen also testified to Ritchie's refusal to meet with potential purchasers. Stasen testified that Ritchie and RIC's refusal to meet potential purchasers of the Stock deterred several potential investors. He stated he was unable to sell the Stock because investors could not make a decision without meeting the executives of RIC.

...

Appellants next assert their conduct as directors that the trial court found to be oppressive was protected from liability by the business judgment rule. We address this argument only in the context of the trial court's conclusion that appellants engaged in oppressive conduct by refusing to cooperate with Ann's attempts to sell the Stock to a third party.

The business judgment rule protects a corporation's directors from personal liability to shareholders for their actions in operating the corporation unless their actions are ultra vires or tainted by fraud. … However, this is not a derivative suit for breach of the duty of care owed to the corporation. Further, the directors of RIC were not held personally liable for the shareholder oppression; nor were the directors or those controlling the corporation directed to buy the Stock themselves. Instead, the trial court's judgment ordered them as directors of RIC and trustees of a majority interest of the shareholders to cause RIC to redeem the Stock. Accordingly, the business judgment rule has no application in this case.

Appellants also contend their conduct was protected by a doctrine similar to the business judgment rule. … *See Willis,* 997 S.W.2d at 801 (referring to need for balancing minority shareholders' reasonable expectations against corporation's need to exercise business judgment). Ritchie testified that he refused to speak to prospective purchasers and directed the rest of RIC's management not to speak to them because of concerns that any statements management made could result in lawsuits by the purchasers. Lutes also testified it would have been possible for Ritchie to meet with outside investors, but that such a meeting might put the corporation at risk of becoming involved in litigation with third parties.

However, the corporation's interest in managing its affairs—or to minimize the possibility of litigation—does not include the right to "substantially defeat" the reasonable expectation of a minority shareholder that she can effectively market her unrestricted stock in the corporation, or the right "to take from holders of unrestricted stock the value of their stock." …

As discussed below, there are several means by which the corporation can protect itself from litigation short of a flat refusal to meet with potential buyers. Applying the definitions of shareholder oppression and balancing the minority shareholder's general reasonable expectations against the corporation's need to exercise business judgment to these facts, we cannot conclude the corporation's desire to avoid any possibility of litigation outweighed Ann's general reasonable expectation of marketing the Stock. Further, other than a general and nonspecific fear of litigation with third parties, appellants do not argue any other justification supporting their contention that their refusal to meet—or allow RIC management to meet—with prospective purchasers of the Stock constitutes a legitimate exercise of business judgment of such necessity as to outweigh the substantial negative effects of their actions on Ann's efforts to sell the Stock.

Under the uncontroverted facts of this case, we conclude appellants acted oppressively toward Ann by refusing to meet or allow any officer or director of RIC to meet with prospective purchasers of the Stock because that conduct in this case substantially defeated Ann's general reasonable expectation of marketing the Stock. We further conclude that the refusal to meet with potential purchasers of the Stock was oppressive because it was "a visible departure from the standards of fair dealing and a violation of fair play on which each shareholder is entitled to rely." ...

In reaching this conclusion, we recognize that the rights of the minority shareholder and the concomitant obligations of the directors or those in control of the corporation are not unlimited. Under the definitions of shareholder oppression, they are limited to such requests and responses necessary to avoid (1) conduct by majority shareholders that "substantially defeats" the minority shareholder's general reasonable expectations (and, if proven, any specific reasonable expectations), as well as (2) conduct that is "burdensome, harsh, or wrongful," or that constitutes "a lack of probity and fair dealing in the company's affairs" or "a visible departure from the standards of fair dealing and a violation of fair play on which each shareholder is entitled to rely." ...

For example, and in the context of a minority shareholder's efforts to sell her stock, the majority shareholders, directors, or those in control of the corporation need not seek potential purchasers for the minority shareholder's stock or otherwise market the stock on her behalf. They need not agree to requests that would unduly disrupt or affect the operation of the business or intrude into issues reserved for corporation's officers and directors. And a shareholder cannot request the corporation's management to speak or act in a manner that would tend to inflate the value of the stock and the corporation, and the shareholder may not request that management mislead potential investors.

Further, reasonable restrictions on the access to and use of business information or property, depending on the nature of the business, will normally be acceptable. Thus, the corporation's management may place reasonable limitations on the corporation's cooperation, including limiting the time spent with potential investors and requiring them to sign confidentiality agreements that protect the company's interests while permitting reasonable due diligence. However, they cannot act in such a way as to substantially defeat the minority shareholder's right to sell her stock to a third party.

We need not opine on the outer limits of what conduct was necessary to avoid substantially defeating Ann's reasonable expectation of marketing the Stock. Here, appellants flatly refused Ann's request that management meet with potential purchasers of the Stock. On its face, this request did not intrude into issues reserved for the directors and officers. There is no evidence the request materially affected the operation of the business or was unreasonable in any other manner. And, most importantly, there is substantial evidence that refusing Ann's request to meet with potential purchasers had the practical effect of precluding her from the opportunity to market the Stock to third parties.

D. Is the Buyout Remedy an Abuse of Discretion as "Unduly Harsh"?

Appellants next assert that, even if Texas law authorizes a buyout as a remedy for shareholder oppression, that remedy is inappropriate here because it is "unduly harsh" under the circumstances, and thus the trial court abused its discretion in imposing such a remedy. As noted earlier, the trial court's decision in fashioning equitable relief is reviewed under an abuse of discretion standard. …

Appellants argue that [t]his unduly harsh "remedy" will force RIC to sell and/or leverage corporate assets to scrape together over $7.3 million for the stock, leaving it vulnerable to the vicissitudes of a collapsing economy. …In short, [the trial court] concluded that RIC should be brought to its knees and placed at risk of bankruptcy to appease Ann. …

[B]ased on the evidence and the record we cannot say that the trial court's order that appellants cause RIC to buy out the Stock as an equitable remedy for their oppressive conduct in connection with Ann's efforts to sell the Stock was so harsh as to constitute an abuse of discretion. We reject appellants' argument to the contrary. …

E. Conclusion

We conclude that a buyout is an available remedy for shareholder oppression under Texas law and that, under the circumstances, appellants' conduct in refusing to meet—or allow RIC management to meet—with prospective purchasers constituted oppressive conduct as to Ann. We also conclude that the trial court did not abuse its discretion in ordering appellants to cause RIC to buy the Stock as an equitable remedy for this oppressive conduct. …

Valuation of the Stock

The jury was asked to find the "fair value" of the Stock. They were instructed that "fair value" meant the value of the Stock, determined:

a. As of June 30, 2006;
b. Using customary and current valuation concepts and techniques generally employed for similar businesses in the context of the transaction requiring appraisal; and
c. Without discounting for lack of marketability or minority status.

In response, the jury found the Stock was worth $7.3 million. Based on this finding, the trial court ordered appellants to cause RIC to pay Ann $7.3 million for the Stock and for Ann to surrender the Stock to RIC. As a part of their first issue, appellants argue the trial court erred in ordering RIC to pay $7.3 million for the Stock because the Stock was wrongly valued. They assert the trial court … erred in failing to discount the value for the Stock's lack of marketability and minority status. …

…

Discounts of the Stock's Value

The trial court ordered RIC to redeem the Stock for "fair value," which the jury determined to be (as of June 30, 2006) $7.3 million without discounts for lack of marketability or minority status. Appellants assert the trial court erred by instructing the jury not to apply any discounts to the Stock's value. They contend the value of the Stock should include discounts for the lack of marketability and the minority status of the Stock.

Case Studies

Two types of "fair value" are enterprise value and fair market value. The enterprise value of stock is determined by the value of the company as a whole and ascribing to each share its pro rata portion of that overall enterprise value. Enterprise value does not include a discount based on the stock's minority status or lack of marketability. In contrast, "fair market value" of corporate stock has been defined as "the price at which the stock would change hands between a willing seller, under no compulsion to sell, and a willing buyer, under no compulsion to buy, with both parties having reasonable knowledge of relevant facts." …

Here, the jury's verdict as to the Stock's "fair value" constitutes their determination of "enterprise value," as they were instructed to value the stock "[w]ithout discounting for lack of marketability or minority status." …

Enterprise value has been seen as the appropriate valuation when a minority shareholder, with no desire to leave the corporation, has been forced to relinquish his ownership position by the oppressive conduct of the majority. … In that situation, "[t]he oppressed minority investor was not looking to sell, and the oppressive majority investor, absent the threat of dissolution or other judicial sanction, was not looking to buy." … Likewise, enterprise value has been held to be the appropriate value for a shareholder dissenting to a merger: in that situation there is a willing buyer, but not a willing seller. … That, however, is not the situation in this case. Here, Ann desired to leave the corporation and sought to market the Stock, first to RIC and then to third parties.

In crafting an equitable remedy for appellants' oppressive conduct in connection with Ann's efforts to sell the Stock, the trial court should have provided the relief prevented by appellants' conduct, i.e., a sale at fair market value. If Ann had been able to sell to a willing buyer under no obligation to purchase, Ann would have obtained the "fair market value" of the Stock. As an equitable remedy for appellants' oppressive conduct, Ann is entitled to no more than that.

Two factors affecting the fair market value of the Stock are its lack of marketability and the fact that it represents a minority position in RIC. … By expressly instructing the jury to exclude these factors in determining the "fair value" of the stock and by basing its equitable remedy on their determination, the trial court ordered appellants to pay Ann more than the fair market value of the Stock. Thus the trial court's judgment provided excessive relief for Ann.

…

Conclusion

We conclude that appellants' refusal to meet with or allow any officer or director of RIC to meet with potential purchasers of the Stock was oppressive conduct and that the trial court did not abuse its discretion by ordering RIC to buyout the Stock as an appropriate equitable remedy. However, we conclude the trial court erred by instructing the jury not to include discounts in determining the fair market value of the Stock. …

Not all courts embrace the oppression doctrine. Most importantly, the Delaware courts adhere to traditional fiduciary duty analysis. For example, in *Nixon v. Blackwell*, 626 A. 2d 1366, 1379–1380 (Del. 1993), the Delaware Supreme Court opined:

> We wish to address [a] matter which was raised at oral argument before this Court: Whether there should be any special, judicially-created rules to "protect" minority stockholders of closely-held Delaware corporations.
>
> The case at bar points up the basic dilemma of minority stockholders in receiving fair value for their stock as to which there is no market and no market valuation. It is not difficult to be sympathetic, in the abstract, to a stockholder who finds himself or herself in that position. A stockholder who bargains for stock in a closely-held corporation and who pays for those shares … can make a business judgment whether to buy into such a minority position, and if so on what terms. One could bargain for definitive provisions of self-ordering permitted to a Delaware corporation through the certificate of incorporation or through by-laws by reason of the provisions in [the Delaware statutes]. Moreover, in addition to such mechanisms, a stockholder intending to buy into a minority position in a Delaware corporation may enter into definitive stockholder agreements, and such agreements may provide for elaborate earnings tests, buy-out provisions, voting trusts, or other voting agreements. …
>
> The tools of good corporate practice are designed to give a purchasing minority stockholder the opportunity to bargain for protection before parting with consideration. It would do violence to normal corporate practice and our corporation law to fashion an ad hoc ruling

which would result in a court-imposed stockholder buy-out for which the parties had not contracted.

SCENARIO

Pam Cakes, Mabel Sirrupp, and Benji Wafel agree to go into the restaurant business together in Baltimore, specializing in breakfast cuisine. Cakes will contribute $25,000, Sirrupp $50,000 and Wafel $5,000. Sirrupp, who lives in Denver, will not manage the business on an ongoing basis, but expects to receive profits from the business. Cakes, who lives in Baltimore, is a dentist for her regular job but also plans to have time to help run the restaurant. Wafel, who has a degree in restaurant management, plans to make the restaurant his regular full-time job.

What provisions do you recommend be included in the "partner/shareholder" agreement? Explain the options and ramifications of the various provisions that may be contained in the agreement.

Chapter 4

PIERCING THE "CORPORATE VEIL"

WE KNOW THE general rule that shareholders in a validly formed corporation enjoy limited liability. They are liable only to the extent of their contributions in the business, including any unrealized gains and capital appreciation. The same holds true for equity holders in other limited liability enterprises, such as limited liability companies. Undoubtedly, shareholder limited liability is a bedrock principle of corporate law: It facilitates economic growth by providing risk-averse shareholders the assurance that they will not be personally responsible to the company's creditors.[1]

As with nearly every general rule, there are exceptions. For example, a creditor (such as a bank) ordinarily is unwilling to extend a loan to a company with few assets. As a condition of providing the loan, the bank normally will insist on a personal guarantee from one or more of the shareholders. By executing a personal guarantee as a result of the contract negotiation process, a subject shareholder becomes personally liable on the loan if the corporation defaults on the payment of this debt obligation.[2]

Another exception to the general rule of limited liability in the corporate setting occurs when a shareholder commits a tort. In this situation, the tortfeasor is personally liable. For example, a shareholder, while carrying on the corporation's business—driving a company vehicle to a customer site in response to a customer's service call—negligently causes an automobile crash. In such case, the corporation as well as the individual shareholder (as the tortfeasor) are liable to the aggrieved victims of the crash.[3]

A third major exception to the general principle of shareholder limited liability is the focus of this Chapter—piercing the "corporate veil."[4] Creditors of a corporation are of two general types—contract creditors and tort creditors. Contract creditors, of course, are "voluntary" creditors. They willingly enter into arrangements (such as the sale of goods, leasing of premises, and servicing of equipment) with the corporation. The second type of creditor—the tort claimant—is an involuntary creditor. Such person may have been injured by falling on a wet floor while shopping at a corporate store, being hit by an auto driven by a corporate employee, or having his/her funds misappropriated by a crooked corporate employee. Clearly, the tort creditor did not bargain for such misfortune.

Nonetheless, in the "piercing" context, both contract and tort creditors have the same objective. Because the corporation does not have sufficient assets to satisfy the debt (or damages) incurred, each of these creditors seek to hold the shareholders personally liable for the amount owed. The manner in which both contract and tort creditors seek to meet this objective is to bring a lawsuit alleging that, due to shareholder domination over the subject corporation as well as equitable considerations, the benefit of shareholder limited liability should be denied. Accordingly, if proven by the plaintiff-creditor, the veil of the corporation is pierced to hold its active shareholders personally liable.[5]

Hence, this situation arises when, although there exists a validly formed corporation, the active shareholders fail to treat the corporation as a separate enterprise. Normally, this showing alone is not enough to pierce the veil. What also must be proven is that equity demands that the veil be pierced—usually, shown by fraud, misrepresentation, or inadequate capitalization. Because of the well established principle of shareholder limited liability, a creditor's task is challenging. Each case must be assessed based on its facts and circumstances. Nonetheless, with some frequency, plaintiff-creditors are victorious in their efforts to pierce the corporate veil, thereby holding active shareholders personally liable.[6]

CONTEXTS IN WHICH PIERCING THE CORPORATE VEIL OCCURS

As seen from the preceding discussion, piercing the corporate veil occurs in both the contract and tort contexts. Cases generally arise in two different settings. The first is where the active shareholders of a closely-held corporation (namely, a corporation comprised of few shareholders whose stock is not publicly traded) are sought to be held personally liable.[7] The second is where a parent corporation is sought to be held financially responsible by creditors for the debt(s) incurred by its subsidiary (note that a parent company ordinarily owns more than 50% of the stock of its subsidiary or its subsidiaries).[8] In this second situation, a creditor also may seek to hold liable not only the parent company but also a number of its other subsidiaries on the basis that they all comprised parts of a single larger business (called the "single business enterprise" doctrine).[9]

Note that in the first instance above, involving shareholders of a close corporation, the specter arises that individuals will be held personally accountable, having to dip into their personal savings to satisfy the judgment entered. Significantly, however, no case has been reported where individual shareholders of a publicly-held corporation (such as one traded on the New York Stock Exchange) have been held personally liable. Or stated another way, the corporate veil has not been pierced with respect to publicly-held companies to hold their shareholders personally liable.[10]

In the second instance, a parent corporation (whose stock may or may not be publicly-held) is sought to be held responsible for the obligations of its subsidiary. In this situation, no personal liability is at stake. Rather, a parent company (which enjoys shareholder limited liability) may be held responsible for the debt(s) of its subsidiary whose veil is sought to be pierced.[11]

From the foregoing discussion, two key inquiries emerge. First, should the corporate veil be pierced more readily with respect to involuntary tort creditors than voluntary contract creditors? Second, should the corporate veil be pierced more readily in the parent-subsidiary (or "corporate group") setting than when individual shareholders are sought to be held personally liable in the closely-held corporation context?

As a general proposition, the same "piercing" analysis applies irrespective whether the creditor is a contract or tort claimant and irrespective whether the case involves a parent-subsidiary or close corporation–individual shareholder scenario. Interestingly, a recent study that analyzed a dataset consisting of nearly 3,000 cases found that tort claimants prevail more often than contract claimants in "piercing" claims. Perhaps surprisingly, that same study also found that individual shareholders in closely-held corporations are at greater risk of successful veil piercing claims than are corporate groups (for example, the parent-subsidiary situation).[12]

PERTINENT FACTORS IN VEIL-PIERCING ANALYSIS

As addressed above, as a generality, veil piercing analysis focuses on two separate inquiries: First, has the subject corporation been treated by its owners as a separate enterprise or have they treated the enterprise in such a manner so that the corporation, in practicality, has lost its separate identity? Second, are there equitable considerations present that merit the corporate veil being pierced, such as the presence of fraud, misrepresentation, or inadequate capitalization?[13] Our discussion next focuses on these considerations.

Domination by a Shareholder over the Corporation

The first step in veil piercing analysis is to assess whether the shareholders have dominated and controlled the corporation to such a degree that the corporation, in practicality, has lost its separate identity. Numerous factors are relevant to this assessment, some of which are more important than others. The following serve as illustrations:

1. The corporation does not adhere to corporate formalities. Examples include not holding board of director and shareholder meetings, not electing officers, and failing to document properly corporate actions (such as the payment of employee salaries, declaration of shareholder dividends, and entering into corporate transactions).[14] This failure to comply with corporate formalities is viewed as relevant by nearly all jurisdictions, except most notably the state of Texas where by statute this factor is deemed irrelevant in both contract and tort veil piercing cases.[15]
2. The corporation fails to open bank accounts in the corporate name and fails to conduct transactions on a corporate basis. For example, checks for payment of a subsidiary corporation's debts are written on a corporate parent's account. As another example, performance of tasks called for in a contract between the subsidiary corporation and third party are conducted by the parent corporation's employees rather than employees of the subsidiary.[16]
3. Perhaps the most important factor with respect to the issue of shareholder domination over a subject corporation is "commingling." Commingling occurs, for instance, when a shareholder shuttles money in and out of the corporation to suit his/her convenience. This may occur when a shareholder takes funds from the corporation without proper authorization to pay personal expenses (such as a home mortgage or a Maui vacation) and subsequently puts funds back into the corporation. Directing corporate employees on the company payroll to perform personal tasks for a shareholder (such as mowing the yard or acting as chauffeur) without additional compensation from the shareholder serves as another example. Another illustration is when corporations in the same corporate family have the same employees without clear identification to the roles that such employees have with respect to each corporation and the amount of compensation that is paid to such employees from each such corporation.[17]

The above discussion provides examples of active shareholders causing the corporation to disregard its separate identity. Slighting corporate formalities, using the parent company's checking account to pay the subsidiary corporation's debts, and commingling of personal and company assets all evince a perception that a separate identity has not been respected by the subject company. Showing such identity of interest between the active shareholders and the subject corporation, however, ordinarily is not sufficient by itself for a plaintiff-creditor to pierce the veil of limited liability. What must also be proven is that equitable considerations militate in favor of veil piercing.

CONSIDERATIONS OF EQUITY

Generally, the corporate veil is pierced only when considerations of equity merit this result. For example, where a subject corporation's agents perpetrate fraud upon a creditor (such as providing deliberate phony financial statements to a bank in order to procure a loan), piercing ordinarily follows.[18] Piercing the corporate veil also frequently occurs when there is misrepresentation. For instance, a parent company's communications with a creditor causing the creditor to reasonably believe that the creditor is contracting with the parent (when in actuality the contract is with the subsidiary corporation) may prompt a court to order that the subsidiary's veil be pierced.[19]

The most problematic issue in this context occurs when the subject corporation is inadequately capitalized. Inadequate capitalization (or undercapitalization) generally signifies that the company does not have sufficient capital levels to cover the debts that are (or foreseeably will be) incurred.[20] In the tort setting, in addition to such criteria as net assets in the business, courts also look to whether the company procured insurance coverage (and the amount thereof). In other words, with respect to ascertaining whether a subject company is adequately capitalized when a tort creditor seeks to pierce the corporate veil, courts will consider both the company's capital levels as well as the amount of insurance coverage that the company has obtained.[21]

Should inadequate capitalization be an important factor favoring veil piercing in contract cases? The cases are divided. On one side is the principle that contract creditors are voluntary. They are in a position to bargain for provisions in the agreement that help protect them from nonperformance by the subject company. These provisions may include receiving personal guarantees from the shareholders, securing the debt with a physical asset of the company (e.g., the company's real property or plant), and limiting the amount of corporate funds (both in compensation and dividends) that can be paid to the shareholders. A state that clearly follows this approach is Texas where piercing is permitted in contract cases only if actual fraud is proven.[22]

On the other hand, many contract creditors are not sophisticated parties. To require such arguably elaborate negotiations prior to entering into routine business agreements would impede commercial deals. Rather, considerations of equity, under this view, demand that shareholders who control a corporation must provide adequate capital to meet expected debts. Actions by shareholders that cause excessive funds to be taken out of the corporation (in the form of either compensation or dividends) and that thereby make the corporation unable to pay its ordinary debts is an abuse of the privilege of limited liability. Such shareholder conduct also places an undue risk on contract creditors. Accordingly, under this view, undercapitalization evidences an abuse of the corporate privilege and serves as a justification for veil piercing.[23]

Should inadequate capitalization be a paramount factor in tort cases? After all, tort claimants are involuntary creditors. Should a corporation or other limited liability enterprise (such as a limited liability company) shift the risk of loss to unknowing members of the public by declining to procure insurance, especially if such insurance is available and is affordable? But what if insurance coverage is not available or at an affordable price? What if some insurance coverage is procured but not nearly sufficient to cover the tort-claimant's losses?

The answers to the foregoing implicate significant issues of public policy. As a generality, where shareholders fail to respect the separate identity of the corporation and no insurance is obtained by such company (assuming that coverage is available), many courts will pierce the corporate veil.[24] This subject becomes more problematic when some insurance coverage is obtained but not a sufficient amount to cover the tort claimant's losses.[25]

Single Business Enterprise Doctrine

In addition to the grounds for veil piercing addressed in this Chapter, an alternative basis for holding corporations in a corporate family liable is based on the single business enterprise doctrine. This doctrine has been advocated by a number of experts but not widely adopted by the courts.[26] As stated by the U.S. Court of Appeals for the Fifth Circuit: "Under that doctrine, when corporations are not operated as separate entities, but integrate their resources to achieve a common business purpose, each constituent corporation may be held liable for the debts incurred in pursuit of that business purpose."[27] Many courts believe that this theory is too expansive, contrary to the public policy of shareholder limited liability that serves as a key source for economic growth.

Hence, that two or more corporations "coordinate operations and combine resources in pursuit of the same business purpose" by itself is an insufficient basis for veil piercing.[28]

CONCLUSION

The general rule of shareholder limited liability has a number of exceptions. The exceptions addressed in this Chapter, and one that often arises in the business world, is that of creditors seeking to pierce the corporate veil to hold its shareholders liable. Although there are certain basic principles that apply in this setting, veil piercing is determined on the facts and circumstances of each case.[29]

To conclude, two propositions are set forth. First, shareholders that cause the corporation to adhere to corporate formalities, maintain separate corporate bank accounts, refrain from commingling, ensure that the corporation is adequately capitalized, and refrain from questionable conduct should have comfort that the corporate veil will not be pierced. Second, on the other hand, where shareholders ignore the separate identity of the corporation by engaging in commingling, slight corporate formalities, cause the undercapitalization of the corporation, and engage in misconduct, such shareholders have a strong likelihood that the corporate veil will be pierced and they will be subject to liability to plaintiff-creditors. In between these two extremes, the law is more uncertain. For that very reason, shareholders should take the necessary steps to help ensure that their limited liability status will be respected by the courts.

NOTES

1. See generally S. Presser, *Piercing the Corporate Veil* (2004).
2. See § 6.22 of the Model Business Corporation Act.
3. See materials in Chapter 1 herein.
4. See *United States v. Milwaukee Refrigerator Transit Co.*, 142 F. 247, 253 (E.D. Wis. 1905) (stating that "a corporation will be looked upon as a legal entity as a general rule, and until sufficient reason to the contrary appears, but when the notion of legal entity is used to defeat public convenience, justify wrong, protect fraud, or defend crime, the law will regard the corporation as an association of persons").
5. See Oh, *Veil-Piercing*, 89 Texas L. Rev. 81, 89–90 (2010).
6. *Id.*
7. See, e.g., *Kinney Shoe Corporation v. Polan*, 909 F. 2d 209 (4th Cir. 1991).

8. See, e.g., *OTR Associates v. IBC Services, Inc.*, 801 A. 2d 407 (N.J. Super. Ct. 2002).
9. See *Walkovszky v. Carlton*, 296 N.Y. 2d 362 (N.Y. Ct. App. 1966).
10. See Thompson, *Piercing the Corporate Veil: An Empirical Study*, 76 Cornell L. Rev. 1036 (1991).
11. See, e.g., *Gardemal v. Westin Hotel Co.*, 186 F. 3d 588 (5th Cir. 1999).
12. See Oh, *Veil-Piercing*, 89 Texas L. Rev. 81, 89–90 (stating that courts "pierce [the corporate veil] almost 50% of the time [and that] veil-piercing claims prevail more often in Tort than Contract").
13. See, e.g., *De Witt Truck Brokers Inc. v. W. Ray Fleming Fruit Co.*, 540 F. 2d 681 (4th Cir. 1976).
14. See *Kinney Shoe Corporation v. Polan*, 939 F. 2d 209 (4th Cir. 1991).
15. See § 21.223(a)(3) of the Texas Business Organization Code.
16. See *National Labor Relations Board v. West Dixie Enterprises, Inc.*, 190 F. 3d 1191 (11th Cir. 1999).
17. See *American Trading and Production Corporation v. Fishback & Moore*, 311 F. Supp. 412 (N.D. Ill. 1970).
18. See *Baker v. Kulczyk*, 732 P. 2d 386 (Idaho Ct. App. 1987).
19. See *OTR Associates v. IBC Services, Inc.*, 801 A. 2d 407 (N.J. Super. 2002).
20. See D. Branson, J. Heminway, M. Loewenstein, M. Steinberg, and M. Warren, *Business Enterprises: Legal Structures, Governance, and Policy* 220 (2009).
21. *Id.* at 220–221.
22. See § 21.223 of the Texas Business Organizations Act.
23. See *Kinney Shoe Corporation v. Polan*, 936 F. 2d 209 (4th Cir. 1991).
24. See *Minton v. Caveney*, 364 P. 2d 473 (Cal. Sup. Ct. 1961). See also, *Baatz v. Arrow Bar*, 452 N.W. 2d 138 (S. Dak. 1989).
25. See *Walkovszky v. Carlton*, 18 N.Y. 2d 414 (N.Y. Ct. App. 1966).
26. For example, the single business enterprise theory has been adopted in Louisiana. See, e.g., *Dishon v. M. Ponthie*, 918 So. 2d 1132 (La. App. 2005). See generally Dearborn, *Enterprise Liability: Reviewing and Revitalizing Liability for Corporate Groups*, 97 Cal. L. Rev. 195 (2009).
27. *Gardemal v. Westin Hotel Co.*, 186 F. 3d 588, 594 (5th Cir. 1999).
28. *SSP Partners v. Gladstrong Investments (USA) Corp.*, 275 S.W. 3d 444, 452 (Tex. 2009).
29. See generally Morrissey, *Piercing All the Veils: Applying an Established Doctrine to a New Business Order*, 32 J. Corp. L. 529 (2007)

THE CASES THAT follow focus on creditors' efforts to pierce the corporate veil in both the contract and tort contexts. In a number of these cases the individual shareholder is sought to be held personally liable while in others the corporate parent is the focus of the veil piercing analysis.

CONTRACT SETTING

BRUNSWICK CORP. V. WAXMAN
UNITED STATES COURT OF APPEALS
599 F.2D 34 (SECOND CIRCUIT 1979)

Mulligan, Circuit Judge:

Brunswick Corporation (Brunswick) appeals from an order and judgment of the Hon. John R. Bartels, United States District Court for the Eastern District of New York, dismissing the complaint and entering judgment for the defendants after a trial without a jury. Brunswick brought this action against the individual defendants seeking over a million dollars in damages. This amount represents the deficiency due under conditional sales contracts entered into between Brunswick and the Waxman Construction Corporation (Construction Corp.) whereby the latter entity purchased bowling lanes and pinsetters. The individual defendants, Harry Waxman and the late Sydney Waxman, signed the contracts as president and secretary of the Construction Corp. The theory of the plaintiff is that the corporate veil of the Construction Corp. should be pierced and the Waxmans held personally liable for the deficiency.

The fact findings of the trial court indicate that in August 1960, the Waxmans formed the Construction Corp. as a no-asset New York corporation [namely, a corporation that has zero assets] to act as signatory and obligor on a series of conditional sales agreements for the purchase of bowling equipment to be operated in five new bowling alleys. The five alleys and the Brunswick equipment were operated by the Waxmans through five separate partnerships, which owned the non-Brunswick equipment and fixtures in the alleys. The Waxmans owned or leased the real property on which the bowling alleys were located, but charged the Construction Corp. no rent for the use of the premises. Nor did the Waxmans pay rent to the Construction Corp. for the use of the bowling equipment. In addition, the Waxmans owned in their individual or partnership capacities all the licenses and permits necessary to operate the alleys. Proceeds from the daily operation of the businesses were deposited in individual bowling alley accounts and later transferred into a central Waxman enterprises bank account from which funds were withdrawn to meet the necessary operating expenses of the alleys. It was from this central bank account that amounts due on the sales contracts with Brunswick were withdrawn and deposited in the Construction Corp. account. The court below found that the Construction Corp.'s sole corporate activity was the transfer of funds into and out of its bank account for the purpose of meeting the installment payments under the Brunswick contracts. The Construction Corp. held no stockholders' or directors' meetings, adopted no bylaws, and issued no stock. While it filed federal and New York State income tax returns, none of these returns showed any income, nor did any report the Brunswick equipment as corporate assets.

Due to a general decline in the bowling industry [when bowling was no longer king-pin], the Construction Corp. was unable to meet its payment obligations under the sales contracts. Pursuant to a 1963 extension agreement, title to the Brunswick equipment was transferred from Construction Corp. to five new corporations, which were also to receive an additional $375,000 in non-Brunswick assets. However, the Waxmans never transferred the additional assets to the five corporations. In addition, these newly formed corporations were as inactive as the Construction Corp. had been. By late 1965, two of the five corporations, Bruckner Lanes, Inc. and Pike Lanes, Inc., were in default. In 1966, Brunswick repossessed its equipment held by Bruckner Lanes and sold it at a substantial deficiency. Although an extension agreement was reached with Pike Lanes in 1966, that corporation continued in substantial default and its equipment was also repossessed and sold by Brunswick at a substantial deficiency.

Although we are persuaded that the district judge reached the proper result here in dismissing the complaint, we cannot subscribe entirely to his views on the law of New York in the field of piercing the corporate veil and the disregard of the corporate fiction. New York law in this area is hardly as clear as a mountain lake in springtime. Since Professor Wormser's initial discussion of the topic in Piercing the Veil of Corporate Entity, 12 Colum.L.Rev. 496 (1912), there have been scores of articles and hundreds of cases discussing the problem, advancing and espousing various theories. In particular we are dubious that, as suggested by the district court, the plaintiff need establish that the Waxmans committed a fraud on Brunswick and that there be a causal connection between the fact that the Waxmans conducted business individually and the contract losses suffered by Brunswick. …

The district judge who tried the case found that Brunswick had knowingly entered into the conditional sales contracts involved in this litigation with a no-asset corporation which was created for the sole purpose of taking title to the equipment which Brunswick sold. Brunswick knew or should be charged with the knowledge that the Waxmans wished to avoid personal liability and that the sole obligor on the sales contract was to be the corporate dummy created for that purpose. Further Brunswick investigated to determine whether the alleys themselves were likely to generate revenues sufficient to make the payments for the equipment purchased by the Construction Corp. Thus, Brunswick was aware or should have known that the dummy corporation was created for the limited purpose of purchase, that the property and buildings in which the equipment was to be installed were owned by the Waxmans in their individual capacities, and that the Waxmans would personally conduct the bowling alley business.

Under these circumstances Brunswick obtained precisely what it bargained for, and it did not bargain for or contemplate the individual liability of the Waxmans which it now seeks to enforce. To pierce the corporate veil here would not in our view accomplish justice or equity but would in fact thwart that end. We therefore refuse to disregard the corporate entity in this case. The creation of the dummy corporation under these circumstances to eliminate personal responsibility should be respected.

AFFIRMED.

BRIDAS S.A.P.I.C V. GOVERNMENT OF TURKMENISTAN UNITED STATES COURT OF APPEALS 477 F. 3D 411 (FIFTH CIRCUIT 2006)

Jones, Chief Judge:

Bridas S.A.P.I.C. ("Bridas") appeals the district court's vacatur of an arbitration award against the Government of Turkmenistan ("Government"), a nonsignatory to an arbitration agreement between Bridas and a government-owned oil and gas company. Because the totality of the record demonstrates that the Government should be bound as an alter ego of State Concern Turkmenneft ("Turkmenneft"), we Reverse and Render for enforcement of the award.

This dispute has been in litigation longer than the agreement that spawned it. Bridas has pursued recovery against the Government for an oil and gas development deal gone awry. The catch has been that the Government was never a signatory to the relevant contractual documents. Bridas has borne the burden, before an arbitration panel and in federal court, of holding the Government liable. This appeal, after remand to the district court, represents the final refinement of numerous theories Bridas advanced against the Government. We review the district court's conclusion on remand that the Government was not an alter ego of Turkmenneft.

I. BACKGROUND

In February 1993, Bridas, an Argentine corporation, entered into a joint venture agreement ("JVA") to exploit oil and gas resources with an entity designated by the Government of Turkmenistan, then recently liberated from the Soviet Union. Turkmenistan was rich in resources, but poor in technical expertise. Bridas was designated as the "foreign party" in the Joint Venture Keimir (named for the region in which exploration would be conducted). The "Turkmenian Party" to the agreement has been an entity wholly owned by the Government, whose identity was designated and re-designated at will by the President of Turkmenistan and has changed a number of times during the life of the joint venture. Turkmenneft is the last entity to step into the role of "Turkmenian Party." Under the JVA, the Turkmenian Party was entitled to receive hydrocarbon production up to the November 1992 levels, while the parties would split any subsequent increase in production. The JVA secured an unlimited export license for hydrocarbons.

Notwithstanding that the JVA was intended to last twenty-five years, the relationship among Bridas, the Turkmenian Party, and the Government soured quickly. The Government insisted, among other things, on raising its share of future proceeds. To force Bridas's submission, the Government ordered Bridas in November 1995 to halt operations in Keimir and cease making imports into and exports from Turkmenistan.

Six months later, Bridas commenced an arbitration proceeding, as provided in the JVA, against the Government and Turkmenneft under the auspices of the International Chamber of Commerce. After Bridas filed its arbitration complaint, the Government dissolved the "Turkmenian Party" in the JVA, replacing it with Turkmenneft. The Government further abolished its Ministry of Oil and Gas. More importantly, the Government decreed that all proceeds from oil and gas exports in the country were to be directed to a special State Oil and Gas Development Fund; the fund's assets were declared immune from seizure.

...

The district court reviewed many of the factors identified by this court as pertinent and held that there was "an insufficient showing of complete domination or extensive control so as to warrant a finding that Turkmenneft was the alter ego of the Government of Turkmenistan." Bridas has appealed from the district court's resulting decision to vacate the award against the Government.

II. DISCUSSION

...

A bedrock of corporate law is that "a parent corporation ... is not liable" for actions taken by its subsidiaries. The same concepts of corporate separateness have been applied to business entities owned by foreign governments. However, courts will apply the alter ego doctrine and hold a parent liable for the actions of its instrumentality in the name of equity when the corporate form is used as a "sham to perpetrate a fraud." In making an alter ego determination, a court is "concerned with reality and not form, [and with] how the corporation operated."...

The alter ego doctrine, like all variations of piercing the corporate veil doctrine, is reserved for exceptional cases. The doctrine applies only if "(1) the owner exercised complete control over the corporation with respect to the transaction at issue and (2) such control was used to commit a fraud or wrong that injured the party seeking to pierce the veil." Given the difficulty of analyzing the control factors in this case, we first address the "fraud or injustice" prong.

A. Fraud or Injustice

To prevail, Bridas had to demonstrate that the Government used its control over Turkmenneft to commit a "fraud or injustice" against Bridas. The Government asserts that only fraud—and no other type of injustice—satisfies this prong of the alter ego test. [Our] cases plainly envision a broader scope that includes the misuse of the corporate form to promote injustice. ... In this contract dispute, Bridas thus had to connect the Government misuse of its "subsidiary" Turkmenneft to the fraud or injustice against it.

In this case, the act of injustice on which the district court focused was the Government's 1995 export ban, which was accomplished through the "Government's exercise of sovereign control of Turkmenistan's borders, not through governmental control of Turkmenneft." The Government's exercise of its sovereign powers may have constituted a wrong to Bridas, but it was not a wrong based on misuse of the corporate organizational form. Contrary to the court's conclusion, the 1995 export ban is not a "fraud or injustice" for alter ego purposes.

This court may, however, affirm the district court's determination that the "fraud or injustice" prong was satisfied if there is other evidence on the record, and argued by Bridas below, to support such a holding.

As it happens, there is ample evidence that after the 1995 export ban the Government misused Turkmenneft to harm Bridas by destroying the value of the JVA. In 1996, when the Government dissolved the Turkmenian Party and replaced it with Turkmenneft, Turkmenneft was initially capitalized with the equivalent of only $17,000 U.S. and was funded by a State Oil and Gas Development Fund expressly rendered immune from seizure under newly enacted Turkmenian law. Yet Turkmenneft became the party bound to arbitrate under the JVA and liable for any adverse award. At the same time, the Government issued a number of decrees distancing itself from the joint venture and attempting to limit its potential exposure to liability. The Government's manipulation of Turkmenneft to prevent Bridas from recovering any substantial damage award satisfies the "fraud or injustice" prong. …

B. Control

The more difficult issue is whether the Government exercised such complete control over Turkmenneft as to be its alter ego. …

[A previous decision] identified twelve "private law" factors commonly utilized by this circuit in making a corporate alter ego determination:

> (1) the parent and subsidiary have common stock ownership; (2) the parent and subsidiary have common directors or officers; (3) the parent and subsidiary have common business departments; (4) the parent and subsidiary file consolidated financial statements; (5) the parent finances the subsidiary; (6) the parent caused the incorporation of the subsidiary; (7) the subsidiary operated with grossly inadequate capital; (8) the parent pays salaries and other expenses of the subsidiary; (9) the subsidiary receives no business except that given by the parent; (10) the parent uses the subsidiary's property as its own; (11) the daily operations of the two corporations are not kept separate; [and] (12) the subsidiary does not observe corporate formalities.

[T]hree more private law factors [are pertinent]: "(1) whether the directors of the 'subsidiary' act in the primary and independent interest of the 'parent'; (2) whether others pay or guarantee debts of the dominated corporation; and (3) whether the alleged dominator deals with the dominated corporation at arm's length." …

The district court ultimately concluded that the Government did not "exercise complete domination or extensive control" over Turkmenneft. The district court conscientiously attempted to analyze the relationship between the Government and Turkmenneft. … We respectfully but firmly disagree with the district court's conclusion and find it clearly erroneous. The court's error lay in elevating the form over the substance of the relationship as it pertained to the transaction with Bridas. …

The court first examined the "formalities factors" in the Government-Turkmenneft relationship. The court observed that the Government caused the incorporation of Turkmenneft and that there was some identity between high-ranking Government and Turkmenneft officials. Furthermore, Government officials attended the JVA's board meetings. More important to the court, however, were that Turkmenneft's "legal status was explicitly recognized on the face of the JVA"; that Turkmenneft is "solely responsible for its own obligations"; and Turkmenneft existed "as a juridical entity long before the events in question." The court also found that Turkmenneft and its predecessors had the right to and did actually hold and use property, and that Turkmenneft can sue and be sued in its own name.

The court did not consider "all of the formalities required by corporation law, including keeping separate books and records and holding regular meetings of shareholders and of the board of directors." Nevertheless, based on the evidence that it considered, the court reached a plausible outcome that Turkmenneft exhibited certain "corporate formalities." Those aspects of the equitable calculation are, however, subordinate to ascertaining the reality of the corporate relationship.

The court found, with regard to the "operations" factors, that Turkmenneft was "operationally separate from the government." The court relied heavily on the assertions that Turkmenneft could trace its origins back many decades within the structure of the then-Soviet Union and that it had engaged in joint ventures with other foreign concerns. …

Although the balance of "formalities factors" and some of the "operational factors" may be consistent with Turkmenneft's existence in an independent and self-supporting entity, the court's skepticism about Turkmenneft's arm's-length status is critical. The Government manipulated Turkmenneft legally and economically to repudiate the contract with Bridas and then render it impossible for Bridas to collect damages. This conclusion is reinforced by the court's review of the "finances" factors [that showed that] not only was the Turkmenian Party financed by the Government, but when the Government created Turkmenneft as the Turkmenian Party's successor, Turkmenneft was grossly undercapitalized with the equivalent of $17,000 U.S., a paltry sum to finance oil and gas exploration and production. The court noted the absence of any financial statement or balance sheet for Turkmenneft, whether under U.S. or local law. Turkmenneft's revenues were diverted to a State Oil and Gas Fund that also collected revenues from other state-owned entities. Although the Government contends that the joint venture, not the Government, paid the joint venture's salaries and expenses, Turkmenneft's costs of [this litigation] have been paid entirely from the State Fund. The court accordingly found that Turkmenneft was not financially independent from the Government and that the Government used the lack of financial separateness "to commit a fraud or another wrong on plaintiffs."

With this conclusion, we concur. Undercapitalization is often critical in alter ego analysis. The fact that Turkmenneft owned producing rights and equipment that it contributed to the joint venture does not in this case support a claim of financial separateness, because such resources could only carry value if the venture were allowed to keep its own revenues, which it was not. Further, the Government changed the law to prevent Turkmenneft's assets from being seized by a creditor such as Bridas, after the initiation of [this litigation]. The fact that a subsidiary maintains what amounts to a "zero balance," and relies exclusively upon another entity to service its debts, is strong evidence that the subsidiary lacks an independent identity.

Despite some indicia of separateness, the reality was that when the Government's export ban forced Bridas out of the joint venture, the Government then exercised its power as a parent entity to deprive Bridas of a contractual remedy. Intentionally bleeding a subsidiary to thwart creditors is a classic ground for piercing the corporate veil. It is true that the standard for this equitable remedy should be more stringent in breach of contract cases, because the creditor has willingly transacted business with a subsidiary and, as here, forewent the opportunity to obtain a guarantee of Turkmenneft's debts by the Government. The standard is met in this case, however, because Turkmenneft assumed full responsibility for its obligations under the joint venture. The Government, as Turkmenneft's owner, made it impossible for the objectives of the joint venture to be carried out.

In this rare case, we are compelled to reverse the district court's finding and conclude that the Government acted as the alter ego of Turkmenneft in regard to this Joint Venture Agreement with Bridas.

...

CASE STUDIES

TORT SETTING

MINTON V. CAVANEY
SUPREME COURT OF CALIFORNIA
364 P.2D 473 (1961)

Traynor, J.:

The Seminole Hot Springs Corporation, hereinafter referred to as Seminole, was duly incorporated in California on March 8, 1954. It conducted a public swimming pool that it leased from its owner. On June 24, 1954, plaintiffs' daughter drowned in the pool, and plaintiffs recovered a judgment for $10,000 against Seminole for her wrongful death. The judgment remains unsatisfied.

On January 30, 1957, plaintiffs brought the present action to hold defendant Cavaney personally liable for the judgment against Seminole. Cavaney died on May 28, 1958, and his widow, the executrix of his estate, was substituted as defendant. The trial court entered judgment for plaintiffs for $10,000. Defendant appeals.

Plaintiffs introduced evidence that Cavaney was a director and secretary and treasurer of Seminole and that on November 15, 1954, about five months after the drowning, Cavaney as secretary of Seminole and Edwin A. Kraft as president of Seminole applied for permission to issue three shares of Seminole stock, one share to be issued to Kraft, another to F. J. Wettrick and the third to Cavaney. The Commissioner of Corporations refused permission to issue these shares unless additional information was furnished. The application was then abandoned and no shares were ever issued. There was also evidence that for a time Seminole used Cavaney's office to keep records and to receive mail. Before his death Cavaney answered certain interrogatories. He was asked if Seminole "ever had any assets?" He stated that "insofar as my own personal knowledge and belief is concerned said corporation did not have any assets." Cavaney also stated in the return to an attempted execution that "[I]nsofar as I know, this corporation had no assets of any kind or character. The corporation was duly organized but never functioned as a corporation."

Defendant introduced evidence that Cavaney was an attorney at law, that he was approached by Kraft and Wettrick to form Seminole, and that he was the attorney for Seminole. Plaintiffs introduced

Cavaney's answer to several interrogatories that he held the post of secretary and treasurer and director in a temporary capacity and as an accommodation to his client.

Defendant contends that the evidence does not support the court's determination that Cavaney is personally liable for Seminole's debts and that the "alter ego" doctrine is inapplicable because plaintiffs failed to show that there was "'(1) … such unity of interest and ownership that the separate personalities of the corporation and the individual no longer exist and (2) that, if the acts are treated as those of the corporation alone, an inequitable result will follow.'"

The figurative terminology "alter ego" and "disregard of the corporate entity" is generally used to refer to the various situations that are an abuse of the corporate privilege. The equitable owners of a corporation, for example, are personally liable when they treat the assets of the corporation as their own and add or withdraw capital from the corporation at will; when they hold themselves out as being personally liable for the debts of the corporation; or when they provide inadequate capitalization and actively participate in the conduct of corporate affairs.

In the instant case the evidence is undisputed that there was no attempt to provide adequate capitalization. Seminole never had any substantial assets. It leased the pool that it operated, and the lease was forfeited for failure to pay the rent. Its capital was "'trifling compared with the business to be done and the risks of loss. …'" The evidence is also undisputed that Cavaney was not only the secretary and treasurer of the corporation but was also a director. The evidence that Cavaney was to receive one-third of the shares to be issued supports an inference that he was an equitable owner and the evidence that for a time the records of the corporation were kept in Cavaney's office supports an inference that he actively participated in the conduct of the business. The trial court was not required to believe his statement that he was only a "temporary" director and officer "for accommodation." In any event it merely raised a conflict in the evidence that was resolved adversely to defendant. Moreover, … the business and affairs of every corporation shall be controlled by, a board of [directors]. Defendant does not claim that Cavaney was a director with specialized duties. It is immaterial whether or not he accepted the office of director as an "accommodation" with the understanding that he would not exercise any of the duties of a director. A person may not in this manner divorce the responsibilities of a director from the statutory duties and powers of that office.

There is no merit in defendant's contentions that the "alter ego" doctrine applies only to contractual debts and not to tort claims. ...

The judgment is reversed.

UNITED STATES V. JON-T CHEMICALS, INC.
UNITED STATES COURT OF APPEALS
768 F. 2D 686 (FIFTH CIRCUIT 1985)

Goldberg, Circuit Judge:

This is the latest installment in a series of cases that threatens to become, in its own small way, a latter-day *Jarndyce and Jarndyce*. [Charles Dickens, *Bleak House* (1853)]. The cases arose as a result of fraudulent misrepresentations by John H. Thomas, Lonnie D. Clark, and Jon-T Farms, Inc., to obtain agricultural subsidies under the [U.S. Government] Upland Cotton Program. Initially, the government sought and obtained criminal convictions against these defendants, which we subsequently affirmed on appeal. ... The government then brought a civil action to recover the erroneously-paid subsidies, obtaining a summary judgment against Thomas, Clark, and Jon-T Farms. ... Now, the government seeks to hold liable the parent company of Jon-T Farms—Jon-T Chemicals—on the ground that Farms was its alter ego or agent.

The district court, sitting without a jury, found that Jon-T Chemicals exercised total domination and control over Jon-T Farms and that consequently Farms was the alter ego of Chemicals. On this basis, it entered judgment against Chemicals in the amount of $4,787,604.20. Because the district court applied the correct legal standard and made findings of fact that are not clearly erroneous, we affirm.

I.

Jon-T Chemicals, an Oklahoma corporation, was incorporated in 1969 as a fertilizer and chemicals business. The following year, John H. Thomas became its majority shareholder as well as its president and board chairman, positions which he retained throughout the 1970 to 1973 period.

In April 1971, Chemicals incorporated Jon-T Farms as a wholly-owned subsidiary to engage in the farming and land-leasing business. Chemicals initially invested $1,000 to establish Farms, but later raised this investment to $10,000. All of the directors and officers of Farms were directors and officers of Chemicals, and Thomas served as the president and chairman of both corporations. In addition, Farms used the offices, computer, and accountant of Chemicals without paying any fee; Chemicals paid the salary of Farms's only regular employee; and Chemicals made ongoing, informal advances to Farms to pay Farms's expenses, reaching $1.8 million by the end of 1973 and $7.1 million in January 1975.

...

II.

Although Chemicals raises nine issues on appeal, these all boil down to a single question: Did the district court err in finding that Farms was the alter ego of Chemicals? If Farms was the alter ego of Chemicals, then Chemicals is liable for torts committed by Farms. ...

A.

Under the doctrine of limited liability, the owner of a corporation is not liable for the corporation's debts. Creditors of the corporation have recourse only against the corporation itself, not against its parent company or shareholders. It is on this assumption that "large undertakings are rested, vast enterprises are launched, and huge sums of capital attracted."

While limited liability remains the norm in American corporation law, certain equitable exceptions to the doctrine have developed. The most common exception is for fraud. If, for example, a corporation is established for a fraudulent purpose or is used to commit an illegal act, or if its shareholders drain the corporation's assets, limited liability may not apply. Another exception arises where, as here, a parent company totally dominates and controls its subsidiary, operating the subsidiary as its business conduit or agent. ...

The complementary theories of limited liability and piercing the corporate veil have provoked consternation among courts and legal scholars alike. They have been variously described as a "legal quagmire," Ballantine, *Separate Entity of Parent and Subsidiary Corporations*, 14 Calif. L. Rev. 12, 15 (1925), and as being "enveloped in the mists of metaphor," *Berkey v. Third Avenue Ry.*, 244 N.Y. 84, 155 N.E. 58, 61 (1926) (Cardozo, J.). … Nowhere is this more true than in the case of the alter ego doctrine. In some sense, every subsidiary is the alter ego of its parent company. Where the subsidiary is wholly-owned by the parent and has the same directors and officers, operating the subsidiary independently of the parent company not only has little practical meaning, it would also constitute a breach both of the subsidiary's duty to further the interests of its owner, and of the directors' and officers' duty towards the parent company. Nevertheless, our cases are clear that one-hundred percent ownership and identity of directors and officers are, even together, an insufficient basis for applying the alter ego theory to pierce the corporate veil. Instead, we maintain the fiction that an officer or director of both corporations can change hats and represent the two corporations separately, despite their common ownership.

In lieu of articulating a coherent doctrinal basis for the alter ego theory, we have instead developed a laundry list of factors to be used in determining whether a subsidiary is the alter ego of its parent. These include whether:

1. the parent and the subsidiary have common stock ownership;
2. the parent and the subsidiary have common directors or officers;
3. the parent and the subsidiary have common business departments;
4. the parent and the subsidiary file consolidated financial statements and tax returns;
5. the parent finances the subsidiary;
6. the parent caused the incorporation of the subsidiary;
7. the subsidiary operates with grossly inadequate capital;
8. the parent pays the salaries and other expenses of the subsidiary;
9. the subsidiary receives no business except that given to it by the parent;
10. the parent uses the subsidiary's property as its own;
11. the daily operations of the two corporations are not kept separate; and
12. the subsidiary does not observe the basic corporate formalities, such as keeping separate books and records and holding shareholder and board meetings.

… Additional factors that are sometimes mentioned are (1) "[w]hether the directors and officers of [the subsidiary] act independently in the interest of that company, or whether they take their orders from the [parent] and act in the [parent's] interest," and (2) the "connection of [the] parent's employee, officer or director to [the] subsidiary's tort or contract giving rise to [the] suit." Analytically, however, these last two factors are on a different plane from the other factors. The first is, in essence, the conclusion that we reach through our alter ego analysis and thus depends on the preceding factors. When the directors and officers of the subsidiary are also directors and officers of the parent, it makes little sense to ask whether they take orders from the parent since they themselves constitute the parent's decisionmaking body and are duty-bound to act in the parent's interest. The second factor relates more to the involvement of the parent itself in the acts giving rise to the suit than to its vicarious liability for the subsidiary's acts in general.

In the present case, there is no doubt that the district court applied the proper legal standard. While recognizing that limited liability represents the general rule, the court noted that, under certain circumstances, courts may pierce the corporate veil—including where a subsidiary is completely dominated by its parent. As the court understood, the alter ego question depends upon the totality of the facts. …

Although Chemicals does not directly challenge the legal standard applied by the court below, it implicitly raises two objections. First, Chemicals contends that a finding of fraud is an essential element of any alter ego determination. According to Chemicals, unless a parent intentionally misleads outsiders, uses the corporate form for fraudulent purposes, or milks the subsidiary's assets, then it is entitled to hide behind the corporate veil of its subsidiary. Chemicals argues that since Farms was established for a proper business purpose—i.e., tax advantages—and since neither Chemicals nor Farms misled outsiders regarding their relationship and finances, the district court erred in piercing the corporate veil.

We disagree. … [W]e do not require a finding of fraud in tort cases. Th[e] distinction [between a contract and a tort claimant] is clear. In a contract case, the creditor has willingly transacted business with the subsidiary. If the creditor wants to be able to hold the parent liable for the subsidiary's debts, it can contract for this. Unless the subsidiary misrepresents its financial condition to the creditor, the creditor should be bound by its decision to deal with the subsidiary; it should not be able to complain later that the subsidiary is unsound. In a tort case, by contrast, the creditor has not voluntarily chosen to deal with the subsidiary; instead, the creditor relationship is forced upon it. Thus, the question of whether the creditor relied on misrepresentations by the subsidiary is irrelevant. Where a parent establishes a subsidiary, undercapitalizes it, and dominates it to such an extent that the subsidiary is a mere conduit for the parent's business, then the parent should not be able to shift the risk of loss due to the subsidiary's tortious acts to innocent third parties.

Here, the Government's claims for fraudulent misrepresentation and conversion sound in tort rather than contract. Moreover, the Government did not voluntarily enter into the relationship with Farms. It did not have the option of granting or not granting the subsidies to the joint ventures. Under the Upland Cotton Program, it was obligated to subsidize applicants who purportedly qualified. The fact that the Government did not rely on any misrepresentations regarding Farms's financial condition or its relationship with Chemicals is thus wholly irrelevant to the question whether Chemicals should be held liable for Farms's misconduct. Unlike the ordinary contracting party, the Government was not dilatory in any duty to investigate Farms's finances, since it had no such duty. As long as Chemicals exercised total domination and control over Farms, it was liable for Farms's acts.

Chemicals also contends that the district court gave insufficient weight to the fact that Farms observed all of the formalities required by corporation law, including keeping separate books and records and holding regular meetings of shareholders and of the board of directors. According to Chemicals, as long as corporate forms were observed by the subsidiary, then the corporate form must also be observed by the courts.

Our only reply is that Chemicals puts form ahead of substance. ... In determining whether a subsidiary is the alter ego of its parent, we apply a multifactor test. One of these factors is whether the corporate formalities were observed—but this is only one of several factors; it is not determinative. Thus, Chemicals' argument that Farms observed the corporate formalities goes merely to the weight of the evidence, not to the correctness of the legal standard applied by the district court.

B.

As we have noted, there is no litmus test for determining whether a subsidiary is the alter ego of its parent. Instead, we must look to the totality of the circumstances. Resolution of the alter ego issue is heavily fact-specific. ...

First, Chemicals challenges the district court's finding that Farms "operated with a grossly inadequate capital." Chemicals claims that although Farms initially had only $10,000 in capital, it subsequently received millions of dollars in advances for working capital from Chemicals. According to Chemicals, Farms could not have been undercapitalized since it had "virtually unlimited access to credit in the form of loans from its parent, Chemicals." Our short answer to this is that if Farms had unlimited access to the coffers of Chemicals, this access should have been sufficient to pay involuntary creditors who were prejudiced by the limited funds in Farms's own coffers. In our view, Chemicals' argument misses the point. The underlying question is whether Farms was an economically viable, independent entity or whether it operated merely as the adjunct or alter ego of Chemicals. The fact that Farms continually had net operating losses and survived due to massive and ongoing transfusions from Chemicals does not indicate that Farms ever stood on its own two feet. Quite the contrary; it reinforces the district court's conclusion that Farms did not have any separate financial existence. As the district court properly concluded, Farms operated primarily on the capital of Chemicals rather than on its own capital.

Chemicals also claims that the district court erred in finding that Chemicals and Farms jointly used and owned property and that they commingled their assets. ... In regard to the joint use of property, it is undisputed that Farms used the offices and computer of Chemicals. It is also undisputed, as the district court found, that Chemicals paid the expenses of several tractors used by Farms. Although Chemicals claims that these expenses were carried on its books as loans to Farms, given the pervasive interconnections between Farms and Chemicals, we do not regard the district court's finding regarding the joint ownership of property to be clearly erroneous.

The district court's finding that there was a commingling of the corporate funds of Chemicals and Farms is similarly supported by the record. It is undisputed that Chemicals made ongoing advances to Farms. Basically, whenever Farms could not pay its bills, Chemicals did so by writing a check. These intercorporate loans were handled informally, without any corporate resolutions authorizing them. Chemicals' accounting department, which also served as the accountant for Farms and for the joint ventures, would prepare daily account balances reflecting the daily balances of Chemicals, Farms, the joint ventures, and Chemicals' other subsidiaries. On the basis of these statements, funds were transferred between the different accounts in order to cover deficiencies.

Although Chemicals claims that there was no commingling of funds because records were kept of each advance made by Chemicals to Farms, we agree with the district court that these records did not reflect the true economic realities and that the officers and directors treated the two corporations as one corporate enterprise. Chemicals admits that no collateral was posted for the "loans" it made to Farms and does not contest that Farms paid no interest on the loans. While we do not denigrate careful recordkeeping of corporate transactions, we do not regard mere records as a philosophers' stone capable of transmuting alter egos into distinct corporations. Records are primarily a memorialization of economic reality, not constitutive of that reality.

Having found the district court's subsidiary findings to be supported by the record, we have little trouble in affirming the court's ultimate finding that Farms is the alter ego of Chemicals. ... To mention just some of the evidence supporting the district court's alter ego holding, all of the directors and officers of Farms served as directors and officers of Chemicals; Farms was wholly owned by Chemicals; Chemicals paid many of the bills, invoices, and expenses of Farms; it covered Farms's overdrafts; it made substantial loans to Farms (at one time amounting to $7 million) without corporate resolutions authorizing the loans and without demanding any collateral or interest; Chemicals and Farms filed consolidated financial statements and tax returns; Farms used the offices and computer of Chemicals without paying any rent; the salary of Farms's one regular employee was paid by Chemicals; and employees of Chemicals performed services for Farms without charging for their time. Chemicals also advanced money and provided services on an informal basis to the joint ventures. Although the evidence in the record does not all point in one direction—the fact, for example, that Farms observed corporate formalities supports its separate corporate existence—it was for the factfinder (in this case the district court) to weigh the evidence and to determine, based on the totality of the evidence, whether an alter ego relationship existed.

Finally, Chemicals argues that the Government never proved that Chemicals participated in the joint ventures, and, in particular, in the wrongdoing resulting in the improper subsidy payments. According to Chemicals, it cannot be held responsible because it did not engage in any wrongdoing. This argument, however, begs the alter ego question. The purpose of the alter ego analysis is to determine whether Chemicals is vicariously liable for Farms's actions—that is, whether actions by Farms are considered to be actions by Chemicals. Thus, even if Chemicals were correct that Thomas filed the false forms and improperly converted the drafts in his capacity as president of Farms rather than of Chemicals, this is irrelevant given the district court's ultimate finding, based on a consideration of the evidence as a whole, that Farms was the alter ego of Chemicals.

...

Affirmed.

GARDEMAL V. WESTIN HOTEL CO.
UNITED STATES COURT OF APPEALS
186 F.3D 588 (FIFTH CIRCUIT 1999)

DeMoss, Circuit Judge:

Plaintiff-appellant, Lisa Cerza Gardemal ("Gardemal"), sued defendants-appellees, Westin Hotel Company ("Westin") and Westin Mexico, S.A. de C.V. ("Westin Mexico"), under Texas law, alleging that the defendants were liable for the drowning death of her husband in Cabo San Lucas, Mexico. The district court dismissed the suit in accordance with the magistrate judge's recommendation that the court grant Westin's motion for summary judgment, and Westin Mexico's motion to dismiss for lack of personal jurisdiction. We affirm the district court's rulings.

I.

In June 1995, Gardemal and her husband John W. Gardemal, a physician, traveled to Cabo San Lucas, Baja California Sur, Mexico, to attend a medical seminar held at the Westin Regina Resort Los Cabos ("Westin Regina"). The Westin Regina is owned by Desarollos Turisticos Integrales Cabo San Lucas, S.A. de C.V. ("DTI"), and managed by Westin Mexico. Westin Mexico is a subsidiary of Westin, and is incorporated in Mexico. During their stay at the hotel, the Gardemals decided to go snorkeling with a group of guests. According to Gardemal, the concierge at the Westin Regina directed the group to "Lovers Beach" which, unbeknownst to the group, was notorious for its rough surf and strong undercurrents. While climbing the beach's rocky shore, five men in the group were swept into the Pacific Ocean by a rogue wave and thrown against the rocks. Two of the men, including John Gardemal, drowned.

Gardemal, as administrator of her husband's estate, brought wrongful death and survival actions under Texas law against Westin and Westin Mexico, alleging that her husband drowned because Westin Regina's concierge negligently directed the group to Lovers Beach and failed to warn her husband of its dangerous condition. Westin then moved for summary judgment, alleging that although it is the parent company of Westin Mexico, it is a separate corporate entity and thus could not be held liable for acts committed by its subsidiary. The magistrate judge agreed with Westin, and recommended that Westin be dismissed from the action. In reaching its decision the magistrate judge rejected Gardemal's assertion that the state-law doctrines of alter-ego and single business enterprise allowed the court to disregard Westin's separate corporate identity. …

In this action Gardemal seeks to hold Westin liable for the acts of Westin Mexico … because Westin Mexico functioned as the alter ego of Westin. … Gardemal next contends that Westin may be held liable on the theory that Westin Mexico operated a single business enterprise. We consider first the issue of whether Westin may be held liable on an alter-ego theory.

1.

Under Texas law [in the tort context] the alter ego doctrine allows the imposition of liability on a corporation for the acts of another corporation when the subject corporation is organized or operated as a mere tool or business conduit. It applies "when there is such unity between the parent corporation and its subsidiary that the separateness of the two corporations has ceased and holding only the subsidiary corporation liable would result in injustice." … Alter ego is demonstrated "by evidence showing a blending of identities, or a blurring of lines of distinction, both formal and substantive, between two corporations." …

An important consideration is whether a corporation is underfunded or undercapitalized, which is an indication that the company is a mere conduit or business tool.

On appeal Gardemal points to several factors which, in her opinion, show that Westin is operating as the alter ego of Westin Mexico. She claims, for example, that Westin owns most of Westin Mexico's stock; that the two companies share common corporate officers; that Westin maintains quality control at Westin Mexico by requiring Westin Mexico to use certain operations manuals; that Westin oversees advertising and marketing operations at Westin Mexico through two separate contracts; and that Westin Mexico is grossly undercapitalized. Gardemal places particular emphasis on the last purported factor, that Westin Mexico is undercapitalized. She insists that this factor alone is sufficient evidence that Westin Mexico is the alter ego of Westin. We are not convinced.

The record, even when viewed in a light most favorable to Gardemal, reveals nothing more than a typical corporate relationship between a parent and subsidiary. It is true, as Gardemal points out, that Westin and Westin Mexico are closely tied through stock ownership, shared officers, financing arrangements, and the like. But this alone does not establish an alter-ego relationship. As we explained in *Jon-T Chemicals, Inc.*, [768 F. 2d 686 (5th Cir. 1985)], there must be evidence of complete domination by the parent.

> The control necessary… is not mere majority or complete stock control but such domination of finances, policies and practices that the controlled corporation has, so to speak, no separate mind, will or existence of its own and is but a business conduit for its principal.

Thus, "one-hundred percent ownership and identity of directors and officers are, even together, an insufficient basis for applying the alter ego theory to pierce the corporate veil." …

In this case, there is insufficient record evidence that Westin dominates Westin Mexico to the extent that Westin Mexico has, for practical purposes, surrendered its corporate identity. In fact, the evidence suggests just the opposite, that Westin Mexico functions as an autonomous business entity. There is evidence, for example, that Westin Mexico banks in Mexico and deposits all of the revenue from its six hotels into that account. The facts also show that while Westin is incorporated in Delaware, Westin Mexico is incorporated in Mexico and faithfully adheres to the required corporate formalities. Finally, Westin Mexico has its own staff, its own assets, and even maintains its own insurance policies.

Gardemal is correct in pointing out that undercapitalization is a critical factor in our alter-ego analysis, especially in a tort case like the present one. But as noted by the district court, there is scant evidence that Westin Mexico is in fact undercapitalized and unable to pay a judgment, if necessary. This fact weighs heavily against Gardemal because the alter ego doctrine is an equitable remedy which prevents a company from avoiding liability by abusing the corporate form. "We disregard the corporate fiction ... when the corporate form has been used as part of a basically unfair device to achieve an inequitable result." ... In this case, there is insufficient evidence that Westin Mexico is undercapitalized or uninsured. Moreover, there is no indication that Gardemal could not recover by suing Westin Mexico directly. As a result, equity does not demand that we merge and disregard the corporate identities of Westin and Westin Mexico. We reject Gardemal's attempt to impute liability on Westin based on the alter-ego doctrine.

2.

Likewise, we reject Gardemal's attempt to impute liability to Westin based on the single business enterprise doctrine. Under that doctrine, when corporations are not operated as separate entities, but integrate their resources to achieve a common business purpose, each constituent corporation may be held liable for the debts incurred in pursuit of that business purpose. Like the alter-ego doctrine, the single business enterprise doctrine is an equitable remedy which applies when the corporate form is "used as part of an unfair device to achieve an inequitable result."

On appeal, Gardemal attempts to prove a single business enterprise by calling our attention to the fact that Westin Mexico uses the trademark "Westin Hotels and Resorts." She also emphasizes that Westin Regina uses Westin's operations manuals. Gardemal also observes that Westin allows Westin Mexico to use its reservation system. Again, these facts merely demonstrate what we would describe as a typical, working relationship between a parent and subsidiary. Gardemal has pointed to no evidence in the record demonstrating that the operations of the two corporations were so integrated as to result in a blending of the two corporate identities. Moreover, Gardemal has come forward with no evidence that she has suffered some harm, or injustice, because Westin and Westin Mexico maintain separate corporate identities.

Reviewing the record in the light most favorable to Gardemal, we conclude that there is insufficient evidence that Westin Mexico was Westin's alter ego. Similarly, there is insufficient evidence that the resources of Westin and Westin Mexico are so integrated as to constitute a single business enterprise. Accordingly, we affirm the district court's grant of Westin's motion for summary judgment on that issue. …

SCENARIO

High-Low Amusement, Inc. is a publicly-held company whose stock is traded on the New York Stock Exchange. It is a parent company that holds 100% of the stock in fifteen subsidiary corporations, each of which operated a major amusement park. Each corporation (namely, the parent corporation and its subsidiaries) complies with corporate formalities, has separate bank accounts, conducts business as a separate corporation, has no commingling issues, and has insurance coverage of $2 million per accident victim, with $50 million in total coverage.

One such subsidiary, Highland Amusement Park, Inc., has a new "thrill" ride that is the first of its kind. The "Hyper-Thriller Titan" is a roller coaster like no other. Its height, drops, curves, and speed makes the "Hyper-Thriller Titan" the most daring amusement park ride in the world. Advertising the thrills of this roller coaster, attendance at the Park has dramatically increased, elevating profits to an all-time high.

Nonetheless, Highland Amusement Park's board of directors and management are concerned about the prospect of serious injuries suffered by riders of the "Hyper-Thriller Titan." This concern is exacerbated by the fact that the Park is near New York City and that as a result thousands of well-paid professionals like the thrill of the ride, including investment bankers, stock brokers, and attorneys.

Concerned that serious injuries will occur on the ride, Highland Amusement Park's board of directors determines to incorporate the "Hyper-Thriller Titan" as a separate corporation (Hyper-Thriller

Titan, Inc.), 100% of whose stock is owned by Highland Amusement Park. This decision has the support of the parent company's (High-Low Amusement, Inc.) board of directors. Hyper-Thriller Titan, Inc. follows corporate formalities, has its own banking accounts, its own employees, and there is no commingling. As anticipated, insurance coverage is more difficult to procure because of the ride's high level of risk—amounting to coverage of $500,000 per accident victim and $10 million coverage in total. Upon customers entering the vicinity of the ride, a metal sign measuring two feet by three feet is posted that reads: "Please Be Aware That the Ride You Are About to Board—The Hyper-Thriller Titan—Is a Separately Incorporated Business. In the Event of Injury on This Ride Caused By Any Negligence of Hyper-Thriller Titan or Any of Its Agents, You Will Not Be Entitled to Recover Damages Against Any Corporation That Owns or Operates This Amusement Park Other Than Hyper-Thriller Titan, Inc."

Three months later, a horrific accident occurs on the Hyper-Thriller Titan allegedly caused by the negligence of an employee of Hyper-Thriller Titan, Inc. Twenty riders suffer catastrophic injuries. They bring suit against Hyper-Thriller Titan, Inc. seeking damages of $250 million. The plaintiff-creditors also seek to pierce the corporate veil of Hyper-Thriller Titan, Inc. to hold its parent corporation (Highland Amusement Park, Inc.) and the ultimate parent corporation, High-Low Amusement, Inc., liable. Moreover, the plaintiffs seek to invoke the single business enterprise doctrine in order to reach the assets of the other fourteen subsidiary corporations, all of whom operate a major amusement park.

What should be the result and why?

Chapter 5

CORPORATE GOVERNANCE

CORPORATE GOVERNANCE MAY be defined: "to describe a system of overlapping legal, regulatory, organizational, and contractual mechanisms designed to protect the interests of a company's owners (the shareholders) and limit opportunistic behavior by corporate managers who control the company's operations."[1] Or, stated differently, corporate governance may be viewed "as a reaction to agency problems, associated with the separation between owners and managers" in a publicly-held enterprise.[2] A robust governance framework, focusing on such attributes as appropriate officer and director conduct, adequacy of internal controls, and sufficiency of disclosure, is vital for corporate and shareholder welfare. Clearly, in view of the financial debacles of the past decade, "the degree to which [a publicly-traded company] observes basic principles of good corporate governance is an increasingly important factor for investors in making investment decisions."[3]

Corporate governance standards today are found in several sources: state common and statutory law, stock exchange rules, Securities and Exchange Commission (SEC) rules, and provisions of the Sarbanes-Oxley Act of 2002 and the Dodd-Frank Act of 2010. In addition to these mandatory sources, companies today voluntarily undertake enhanced governance practices in efforts to improve their oversight and disclosure systems.

TO WHOM IS THE DUTY OWED?

Traditionally, the general focus of the board of directors is to seek in a lawful manner to maximize profit for the benefit of the corporation and its owners—the shareholders.[4] In this regard, may the board also consider the interests of other constituencies, such as the company's employees, communities in which it transacts business, and the public with respect to, for example, environmental practices? What if by taking these interests into account, shareholder profit maximization is lessened to some degree? Significantly, in the past twenty years, many states have enacted "constituency" statutes which authorize a corporation's board of directors to consider interests in addition to those of shareholders.[5] Generally, under these statutes, when exercising their business judgment in acting in the corporation's best interests (which may be the company's best interests in the short-term or long-term),[6] directors may take into account such interests as those of employees, affected communities, and the public welfare.[7] Interpreted flexibly, these statutes provide directors broad discretion to consider constituent interests so long as shareholders are not unduly prejudiced.[8]

On the other hand, a number of states permit other constituent interests to be considered by the board of directors only if shareholder welfare is not compromised. Director conduct that adversely impacts shareholders for the purpose of benefitting other constituents is improper.[9] Nonetheless, in view of the broad business judgment that directors have,[10] courts frequently uphold director action based on the view that a board of director's determination is in the shareholders' best *long-term* interests (even though such action that benefits other constituencies is not consistent with *short-term* maximization of profit).[11]

With respect to debt holders (such as bonds and debentures) and preferred shareholders, their rights generally are determined by contract and other sources of creditor rights.[12] Looking to contractual provisions that are contained in subscription agreements, stock certificates, debt covenants, a subject company's articles of incorporation and other contractual agreements, the parties' rights and obligations are set forth.[13] Hence, in the corporate context, directors and officers generally owe fiduciary duties to the corporation and to the common shareholders collectively.[14]

ROLE OF THE BOARD OF DIRECTORS: OVERVIEW

A focus of corporate governance is on the accountability owed by a subject corporation's executive officers to shareholders. Three ways in which transparency and managerial accountability can be achieved are: (1) direct review by the company's shareholders of officer conduct and actions; (2) government or self-regulatory organization (SRO) oversight of the stock markets; and (3) monitoring of the management by the board of directors and its committees.[15] Generally, other than in a close corporation,[16] direct review by shareholders of management normally is not a feasible alternative.[17] As stated by former Federal Reserve Board chairman Alan Greenspan, in a publicly-traded company, "[o]wnership [is] more dispersed, and few shareholders have sufficient stakes to individually influence the choice of boards of directors or chief executive officers. The vast majority of corporate share ownership is for investment, not for operating control of a company."[18]

Government and SRO regulation of the securities markets positively impact good corporate governance practices. As examples, pursuant to such regulation: publicly-held companies must disclose to their shareholders and the investing public material information on a continual basis; a majority of the directors of companies whose stock is listed on a national stock exchange must be independent; the audit and compensation committees must be comprised entirely of independent directors; and certain "sharp" practices, such as insider trading and stock manipulation, are prohibited.[19] These mandates enhance corporate accountability and governance.

With respect to the implementation of sound corporate accountability and governance, the board of directors and its committees are the critical players. The integrity and ability of directors, the structure and processes of the board and its committees, and director independence are key components in evaluating a board's effectiveness.[20]

Nonetheless, normally the board of directors of a publicly-traded company is not expected to manage the enterprise on a daily basis. Its role is to supervise management "in an environment of loyal but independent oversight."[21] As the New Jersey Supreme Court held: "Directorial management does not require a detailed inspection of day-to-day activities, but rather a general monitoring of corporate affairs and policies."[22]

DUTIES OF THE BOARD OF DIRECTORS

Generally, key functions of a board of directors in a publicly-held company include strategic planning, selection (and termination) of executive officers, risk identification, oversight and compensation of senior management, succession planning, communications with shareholders, overseeing the implementation of reasonably extensive financial controls, and adoption and application of law compliance programs. In undertaking these tasks, "the Board should incorporate strong corporate governance mechanisms, such as independent audit committees, board approval requirements for related-party transactions [and] legal protections for minority shareholders. …"[23]

The Business Roundtable sets forth the following important functions for a board of directors to undertake:

1. Select, regularly evaluate and, if necessary, replace the chief executive officer. Determine management compensation. Review succession planning.
2. Review and, where appropriate, approve the financial objectives, major strategies, and plans of the corporation.
3. Provide advice and counsel to top management.
4. Select and recommend to shareholders for election an appropriate slate of candidates for the board of directors; evaluate board process and performance.
5. Review the adequacy of systems to comply with all applicable laws/ regulations.[24]

A corporation's board of directors normally should approve (or disapprove) all major corporate plans.[25] These would include, for example, entering into new lines of business, acquiring another business enterprise, declaring a dividend to shareholders, and disposing of a major asset. Other examples where Board attention should be focused include issues raising significant questions with respect to the company's financial or operational standing, accounting practices, lawsuits, and regulatory concerns.[26]

Additionally, a corporation's board of directors should help ensure that appropriate corporate policies are in place concerning the company's compliance and disclosure practices. For example, "public companies [today] establish specific policies and procedures dealing with public communications, share ownership reporting, and insider trading. These programs are designed to ensure that the corporation makes complete, accurate and timely disclosure of material information, complies with the registration requirements, and satisfies other securities law obligations."[27] Other programs focus on the corporation's compliance with the antitrust laws, environmental regulations, food and drug laws, the Foreign Corrupt Practices Act, and a host of other statutes and regulations.[28]

In carrying out its responsibilities, the Board must rely on information received from the company's officers, employees, and various corporate departments. For example, with respect to the company's financial statements, the Board (and the audit committee) relies on information from the company's internal staff, its financial officers (including the chief financial officer and the comptroller) and the outside auditors. Therefore, it is crucial for the Board to have confidence that the internal control mechanisms that are in place are adequate in order to help effectuate the efficient flow of relevant and correct information.[29]

INDEPENDENCE OF THE BOARD

As stated by a respected source, "[a] board of directors of a publicly traded company is the first, best line of defense protecting shareholder interest."[30] However, where the Board's composition is aligned with that of the company's management, the Board's oversight function is compromised. This gives rise to the potential for managerial misconduct and lack of objective scrutiny. To reduce these risks, emphasis is placed on the concept of "independent" directors serving on corporate boards.[31] In this regard, the major securities markets have rules requiring that all listed companies have a majority of independent directors.[32] For example, the New York Stock Exchange (NYSE) and the NASDAQ Stock Market (NASDAQ) require that listed companies have "a majority of independent directors" as part of their corporate governance requirements.[33] In the NYSE's commentary, it explains that requiring independent directors "will increase the quality of board oversight and lessen the possibility of damaging conflicts of interest."[34] NYSE rules also require that the nominating/corporate governance committee, compensation committee, and the audit committee be comprised entirely of independent directors.[35] Today, pursuant to the Sarbanes-Oxley Act of 2002 and the Dodd-Frank Act of 2010, the membership of the audit and compensation committees of a publicly-traded company must be comprised entirely of independent directors.[36]

Both the NYSE and NASDAQ have specific requirements for what qualifies as "independence" for the purposes of director qualification. For example, NYSE rules require that the company's board of directors affirmatively establish that the director in question has no "material relationship" with the company in order to meet the standard for independence.[37] In addition, the NYSE rules identify certain relationships that defeat independence.[38] Such relationships include: being an employee of the company within the previous three years or having an immediate family member that was an executive officer within those three years, receiving $120,000 in direct compensation (other than directors' fees and pensions) from the company during any twelve-month period within the previous three years, working for the company's auditor under certain circumstances, serving as an executive officer of another company with respect to which any of the company's present executive officers serve on such other company's compensation committee, and being a current employee of an entity that made payments to or received payments from the subject company within the past three years if those payments exceed the greater of $1 million or 2% of the company's consolidated gross revenues.[39] Each of these disqualifications also implicates directors whose immediate family members meet such criteria.[40] NASDAQ rules contain similar requirements and tests for director independence.[41]

For purposes of serving on a subject company's audit committee, the Sarbanes-Oxley Act has its own definition of "independence." Under Sarbanes-Oxley, a director is not considered independent for qualification as an audit committee member if such director accepts any compensatory remuneration (other than director fees) from the company, or is an affiliated person[42] of the company or any of its subsidiaries.[43] Interestingly, however, a close personal relationship with a company executive does not necessarily make a director "interested." In other words, a director, who is the CEO's best friend since childhood and who regularly socializes (or plays golf) with the CEO, may be viewed as independent where no significant financial ties exist.[44]

Based upon these developments in the law, the American Bar Association's Corporate Director's Guidebook[45] states that in order to function most effectively, the board of directors of a public corporation "must exercise independent judgment in carrying out its responsibilities."[46] Thus, director independence today "is a prevailing theme in corporate governance, if not always in corporate law."[47] Indeed, in reviewing his twelve-year term on the Delaware Supreme Court, former Chief Justice E. Norman Veasey recognized the "courts' deepened reliance on independent directors and an expectation that directors will act thoughtfully and in good faith."[48] Other observers also have reflected that the "move to independent directors, which began as a 'good governance' exhortation, has become in some respects a mandatory element of corporate law."[49] The Sarbanes-Oxley and Dodd-Frank Acts, stock exchange rules, and court decisions have thus brought about many reforms; the impact of these reforms is to elevate the importance of the independent director in the corporate governance framework.[50]

Thus, courts recognize, and indeed emphasize, the importance of independent directors. Delaware Vice Chancellor Strine has acknowledged "the strong role that our law gives to independent directors."[51] For example, in related party transactions (e.g., where a director engages in a transaction with the corporation on whose board she sits), the role of disinterested directors in the quest to achieve fairness has been stressed.[52] In the shareholder derivative suit context, in ascertaining whether demand on the board of directors is executed as being futile, courts examine the disinterestedness and independence of the subject directors.[53] In this setting, courts place great emphasis specifically on the independence of special litigation committees in seeking the termination of shareholder derivative actions.[54] Furthermore, in change of control transactions, courts focus on the particularly critical role that independent directors play, emphasizing the importance of independent directors in determining the good faith use of defensive measures in corporate takeovers.[55]

With the current climate of corporate governance in mind, the emphasis on director "independence" has been recognized by legislators, courts, regulators, the private sector, scholars, and observers alike. Reforms have accentuated the need for "independent" directors to serve on boards in order to improve corporate governance in the United States.

INDEPENDENT COMMITTEES

AUDIT COMMITTEE

In order for a company's stock to be traded on a national securities exchange (such as the NYSE or the NASDAQ Stock Market), it must have an audit committee comprised entirely of independent directors.[56] Audit committee members thus should not have any relationship that interferes with the exercise of independent judgment. One of the audit committee's primary functions is to review the company's financial reporting processes. "Because the corporation's financial data concerns the performance of management, it is important to have an independent forum for discussing this data [both with the company's staff and with the outside audit firm] and the manner of its preparation, in which management participates only on request."[57]

The audit committee thus has general oversight responsibility in reviewing the practices and processes adopted for producing financial data and for setting up and monitoring internal controls.[58] It also will oversee, at times, internal corporate investigations based on possible financial irregularities and the lodging of whisteblower complaints by employees.[59] The audit committee moreover has the responsibility for overseeing the performance of the company's external auditor and providing a forum for dialogue between the company's senior internal accounting staff and the external auditor.[60] In this respect,

> an independent audit committee provides a forum for regular, informal, and private discussion between the external auditor and directors who have no significant relationships with management. In the absence of such a forum, an external auditor would often be reluctant to call for a meeting at the board level unless a problem of great magnitude had arisen. In contrast, the provision of an institutionalized forum facilitates and indeed encourages the external auditor to raise

> potentially troublesome issues at a relatively early stage, allows the auditor to broach sensitive problems in an uninhibited and private fashion, and gives the auditor assurance that it can readily get a hearing in the event of a disagreement with management.[61]

Accordingly, the audit committee is an important part of a corporation's internal control and risk management activities.

The American Law Institute (ALI) recommends the following responsibilities for an audit committee of a publicly-held corporation:

> a. Recommend the firm to be employed as the corporation's external auditor and review the proposed discharge of any such firm;
> b. Review the external auditor's compensation, the proposed terms of its engagement, and its independence;
> c. Review the appointment and replacement of the senior internal auditing executive, if any;
> d. Serve as a channel of communication between the external auditor and the board and between the senior internal auditing executive, if any, and the board;
> e. Review the results of each external audit of the corporation ...;
> f. Review the corporation's annual financial statements, any certification, report, opinion, or review rendered by the external auditor in connection with those financial statements, and any significant disputes between management and the external auditor that arose in connection with the preparation of those financial statements;
> g. Consider, in consultation with the external auditor and the senior internal auditing executive, if any, the adequacy of the corporation's internal controls; [and]
> h. Consider major changes and other major questions of choice respecting the appropriate auditing and accounting principles and practices to be used in the preparation of the corporation's financial statements. ...[62]

COMPENSATION COMMITTEE

Pursuant to SRO rules and the Dodd-Frank Act of 2010, publicly traded companies whose stock is traded on a national securities exchange must have a compensation committee comprised entirely of independent directors.[63] The requirement of a compensation committee comprised solely of independent directors who have no material financial ties to the corporation or its insiders is viewed as necessary in view of recent excessive executive compensation practices, including stock option backdating.[64] These abusive practices resulted in government enforcement actions and public ire.[65]

The compensation committee accordingly provides support for the Board's oversight function. It is responsible for reviewing and approving the executive compensation policies, plans and programs of the company. Generally, the compensation paid to senior executives of a subject company should be balanced—namely, attractive to the executive, consistent with his/her performance and position, and in the company's best interests.[66]

An independent compensation committee is a necessary vehicle to eliminate the conflict of interest management has in deciding its own remuneration package.[67] After all, executive officers, like the CEO, cannot review their own compensation packages as board members in an impartial manner. Accordingly, a compensation committee with independent and diligent members, who act with integrity and fairness, is superior in determining the appropriate compensation for the company's executives.[68] To effectively perform its function, the committee should periodically update itself with respect to the current compensation trends and practices in the market.[69]

Today, pursuant to the Dodd-Frank Act of 2010, shareholders of publicly-held companies have an advisory vote with respect to executive compensation.[70] This non-binding "Say on Pay" shareholder vote should be influential in a compensation committee's determination of appropriate remuneration for senior executives. A shareholder vote disapproving the compensation awarded will signal shareholder dissatisfaction that may well reach far beyond remuneration issues to encompass fundamental issues that focus on the corporation's performance and stock price.[71]

NOMINATING/CORPORATE GOVERNANCE COMMITTEE

A nominating/corporate governance committee is central to the effective functioning of the Board.[72] The presence of such a committee comprised of independent directors is common today.[73] The nominating/corporate governance committee, like the audit and compensation committees, also assists in overseeing the functions of the Board and the management of the company. One of the important functions of this committee is to select and nominate director candidates for the Board and its committees, based on established procedure and selection criteria.[74] The committee reviews each nominee's candidacy focusing on such factors as competence, experience, integrity, and independence. The committee also should periodically review each director's performance and recommend whether such director should be renominated.[75]

Pursuant to rules adopted by the SEC, a company's largest shareholder, owning at least three percent of its stock for at least three years duration, may nominate the greater of up to 25% of directors or one director to serve on the corporation's board of directors. Such shareholder cannot use the process to institute a change of control.[76] These SEC rules were successfully challenged and invalidated by a federal appellate court.[77]

DOES ENHANCED CORPORATE GOVERNANCE IMPACT STOCK PRICE?

Although not without disagreement,[78] reputable studies have found that investors will pay a premium for the common stock of companies that enjoy high corporate governance standards. For example, a report issued in 2011 found that "empirical research has brought evidence of the measurable payoff of CSE [corporate social responsibility] initiatives on firms as well as their stakeholders."[79] A McKinsey & Company survey found that in North America investors will pay an average premium of 12 to 14% "for companies exhibiting high corporate governance standards."[80] A study issued by Deutsche Bank concluded that "the influence of corporate governance standards in a company's long-term equity performance is beyond doubt."[81] And, in yet another study, it was found that companies with the strongest corporate governance had abnormal positive returns of up to 8.5% contrasted with companies with weak corporate governance.[82] Hence, reputable studies have found that strong corporate governance may not only promote greater corporate accountability to a company's shareholders—it may in fact result in a higher price for the company's common stock.

SUMMATION

As set forth by one premier source, the "hot topics" for the corporate boardroom today are as follows:

1. Set appropriate executive compensation in the midst of increased regulatory and shareholder scrutiny.
2. Oversee enterprise-wide risk management, including all facets of the company's risk profile and crisis response plans.
3. Oversee the development of short-term and long-term strategy in an increasingly interdependent world economy.
4. Monitor challenges to the new SEC proxy access rules. …
5. Review existing board members' qualifications and ensure appropriate board composition.

6. Cultivate shareholder relations as investors push for more board transparency and accountability.
7. Consider M&A [merger and acquisition] opportunities as the capital markets continue to rebound.
8. Review and revise, if appropriate, takeover defenses in response to recent judicial decisions and the rise in M&A activity.
9. Ensure that an effective succession plan is in place.
10. Monitor legislative developments and prepare for more government regulation.[83]

NOTES

1. International Organization of Securities Commissions (IOSCO), June 2009 Final Report of the Task Force, "Protection of Minority Shareholders in Listed Issuers," and February 2005 Final Report of the Task Force, "Strengthening Capital Markets Against Financial Fraud," available at www.iosco.org/library/pubdocs/pdf/IOSCOPD295.pdf and www.iosco.org/library/pubdocs/pdf/IOSCOPD192.pdf.
2. *Id.* Beltratti, *The Complementarity Between Corporate Governance and Corporate Social Responsibility,* The Geneva Papers 373, 375 (2005).
3. Organization for Economic Co-operation and Development (OECD), *OECD Principles of Corporate Governance* (2004), *available at* http://www.oecd.org/dataoecd/32/18/31557724.pdf
4. See *Dodge v. Ford Motor Co.*, 170 N.W. 668 (Mich. 1919).
5. To date, approximately 30 states have passed constituency statutes. See, e.g., Ariz. Rev. Stat. Ann. § 10-2702; Conn. Gen. Stat. Ann. § 33-756(d); Fla. Stat. Ann. ch. 607.0830; Ind. Code Ann. § 23-1-35-1; Mass. Ann. Laws ch. 156B, § 65; N.J. Stat. Ann. § 14A:6-1; N.Y. Bus. Corp. Law § 717; Ohio Rev. Code Ann. § 1701.59; 15 Pa. Cons. Stat. §§ 515–517, 1715–1717; Tenn. Code Ann. § 48-35-204; Wyo. Stat. § 17-16-830. See generally Hansen, *Other Constituency Statutes: A Search for Perspective,* 46 Bus. Law. 1355 (1991).
6. See sources in note 5 *supra.*
7. See, e.g., Conn. Gen. Stat. Ann. § 33-756(d); Fla. Stat. Ann. ch. 607-0830; Ga. Code Ann. § 14-2-202(b)(5); Ill. Rev. Stat. ch. 32, para. 8.85; Ind. Code Ann. § 23-1-35-1; sources cited in note 5 *supra.*
8. For example, constituency statutes of three states, Indiana, Iowa, and Pennsylvania, raise the issue whether the directors are authorized to make decisions which have "no benefit whatever to the shareholders." *See* Hansen, *supra* note 5, at 1375. These statutes "expressly negate the concept that the interests of the shareholders are the primary among the spectrum of corporate constituencies." *Id.*
9. "No statute authorizes directors to ignore the shareholders' interests. Instead, the statutes merely authorize directors to consider a variety of additional interests.

The right to consider a wider variety of interests does not equal the right to ignore the shareholders' interests." Bainbridge, *Interpreting Nonshareholder Constituency Statutes,* 19 Pepp. L. Rev. 971, 989 (1992). In fact, most statutes provide that the interest of other constituencies can be taken into account "in addition to the shareholders' interests." *Id.* See Ariz. Rev. Stat. Ann. § 10-2702; Fla. Stat. Ann. ch. 607.0830; Ga. Code Ann. § 14-2-202(b)(5); Wis. Stat. § 180.0827.

10. See, e.g., *Aronson v. Lewis,* 473 A. 2d 805 (Del. 1983).
11. See, e.g., *Paramount Communications, Inc. v. Time*, 571 A. 2d 1140 (Del. 1989).
12. See, e.g., *North American Catholic Educational Programming Foundation, Inc. v. Gheewala,* 930 A. 2d 92, 100 (Del. 2007) (stating that "creditors are afforded protection through contractual agreements, fraud and fraudulent conveyance law, implied covenants of good faith and fair dealing, bankruptcy law, general commercial law, and other sources of creditor rights"). *Waggoner v. Laster,* 581 A. 2d 1127, 1135 (Del. 1990) (rights of preferred shareholders are contractual in nature).
13. See sources cited in note 12 *supra.*
14. See *Smith v. Van Gorkom*, 488 A. 2d 858 (Del. 1985).
15. See American Law Institute, Principles of Corporate Governance: Analysis and Recommendations, Introductory Note To Parts III And III-A (Structure Of The Corporation) (1994) (hereinafter *ALI Principles of Corporate Governance*).
16. Generally, a closely-held corporation is one in which: there are few shareholders; the shareholders directly participate in the corporation's management and operation; and no liquid market exists for shareholders to sell their stock. See generally *Donahue v. Rodd Electrotype Co.,* 328 N.E. 2d 505 (Mass. 1975).
17. *ALI Principles of Corporate Governance*, *supra* note 15, at § 4.01(c).
18. Remarks by Chairman Alan Greenspan, *Corporate Governance,* at the Stern School of Business, New York University, New York, March 26, 2002, *available at* http://www.federalresesrve.gov/boarddocs/speeches/2002/200203262/default.htm
19. NYSE, Inc., Listed Company Manual § 303A.10 Comment; NASDAQ, Inc., Manual Rules 4611(5)(B), 5635.
20. See *ALI Principles of Corporate Governance*, note 15 *supra.*
21. *Id.* § 3.01(c) cmt. a.
22. *Francis v. United Jersey Bank*, 87 N.J. 15, 432 A.2d 814 (1981).
23. *See* IOSCO, February 2005 Final Report of the Task Force, *Strengthening Capital Markets Against Financial Fraud,* available at www.iosco.org/library/pubdocs/pdf/IOSCOPD192pdf (hereinafter IOSCO Report).
24. The Business Roundtable, *Corporate Governance and American Competitiveness* (New York: The Business Roundtable 1990, 2002).
25. *ALI Principles of Corporate Governance, supra* note 15, § 3.02 cmt. f.
26. *Id.*

27. ABA Guidebook Comm. on Corporate Laws, *Corporate Director's Guidebook* 103 (5th ed. 2007) (hereinafter *ABA Guidebook*).
28. See, e.g., Webb and Molo, *Some Practical Considerations in Developing Effective Compliance Programs,* 71 Wash. U.L.Q. 375 (1993).
29. The Conference Board, *Conference Board Commission on Public Trust and Private Enterprise* (Jan. 9, 2003), *available at* http://www.conference-board/org/pdf_free/sr-03-04.pdf
30. *ISOCO Report*, *supra* note 23, at 4.
31. See *ABA Guidebook, supra* note 27, at 73.
32. NYSE, Inc., Listed Company Manual § 303A.01; NASDAQ, Inc., Manual Rule 4350(c).
33. *Id.*
34. *Id.* § 303A.01 cmt.
35. *Id.* §§ 303A.04(a), 303A.05, 303A.07(b).
36. Securities Exchange Act of 1934 § 10C, Pub. L. No. 111-203, § 952, 124 Stat. 1376, 1900 (codified as amended at 15 U.S.C. § 78j-3 (2010)).
37. NYSE, Inc., Listed Company Manual § 303A.02(a).
38. *Id.* § 303A.02(b).
39. *Id.*
40. *Id.*
41. A director will not be considered "independent" if, during the preceding three years: he was employed by the company; with certain exceptions, he or a family member received over $120,000 from the company over any twelve-month period; his family member was an executive of the company; he or a family member was a partner, controlling shareholder, or executive of a company that paid or received the greater of $200,000 or 5% of the recipient's gross revenues; he or a family member served as an executive of another company for which an executive of the present company served on the compensation committee; he or a family member participated in the outside audit of the company; or he is an "interested person" according to the Investment Company Act of 1940. NASDAQ, Inc., Manual Rule 4200(a)(15).
42. Clearly, for example, directors who also are officers of the company or any of its subsidiaries are affiliated persons.
43. Securities Exchange Act of 1934 § 10A(m)(3)(B); cf. NASDAQ, Inc., Manual Rule 4200(a)(15); NYSE, Inc., Listed Company Manual § 303A.02(b).
44. However, when a director meets the applicable standards of "independence" requirements, if there are close personal or business ties between the director and the CEO, the director may not be an appropriate choice for membership on the committee. See ABA Guidebook, *supra* note 27, at 71.
45. The Corporate Director's Guidebook is a guidebook published by the ABA Committee on Corporate Laws of the ABA Section of Business Law. *Id.* at vii. The Guidebook espouses the theme of the "increasingly vital role that directors play in protecting investors' interests and in directing and overseeing corporate strategy

and its execution by senior officers." *Id.* The Committee was chaired by former Chief Justice of the Delaware Supreme Court, E. Norman Veasey. *Id.* at viii.

46. *Id.* at 38.
47. Veasey and Di Guglielmo, *What Happened in Delaware Corporate Law from 1992–2004? A Retrospective on Some Key Developments,* 153 U. Pa. L. Rev. 1399, 1472 (2005).
48. *Id.* at 1406.
49. Gordon, *The Rise of Independent Directors in the United States, 1950–2005: Of Shareholder Value and Stock Market Prices,* 59 Stan. L. Rev. 1465, 1468 (2007). In 1978, then SEC Chairman Harold M. Williams emphasized the importance of independent directors in the corporate governance framework. Harold M. Williams, Chairman, Securities Exch. Comm'n, Address at the Fifth Annual Securities Regulation Institute: Corporate Accountability (Jan. 18, 1978). *See generally* Ferrara and Steinberg, *A Reappraisal of Santa Fe: Rule 10b-5 and the New Federalism,* 129 U. Pa. L. Rev. 263 (1980).
50. Gordon, *supra* note 49, at 1539. *See also Paramount Commc'ns v. QVC Network,* 637 A. 2d 34, 44 (Del. 1994) (discussing the importance of independent directors in sale of control transaction); *Mills Acquisition Co. v. MacMillan, Inc.,* 559 A. 2d 1281, 1285 (Del. 1989) (discussing the role of independent directors in scrutinizing transactions); *Unocal Corp. v. Mesa Petroleum Co.,* 493 A. 2d 946, 955 (Del. 1985) (discussing the role of independent directors in the use of defensive tactics in corporate takeovers); *Zapata Corp. v. Maldonado,* 430 A. 2d 779, 788–789 (Del. 1981) (establishing independence as the first part of a two-part test for determining the legitimacy of a special litigation committee).
51. *In re Cox Commc'ns, Inc. S'holders Litig.*, 879 A. 2d 604, 647 (Del. Ch. 2005).
52. *See, e.g., Krasner v. Moffett,* 826 A. 2d 277, 286 (Del. 2003) (holding that, where the majority of the board had potential self-interest in a merger, the independence of a special committee of disinterested directors used to approve the merger is a fact-sensitive inquiry); *Marciano v. Nakiash,* 535 A. 2d 400, 404 (Del. 1987) (referring to the importance of majority approval of disinterested directors for interested director transactions); *Weinberger v. UOP, Inc.,* 457 A. 2d 701, 710–711 (Del. 1983) (applying the general test of fairness that should be applied to related-party transactions, and specifically cash-out mergers).
53. *See, e.g., Fagin v. Gilmartin,* 432 F. 3d 276, 283 (3d Cir. 2005) (applying Delaware law in finding that demand was not excused because the mere fact that a director is also an officer does not by itself defeat that director's independence); *Stone v. Ritter,* 911 A. 2d 362, 366–367 (Del. 2006) (discussing the standards for finding demand futility if the directors are not disinterested and independent); *Braddock v. Zimmerman,* 906 A. 2d 776, 786 (Del. 2006) (discussing the role of a "new" board of independent directors determining demand-excuse); *Beam v. Stewart,* 845 A. 2d 1040, 1049 (Del. 2004) (discussing the standards for establishing interest or lack of independence in demand futility cases); *Desimone v. Barrows,* 924 A. 2d 908, 943 (Del. Ch. 2007) (finding that plaintiff had not pleaded facts with sufficient particularity to establish demand excusal).

54. *See, e.g., Zapata*, 430 A. 2d at 788–789 (establishing independence as the first part of a two-part test for determining the legitimacy of a special litigation committee).
55. *See, e.g., Paramount Commc'ns*, 637 A. 2d at 44; *Mills Acquisition*, 559 A. 2d at 1285; *Unocal*, 493 A. 2d at 955.
56. NYSE, Inc. Listed Company Manual § 303A.07(a); NASDAQ, Inc., Manual Rule 4350(d)(2)(A)(i).
57. *ALI Principles of Corporate Governance, supra* note 15, § 3.05 cmt. c(i).
58. *Id.* § 3.05 cmt. d.
59. See NYSE, Inc., Listed Company Manual § 303A.07(f); NASDAQ, Inc., Manual Rule 4350(d)(3).
60. See *ALI Principles of Corporate Governance, supra* note 15, § 3.05 cmt. c(i).
61. *Id.* § 3.05 cmt. c(iii).
62. *Id.* § 3A.03.
63. Securities Exchange Act of 1934 § 10C, Pub. L. No. 111-203, § 952, 124 Stat. 1900 (codified as amended at 15 U.S.C. § 78j-3 (2010)).
64. See, e.g., *In re Tyson Foods Inc. Consolidated Shareholder Litigation*, 919 A. 2d 563 (Del. 2007); *Ryan v. Gifford*, 918 A. 2d 341 (Del. 2007). See generally Morrissey, *The Path of Corporate Law: Of Options Backdating, Derivative Suits, and the Business Judgment Rule*, 86 Oregon L. Rev. 973 (2008).
65. See, e.g., *SEC v. McGuire*, 39 Sec. Reg. & L. Rep. (BNA) 1909 (D. Minn. 2007) (chief executive officer of United Health Group Inc. paid $468 million to settle SEC charges of illegal stock option backdating). See generally, Bebchuk, Grinstein, and Peyer, *Lucky CEOs and Lucky Directors*, 65 J. Fin. No. 6, at 2363 (Dec. 2010); Fried, *Option Backdating and Its Implications*, 65 Wash. & Lee L. Rev. 853 (2008).
66. The Conference Board, *The Conference Board Task Force on Executive Compensation*, available at http://www.conference-board.org/pdf_free/ExecCompensation2009.pdf
67. See *ALI Principles of Corporate Governance, supra* note 15, § 3A.05 cmt. c.
68. *Id.*
69. *Id.* cmt. d.
70. Securities Exchange Act of 1934 § 14A, Pub. L. No. 111-203, § 951, 124 Stat. 1376 (2010).
71. See Murray, *What Hath Dodd (and Frank) Wrought? Preparing for the 2011 and Future Proxy Seasons in a Dodd-Frank Environment*, 38 Sec. Reg. L.J. 303, 315–327 (2010).
72. See NYSE, Inc., Listed Company Manual § 303A.04 cmt.
73. Companies listed on the NYSE are required to have a nominating committee that is comprised entirely of independent directors, while the NASDAQ has a comparable requirement. *Id.* § 303A.04(a); NASDAQ, Inc., Manual Rule 4350(c)(3).
74. NYSE, Inc. Listed Company Manual § 303A.04(b).
75. See *ALI Principles of Corporate Governance, supra* note 15, § 3A.04 cmt. e.

76. Securities Exchange Act of 1934 § 14(a), Pub. L. No. 111-203, § 971, 124 Stat. 1915 (codified as amended at 15 U.S.C. 78n(a)1 (2010).
77. Business Roundtable, et al. v. SEC, 647 F.3d 1144 (D.C. Cir. 2011).
78. See e.g., Kim, *Stock Returns, Corporate Governance, and Long-Term Economic Growth,* 35 Ohio North U.L. Rev. 685 (2009).
79. Carroll and Shabana, *The Business Case for Corporate Social Responsibility*, Director Notes, The Conference Board, No. DN-V3N11 (June 2011), available at http://www.conferenceboard.org.
80. McKinsey & Company, *Global Investor Opinion Survey: Key Findings* (July 2002).
81. Deutsche Bank, *Beyond the Numbers: Materiality of Corporate Governance* (Nov. 25, 2005).
82. Gompers and Ishii, *Corporate Governance and Equity Prices,* 118 Quart. Jour. Econ. 107 (Feb. 2003). See generally Brown and Caylor, *Corporate Governance and Firm Valuation*, 25 J. Accounting and Pub. Pol. 409 (2006).
83. Akin Gump Strauss Hauer & Feld LLP, *Corporate Alert—Top 10 Topics for Directors in 2011* (Dec. 6, 2010).

THE FOLLOWING EXCERPTS highlight topical subjects in corporate governance.

THE CONFERENCE BOARD COMMISSION ON PUBLIC TRUST AND PRIVATE ENTERPRISE FINDING AND RECOMMENDATIONS—PART 2: CORPORATE GOVERNANCE*

The Compact as Foundation for the Corporation

Investor trust in our corporate system is premised on a series of relationships among shareowners,[1] board of directors and management. Shareowners invest their assets in corporations managed by professionals. This separation of owners from managers is an important feature of the modern public corporation. A key role of the board of directors is to provide oversight to ensure that management acts in the best long-term interests of the corporation and thus in the best long-term interests of its shareowners.

A view toward the long term serves the best interests not only of the company's shareowners, but also of the company's other constituencies, such as employees, customers, suppliers and communities. We recognize the challenge executives face in meeting short-term goals for some constituencies while at the same time achieving the company's long-term goals. However, we firmly believe that managing the corporation for continued long-term viability as a productive organization on behalf of its shareowners can be generally beneficial for other stakeholders. (See discussion on constituencies below.)

The Commission also notes that the corporation's interests, as well as those of its other stakeholder constituencies, are best served

1 The Commission recognizes the importance of holders of a company's stock developing a perspective for long-term growth and retaining their stock to realize these objectives; accordingly, this report uses the term "shareowner" for such holders.

with a shareowner base that holds its investment for the long term. Shareowners who keep their investment over an extended period of time strengthen the corporate compact and provide management with incentives to manage the corporation in ways that benefit the interests of both shareowners and other constituencies. Retaining a long-term shareowner base and strengthening the compact works effectively only when shareowners have a high level of trust that the business is being managed honestly and in their best long-term interests.

In order to provide the oversight and guidance required of them, directors must have a firm grasp of the central business issues that drive the success of the company. They must understand how capital is spent and why, as well as other key strategic issues such as debt and other balance sheet structures, the deployment of resources, the company's focus, and the definition and assessment of the company's business risks, to name just a few. In addition, they must always remember that, just as managers work on behalf of the corporation and its shareowners, the board's efforts must be thus directed as well. Only a strong, diligent board, with a substantial majority[2] of independent directors that both understands the key issues and asks management the tough questions, is capable of ensuring that shareowner interests are properly served.

...

The Importance of Other Constituencies

Although most state corporation laws establish that corporations should be run to enhance that corporation's economic interests, and therefore the interests of its shareowners, corporation are also expected to fulfill their legal and ethical obligations to other constituencies.[3] As noted previously, respect and concern for a range of corporate constit-

---

2 The Commission goes beyond the recommendations of the New York Stock Exchange that companies, other than controlled companies, have a "majority" of independent directors to recommend that a "substantial majority" of directors be independent. A controlled company is one for which more than 50 percent of the voting power is held by an individual, a group, or another company. New York Stock Exchanges, Sec. 1 of proposed amendments to Sec. 303A of Listing Standards.

3 For a list of states which by statute permit or require boards to consider interests of other constituencies in reaching their decisions, see Guhan Subramanian, "The Influences of Antitakeover Statutes on Incorporation Choice: Evidence on the 'Race

uencies, including employees, customers, communities and suppliers, contributes to a positive climate for optimal corporate behavior. In such a climate, the corporation can then continue to provide the jobs which sustain employees and, by extension, the communities in which they live. It can provide communities not only with an employer for its residents, but also with a more solid tax base and with an organization that can contribute money, talent, and vitality to civic life. It can also continue to serve the customer and supplier constituencies that depend on the products it makes or services it provides.

Furthermore, public opinion widely endorses the view that companies should not neglect the expectations of the constituencies. In a *Business Week* survey, 95 percent of respondents felt that U.S. corporations have responsibilities to constituencies such as employees and communities in which they operate, even at the sacrifice of some profit.[4] In the final analysis, the free enterprise system exists at the pleasure of society, and the trust and confidence of these other constituencies is crucial to its productive functioning.

A Long-Term Ownership Focus

The Commission believes that a strong focus on the corporation's long-term economic growth and viability is essential to the restoration of trust in public corporations. This focus involves not only the board's and management's long-term strategies and conduct of the business to create lasting value, but also the development of a base of shareowners whose investment is similarly for long-term growth and gain. (See discussion below on shareowner obligations.) Such a long-term ownership focus provides an impetus to avoid management focused exclusively on short-term gain. The Commission believes that managing for short-term earnings and stock price results has led to many of the behaviors and manipulations that have resulted in the recent corporate crises and loss of investor confidence.[5]

Debate' and Antitakeover Overreaching," 150 U. Pa. L. Rev. 1795 (June 2002), at p. 1828.

4 A. Bernstein, "Too Much Corporate Power?," *Business Week*, September 11, 2000: http://www.businessweek.com:/2000/00_37/b3698004.htm.

5 In its report on executive compensation (see note 1, *supra*), the Commission explained the relationship between managing for short-term stock price results and abuses in executive compensation.

The Roles of the CEO and Chairman

The Commission is profoundly troubled by the corporate scandals of the recent past. The primary concern in many of these situations is that strong CEOs appear to have exerted a dominant influence over their boards, often stifling the efforts of directors to play the central oversight role needed to ensure a healthy system of corporate governance. In such circumstances, boards have often either lacked the structure and information to perform their roles properly, or they have simply abdicated their responsibilities to provide the oversight required of them. In such circumstances, the board cannot properly oversee the CEO's performance.

The ultimate responsibility for good corporate governance rests with the board of directors. Only a strong, diligent and independent board of directors that understands the key issues, provides wise counsel and asks management the tough questions is capable of ensuring that the interests of shareowners as well as other constituencies are being properly served.

If boards are to be accountable for good corporate governance, they must have the information and flexibility to work with senior management in choosing how best to achieve good governance within the framework of the unique personal chemistry in the company, as well as its distinctive history and culture. Moreover, the relationship between the board and management need not be and should not be, except in unusual circumstances, adversarial. Rather, the relationship should be open, honest and constructive. The Commission also notes that having frequent, regular meetings of the non-management directors is a key structural component for oversight of the CEO function.[6]

The responsibilities of leading the board and of managing the company are distinct. The CEO is the highest-ranking member of the management team. As such, he or she is accountable for the corporation's management and performance. As noted above, the board is charged with ensuring that management is carrying out its responsibilities in the company's and the shareowners' best long-term interests. Typically, the CEO is a member of the board, but he or she is also part of the management team that the board oversees. This dual role can provide a potential for conflict, particularly in those cases in

6 Section 3 of the NYSE's proposed amendments to its listing standards would make "regularly scheduled executive sessions" of the non-management directors a requirement.

which the CEO attempts to dominate both the management of the company and the exercise of the responsibilities of the board.

The Commission believes that a crucial governance challenge facing American corporations involves establishing an appropriate balance between managing the corporation and providing the independent directors with the powers and resources they need to perform their role. The Act and the amendments to the New York Stock Exchange ("NYSE") listing standards[7] recognize this conundrum, and they endeavor to resolve it be requiring a relationship between the CEO and the independent directors in which the independent directors can—and must—exercise certain responsibilities without management interference. These initiatives have attempted to create a better balance in the relationship between senior management, including the CEO, and the independent directors, facilitating the exercise of the roles and powers of each.[8]

Therefore, each board of directors should adopt a structure that provides an appropriate balance between the powers of the CEO and those of the independent directors in which the ability of the independent directors to be informed, to discuss and debate issues they deem important, and to act objectively on an informed basis is not compromised. In creating such a structure, the Commission recognizes that: (1) the objective is to strengthen the independence and role of the board with appropriate checks and balances on the power, actions and performance of the CEO; (2) board structures vary greatly among American corporations; and (3) no single board structure has yet been demonstrated to be superior in providing the oversight that leads to corporate success.

---

7 New York Stock Exchange, Proposed Amendments to Listing Standards Manual, http://www.real.com/ads/html/gator_770x300_us2_html.

8 For example, the New York Stock Exchange proposes to require that the independent directors compose a majority of the board and that they meet regularly in executive session. New York Stock Exchange, Proposed Amendments to Listing Standards Manual, http://www.real.com/ads/html/gator_770x300_us2_html. (For clarification, and as noted above, The Commission recommends that a "substantial majority" of directors be independent.) As another example, the Act requires audit committees, composed solely of independent directors, to take a more active role in ensuring the accuracy and integrity of the corporation's financial statements. See, for example, Section 301 of this Act.

In order to achieve the objectives of board independence, each board must be sensitive to any relationships between the CEO and the leaders of the non-management directors that could impair the appropriate balance between the Board's and CEO's roles. Each Board should be particularly sensitive to the possibility of such relationships and should tailor its inquiries about these relationships to its company's particular circumstances.

The Commission notes three principal approaches that could be taken to provide the appropriate balance between board and CEO functions:

1. The Roles of Chairman and CEO would be performed by two separate individuals, and the Chairman would be one of the independent directors. The Commission recommends that each corporation give careful consideration, based on its particular circumstances, to separating the offices of the Chairman and Chief Executive Officer. The Commission believes that separating the positions of Chairman and CEO is fully consistent with the objectives of the Act, the New York Stock Exchange listing requirements, and the NASDAQ requirements,[9] and that separating the roles of Chairman and CEO enhances the implementation of the Act and stock exchange reforms.
2. The roles of Chairman and CEO would be performed by two separate individuals. However, if the Chairman is not an independent director under stock exchange standards, (a situation which often occurs when the founder or a major stockholder is Chairman), he or she should not be a member of the management team and should not report to the CEO. In this case, a Lead Independent Director ("LID") position (or other equivalent designation) should also be established.

   Under this approach, it is essential that the Chairman, while perhaps not meeting the technical requirements of independence under stock exchange standards, does not, in fact, have any relationships with the CEO or other members of management that compromises his or her ability to act free from the control of the CEO and management. In this situation, the board must be particularly diligent in making that determination. The Commission believes that this separateness in status and reporting relationships, coupled with the creation of the LID or equivalent position, can provide an appropriate balance between the leadership of the board and the management of the company.

9 For summary, see NASDAQ website: www.nasdaq.com—Inside NASDAQ, Legal and Compliance, Proposed Rule Changes.

3. Where a board does not choose to separate the Chairman and CEO position, or when such boards are in transition to a structure where the positions will be separated, a Presiding Director position should be established.[10]

Boards that choose not to take any of these approaches should explain their reasons for doing so, as well as the board structure which they employ to achieve the objectives of strong, independent board leadership.

In each of the three situations described above, the roles of Chairman, Lead Independent Director, and Presiding Director should be clearly defined. In the first case, at a minimum, the Chairman should preside at board meetings, have ultimate approval over information flow to the board, meeting agendas, and meeting schedules to ensure that the independent directors have sufficient time for discussion of all agenda items.

In the second case, where the Chairman is not one of the independent directors, the Lead Independent Director should work closely with the Chairman to finalize information flow, meeting agendas, and meeting schedules. The Lead Independent Director should also chair meetings of the non-management directors and serve as the principal liaison between the independent directors and the Chairman. The non-CEO Chairman and Lead Independent Director (or other equivalent designation) could also take a lead role, in conjunction with the Chairman, in the board evaluation process. (See discussion below.)

In the third case, the responsibilities of the Presiding Director should, at a minimum, include presiding at board meetings when the

---

10 The concept of a "lead" or "senior" director who chairs meetings of the non-management directors and who serves as the liaison between the CEO and the independent directors has been discussed for many years and has been adopted by some, albeit a limited number of, companies. The number of companies ranges from 2.4 percent to 6 percent to 13 percent, depending on the variety and number of companies surveyed (data from Investor Responsibility Research Center *Board Practices/Board Pay 2001* survey, the Conference Board's Directors' *Compensation and Board Practices 2002* survey, and the American Society of Corporate Secretaries *Current Board Practices 2002* survey, respectively). Here, the Commission takes this lead director concept further and recommends that the Presiding Director, who effectively functions as the "lead" or "senior" director, also takes on certain functions previously reserved to the Chairman.

Chairman/CEO is not present, presiding at meetings of the independent directors, and having ultimate approval over information flow to the board, meeting agendas, and meeting schedules. It may also be desirable for the Presiding Director to take a lead role, in conjunction with the Chairman, in the board evaluation process. (See discussion below.)

The Role of the Board of Directors

Effective boards require the right structure, the right processes, and the right people to ensure independent and objective decision making. Boards must be composed of qualified individuals, a substantial majority[11] of whom are free from disqualifying conflicts of interest, who have and will devote the necessary time to fulfill their responsibilities, and who are able to understand the issues facing the company, challenge management with tough questions and goals, and take action when needed. To perform their functions effectively, directors must act diligently and independently of management. Each board committee must also be given the authority necessary to carry out its intended functions. Finally, as noted above, the independent directors must have adequate information to make good decisions, the ability to put key questions on the agenda, and adequate time to deal with the central issues they are confronting. Companies will certainly have to develop ways to motivate and attract such independent directors in an era of rapidly increasing governance requirements.

In fulfilling its oversight function, boards must monitor management's operating performance as well as ethical and legal compliance. In approving strategies, boards need to understand, among other things, the corporation's capital allocation, debt levels, risks and vulnerabilities, compensation strategy, and growth opportunities. Importantly, they must engage management on the central issues facing the company and have a firm grasp on the tradeoffs that lie at the heart of a corporate enterprise. Management should also look to the board for support and help as issues arise in particular circumstances.

Each director brings certain skills, backgrounds, and expertise to the board. In addition, boards have both a collective expertise as well as particular areas on knowledge of each of its members that

11 This requirement would not necessarily apply to controlled companies. See footnote 4, *supra*.

can be used to solve problems and address issues on an as-needed basis.

To discharge their responsibilities most effectively, directors should:

- Exercise objectivity and autonomy to make independent, informed decisions;
- Develop the knowledge and expertise to provide effective board oversight;
- Display the character, integrity, and will to assert their points of view, and demonstrate loyalty exclusively to the corporation and its shareowners;
- Devote the time necessary to fulfill the legal, regulatory and stock exchange requirements imposed upon them; and
- Have the ability to retain, to the extent they deem necessary, advisors and independent staff support.

The Nominating/Governance Committee

The Commission believes that it is important that each corporation establish a committee of independent directors to oversee corporate governance issues, including the statement of corporate governance principles and the performance evaluations of the board, its committees, and each director, as necessary. The Commission therefore endorses the principle that each listed company, other than controlled companies,[12] have a nominating/corporate governance committee composed entirely of independent directors (or functional equivalent consisting solely of independent directors).[13] As the NYSE notes, "[a] nominating/corporate governance committee is central to the effective functioning of the board."[14]

Board Evaluation

The Commission believes that each board should develop a three-tier director evaluation mechanism which includes evaluation of the performance of the board as a whole, the performance of each

---

12 See footnote 4, *supra*.

13 New York Stock Exchange, Section 4 of the proposed amendments to Rule 303A.

14 *Id.*

committee and the performance of each individual director, as necessary. The Commission does not believe there is any one approach to evaluation that is appropriate for all corporations. At a minimum, evaluation of directors should ensure that each director meets the board's qualification for membership when the director is nominated or renominated to the board. Evaluation of the board and its committees should also determine whether each has fulfilled its basic, required functions.

Beyond meeting baseline standards, evaluation can be a powerful tool for directors to improve their performance by understanding areas which require further development or training. Evaluations should provide feedback to develop more effective director, committee, and board functions. Each board should establish evaluation processes and criteria that best reflect the board's own requirements.

Responsibility for development of evaluation methods and criteria should reside with the nominating/governance committee or equivalent committee of independent directors or their designee, depending on the governance model adopted by the board.[15] It may be desirable for the independent Chairman, the Lead Independent Director, or the Presiding Director, depending on the company's board structure, to take a lead role, in conjunction with the Chairman, in the board evaluation process.

. . .

---

15 The Commission recognizes that it is the responsibility of the full board to evaluate the CEO.

*AMERICAN LAW INSTITUTE PRINCIPLES OF CORPORATE GOVERNANCE: ANALYSIS AND RECOMMENDATIONS**

§ 2.01 The Objective and Conduct of the Corporation

> *(a) Subject to the provisions of Subsection (b) and § 6.02 (Action of Directors That Has the Foreseeable Effect of Blocking Unsolicited Tender Offers), a corporation should have as its objective the conduct of business activities with a view to enhancing corporate profit and shareholder gain.*
> *(b) Even if corporate profit and shareholder gain are not thereby enhanced, the corporation, in the conduct of its business:*
> *(1) Is obliged, to the same extent as a natural person, to act within the boundaries set by law;*
> *(2) May take into account ethical considerations that are reasonably regarded as appropriate to the responsible conduct of business; and*
> *(3) May devote a reasonable amount of resources to public welfare, humanitarian, educational, and philanthropic purposes.*

Comment

Corporate Objective and Corporate Conduct

The subject matter of these Principles is the governance of business corporations. The business corporation is an instrument through which capital is assembled for the activities of producing and distributing goods and services and making investments. These Principles take as a basic proposition that a business corporation should have as its objective the conduct of such activities with a view to enhancing corporate profit and shareholder gain. ... The basic proposition is qualified in the manner stated in Subsection (b), which speaks to the conduct of the corporation. The provisions of Subsection (b) reflect a recognition that the corporation is a social as well as an economic institution, and

* Principles of Corporate Governance: Analysis and Recommendations, © 1994 by the American Law Institute. Reprinted with permission. All rights reserved.

accordingly that its pursuit of the economic objective must be constrained by social imperatives and may be qualified by social needs.

The Economic Objective

In very general terms, Subsection (a) may be thought of as a broad injunction to enhance economic returns, while Subsection (b) makes clear that certain kinds of conduct must or may be pursued whether or not they enhance such returns (that is, even if the conduct either yields no economic return or entails a net economic loss). In most cases, however, the kinds of conduct described in Subsection (b) could be pursued even under the principle embodied in Subsection (a). Such conduct will usually be consistent with economic self-interest, because the principle embodied in Subsection (a)—that the objective of the corporation is to conduct business activities with a view to enhancing corporate profit and shareholder gain—does not mean that the objective of the corporation must be to realize corporate profit and shareholder gain in the short run. Indeed, the contrary is true: long-run profitability and shareholder gain are at the core of the economic objective. Activity that entails a short-run cost to achieve an appropriately greater long-run profit is therefore not a departure from the economic objective. An orientation toward lawful, ethical, and public-spirited activity will normally fall within this description. The modern corporation by its nature creates interdependencies with a variety of groups with whom the corporation has a legitimate concern, such as employees, customers, suppliers, and members of the communities in which the corporation operates. The long-term profitability of the corporation generally depends on meeting the fair expectations of such groups. Short-term profits may properly be subordinated to recognition that responsible maintenance of these interdependencies is likely to contribute to long-term corporate profit and shareholder gain. The corporation's business may be conducted accordingly.

...

Compliance with Legal Rules

Under § 2.01(b)(1), the corporation is obliged, to the same extent as a natural person, to act within the boundaries set by law. It is sometimes maintained that whether a corporation should adhere to a given legal rule may properly depend on a kind of cost-benefit analysis, in which probable corporate gains are weighed against either probable social costs, measured by the dollar liability imposed for engaging in such conduct, or probable corporate losses, measured by potential dollar liability discounted for likelihood of detection. Section 2.01 does not adopt this position. With few exceptions, dollar liability is not a "price" that can properly be paid for the privilege of engaging in legally wrongful conduct. Cost-benefit analysis may have a place in the state's determination whether a given type of conduct should be deemed legally wrongful. Once that determination has been made, however, the resulting legal rule normally represents a community decision that the conduct is wrongful as such, so that cost-benefit analysis whether to obey the rule is out of place.

Accordingly, in conducting its business, the corporation, like all other citizens, is under an obligation to act within the boundaries set by law. ...

Ethical Considerations

Section 2.01(b)(2) provides that a corporation may take into account ethical considerations that are reasonably regarded as appropriate to the responsible conduct of business. It is sometimes argued that because adherence to ethical principles typically involves long-run financial benefits, the concept of the long run dissolves any apparent tension between financial and ethical considerations. Certainly, a long-run profit motive may often explain conduct that appears to be based on ethical grounds. Furthermore, when ethical considerations enter into corporate decisions, they are usually mixed with, rather than opposed to, long-run profit considerations. Nevertheless, observation suggests that corporate decisions are not infrequently made on the basis of ethical considerations even when doing so would not enhance corporate profit or shareholder gain. Such behavior is not only appropriate, but desirable. Corporate officials are not less morally obliged than any other citizens to take ethical considerations into account, and it would be unwise social policy to preclude them from doing so.

This does not mean that corporate officials can properly take into account any ethical consideration, no matter how idiosyncratic. Because such officials are dealing with other people's money, they will act properly in taking ethical principles into account only where those considerations are reasonably regarded as appropriate to the responsible conduct of business. In this connection, however, it should be recognized that new principles may emerge over time. A corporate official therefore should be permitted to take into account emerging ethical principles, reasonably regarded as appropriate to the responsible conduct of business, that have significant support although less-than-universal acceptance.

The ethical considerations reasonably regarded as appropriate to the responsible conduct of business necessarily include ethical responsibilities that may be owed to persons other than shareholders with whom the corporation has a legitimate concern, such as employees, customers, suppliers, and members of the communities within which the corporation operates. The content of these responsibilities may vary according to the type of business in question and the history and established standards of the particular corporation. For example, a manufacturer of consumer goods may owe an ethical obligation to produce safe products, while newspapers may owe ethical obligations that are defined in part by the moral standards of journalism. Similarly, the content of the fairness obligation owed to groups such as employees may depend in part on past statements and practices that have engendered reasonable reliance or legitimate expectations. ...

Public Welfare, Humanitarian, Educational, and Philanthropic Purposes

Section 2.01(b)(3) permits the corporation to devote a reasonable amount of resources to public welfare, humanitarian, educational, and philanthropic purposes, even if corporate profit and shareholder gain are not thereby enhanced. As in the case of ethical considerations, conduct that appears to be based on public welfare, humanitarian, educational, or philanthropic considerations may be intended to enhance corporate profit and shareholder gain. For example, a donation to public television may be made for reasons comparable to those for sponsoring a commercial, and a contribution to local Red Cross or Community Chest activities may be made for reasons of employee well-being and morale. Furthermore, when considerations of the type described in § 2.01(b)(3) enter into corporate decisions, they are usually mixed with, rather than separable from, considerations of profitability and ethics. In such cases the activity may be justified under § 2.01(a) or § 2.01(b)(2).

Section 2.01(b)(3) goes beyond these justifications and allows corporate resources to be devoted to public welfare, humanitarian, educational, and philanthropic purposes even without a showing of expected profits or ethical norms. It is now widely accepted that the corporation should at least consider the social impact of its activities, so as to be aware of the social costs those activities entail. By implication, the corporation should be permitted to take such costs into account, within reason. For example, the corporation may take into account, within reason, public-welfare concerns relevant to groups with whom the corporation has a legitimate concern, such as employees, customers, suppliers, and members of the communities within which the corporation operates. Furthermore, because of the central position of corporations in the economic structure, the cooperation of corporations in furthering established governmental policies is often critical to the success of such policies. Social policy also favors humane behavior by major social institutions. Finally, social policy favors the maintenance of diversity in educational and philanthropic activity, and this objective would be more difficult to achieve if corporations, which control a great share of national resources, were not allowed to devote a portion of these resources to those ends. However, corporate activity that is justified solely by social considerations should be subject to a limit of reasonableness, because the activity is by hypothesis not solely in furtherance of the corporate business, the relevant considerations do not necessarily bear on the manner in which business should be conducted, and (partly for those reasons) there is no limit inherent in the considerations themselves on the extent to which corporate resources may be devoted to such purposes.

The determination whether the amount of resources used for purposes stated in § 2.01(b)(3) is reasonable in any given case, like other questions of reasonableness in the law, depends on all the circumstances of the case. ...

§ 3.01 Management of the Corporations's Business: Functions and Powers of Principal Senior Executives and Other Officers

> *The management of the business of a publicly held corporation should be conducted by or under the supervision of such principal senior executives as are designated by the board of directors, and by those other officers and employees to whom the management function is delegated by the board or those executives, subject to the functions and powers of the board under § 3.02.*

Comment

a. Comparison with Present Law

The formation of § 3.01 differs from the literal terms of the older statutory formulations (which commonly provided that the business of the corporation "shall be managed by [its] board") and, to a much lesser extent, from the more modern formulations, such as Delaware Gen. Corp. Law § 141 ("[t]he business and affairs of every corporation ... shall be managed by or under the direction of" the board), or Model Act § 8.01(b) ("[a]ll corporate powers shall be exercised by or under authority of, and the business and affairs of a corporation shall be managed under the direction of," the board). However, § 3.01 reflects long-established corporate practice under both types of statutory formulation. For example, the *Corporate Director's Guidebook* states:

> It is generally recognized that the board of directors is not expected to operate the business. Even under statutes providing that the business and affairs shall be "managed" by the board of directors, it is recognized that actual operation is a function of management. The responsibility of the board is limited to overseeing such operation. ...
>
> It is important to emphasize that the role of the director is to monitor, in an environment of loyal but independent oversight, the conduct of the business and affairs of the corporation in behalf of those who invest in the corporation.

Similarly, the *Business Roundtable Statement* (pp. 2094–98) comments:

> It is plainly impossible for a board composed partly of "outsiders," that is partly of persons who are not full-time employees, to conduct ... day-to-day [corporate] affairs. ...
>
> Although the board cannot effectively conduct day-to-day operations, The board does have a major role in, and a major accountability for, the financial performance of the enterprise. This clearly requires a continuing check on corporate financial results and prospects, including profit and loss and cash flow by major business segments.

...

§ 3.02 Functions and Powers of the Board of Directors

Except as otherwise provided by statute:

(a) The board of directors of a publicly held corporation should perform the following functions:

(1) Select, regularly evaluate, fix the compensation of, and, where appropriate, replace the principal senior executives;

(2) Oversee the conduct of the corporation's business to evaluate whether the business is being properly managed;

(3) Review and, [as a general matter], approve the corporation's financial objectives and major corporate plans and actions;

(4) Review and, [as a general matter], approve major changes in, and determinations of other major questions of choice respecting, the appropriate auditing and accounting principles and practices to be used in the preparation of the corporation's financial statements;

(5) Perform such other functions as are prescribed by law, or assigned to the board under a standard of the corporation.

(b) A board of directors also has power to:

(1) Initiate and adopt corporate plans, commitments, and actions;

(2) Initiate and adopt changes in accounting principles and practices;

(3) Provide advice and counsel to the principal senior executives;

(4) Instruct any committee, principal senior executive, or other officer, and review the actions of any committee, principal senior executive, or other officer;

(5) Make recommendations to shareholders;

(6) Manage the business of the corporation;

(7) Act as to all other corporate matters not requiring shareholder approval.

(c) Subject to the board's ultimate responsibility for oversight under Subsection (a)(2), the board may delegate to its committees authority to perform any of its functions and exercise any of its powers.

Comment

a. Comparison with Present Law

Section 3.02 differs from the literal terms of statutory formulations of the role of the board (see Comment *a* to § 3.01), but provides an articulation of the board's basic functions and powers that almost certainly would be arrived at by the courts in light of the language of these statutes read in the context of modern corporate practice. Although the statutes literally seem to require the board to either manage or direct the management of the corporation, it is widely understood that the board of a publicly held corporation normally cannot and does not perform those functions in the usual sense of those terms. ... Thus, the Business Roundtable's *Corporate Governance and American Competitiveness* states that:

> The board of directors has five primary functions:
>
> 1. Select, regularly evaluate and, if necessary, replace the chief executive officer. Determine management compensation. Review succession planning.
> 2. Review and, where appropriate, approve the financial objectives, major strategies, and plans of the corporation.
> 3. Provide advice and counsel to top management.
> 4. Select and recommend to shareholders for election an appropriate slate of candidates for the board of directors; evaluate board processes and performance.
> 5. Review the adequacy of systems to comply with all applicable laws/regulations.

Accordingly, it seems clear that, as provided in § 3.02, the board can normally satisfy the requirements of present statutes without either actively managing or directing the management of the corporation, as long as it oversees management and retains the decisive voice on major corporate actions. As stated by the New Jersey Supreme Court in Francis v. United Jersey Bank, 87 N.J. 15, 432 A.2d 814 (1981), "Directorial management does not require a detailed inspection of day-to-day activities, but rather a general monitoring of corporate affairs and policies." ...

The Oversight Function

In the publicly held corporation, the management function is normally vested in the principal senior executives. A basic function of the board is to select these executives and to oversee their performance (using the term "oversee" to refer to general observation and oversight, not active supervision or day-to-day scrutiny) to determine whether the business is being properly managed. ... This oversight function is usually performed, not directly by actively supervising the principal senior executives, but indirectly by evaluating the performance of those executives and replacing any who are not meeting reasonable expectations concerning job performance. ...

The board's obligation to oversee the performance of the principal senior executives does not imply an antagonist relationship between the board and the executives. Rather, it contemplates a collegial relationship that is supportive as well as watchful. To paraphrase the *Business Roundtable Statement,* the relationship between the board and the executives should be challenging yet positive, arm's length but not adversary.

A significant aspect of oversight by the board is continuing attention to the conduct of the corporation's business. As stated in the *Corporate Director's Guidebook:*

> The corporate director should be concerned that the corporation has programs looking toward compliance with applicable laws and regulations, both foreign and domestic, that it circulates (as appropriate) policy statements to this effect to its employees, and that it maintains procedures for monitoring such compliance.

Similarly, the Business Roundtable's *Corporate Governance and American Competitiveness* lists as one of the board's five primary functions: "Review the adequacy of systems to comply with applicable laws/regulations."

Selection, Evaluation, Compensation, and Replacement of Principal Senior Executives

Section 3.02(a)(1) provides that the board should select, regularly evaluate, fix the compensation of, and, where appropriate, replace the principal senior executives. ... The evaluation of the principal senior executives need not be formal. In determining the compensation of and in evaluating principal senior executives, the board or its committee is entitled to rely on the chief executive officer's formal or informal evaluations of principal senior executives who are the chief executive officer's subordinates.

In most cases, recommendations of candidates for principal senior executive offices will be initiate by the chief executive. The board will normally be entitled to rely on such recommendations, and in any event the board should normally give great weight, or even defer, to such recommendations. However, ultimate responsibility for the selection of principal senior executives rests with the board, unless otherwise provided by statute.

The process of selecting and evaluating officers below the level of the principal senior executives is normally conducted by the principal senior executives, but the board should oversee that process, or its results, both as part of its general oversight function and to help ensure that the ranks of top management are capably staffed and that lines of succession are adequately maintained.

Review of Major Corporate Plans and Actions

Section 3.02(a)(3) provides that the board should review and, [as a general matter], approve the corporation's financial objectives and major corporate plans and actions. What constitutes a major corporate plan or action is a matter of business judgment. Moreover, as a functional matter these judgments will normally be made, at least in the first instance, by the principal senior executives, and more particularly the chief executive officer, because in most cases the executives shape the board's agenda. However, the board may determine as a matter of business judgment either that a proposed plan or action that comes to its attention other than through the principal senior executives should receive board review, or that a plan or action that the principal senior executives believe should receive board review does not in fact need board time and should be recommitted to the principal senior executives for decision.

Examples of major corporate plans would normally include long-term strategic and investment plans, annual capital and operating budgets, and targeted rates of return. Examples of major corporate actions would normally include the creation or retirement of significant long-term debt, programs for the issuance or reacquisition of significant amounts of equity, significant capital investments, significant acquisitions of stock in other corporations, business combinations including those effected for cash, and the disposition of significant businesses. In general, the board should also address any matters that would in its judgment, or in the judgment of the principal senior executives, expose the corporation to significant litigation or significant new regulatory problems, or have or promise to have major public impact.

As a practical matter, the initiation and formulation of major corporate plans and actions must depend in large part on an intimate knowledge of the business of the corporation, and this knowledge is more likely to be possessed by the senior executives than by the board. Section 3.02(a)(3) therefore contemplates that, while ultimate responsibility for approving major corporate plans and actions is vested in the board, and the board also has power to initiate their formulation, in practice these plans and actions will usually be initiated and formulated by the senior executives. By the same token, the board may properly approve several options and leave it to the senior executives to decide, in light of emergent conditions, which option to execute. In making such determinations, the board and the senior executives would be entitled to the protection of the business judgment rule when they satisfy the standards of that rule. ... [As explained in other chapters of this book, the business judgment rule generally protects a determination made by a board of directors from successful challenge. The rule is a presumption that the Board made an adequately informed deliberative decision in good faith without a disabling conflict of interest. The standard for rebutting the presumption of the business judgment rule is that of gross negligence.]

Delegation of Board Powers and Functions

It is commonly provided by statute that the board may delegate to a committee the authority to exercise any of its powers, subject to certain limitations. Section 3.02(c) recognizes the permissibility of such delegation, within the limitations imposed by those statutes. Section 3.02(c) also recognizes that the board's functions can be delegated to its committees. Although the board can (and normally will) delegate to committees the performance of parts of the oversight function, and employ committees to implement and support that function, this delegation and employment is subject to the constraint that, because of the critical nature of the oversight function, the board must maintain a continuing presence in and ultimate responsibility for the overall performance of that function. ...

Certain powers and functions, most notably the power to manage the business of the corporation, may also be delegated to officers, as is made clear by § 3.01.

As a matter of corporate practice, actions taken by a committee to which a significant part of the authority of the board has been delegated should be reported to the board at its next meeting, usually by distribution of committee minutes or by a written or oral report. This procedure is intended ... to give the board a means of [being informed and] supervising its committees. ...

...

§ 3.05 Audit Committee in Large Publicly Held Corporations

> *Every ... publicly held corporation [must] have an audit committee to implement and support the oversight function of the board by reviewing on a periodic basis the corporation's processes for producing financial data, its internal controls, and the independence of the corporation's external auditor. The audit committee should consist of at least three members, and should be composed exclusively of [independent outside] directors. ...*

...

Rationale and Operation

An independent audit committee serves to implement and support the oversight function of the board in several ways.

(i) Such a committee provides a means for review of the corporation's processes for producing financial data, its internal controls, and the independence of the corporation's external auditor, and a forum for dialogue with the corporation's external and internal auditors. In theory, the full board might execute these functions itself, because the board is obliged in any event to be conversant with those matters. In practice, however, there are several reasons why an audit committee would normally constitute a preferable location for these functions. For one thing, a focused review and detailed discussion of the corporation's processes for producing financial data, its internal controls, and the independence of its external auditor might be too time-consuming for the full board. For another, because the corporation's financial date concerns the performance of management, it is important to have a forum for [the independent outside directors who comprise the committee to] discuss this data, and the manner of its preparation, in which management participates only on request.

(ii) An independent audit committee reinforces the independence of the corporation's external auditor, and thereby helps assure that the auditor will have free rein in the audit process. This reinforcement is achieved in part by conferring, on an organ that is independent of the management whose financial results are being audited, a vital role in the retention, discharge, and compensation of the external auditor. In addition, such a committee provides tangible embodiment of the concept that, within the framework of corporate relationships, the external auditor is responsible to the board and to the shareholders.

(iii) An independent audit committee provides a forum for regular, informal, and private discussion between the external auditor and directors who have no significant relationships with management. In the absence of such a forum, an external auditor would often be reluctant to call for a meeting at the board level unless a problem of great magnitude had arisen. In contrast, the provision of an institutionalized forum facilitates and indeed encourages the external auditor to raise potentially troublesome issues at a relatively early stage, allows the auditor to broach sensitive problems in an uninhibited and private fashion, and gives the auditor assurance that it can readily get a hearing in the event of a disagreement with management.

(iv) An independent audit committee reinforces the objectivity of the internal auditing department. If that department reports primarily to management ... and has no regular access to the board or to a board committee, it may encounter resistance to recommendations that do not meet with management's approval. Regular access to an audit committee may help ameliorate such resistance. A working relationship with an audit committee is also likely to increase the status and therefore the effectiveness of the internal auditing department.

...

At times, the U.S. Securities and Exchange Commission (SEC) may institute enforcement actions against outside directors for their alleged deficient oversight. The following SEC release provides a recent example.

SEC CHARGES MILITARY BODY ARMOR SUPPLIER AND FORMER OUTSIDE DIRECTORS WITH ACCOUNTING FRAUD

SEC Press Release No. 2011-52

Washington, D.C., Feb. 28, 2011—The Securities and Exchange Commission today charged a major supplier of body armor to the U.S. military and law enforcement agencies for engaging in a massive accounting fraud. The agency separately charged three of the company's former outside directors and audit committee members for their complicity in the scheme.

The SEC alleges that Pompano Beach, Fla.-based DHB Industries (now known as Point Blank Solutions) engaged in pervasive accounting and disclosure fraud through its senior officers and misappropriated company assets to personally benefit the former CEO. This resulted in the filing of materially false and misleading periodic reports to investors. The SEC further alleges that outside directors Jerome Krantz, Cary Chasin, and Gary Nadelman were willfully blind to numerous red flags signaling the accounting fraud, reporting violations, and misappropriation at DHB.

The SEC previously charged former DHB CEO David Brooks as well as two other former DHB senior officers for their roles in the fraud.

"We will not second-guess the good-faith efforts of directors. But in stark contrast, Krantz, Chasin and Nadelman were directors and audit committee members who repeatedly turned a blind eye to warning signs of fraud and other misconduct by company officers," said Robert Khuzami, Director of the SEC's Division of Enforcement.

Eric I. Bustillo, Director of the SEC's Miami Regional Office, added, "This massive accounting fraud permeated throughout an entire company and was facilitated by the egregious, wholesale failure of the company's board to act in the face of mounting red flags. As the fraud swirled around them, Krantz, Chasin, and Nadelman ignored the obvious and submitted to the directives and decisions of DHB's senior management while themselves profiting from sales of the company's securities."

The SEC filed two separate complaints in the U.S. District Court for the Southern District of Florida against DHB and the former outside directors. According to the SEC's complaint against Krantz, Chasin, and Nadelman, their willful blindness to red flags allowed senior management to manipulate the company's reported gross profit, net income, and other key figures in its earnings releases and public filings between 2003 and 2005. The company overstated inventory values, failed to include appropriate charges for obsolete inventory, and falsified journal entries. By ignoring red flags, the three outside directors also facilitated the misconduct by Brooks, who diverted at least $10 million out of the company through fraudulent transactions with a related entity that he controlled. Their willful blindness to red flags additionally facilitated DHB's improper payment of millions of dollars in personal expenses for Brooks, including luxury cars, jewelry, art, real estate, extravagant vacations, and prostitution services. Despite being confronted with the red flags indicating fraud, Krantz, Chasin, and Nadelman approved or signed DHB's false and misleading filings.

The SEC's complaints against DHB, Krantz, Chasin, and Nadelman charge them with violating or aiding and abetting the antifraud, reporting, books and records, and other provisions of the federal securities laws. DHB has agreed to settle with the SEC and agreed to a permanent injunction from future violations. The proposed settlement took into account the remedial measures already taken by the company. The company is currently in bankruptcy and its settlement with the SEC is pending the approval of the bankruptcy court. The SEC seeks injunctive relief, disgorgement of ill-gotten gains, monetary penalties, and officer and director bars against Krantz, Chasin, and Nadelman.

...

SCENARIO

Leg-Up Toys, Inc., is a publicly held company whose stock is traded on the NASDAQ Stock Exchange. It is a leading toy producer with its principal executive office and sole manufacturing site located in Twin Falls, Idaho. The company is a major employer in Twin Falls, employing about 3,000 of the city's total population in its manufacturing unit. The company has a capitalized net worth of $125 million. Based on thorough research and analysis by retained experts, the company's board of directors is now considering outsourcing the company's manufacturing operations to China. The experts' reports forecast that this overseas outsourcing plan would likely reduce the cost of production and operation by 20% and thereby should significantly increase the company's earnings per share. However, closing the manufacturing plant in Twin Falls would result in loss of employment for thousands of the city's residents. Moreover, whether the quality of the products made and transportation costs remain as projected with respect to the prospective relocation of manufacturing to China are, of course, somewhat uncertain.

The board and management of the company want to behave in a socially responsible way and avoid such a huge unemployment blow to Twin Falls and its approximate 34,500 residents. But they also know that they have the primary duty to act for the long-term profit maximization for the company's shareholders.

If the board of directors decides not to relocate the company's manufacturing operations to China, would the Board be acting improperly by not seeking to maximize shareholder return? Or alternatively, should the company forego this potential (but not certain) increase in corporate profits by continuing its production operations in Twin Falls?

Chapter 6

FIDUCIARY DUTIES

IN THE CORPORATE law setting, directors and officers owe two general fiduciary duties: the duty of care and the duty of loyalty. These duties also apply in other business enterprises, such as with respect to general partners in a partnership and to managers in a limited liability company (LLC). While these duties cannot be eliminated by contract, they can be reduced to a significant degree by the governing document (such as the corporation's articles of incorporation) or by written agreement of the owners (such as pursuant to a partnership, LLC, or shareholder agreement). Moreover, as a general matter, these duties are owed in the corporate setting only to the corporation and to common stockholders collectively. By contrast, the rights of preferred stockholders and debt holders ordinarily are determined by contract.[1]

We will begin our discussion with the internal affairs doctrine and the preference of incorporating in Delaware for publicly-held companies. The Chapter will then focus on the duty of care followed by the duty of loyalty. In this respect, the materials contained in Chapter 7, focusing on shareholder litigation, are pertinent to this discussion.

THE INTERNAL AFFAIRS DOCTRINE AND DELAWARE INCORPORATION

The internal affairs doctrine generally posits that the law of the state of incorporation governs the relations between the corporation, its fiduciaries (e.g., its directors and officers), and the shareholders.[2] For example, assume that a corporation is incorporated in Delaware, conducts business globally, has its headquarters in Chicago, and has most of its physical assets situated in Indiana. Further assume that shareholders bring a lawsuit against the directors alleging that the directors breached their duty of loyalty by authorizing the corporation to engage in an improper transaction with the chief executive officer (e.g., the sale of property to the CEO at an unfair price that improperly benefits the CEO). The law to be applied in assessing the propriety of the directors' conduct is the law of the state of incorporation—here, Delaware.

One key question is why would a state desire business enterprises to incorporate within its borders. The simple answer is that "it's all about the money." Companies must pay incorporation fees, franchise taxes and other episodic fees (e.g., such as a filing fee for amendment of the articles of incorporation) to the incorporating state. Indeed, states like Delaware derive tens of millions of dollars from these payments,[3] resulting in these fees serving a vital role in a state's economic vitality.[4]

But why Delaware—a relatively small state with lovely beaches (e.g., Rehoboth Beach)? The reason generally is that Delaware for decades has been perceived as the premier state for publicly-held companies to incorporate. This is so for numerous reasons. First, the Delaware legislature and courts are viewed as sophisticated and responsive to corporate needs. Second, Delaware's corporate law has strong judicial precedent on many issues, thereby making it well developed and understood. Third, Delaware law is perceived as predictable.[5] And, fourth, in the view of critics, the Delaware courts and legislature unduly favor management interests over those of shareholders. This favoritism induces boards of directors and executive officers to seek Delaware incorporation.[6] As stated by one critic:

> The sovereign state of Delaware is in the business of selling its corporation law. This is profitable business, for corporation law is a good commodity to sell. The market is large, and relatively few producers compete on a national scale. The consumers of this commodity are corporations, and as we shall see, Delaware, like any other good businessman, tries to give the consumer what he wants. In fact, those who will buy the product are not only consulted about their preferences, but are also allowed to design the product and run the factory.[7]

Although this statement exaggerates the managerial bias of state company law, it reflects the view held by many that state corporation law is a "race for the bottom" that Delaware has won.[8]

DUTY OF CARE

The duty of care may be defined as the "amount of care exercised by like persons in similar circumstances."[9] In order to successfully claim a breach of the duty of care, one must show that the duty was owed to the complainant, a breach of that duty, causation and, if money damages are sought, damages.[10] The case of *Francis v. United Jersey Bank*[11] is a good example of how a director can breach his/her duty of care. In that case the CEO of a reinsurance broker in charge of segregating and protecting funds died. His wife (Mrs. Pritchard) and two sons became the sole directors. Without their mother's knowledge, the two sons began using client funds to grant loans to themselves. When the plaintiffs became aware of these loans, they sued Mrs. Pritchard for breach of the duty of care. The court determined that she was negligent as a director. As a director, one must "acquire at least a rudimentary understanding of the business of the corporation."[12] Elaborating, the New Jersey high court opined:

> [A] director should become familiar with the fundamentals of the business in which the corporation is engaged. … Because directors are bound to exercise ordinary care, they cannot set up as a defense lack of the knowledge needed to exercise the requisite degree of care. If one feels that he has not had sufficient business experience to qualify him to perform the duties of a director, he should either acquire the knowledge by inquiry or refuse to act. …
>
> Directors are under a continuing obligation to keep informed about the activities of the corporation. Otherwise, they may not be able to participate in the overall management of corporate affairs. …
>
> Directorial management does not require a detailed inspection of day-to-day activities, but rather a general monitoring of corporate affairs and policies. Accordingly, a director is well advised to attend board meetings regularly. Indeed, a director who is absent from a board meeting is presumed to concur in the action taken on a corporate matter, unless he files a "dissent with the secretary of the corporation within a reasonable time after learning of such action." … Regular attendance does not mean that directors must attend every meeting, but that directors should attend meetings as a matter of practice. …
>
> While directors are not required to audit corporate books, they should maintain familiarity with the financial status of the corporation by a regular review of financial statements. … The review of financial statements … may give rise to a duty to inquire further into

> matters revealed by those statements. A director is not an ornament, but an essential component of corporate governance. …[13]

Mrs. Pritchard's ignorance was not a defense. Next, the court held that she had the ability and leverage to stop her sons' actions, but did not do so. She accordingly breached her duty of care and caused the plaintiffs' losses.[14]

THE BUSINESS JUDGMENT RULE

An important shield from liability afforded to fiduciaries (like officers and directors) is the business judgment rule. The business judgment rule is "a presumption that in making a decision, the [fiduciaries] of a corporation acted on an informed basis and in good faith."[15] The rationale underlying the rule is that courts should not interfere, second-guess, or be "Monday morning quarterbacks" when directors or officers make their good faith impartial business decisions.[16] In short, the rule is one of judicial non-review of such decisions.[17] Generally, in order for the business judgment rule to be invoked, the following must be present: First, the board of directors, committee or other such representative must have made a deliberative decision. Not only affirmative decisions to act come within the rule—determinations to abstain from taking action (such as deciding not to develop a new product or not to purchase certain assets) come within the rule.[18] Second, there cannot be a disabling conflict of interest. This generally means that the fiduciaries are not engaged in financial self-dealing[19] and are not controlled or dominated by another so as to prevent that person from exercising independent judgment.[20] Third, the decision must be sufficiently informed. The standard applied for ascertaining whether a decision is sufficiently informed is rather lax: that of gross negligence.[21] A fourth element is required by some (perhaps a majority of) courts: namely, that the decision had a rational basis. This is another rather lax inquiry: focusing on whether the decision was made without gross negligence.[22] The business judgment is a presumption that the above elements were met by the subject fiduciaries. It is the plaintiff's burden to rebut the presumption that the business judgment rule applies.[23]

A controversial case that showcases the duty of care in conjunction with the business judgment rule is *Smith v. Van Gorkom.*[24] Stated briefly, Van Gorkom was the chief executive officer and chairman of the board of directors of Trans Union, a New York Stock Exchange listed company. Seeking to find a buyer for the company, Van Gorkom approached financier Jay

Pritzker. With minimal discussions, Van Gorkom and Pritzker arrived at a price of $55 per Trans Union share. In addition, Pritzker successfully negotiated for certain deal protective benefits (called "lock-ups").[25] The Trans Union board of directors recommended the merger which subsequently was approved by the shareholders. Aggrieved shareholders thereupon brought suit against the directors. The court held that the directors had breached their duty of care and were not protected by the business judgment rule. The court determined that the directors: (1) did not adequately inform themselves as to Van Gorkom's role with respect to the "sale" of the company and in establishing the per share purchase price; (2) were uninformed as to the intrinsic value of the company; and (3) given these circumstances, at a minimum, were grossly negligent in approving Trans Union's "sale" upon two hours' consideration without prior notice and without the presence of a crisis or emergency.[26]

DIRECTOR PROTECTION STATUTES (OR "RAINCOAT PROVISIONS")

The Delaware Supreme Court's decision signified that the Trans Union directors incurred millions of dollars of liability in a merger transaction when they did not personally benefit and where shareholders received a 50% premium over the stock's market price measured on the day of the deal's announcement.[27] As a consequence of that decision, directors became fearful of undue liability exposure, thereby generating apprehension in Delaware that many corporations would "leave" Delaware and incorporate elsewhere. Responding to this "opportunity," states promoted the benefits of incorporation in their respective states, seeking the significant franchise and other fees paid by subject companies.[28] This led Delaware and dozens of other states to enact director limitation of liability statutes, called "raincoat provisions."

The Delaware statute, which has been widely adopted by many other states, permits that a company's articles of incorporation may "eliminat[e] or limit the personal liability of a director to the corporation or its stockholders for monetary damages for breach of fiduciary duty as a director, provided that such provision shall not eliminate or limit the liability of a director" for breaches of the duty of loyalty, reckless misconduct, or violation of another applicable law (such as antitrust, environmental, or securities law).[29] This statute thus makes it much more difficult for plaintiffs to successfully pursue breach of duty of care actions seeking money damages.

As enacted by the vast majority of states, these statutes are not self-enabling: the corporation must affirmatively incorporate the provision in its articles of incorporation. This normally is accompanied by a majority of the company's shares voting in favor of the raincoat provision's inclusion in the subject corporation's articles of incorporation.[30] A not surprising outcome of the raincoat provision is to prompt more plaintiffs to attempt to frame their claims as breaches of the duty of loyalty (rather than the duty of care).

DUTY OF LOYALTY

The duty of loyalty arises when a corporate fiduciary, such as a director, officer, or controlling shareholder, benefits at the expense of the corporation or otherwise fails to act in the best interests of the corporation. In these situations, the fiduciary may place the interests of self, family, friends, or associates over those of the corporation. The duty of loyalty may be implicated in several contexts, including where the director or officer engages in a related party transaction (including an interested director transaction), usurps a corporate opportunity, improperly competes with the corporation, is controlled or dominated by another, or receives excessive executive compensation.[31] The duty of loyalty also arises when a parent company, exercising its control over the subsidiary, causes the subsidiary to engage in a transaction that unduly benefits the parent company.[32]

RELATED PARTY TRANSACTIONS

Improper related party transactions may be defined as a controlling shareholder or other fiduciary (such as a director or the chief executive officer) causing the corporation to provide such fiduciary with a benefit to the detriment of the corporation and its shareholders.[33] The controlling shareholder can be a director, an officer, or a shareholder holding a material financial interest (such as an individual or business enterprise owning more than 50% of the subject company's stock). Note that when a director or officer engages in a transaction with the corporation either personally or through another enterprise of which he is a fiduciary or owns a material financial interest, such transaction is a related party transaction (and in the director context is called an "interested director transaction").[34] It is important to observe that such transactions are proper if they are fair. Disinterested director or shareholder approval of the transaction with adequate disclosure significantly enhances the likelihood that a court will uphold the transaction as appropriate. Fairness means "entire fairness"—fair dealing and fair price.[35] Generally, disinterested director approval of the transaction after such directors are informed of all material facts shifts the burden of proving unfairness to the complainant or, in the alternative, invokes the business judgment rule.[36] Without informed disinterested director or shareholder approval, the burden rests with the defendant fiduciary to prove the transaction's fairness.[37]

USURPING A CORPORATE OPPORTUNITY

Directors, officers or other fiduciaries may not improperly take or usurp a corporate opportunity belonging to the corporation. Debate exists among different jurisdictions regarding how broadly or narrowly to construe this principle. Different tests have been employed. One is the "line of business" test, which posits that any opportunity that is in the same or closely-related line of business as the corporation is a corporate opportunity.[38] Applying this test, many courts look not only to the existing lines of business but also to the company's prospective plans so long as they are sufficiently concrete.[39] A second test is the "interest or expectancy" test. This test generally focuses on whether the corporation has expressed an interest in the specific opportunity that the fiduciary takes.[40] A third test is the "fairness" test. This test looks to see if the transaction was a corporate opportunity, either by the line of business test or the expectancy test, and then the court applies a fairness test. The fairness test looks to factors such as whether the fiduciary learned of the opportunity in her personal or official capacity, whether the fiduciary is an inside or outside director, whether the corporation had the financial ability to exploit and profit from the opportunity, and whether the fiduciary used any corporate resources to gain the opportunity.

If an opportunity is deemed a corporate opportunity, the subject director or executive officer ordinarily may take the opportunity only after making appropriate disclosure to the board of directors and having the board reject the opportunity. In situations where a fiduciary usurps a corporate opportunity, restitution may be ordered for the benefit of the corporation by means of a constructive trust, thereby ordering the wrongdoer to transfer the opportunity (such as real property) to the corporation.[41]

COMPETING WITH THE CORPORATION

Another situation in which a breach of duty of loyalty may arise is when a fiduciary unfairly competes with the corporation. Unless properly authorized by the corporation (such as through a shareholder agreement or board of director resolution), a fiduciary seeking to compete with the corporation should not use any corporate time, assets or facilities with respect to this competitive endeavor. Nor should the fiduciary seek to lure prospective clients before termination of employment. Accordingly, certain actions that are not allowed to be taken by a fiduciary seeking to compete with the corporation include the use of proprietary client lists, taking of confidential information, making disparaging comments about the corporation, or engaging in tortious conduct such as interfering with a contractual arrangement with an existing corporate client.[42] Nonetheless, confining oneself to the planning stage or making minor use of corporate assets may be tolerated by a court (such as minor use of the company's printers and duplicating equipment).[43]

Excessive Executive Compensation

Another example of breach of the duty of loyalty involves excessive executive compensation. Such compensation today in publicly-held companies is effected through a compensation committee comprised entirely of independent directors.[44] Nonetheless, when the compensation awarded has no reasonable relationship to the services performed or when directors serving on the compensation committee act without good faith or are otherwise conflicted, the duty of loyalty (as well as the duty of care) will be implicated.[45]

Domination and Control

The duty of loyalty also is implicated when a director is controlled or dominated by another, such as being dominated by the company's chief executive officer. A director who is beholden to another does not have to financially benefit to be interested. Such director is interested if, due to such domination or control, such director does not exercise independent judgment.[46]

Parent Subsidiary Domination

Another type of duty of loyalty issue arises when a parent company, because of its control over the subsidiary, causes the subsidiary to engage in actions that unfairly benefit the parent company. When self-dealing arises—to determine if the actions of the parent company constitute a breach of the duty of loyalty—courts frequently apply the entire fairness test. This test is comprised of two parts: that the transaction was negotiated and consummated by means of fair dealing and that the price paid was within the range of fairness.[47] For example, a parent company that causes its subsidiary to sell an asset of the subsidiary to the parent at a price materially lower than the fair market value (namely, what a non-affiliated party in an arm's length transaction would pay for such asset), would, in all likelihood, breach the duty of loyalty.[48]

TWO OTHER FIDUCIARY DUTIES

Two other fiduciary duties categorized under the duty of loyalty are the duty to disclose and the duty of good faith. A tactical reason why they would be pleaded as duty of loyalty breaches is to enable plaintiffs to avoid state statutory raincoat provisions (discussed earlier in this chapter) which limit or eliminate monetary liability for a breach of the duty of care.[49]

THE DUTY TO DISCLOSE/THE DUTY OF CANDOR

The duty to disclose generally means that fiduciaries (such as directors or officers), when communicating with shareholders, must accurately disclose all material information that is reasonably available.[50] Material information is defined as information that a reasonable shareholder would consider important in making an investment or voting decision.[51] This disclosure obligation can implicate both the duty of care and the duty of loyalty.[52] Clearly, if directors knowingly or intentionally convey to shareholders materially false information, the duty of loyalty applies.[53]

THE DUTY OF GOOD FAITH

A breach of the duty of good faith that also constitutes a breach of the duty of loyalty arises when a director acts with conscious indifference or recklessly disregards the corporation's best interests.[54] With respect to establishing lack of good faith based on director neglect to establish reasonably adequate safeguards to protect against loss, either due to violations of law (e.g., environmental penalties) or market risks (e.g., failure to hedge a key commodity in the company's business), a sustained or systematic failure of the board to exercise oversight ordinarily must be proven.[55] For example, concerning law compliance, a plaintiff must show that the subject directors had utterly failed to implement any reporting system of control.[56] Second, if the board had implemented such a system, liability may ensue based on conscious failure to monitor its operations.[57] In practical effect, liability based on a director's failure to act in good faith normally will arise only when such directors consciously looked the other way—or, in other words, had a "head in the sand" or "ostrich" approach to their fiduciary duties.[58]

Aiding and Abetting

Significantly, a person who is not a fiduciary may be held liable for aiding and abetting a breach of a fiduciary duty. Auditors, bankers and attorneys are among those who should be wary of becoming aiders and abettors. There are three elements that must be present for aiding and abetting liability: (1) a breach of fiduciary duty was committed by the primary violator (e.g., a director); (2) knowledge of that breach by the aider and abettor; and (3) the rendering of substantial assistance by the aider and abettor.[59] Due to that any money judgment against primary violators may be insufficient to compensate plaintiffs, auditors, bankers, and lawyers are sued as "deep pockets" with some frequency.[60] Accordingly, care and good judgment must be exercised by these professionals.[61]

"Close" Corporations: Shareholder Oppression

As addressed in Chapter 3, according to many courts, shareholders comprising a controlling group in a close corporation must treat the minority shareholder(s) with fairness.[62] Applying this rationale, these courts protect a minority shareholder's "reasonable expectations" when entering into the venture and as those reasonable expectations evolve over the course of the company's history.[63] These reasonable expectations, for example, may include: status as a director and officer; payment of dividends at a customary level; right to employment; and payment of a reasonable salary.[64] When these reasonable expectations are frustrated by those in control of the corporation (even when such conduct may not constitute a breach of the duty of care or loyalty under applicable state corporate law), a court may order a buy-out of the minority's shares at a fair price.[65]

Conclusion

The duties of care and loyalty as well as application of the business judgment rule arise with regularity with respect to director and officer conduct. Those who serve in these positions as well as those who advise these fiduciaries should be knowledgeable of the applicable standards. By conducting themselves within the confines of permissible conduct (and hopefully compliant with "best practices"), avoidance of adverse legal consequences is far more likely. In these times of government as well as private lawsuits, appropriate standards should be effectively implemented to lessen the risk of liability and promote the corporation's best interests.

NOTES

1. See §§ 103(b)(3)–(4), 404 of the Revised Uniform Partnership Act; *North American Catholic Educational Programming Foundation, Inc. v. Gheewalla*, 930 A. 2d 92 (Del. 2007); *Fletcher International Ltd. v. Ion Geophysical Corp.*, 2011 Del. Ch. LEXIS 53 (Del. Ch. 2011); *Singer v. Singer*, 634 P. 2d 766 (Okla. App. 1981).
2. See *CTS Corp. v. Dynamics Corp. of America*, 481 U.S. 69 (1987).
3. See Williams, *Delaware's Sedate Chancery Court Is a Major Corporate Battleground*, Wall St. J., May 10, 1984, at p. 37.
4. *Id.*
5. See duPont, *Incorporated in Delaware*, Directors & Boards at 12 (Fall 1981).
6. See Cary, *Federalism and Corporate Law: Reflections Upon Delaware*, 83 Yale L.J. 663 (1974).
7. Comment, *Law for Sale: A Study of the Delaware Corporation Law of 1967*, 117 U. Pa. L. Rev. 861, 861–862 (1969).
8. See Cary, *supra* note 6, at 664.
9. See D. Branson, J. Heminway, M. Lowenstein, M. Steinberg and W. Warren, *Business Enterprises: Legal Structures, Governance, and Policy* 382 (2009).
10. See *Brane v. Roth*, 590 N.E. 2d 587 (Ind. App. 1993); *Barnes v. Andrews*, 298 F. 614 (S.D.N.Y. 1924).
11. 432 A. 2d 814 (N.J. 1981).
12. *Id.* at 821.
13. *Id.* at 821–822.
14. *Id.* at 822–826.
15. *Aronson v. Lewis*, 473 A. 2d 805, 812 (Del. 1984).
16. See *Cede & Co. v. Technicolor, Inc.*, 634 A. 2d 345, 361 (Del. 1993).
17. See Johnson, *The Modest Business Judgment Rule*, 55 Bus. Law. 625 (2000).
18. See American Law Institute, Principles of Corporate Governance: Analysis and Recommendations § 4.01 (1994); Branson et. al., *supra* note 9, at 417.
19. See *Clark v. Lomas & Nettleton Financial Corp.*, 581 F. 2d 516 (5th Cir. 1978).
20. See *Aronson v. Lewis*, 473 A. 2d 805 (Del. 1984).
21. See *Smith v. Van Gorkom*, 488 A. 2d 858 (Del. 1985).
22. See *Gimbal v. Signal Companies*, 316 A. 2d 599 (Del. Ch.), *aff'd*, 316 A. 2d 619 (Del. 1974).

23. See Branson, *The Rule That Isn't a Rule—The Business Judgment Rule,* 36 Valpariso L. Rev. 631, 645 (2002).
24. 488 A. 2d 858 (Del. 1985).
25. *Id.* at 865–867.
26. *Id.* at 873–880.
27. See Manning, *Reflections and Practical Tips on Life in the Boardroom After Van Gorkom,* 41 Bus. Law. 1 (1985).
28. See Steinberg, *The Evisceration of the Duty of Care,* 42 Sw. L.J. 919 (1988).
29. See § 102(b)(7) of the Delaware General Corporation Law. See also §§ 2-405.2, 2-418 of the Maryland Corporation Law. §§13.1-690, 13.1-692.1 of the Virginia Corporation Law.
30. See § 102(b)(7) of the Delaware General Corporation Law.
31. See, e.g., *Enstar Group, Inc. v. Grassgreen,* 812 F. Supp. 1562 (M.D. Ala. 1993).
32. See *Sinclair Oil Corp. v. Levien,* 280 A. 2d 717 (Del. 1971).
33. *Id.* at 720–723.
34. See § 144 of the Delaware General Corporation Law.
35. See *Fliegler v. Lawrence,* 361 A. 2d 218 (Del. 1976); *Remillard Brick Co. v. Remillard-Dandini Co.,* 241 P. 2d 66 (Cal. App. 1952).
36. See *Marciano v. Nakash,* 535 A. 2d 400 (Del. 1987).
37. See *Lewis v. S.L & E., Inc.,* 629 F. 2d 764 (2d Cir. 1980).
38. See *Broz v. Cellular Information Systems,* 673 A. 2d 148 (Del. 1996).
39. See *PJ Acquisition Corp. v. Skoglund,* 453 N.W. 2d 1 (Minn. 1990).
40. See *Farber v. Servan Land Co.,* 662 F. 2d 371 (5th Cir. 1981).
41. See *Today Homes, Inc. v. Williams,* 634 S.E. 2d 737 (Va. 2006); *Brandt v. Somerville,* 692 N.W. 2d 144 (N.D. 2005); *Miller v. Miller,* 222 N.W. 2d 71 (Minn. 1974); *Graham v. Mimms,* 444 N.E. 2d 549 (Ill. App. 1982).
42. See *PepsiCo, Inc. v. Redmond,* 54 F. 3d 1262 (7th Cir. 1995); ALI Corporate Governance Project, *supra* note 18, at § 5.06.
43. See *Voss Engineering, Inc. v. Voss Industries,* 481 N.E. 2d 63 (Ill. App. 1985).
44. See § 10A of the Securities Exchange Act, as amended by the Dodd-Frank Act of 2010.
45. See *Rogers v. Hill,* 289 U.S. 582 (1933); *In re the Walt Disney Company Derivative Litigation,* 906 A. 2d 27 (Del. 2006); *Hall v. Staha,* 858 S.W. 2d 672 (Ark. 1993).
46. See *Aronson v. Lewis,* 473 A. 2d 805 (Del. 1984).
47. See *Weinberger v. UOP, Inc.,* 457 A. 2d 701 (Del. 1983).
48. See *Sinclair Oil Corp. v. Levien,* 280 A. 2d 717 (Del. 1971).
49. See *supra* notes 27-30 and accompanying text.
50. See *Brehm v. Eisner,* 746 A. 2d 244 (Del. 2000).
51. See *Malone v. Brincat,* 722 A. 2d 5 (Del. 1998).
52. See *Zirn v. VLI Corp.,* 621 A. 2d 773 (Del. 1993).
53. See *In re Reliance Securities Litigation,* 91 F. Supp. 2d 706 (Del. 2000).

54. See *Stone v. Ritter*, 911 A. 2d 362 (Del. 2006); *In re the Walt Disney Company Derivative Litigation*, 906 A. 2d 27 (Del. 2006).
55. *Stone v. Ritter*, 911 A. 2d at 370.
56. *Id.*
57. *Id.* See *In re Abbott Laboratories Derivative Shareholders Litigation*, 325 F. 3d 795 (7th Cir. 2003); *McCall v. Scott*, 239 F. 3d 808, amended, 250 F. 3d 997 (6th Cir. 2001).
58. See cases cited note 57 *supra*.
59. A number of jurisdictions require that the aider and abettor must have actual knowledge. See *Eurycleia Partners LP v. Seward & Kissel, LLP*, 883 N.Y. 2d 147 (2009).
60. See Mason, *Civil Liability for Aiding and Abetting*, 61 Bus. Law. 1135 (2006).
61. See M. Steinberg, *Attorney Liability After Sarbanes-Oxley* (2011).
62. See cases cited in Chapter 3, at notes 40-45.
63. See, e.g, *Meiselman v. Meiselman,* 307 S.E. 2d 551 (N.C. 1983).
64. See *Wilkes v. Springdale Nursing Home, Inc.*, 353 N.E. 2d 657 (Mass. 1976).
65. See, e.g., *In the Matter of Kemp & Beatley, Inc.*, 473 N.E. 2d 1173 (N.Y. 1984).

CASE STUDIES

THE CASES THAT follow provide different factual contexts in which corporate fiduciaries allegedly breached their duties of care and loyalty. We will begin with a popular case that implicates the *business judgment rule* involving the infamous Chicago Cubs who last won a World Series title over 100 years ago (in 1908):

SHLENSKY V. WRIGLEY
ILLINOIS COURT OF APPEALS
237 N.E. 2D 776 (1968)

Sullivan, J.:

This is an appeal from a dismissal of plaintiff's amended complaint on motion of the defendants. The action was a stockholders' derivative suit against the directors for negligence and mismanagement. The corporation was also made a defendant. Plaintiff sought damages and an order that defendants cause the installation of lights in Wrigley Field and the scheduling of night baseball games.

Plaintiff is a minority stockholder of defendant corporation, Chicago National League Ball Club (Inc.), a Delaware corporation with its principal place of business in Chicago, Illinois. Defendant corporation owns and operates the major league professional baseball team known as the Chicago Cubs. The corporation also engages in the operation of Wrigley Field, the Cubs' home park, the concessionaire sales during Cubs' home games, television and radio broadcasts of Cubs' home games, the leasing of the field for football games and other events and receives its share, as visiting team, of admission moneys from games played in other National League stadia. The individual defendants are directors of the Cubs and have served for varying periods of years. Defendant Philip K. Wrigley is also president of the corporation and owner of approximately 80% of the stock therein. Plaintiff alleges that since night baseball was first played in 1935 nineteen of the twenty major league teams have scheduled night games. In 1966, out of a total of 1,620 games in the major leagues, 932 were played at night. Plaintiff alleges that every member of the major leagues, other than the Cubs, scheduled substantially all of its home games in 1966 at night, exclusive of opening days, Saturdays, Sundays, holidays and days prohibited by league rules. Allegedly this has been done for the specific purpose of maximizing attendance and thereby maximizing revenue and income.

The Cubs, in the years 1961–65, sustained operating losses from its direct baseball operations. Plaintiff attributes those losses to inadequate attendance at Cubs' home games. He concludes that if the directors continue to refuse to install lights at Wrigley Field and schedule night baseball games, the Cubs will continue to sustain comparable losses and its financial condition will continue to deteriorate.

Plaintiff alleges that, except for the year 1963, attendance at Cubs' home games has been substantially below that at their road games, many of which were played at night.

Plaintiff compares attendance at Cubs' games with that of the Chicago White Sox, an American League club, whose weekday games were generally played at night. The weekend attendance figures for the two teams were similar; however, the White Sox week-night games drew many more patrons than did the Cubs' weekday games.

Plaintiff alleges that the funds for the installation of lights can be readily obtained through financing and the cost of installation would be far more than offset and recaptured by increased revenues and incomes resulting from the increased attendance.

Plaintiff further alleges that defendant Wrigley has refused to install lights, not because of interest in the welfare of the corporation but because of his personal opinions "that baseball is a 'daytime sport' and that the installation of lights and night baseball games will have a deteriorating effect upon the surrounding neighborhood." It is alleged that he has admitted that he is not interested in whether the Cubs would benefit financially from such action because of his concern for the neighborhood, and that he would be willing for the team to play night games if a new stadium were built in Chicago.

Plaintiff alleges that the other defendant directors, with full knowledge of the foregoing matters, have acquiesced in the policy laid down by Wrigley and have permitted him to dominate the board of directors in matters involving the installation of lights and scheduling of night games, even though they knew he was not motivated by a good faith concern as to the best interests of defendant corporation, but solely by his personal views set forth above. It is charged that the directors are acting for a reason or reasons contrary and wholly unrelated to the business interest of the corporation; that such arbitrary and capricious acts constitute mismanagement and waste of corporate assets, and that the directors have been negligent in failing to exercise reasonable care and prudence in the management of the corporate affairs.

The question on appeal is whether plaintiff's amended complaint states a cause of action. It is plaintiff's position that fraud, illegality and conflict of interest are not the only bases for a stockholder's derivative action against the directors. Contrariwise, defendants argue that the courts will not step in and interfere with honest business judgment of the directors unless there is a showing of fraud, illegality or conflict of interest.

The cases in this area are numerous and each differs from the others on a factual basis. However, the courts have pronounced certain ground rules which appear in all cases and which are then applied to the given factual situation. ... [For example, one court has opined:]

> "We have then a conflict in view between the responsible managers of a corporation and an overwhelming majority of its stockholders on the one hand and a dissenting minority on the other—a conflict touching matters of business policy, such as has occasioned innumerable applications to courts to intervene and determine which of the two conflicting views should prevail. The response which courts make to such applications is that it is not their function to resolve for corporations questions of policy and business management. The directors are chosen to pass upon such questions and their judgment [absent improper conduct] is accepted as final. The judgment of the directors of corporations enjoys the benefit of a presumption that it was formed in good faith and was designed to promote the best interest of the corporation they serve."

...

Plaintiff argues that the allegations of his amended complaint are sufficient to set forth a cause of action under the principles set out in *Dodge v. Ford Motor Co.*, 204 Mich. 459. ... In that case plaintiff, owner of about 10% of the outstanding stock, brought suit against the directors seeking payment of additional dividends and the enjoining of further business expansion. In ruling on the request for dividends the court indicated that the motives of Ford in keeping so much money in the corporation for expansion and security were to benefit the public generally and spread the profits out by means of more jobs, etc. The court felt that these were not only far from related to the good of the stockholders, but amounted to a change in the ends of the corporation and that this was not a purpose contemplated or allowed by the corporate charter. …

Plaintiff in the instant case argues that the directors are acting for reasons unrelated to the financial interest and welfare of the Cubs. However, we are not satisfied that the motives assigned to Philip K. Wrigley, and through him to the other directors, are contrary to the best interests of the corporation and the stockholders. For example, it appears to us that the effect on the surrounding neighborhood might well be considered by a director who was considering the patrons who would or would not attend the games if the park were in a poor neighborhood. Furthermore, the long run interest of the corporation in its property values at Wrigley Field might demand all efforts to keep the neighborhood from deteriorating. By these thoughts we do not mean to say that we have decided that the decision of the directors was a correct one. That is beyond our jurisdiction and ability. We are merely saying that the decision is one properly before directors and the motives alleged in the amended complaint showed no fraud, illegality or conflict of interest in their making of that decision.

…

[W]e do not agree with plaintiff's contention that failure to follow the example of the other major league clubs in scheduling night games constituted negligence. Plaintiff made no allegation that these teams' night schedules were profitable or that the purpose for which night baseball had been undertaken was fulfilled. Furthermore, it cannot be said that directors, even those of corporations that are losing money, must follow the lead of the other corporations in the field. Directors are elected for their business capabilities and judgment and the courts cannot require them to forego their judgment because of the decisions of directors of other companies. Courts may not decide these questions in the absence of a clear showing of dereliction of duty on the part of the specific directors and mere failure to "follow the crowd" is not such a dereliction.

For the foregoing reasons the order of dismissal entered by the trial court is affirmed.

The next case focuses on the *corporate opportunity doctrine*. Rather than adopting the traditional line of business test, the interest or expectancy test, or the fairness test, the court opted for the test promulgated by the American Law Institute (ALI). As set forth in Section 5.05(b) of the ALI's Principles of Corporate Governance, a corporate opportunity is defined as:

> (1) Any opportunity to engage in a business activity of which a director or senior executive becomes aware, either:
> (A) In connection with the performance of functions as a director or senior executive, or under circumstances that should reasonably lead the director or senior executive to believe that the person offering the opportunity expects it to be offered to the corporation; or
> (B) Through the use of corporate information or property, if the resulting opportunity is one that the director or senior executive should reasonably be expected to believe would be of interest to the corporation; or
> (2) Any opportunity to engage in a business activity of which a senior executive [thereby excluding an outside director] becomes aware and knows is closely related to a business in which the corporation is engaged or expects to engage.

NORTHEAST HARBOR GOLF CLUB, INC. V. HARRIS
SUPREME COURT OF MAINE
725 A. 2D 1018 (1999)

Clifford, J.:

Nancy Harris appeals from a judgment ordering equitable relief in favor of Northeast Harbor Golf Club, Inc., following a non-jury trial. Harris contends that the court incorrectly determined that her purchase and development of property surrounding the Club was a corporate opportunity that she usurped, and further contends that any cause of action against her is barred by the statute of limitations and by laches. The Club cross-appeals, contending that, independent of usurping a corporate opportunity, Harris breached her fiduciary duty to the Club when she began developing the property in 1988. Because we conclude that the court correctly determined that Harris usurped a corporate opportunity, but that the statute of limitations period within which the Club could have brought an action against Harris expired … we vacate the judgment.

The Northeast Harbor Golf Club is a Maine corporation operating a golf course located in Mt. Desert. Nancy Harris served as president of the Club from 1971 until August of 1990. The Club is managed by the president and a board of directors. Although the board of directors was empowered to approve policy decisions, it was content to have Harris assume much of the responsibility for the Club's operation. Harris generously contributed to the Club throughout her tenure as president. In addition to her duties as president, she performed other tasks, including mowing and gardening. Moreover, to alleviate the Club's financial difficulties, Harris often purchased equipment for the Club with her own money and either leased or sold it to the corporation for a reduced price to ensure that the Club would not be forced to make substantial cash outlays.

From 1972 until 1984, the board, at Harris's insistence, discussed either purchasing and developing land surrounding the Club or developing some of the Club's real estate in order to raise money. At the 1976 annual meeting, the Club was informed that a consultant, after investigating the matter, had concluded that the Club's land, surrounding the golf course, was suitable for development. In 1977, the board authorized Harris to form a committee to study in more detail developing some of the Club's land. The purpose of development was to improve the financial condition of the Club.

At the 1982 meeting, Harris made it clear that she strongly advocated housing development on Club property and volunteered to finance construction of the first house. Although some directors opposed development, the board eventually approved building houses on Club property by a 14 to 4 vote. At the 1984 annual meeting, Harris presented an "Outline of Proposal for Sale and Management of Excess Land" and the board approved her proposal to sell two lots of Club land to raise revenue. No lots were ever sold.

The subject of this lawsuit is land surrounding the Club that Harris purchased in her own name, some in 1979, and more in 1985. In 1979, in her capacity as Club president, Harris learned of an opportunity to purchase property owned by Lucy Gilpin. The Gilpin property adjoins Club property, including the driveway which provided access to the golf course, the clubhouse, and a portion of the Club's parking lot. Moreover, the Gilpin property is encumbered by an easement that allows golfers to travel from the green of one hole to the tee area of the next hole.

Harris purchased the Gilpin property in her own name for $45,000. She did not disclose her plans to the board prior to acquiring the property. The minutes from the Club's 1979 Board of Directors' meeting stated that "Harris reported that she had recently acquired the Gilpin land adjacent to the old first, second and third holes. Though she intends to hold the land for herself, the golf club will be protected." Harris contends that her statements were made to assure the Club that she would act responsibly, not that she would never develop the land. The board took no action in response to Harris's purchase. Harris testified that at the time she bought the land she had no plans to develop the property and that no such plans were formulated until 1988.

In 1984, Harris, independent of her position with the Club, learned of the availability of property owned by the Smallidge family. The property was surrounded on three sides by the Club and on the fourth side by a house. Harris contracted to purchase eight of the ten interests of the Smallidge heirs in February of 1985, another in March, and the last in June of 1985, for a total of $60,000. Harris disclosed the purchase to the board of directors at the Club's annual meeting on August 28, 1985. At the meeting, she apologized for delaying the construction of a shed approved the previous year, explaining that the construction was delayed because the site was adjacent to the Smallidge property and she did not want to "rock the boat" in her negotiations to purchase the land. She justified the purchase by stating that she wanted the land to remain in "friendly hands." The board took no formal action with respect to Harris's purchase.

In December of 1988, Harris's son filed an application with the Mt. Desert Planning Board to subdivide part of the Gilpin property into five house lots to be named Bushwood. The plan was approved in June of 1991. The board of directors of the Club took no action to oppose the subdivision. A group of the Club's directors, however, formed a separate organization to oppose the subdivision, contending that it violated local zoning ordinances. The effort to oppose the subdivision did not succeed. Eventually the board became divided over development. In 1989, however, the board agreed that it "would not adopt any position" on Harris's son's pending subdivision application. Harris was asked for and gave her resignation in 1990. In 1991, the Club voted to challenge the Bushwood subdivision. The challenge, however, was not successful. … The Club commenced this suit against Harris, on

May 23, 1991, alleging that by purchasing the Gilpin and Smallidge properties she usurped an opportunity that belonged to the Club.

The [trial court called the] Superior Court initially concluded that Harris had not usurped a corporate opportunity because it found that the Club was not in the business of purchasing property and lacked the financial ability to do so. The Club appealed, and we adopted the American Law Institute's (ALI) definition of taking a corporate opportunity, vacated the judgment, and remanded the case to the Superior Court for trial of the facts pursuant to the ALI definition. *See Northeast Harbor Golf Club, Inc. v. Harris,* 661 A. 2d 1146 (Me. 1995). After remand, the Superior Court found that Harris had usurped a corporate opportunity and that the Club's claim was not barred by the statute of limitations. The court entered a judgment for the Club, imposed a constructive trust on the property owned by Harris, and ordered Harris to convey the properties to the Club on payment of the purchase price and interest and taxes. These appeals by Harris and the Club followed.

I . Appeal by Harris

A. Corporate Opportunity

Harris concedes that, because she learned of the opportunity to purchase the Gilpin property in her capacity as president of the Club, her purchase of that property in 1979 constituted the taking of a corporate opportunity. She disputes liability, relying on the statute of limitations and laches. Harris contends that because she learned of the availability of the Smallidge property independent of her position as an officer of the Club, and because the purchase of that land was not closely related to the Club's business, that there was no usurpation of a corporate opportunity. In reviewing the decision of the Superior Court, we defer to the historical factual findings of the court, but the determination of whether an opportunity is a "corporate opportunity" is a question of law that we review *de novo.*

Even if the opportunity to engage in a business activity, in which the officer or director becomes involved, is not learned of through her connection to the business of the corporation, nevertheless, such an opportunity may be considered a corporate opportunity if the officer or director knows it "is closely related to a business in which the corporation is engaged or expects to engage." [American Law Institute,] Principles of Corporate Governance § 5.05(b)(2).

The central feature of the ALI test is the strict requirement of full disclosure prior to taking advantage of any corporate opportunity. This feature was designed to prevent individual directors and officers from substituting their own judgment for that of the corporation when determining whether it would be in the corporate interest, or whether the corporation is financially or otherwise able to take advantage of an opportunity. ... Doubt about the financial capacity of a corporation to pursue an opportunity may affect the incentive of a director of officer to solve corporate financing problems, and evidence regarding the corporation's financial status is often controlled by the usurping corporate director or officer. ... The ALI approach recognizes the danger in allowing an individual director or officer to determine whether a corporation has the ability to take an opportunity, and accordingly disclosure to the corporation is required.

Full disclosure is likewise important to prevent individual directors and officers from using their own unfettered judgment to determine whether the business opportunity is related to the corporation's business, such that it would be in the corporate interest to take advantage of that opportunity. "The appropriate method to determine whether or not a corporate opportunity exists is to let the corporation decide at the time the opportunity is presented." ... This rule protects individual directors and officers because after disclosing the potential opportunity to the corporation, they can pursue their own business ventures free from the possibility of a lawsuit. If there is doubt as to whether a business opportunity is closely related to the business of the corporation, that doubt must be resolved in favor of the corporation so that the officer or director will have a strong incentive to disclose any business opportunity even remotely related to the business of the corporation.

In this case, the Club's normal business is maintaining and operating a golf course. That business is dependent on having sufficient land for the course itself and ensuring that the activity of golf is not hindered or affected by development of adjacent and surrounding property. The Club had frequently discussed developing some of its own land and on one occasion talked about the possibility of purchasing and developing adjacent land. The purchase of the Smallidge land, surrounded as it is on three sides by the Club's land and adjacent to three of its golf holes, ... is sufficiently related to the Club's business to constitute a corporate opportunity. Accordingly, Harris would be liable to the Club for taking advantage of a corporate opportunity for purchases of both the Gilpin and Smallidge properties unless the Club's action is barred by the statute of limitations, or is otherwise barred by laches.

...

[The court thereafter held that the statute of limitations had expired and ordered entry of judgment for the defendant Harris.]

The two cases that follow likewise focus on alleged breaches of the fiduciary duty of loyalty—either due to alleged self dealing transactions or other alleged misconduct that improperly benefitted the defendant fiduciaries.

BENIHANA OF TOKYO, INC. V. BENIHANA, INC.
SUPREME COURT OF DELAWARE
906 A. 2D 114 (2006)

Berger, J.:

In this appeal, we consider whether Benihana, Inc. was authorized to issue $20 million in preferred stock and whether Benihana's board of directors acted properly in approving the transaction. We conclude that the Court of Chancery's factual findings are supported by the record and that it correctly applied settled law in holding that the stock issuance was lawful and that the directors did not breach their fiduciary duties. Accordingly, we affirm.

Factual and Procedural Background

Rocky Aoki founded Benihana of Tokyo, Inc. (BOT), and its subsidiary, Benihana, which own and operate Benihana restaurants in the United States and other countries. Aoki owned 100% of BOT until 1998, when he pled guilty to insider trading charges. In order to avoid licensing problems created by this status as a convicted felon, Aoki transferred his stock to the Benihana Protective Trust. The trustees of the Trust were Aoki's three children (Kana Aoki Nootenboom,

Kyle Aoki, and Kevin Aoki) and Darwin Dornbush (who was then the family's attorney, a Benihana director, and, effectively, the company's general counsel).

Benihana, a Delaware corporation, has two classes of common stock. There are approximately 6 million shares of Class A common stock outstanding. Each share has 1/10 vote and the holders of Class A common are entitled to elect 25% of the directors. [Regarding the second class, there] are approximately 3 million shares of Common stock outstanding. Each share of Common has one vote and the holders of Common stock are entitled to elect the remaining 75% of Benihana's directors. Before the transaction at issue, BOT owned 50.9% of the Common stock and 2% of the Class A stock. The nine member board of directors is classified and the directors serve three-year terms.

In 2003, shortly after Aoki married Keiko Aoki, conflicts arose between Aoki and his children. In August, the children were upset to learn that Aoki had changed his will to give Keiko control over BOT. Joel Schwartz, Benihana's president and chief executive officer, also was concerned about this change in control. He discussed the situation with Dornbush, and they briefly considered various options, including the issuance of sufficient Class A stock to trigger a provision in the certificate of incorporation that would allow the Common and Class A to vote together for 75% of the directors.

The Aoki family's turmoil came at a time when Benihana also was facing challenges. Many of its restaurants were old and outmoded. Benihana hired WD Partners to evaluate its facilities and to plan and design appropriate renovations. The resulting Construction and Renovation Plan anticipated that the project would take at least five years and cost $56 million or more. Wachovia offered to provide Benihana a $60 million line of credit for the Construction and Renovation Plan, but the restrictions Wachovia imposed made it unlikely that Benihana would be able to borrow the full amount. Because the Wachovia line of credit did not assure that Benihana would have the capital it needed, the company retained Morgan Joseph & Co. to develop other financing options.

On January 9, 2004, after evaluating Benihana's financial situation and needs, Fred Joseph, of Morgan Joseph, met with Schwartz, Dornbush and John E. Abdo, the board's executive committee. Joseph expressed concern that Benihana would not have sufficient available capital to complete the Construction and Renovation Plan and pursue appropriate acquisitions. Benihana was conservatively leveraged, and Joseph discussed various financing alternatives, including bank debt, high yield debt, convertible debt or preferred stock, equity and sale/leaseback options.

The full board met with Joseph on January 29, 2004. He reviewed all the financing alternatives that he had discussed with the executive committee, and recommended that Benihana issue convertible preferred stock. Joseph explained that the preferred stock would provide the funds needed for the Construction and Renovation Plan and also put the company in a better negotiating position if it sought additional financing from Wachovia.

Joseph gave the directors a board book, marked "Confidential," containing an analysis of the proposed stock issuance (the Transaction). ...

The board met again on February 17, 2004, to review the terms of the Transaction. The directors discussed Benihana's preferences and Joseph predicted what a buyer likely would expect or require. For example, Schwartz asked Joseph to try to negotiate a minimum on the dollar value for transactions that would be deemed "material corporation transactions" and subject to the buyer's approval. Schwartz wanted to give the buyer only one board seat, but Joseph said that Benihana might have to give up two. Joseph told the board that he was not sure that a buyer would agree to an issuance in two tranches, and that it would be difficult to make the second tranche non-mandatory. As the Court of Chancery found, the board understood that the preferred terms were akin to a "wish list."

Shortly after the February meeting, Abdo contacted Joseph and told him that BFC Financial Corporation was interested in buying the new convertible stock. In April 2005, Joseph sent BFC a private placement memorandum. Abdo negotiated with Joseph for several weeks. They agreed to the Transaction on the following basic terms: (i) $20 million issuance in two tranches of $10 million each, with the second tranche to be issued one to three years after the first; (ii) BFC obtained one seat on the board, and one additional seat if Benihana failed to pay dividends for two consecutive quarters; (iii) BFC obtained preemptive rights on any new voting securities; (iv) 5% dividend; (v) 15% conversion premium; (vi) BFC had the right to force Benihana to redeem the preferred stock in full after ten years; and (vii) the stock would have immediate "as if converted" voting rights. Joseph testified that he was satisfied with the negotiations, as he had obtained what he wanted with respect to the most important points.

On April 22, 2004, Abdo sent a memorandum to Dornbush, Schwartz and Joseph, listing the agreed terms of the Transaction. He did not send the memorandum to any other members of the Benihana board. Schwartz did tell [directors] Becker, Sturges, Sano, and possibly Pine that BFC was the potential buyer. At its next meeting, held on May 6, 2004, the entire board was officially informed of BFC's involvement in the Transaction. Abdo made a presentation on behalf of BFC and then left the meeting. Joseph distributed an updated board book, which explained that Abdo had approached Morgan Joseph on behalf of BFC, and included the negotiated terms. The trial court found that the board was not informed that Abdo had negotiated the deal on behalf of BFC. But the board did know that Abdo was a principal of BFC. After discussion, the board reviewed and approved the Transaction, subject to the receipt of a fairness opinion.

On May 18, 2004, after he learned that Morgan Joseph was providing a fairness opinion, Schwartz publicly announced the stock issuance. Two days later, Aoki's counsel sent a letter asking the board to abandon the Transaction and pursue other, more favorable, financing alternatives. The letter expressed concern about the directors' conflicts, the dilutive effect of the stock issuance, and its "questionable legality." Schwartz gave copies of the letter to the directors at the May 20 board meeting, and Dornbush advised that he did not believe that Aoki's concerns had merit. Joseph and another Morgan Joseph representative then joined the meeting by telephone and opined that the Transaction was fair from a financial point of view. The board then approved the Transaction.

During the following two weeks, Benihana received three alternative financing proposals. Schwartz asked Becker, Pine and Sturges to act as an independent committee and review the first offer. The committee decided that the offer was inferior and not worth pursuing. Morgan Joseph agreed with that assessment. Schwartz referred the next two proposals to Morgan Joseph, with the same result.

On June 8, 2004, Benihana and BFC executed the Stock Purchase Agreement. On June 11, 2004, the board met and approved resolutions ratifying the execution of the Stock Purchase Agreement and authorizing the stock issuance. Schwartz then reported on the three alternative proposals that had been rejected by the ad hoc committee and Morgan Joseph. On July 2, 2004, BOT filed this action against all of Benihana's directors, except Kevin Aoki, alleging breaches of fiduciary duties; and against BFC, alleging that it aided and abetted the fiduciary violations. Three months later, as the parties were filing their pre-trial briefs, the board again reviewed the Transaction. After considering the allegations in the amended complaint, the board voted once more to approve it. The Court of Chancery held a four day trial in November 2004. In December 2005, after post-trial briefing and argument, the trial court issued an opinion holding that Benihana was authorized to issue the preferred stock with preemptive rights, and that the board's approval of the Transaction was a valid exercise of business judgment. This appeal followed.

Discussion

...

BOT maintains that the trial court erred in finding that [the Benihana board of directors] acted properly in approving the Transaction. Specifically, BOT argues that the Court of Chancery erred: (1) by applying 8 Del. C. § 144(a)(1), because the board did not know all material facts before it approved the Transaction; (2) by applying the business judgment rule, because Abdo breached his fiduciary duties; and (3) by finding that the board's primary purpose in approving the Transaction was not to dilute BOT's voting power.

A. Section 144(a)(1) Approval

Section 144 of the Delaware General Corporation Law provides a safe harbor for interested transactions, like this one, if "[t]he material facts as to the director's ... relationship or interest and as to the contract or transaction are disclosed or are known to the board of directors ... and the board ... in good faith authorizes the contract or transaction by the affirmative votes of a majority of the disinterested directors. ... " After approval by disinterested directors, courts review the interested transaction under the business judgment rule, which "is a presumption that in making a business decision, the directors of a corporation acted on an informed basis, in good faith and in the honest belief that the action taken was in the best interest of the company."

BOT argues that § 144(a)(1) is inapplicable because, when they approved the Transaction, the disinterested directors did not know that Abdo had negotiated the terms for BFC. Abdo's role as negotiator is material, according to BOT, because Abdo had been given the confidential term sheet prepared by Joseph and knew which of those terms Benihana was prepared to give up during negotiations. We agree that the board needed to know about Abdo's involvement in order to make an informed decision. The record clearly establishes, however, that the board possessed that material information when it approved the Transaction on May 6, 2004 and May 20, 2004.

Shortly before the May 6 meeting, Schwartz told Becker, Sturges and Sano that BFC was the proposed buyer. Then, at the meeting, Abdo made the presentation on behalf of BFC. Joseph's board book also explained that Abdo had made the initial contact that precipitated the negotiations. The board members knew that Abdo is a director, vice-chairman, and one of two people who control BFC. Thus, although no one ever said, "Abdo negotiated this deal for BFC," the directors understood that he was BFC's representative in the Transaction. As Pine testified, "whoever actually did the negotiating, [Abdo] as a principal would have to agree to it. So whether he sat in the room and negotiated it or he sat somewhere else and was brought the results of someone else's negotiation, he was the ultimate decision-maker." Accordingly, we conclude that the disinterested directors possessed all the material information on Abdo's interest in the Transaction, and their approval at the May 6 and May 20 board meetings satisfies § 144(a)(1).

B. Abdo's Alleged Fiduciary Violation

BOT next argues that the Court of Chancery should have reviewed the Transaction under an entire fairness standard because Abdo breached his duty of loyalty when he used Benihana's confidential information to negotiate on behalf of BFC. This argument starts with a flawed premise. The record does not support BOT's contention that Abdo used any confidential information against Benihana. Even without Joseph's comments at the February 17 board meeting, Abdo knew the terms a buyer could expect to obtain in a deal like this. Moreover, as the trial court found, "the negotiations involved give and take on a number of points" and Benihana "ended up where [it] wanted to be" for the most important terms. Abdo did not set the terms of the deal; he did not deceive the board; and he did not dominate or control the other directors' approval of the Transaction. In short, the record does not support the claim that Abdo breached his duty of loyalty.

C. Dilution of BOT's Voting Power

Finally, BOT argues that the board's primary purpose in approving the Transaction was to dilute BOT's voting control. BOT points out that Schwartz was concerned about BOT's control in 2003 and even discussed with Dornbush the possibility of issuing a huge number of Class A shares. Then, despite the availability of other financing options, the board decided on a stock issuance, and agreed to give BFC "as if converted" voting rights. According to BOT, the trial court overlooked this powerful evidence of the board's improper purpose.

It is settled law that, "corporate action ... may not be taken for the sole or primary purpose of entrenchment." Here, however, the trial court found that "the primary purpose of the ... Transaction was to provide what the directors subjectively believed to be the best financing vehicle available for securing the necessary funds to pursue the agreed upon Construction and Renovation Plan for the Benihana restaurants." That factual determination has ample record support, especially in light of the trial court's credibility determinations. Accordingly, we defer to the Court of of Chancery's conclusion that the board's approval of the Transaction was a valid exercise of its business judgment, for a proper corporate purpose.

Conclusion

Based on the foregoing, the judgment of the Court of Chancery is affirmed.

GILDER V. PGA TOUR, INC.
UNITED STATES COURT OF APPEALS
936 F. 2D 417 (NINTH CIRCUIT 1991)

Tang, Circuit Judge:

Karsten Manufacturing Corporation and eight professional golf players challenge the implementation of a new rule by the PGA Tour

(PGA) banning clubs with U-shaped grooves. Karsten and the professional player plaintiffs challenge the actions of the PGA on antitrust and state law grounds. After a three day hearing, the district court granted a preliminary injunction enjoining the PGA from implementing the rule. The PGA appeals. We affirm.

Factual and Procedural Background

This action concerns a rule change implemented by the PGA that bans all clubs on which the cross-section of the grooves on the face of the club is in the shape of a square or "U" as opposed to a "V":

Karsten Manufacturing Corporation (Karsten) designs, manufactures, and sells a variety of golf equipment including: putters, woods, golf bags, and "Ping Eye 2" golf clubs. All of Karsten's Ping Eye 2 golf clubs have U-shaped grooves. Karsten's marketing strategy is that it supplies the same equipment to the amateur as to the professional. Karsten maintains that the U-groove rule will harm its reputation if it is forced to make what the company feels is an inferior product with V-grooves.

Bob Gilder and the seven other plaintiffs in this action are eight professional golfers who are members of the PGA. Each of the eight professionals players uses Karsten's Ping Eye 2 clubs on the Tour.

The defendants in this action are the PGA; Dean A. Beman, the Commissioner and Chief Executive Officer of the PGA; and E. Mandell de Windt, Roger E. Birk, and Hugh E. Culverhouse, members of the PGA Tour Tournament Policy Board. The PGA is the organization which administers professional golf tournaments for the regular Tour and the Senior Tour.

The PGA Policy Board is composed of ten directors. Four of the directors are players elected from the membership of the PGA. The board also includes three officers of the PGA of America and three independent directors with no ties to golf. The independent directors volunteer their time.

In 1984, the United States Golf Association (USGA) changed the rules of golf to allow grooves in the shape of a U. Karsten developed its U-groove club. In 1985, players on the Tour began to complain that the U-groove golf clubs were detracting from the skill level of the game. These players complained that the U-grooves imparted more spin on the golf ball and thus provided greater control for shots from grassy lies of the rough. This characteristic offsets the advantage of players with the skill necessary to keep the golf shot in the fairways.[1]

In January 1987, the USGA conducted tests and concluded that the U-grooves impart more spin on the ball than V-grooves. However, in June 1987, the USGA concluded that there was not enough information to bar clubs with the U-grooves.

On August 10, 1987, the PGA released the results of an equipment survey. One hundred seventy-one of the two hundred golfers on the tour had responded. Of those, seventy-three percent responded that they used U-groove clubs. When asked the advantages of the club, seventy-four percent indicated that the grooves provide for greater control from the wet grass and rough. When asked if the PGA should ban the U-groove, sixty percent responded in the affirmative.

In September 1987, Commissioner Beman wrote to all the gold club manufacturers advising them that the PGA had engaged two technical experts to study the issue of the U-groove. The letter asked the manufacturers to provide pertinent information and relevant data. Karsten did not respond to this request.

In November of 1987, the independent testing expert conducted elaborate field tests trying to localize the effect of the groove. The PGA gave the resulting data to two separate consulting groups, one at the University of Texas and one at the University of Delaware. Each of the Universities devised its own methodology to interpret the data. Both studies concluded that the U-grooves impart more spin to the golf ball than the V-grooves. …

On May 12, 1988, Commissioner Beman recommended to the board that a proposed rule change banning U-grooves be circulated for public comment. On May 24, 1988, the board accepted Beman's recommendation. The PGA received comments from some manufacturers and the PGA made some changes in the rule.

On August 16, 1988, the PGA deferred action on the proposed rule until the USGA conducted further player study. The USGA tests confirmed that balls hit from the rough with U-grooves have a different spin rate than those hit with the V-grooves. The USGA determined, however, that the tests did not show a significant enough difference to ban the clubs with U-grooves.

1. The grass on the fairways is kept short enough to provide a good lie for the golf ball. The areas of the "rough" have taller grass which provides for a bad lie for the golf ball. A golfer in the fairway has an advantage over a golfer whose ball lands in the grassy area of the "rough."

Beman recommended that the PGA Policy Board adopt the U-groove ban. The PGA's bylaws at that time required a majority of the directors present and three of the player directors to vote on any rule change. At its February 28, 1989 meeting, the four player directors and the PGA officer directors abstained from voting because of conflicts of interest. Each of the abstaining directors had ties to golf club manufacturers. The three independent directors unanimously voted for the rule. The effective date of the rule was January 1, 1990.

Karsten contracted the PGA on June 23, 1989. Karsten met with the PGA to express its concerns on August 14, 1989. At that meeting, Karsten argued, based on its own testing, that the U-grooves do not affect the spin of the ball.

...

On December 5, 1989, all ten members of the PGA board met in a special session. At that meeting, all ten directors voted to change the bylaws of the PGA so that the disinterested members could take binding action on behalf of the PGA policy board when the majority of the directors could not vote because of a conflict. The three disinterested directors then unanimously voted to readopt the groove rule.

Karsten's suit came on for an evidentiary hearing on December 15, 19, and 20, 1989. At the hearing, John Solheim, Karsten's Vice-President, testified that the believes that the U-grooves do not improve player performance.

At the hearing, Karsten presented an economist from Arizona State University, Dr. Richard Smith, who testified that the grooves had not had a negative effect on the PGA. ...

Two of the plaintiff players testified at the hearing. Bob Gilder testified that switching clubs would hurt his game, which in turn would affect his endorsement income. Gilder has been using Ping clubs since 1970. He likes the design and dynamics of the club. He cannot identify a difference in the club based on the shape of the grooves. He had switched to the Ping Eye 2 clubs in October of 1989. Gilder testified that he would probably use the Ping Eye 2 clubs with V-grooves if Karsten manufactured them.

George Lanning testified that he is a left-handed golfer. Lanning testified to his belief that Karsten makes the only quality left-handed clubs on the market. He further testified that he might lose his exemption card, which allows him to play on the Tour, if he is forced to change clubs.

Tom Kite, the all-time leading money winner on the Tour, testified that U-grooves diminished the skill factor of the game because the clubs offset the traditional advantage of being able to hit the ball in the fairway of the golf course.

Commissioner Beman testified that the issuance of the preliminary injunction would have dire consequences for the PGA. He testified that the PGA would not be able to propagate any rules for the professional tournaments that it oversees.

After this lengthy evidentiary hearing, the district court held that Karsten and the professional player plaintiffs had demonstrated that (1) they had a reasonable chance of success on the merits, (2) they would suffer irreparable injury if the injunction were not imposed, (3) the balance of hardships tips sharply in favor of the plaintiffs, and (4) there are serious questions for litigation. The PGA appeals.

...

Discussion

...

The district court concluded that the professional player plaintiffs would be irreparably harmed if they were forced to abandon their Ping Eye 2 clubs and use different clubs. Testimony supported this conclusion. The players' testimony showed that the ban would affect the ability of the professional player plaintiffs to qualify in future tournaments and their ability to secure endorsements.

...

Here, the district court found that the professional player plaintiffs have demonstrated they will suffer an immediate threatened injury. The professionals will be irreparably harmed if they are forced to change clubs because they would be at a competitive disadvantage. They testified that the ban on clubs will force them to change their club selection and will have a detrimental effect on their golf game. They further testified that this forced club change would have an immediately discernible but unquantifiable adverse impact on their earnings, their ability to maintain their eligibility for the tour, and for endorsement contracts. This testimony was supported by cross-examination of Commissioner Beman and Tom Kite. The difficulty in quantifying the injury done to the professionals does not make their injuries speculative. ... Therefore, the district court's conclusion that the professionals have established that they will suffer irreparable harm if the ban is enforced is not clearly erroneous.

With regard to Karsten Manufacturing, the district court found that Karsten would be required to redesign its clubs, retool its manufacturing process, and abandon its well-established U-groove market. Additionally, Karsten has produced evidence tending to show that the U-groove ban appears to have harmed Karsten's reputation as a golf club manufacturer.

...

Fiduciary Duty and By-Law Analysis

The district court held that there were substantial questions raised about the propriety of the manner in which the board passed the U-groove ban. The individual professional player plaintiffs have alleged that the PGA directors breached their fiduciary duties by breaching the by-laws, directly and indirectly, and by voting on an issue in which they had conflicting financial interests.

To the extent that the individual plaintiffs are members of the PGA organization, the individual plaintiffs argue that the members of the board of directors owe them a fiduciary duty. The professional player plaintiffs argue that the player directors and the officer directors have a duty to act "in the best interests of the corporation and [they are] prohibited from using [their] position ... for [their] private gain." ... The PGA argues that Maryland law allows interested directors to act after full disclosure to the board and approval by the non-interested directors. ... However, that statute only states that a contract or transaction is not void or voidable *solely* on the basis that an interested director voted on it. That section does not address whether there is a violation of the director's fiduciary duties when the interested director votes. ...

The district court held that the first vote of the PGA Policy Board violated the by-laws of the PGA. The by-laws required the player directors to vote on rule changes. However, the district court found that none of the player directors voted to adopt the U-groove ban in violation of those by-laws because each of the player directors had a financial conflict. This conflict was due to ties to competing manufacturers of gold clubs. Subsequently, each of the directors voted to change the by-laws to allow the noninterested directors to vote, in the very same meeting and possibly with the intention of allowing the other directors to pass the regulation. Voting on a matter on which a director has a conflict of interest may violate that director's fiduciary duty. A court "may intervene to prevent (or annul) conduct on the part of directors that is fraudulent or represents a breach of their fiduciary obligations." ...

We are not prepared to rule on the merits of these questions at this stage of the litigation and on this undeveloped record. We hold only that the district court did not abuse its discretion in determining that this case raises serious questions that must be resolved at trial.

The next case is one of the premier decisions in Delaware company law. The Delaware Supreme Court resolves a fundamental issue—what constitutes self-dealing by a corporate fiduciary. The court answers this question in the context of a parent corporation that allegedly exercised control over its subsidiary in order to receive improper financial benefits to the detriment of the subsidiary and the subsidiary's other shareholders.

SINCLAIR OIL CORPORATION V. LEVIEN
SUPREME COURT OF DELAWARE
280 A. 2D 717 (1971)

Wolcott, J.

This is an appeal by the defendant, Sinclair Oil Corporation (hereafter Sinclair), from an order of the Court of Chancery in a derivative action requiring Sinclair to account for damages sustained by its subsidiary, Sinclair Venezuelan Oil Company (hereafter Sinven), organized by Sinclair for the purpose of operating in Venezuela, as a result of dividends paid by Sinven, the denial to Sinven of industrial development, and a breach of contract between Sinclair's wholly-owned subsidiary, Sinclair International Oil Company, and Sinven.

Sinclair, operating primarily as a holding company, is in the business of exploring for oil and of producing and marketing crude oil and oil products. At all times relevant to this litigation, it owned about 97% of Sinven's stock. The plaintiff owns about 3000 of 120,000 publicly held shares of Sinven. Sinven, incorporated in 1922, has been engaged in petroleum operations primarily in Venezuela and since 1959 has operated exclusively in Venezuela.

Sinclair nominates all members of Sinven's board of directors. The Chancellor found as a fact that the directors were not independent of Sinclair. Almost without exception, they were officers, directors, or employees of corporations in the Sinclair complex. By reason of Sinclair's domination, it is clear that Sinclair owed Sinven a fiduciary duty.

The Chancellor held that because of Sinclair's fiduciary duty and its control over Sinven, its relationship with Sinven must meet the test of intrinsic fairness. The standard of intrinsic fairness involves both a high degree of fairness and a shift in the burden of proof. Under this standard the burden is on Sinclair to prove, subject to careful judicial scrutiny, that its transactions with Sinven were objectively fair.

Sinclair argues that the transactions between it and Sinven should be tested, not by the test of intrinsic fairness with the accompanying shift of the burden of proof, but by the business judgment rule under which a court will not interfere with the judgment of a board of directors unless there is a showing of gross and palpable overreaching. A board of directors enjoys a presumption of sound business judgment, and its decisions will not be disturbed if they can be attributed to any rational business purpose. A court under such circumstances will not substitute its own notions of what is or is not sound business judgment.

We think, however, that Sinclair's argument in this respect is misconceived. When the situation involves a parent and a subsidiary, with the parent controlling the transaction and fixing the terms, the test of intrinsic fairness, with its resulting shifting of the burden of proof, is applied. The basic situation for the application of the rule is the one in which the parent has received a benefit to the exclusion and at the expense of the subsidiary.

[T]his court dealt with the question of fairness in parent-subsidiary dealings in *Getty Oil Co. v. Skelly Oil Co.*, [267 A. 2d 883 (Del. 1970)]. In that case, both parent and subsidiary were in the business of refining and marketing crude oil and crude oil products. The Oil Import Board ruled that the subsidiary, because it was controlled by the parent, was no longer entitled to a separate allocation of imported crude oil. The subsidiary then contended that it had a right to share the quota of crude oil allotted to the parent. We ruled that the business judgment standard should be applied to determine this contention. Although the subsidiary suffered a loss through the administration of the oil import quotas, the parent gained nothing. The parent's quota was derived solely from its own past use. The past use of the subsidiary did not cause an increase in the parent's quota. Nor did the parent usurp a quota of the subsidiary. Since the parent received nothing from the subsidiary to the exclusion of the minority stockholders of the subsidiary, there was no self-dealing. Therefore, the business judgment standard was properly applied.

A parent does indeed owe a fiduciary duty to its subsidiary when there are parent-subsidiary dealings. However, this alone will not evoke the intrinsic fairness standard. This standard will be applied only when the fiduciary duty is accompanied by self-dealing—the situation when a parent is on both sides of a transaction with its subsidiary. Self-dealing occurs when the parent, by virtue of its domination of the subsidiary, causes the subsidiary to act in such a way that the parent receives something from the subsidiary to the exclusion of, and detriment to, the minority stockholders of the subsidiary.

We turn now to the facts. The plaintiff argues that, from 1960 through 1966, Sinclair caused Sinven to pay out such excessive dividends that the industrial development of Sinven was effectively prevented, and it became in reality a corporation in dissolution.

From 1960 through 1966, Sinven paid out $108,000,000 in dividends ($38,000,000 in excess of Sinven's earnings during the same period). The Chancellor held that Sinclair caused these dividends to be paid during a period when it had a need for large amounts of cash. Although the dividends paid exceeded earnings, the plaintiff concedes that the payments were made in compliance with 8 Del. C. § 170, authorizing payment of dividends out of surplus or net profits. However, the plaintiff attacks these dividends on the ground that they resulted from an improper motive—Sinclair's need for cash. The Chancellor, applying the intrinsic fairness standard, held that Sinclair did not sustain its burden of proving that these dividends were intrinsically fair to the minority stockholders of Sinven.

Since it is admitted that the dividends were paid in strict compliance with 8 Del. C. § 170, the alleged excessiveness of the payments alone would not state a cause of action. Nevertheless, compliance with the applicable statute may not, under all circumstances, justify all dividend payments. If a plaintiff can meet his burden of proving that a dividend cannot be grounded on any reasonable business objective, then the courts can and will interfere with the board's decision to pay the dividend.

Sinclair contends that it is improper to apply the intrinsic fairness standard to dividend payments even when the board which voted for the dividends is completely dominated. …

We do not accept the argument that the intrinsic fairness test can never be applied to a dividend declaration by a dominated board, although a dividend declaration by a dominated board will not inevitably demand the application of the intrinsic fairness standard. If such a dividend is in essence self-dealing by the parent, then the intrinsic fairness standard is the proper standard. For example, suppose a parent dominates a subsidiary and its board of directors. The subsidiary has outstanding two classes of stock, X and Y. Class X is owned by the parent and Class Y is owned by minority stockholders of the subsidiary. If the subsidiary, at the direction of the parent, declares a dividend on its Class X stock only, this might well be self-dealing by the parent. It would be receiving something from the subsidiary to the exclusion of and detrimental to its minority stockholders. This self-dealing, coupled with the parent's fiduciary duty, would make intrinsic fairness the proper standard by which to evaluate the dividend payments.

Consequently it must be determined whether the dividend payments by Sinven were, in essence, self-dealing by Sinclair. The dividends resulted in great sums of money being transferred from Sinven to Sinclair. However, a proportionate share of this money was received by the minority shareholders of Sinven. Sinclair received nothing from Sinven to the exclusion of its minority stockholders. As such, these dividends were not self-dealing. We hold therefore that the Chancellor erred in applying the intrinsic fairness test as to these dividend payments. The business judgment standard should have been applied.

We conclude that the facts demonstrate that the dividend payments complied with the business judgment standard. … The motives for causing the declaration of dividends are immaterial unless the plaintiff can show that the dividend payments resulted from improper motives and amounted to waste. The plaintiff contends only that the dividend payments drained Sinven of cash to such an extent that it was prevented from expanding.

The plaintiff proved no business opportunities which came to Sinven independently and which Sinclair either took to itself or denied to Sinven. As a matter of fact, with two minor exceptions which resulted in losses, all of Sinven's operations have been conducted in Venezuela, and Sinclair had a policy of exploiting its oil properties located in different countries by subsidiaries located in the particular countries.

From 1960 to 1966 Sinclair purchased or developed oil fields in Alaska, Canada, Paraguay, and other places around the world. The plaintiff contends that these were all opportunities which could have been taken by Sinven. The Chancellor concluded that Sinclair had not proved that its denial of expansion opportunities to Sinven was intrinsically fair. He based this conclusion on the following findings of fact. Sinclair made no real effort to expand Sinven. The excessive dividends paid by Sinven resulted in so great a cash drain as to effectively deny to Sinven any ability to expand. During this same period Sinclair actively pursued a company-wide policy of developing through its subsidiaries new sources of revenue, but Sinven was not permitted to participate and was confined in its activities to Venezuela.

However, the plaintiff could point to no opportunities which came to Sinven. Therefore, Sinclair usurped no business opportunity belonging to Sinven. Since Sinclair received nothing from Sinven to the exclusion of and detriment to Sinven's minority stockholders, there was no self-dealing. Therefore, business judgment is the proper standard by which to evaluate Sinclair's expansion policies.

Since there is no proof of self-dealing on the part of Sinclair, it follows that the expansion policy of Sinclair and the methods used to achieve the desired result must, as far as Sinclair's treatment of Sinven is concerned, be tested by the standards of the business judgment rule. Accordingly, Sinclair's decision, absent fraud or gross overreaching, to achieve expansion through the medium of its subsidiaries, other than Sinven, must be upheld.

Even if Sinclair was wrong in developing these opportunities as it did, the question arises, with which subsidiaries should these opportunities have been shared? No evidence indicates a unique need or ability of Sinven to develop these opportunities. The decision of which subsidiaries would be used to implement Sinclair's expansion policy was one of business judgment with which a court will not interfere absent a showing of gross and palpable overreaching. ... No such showing has been made here.

Next, Sinclair argues that the Chancellor committed error when he held it liable to Sinven for breach of contract.

In 1961 Sinclair created Sinclair International Oil Company (hereafter International), a wholly owned subsidiary used for the purpose of coordinating all of Sinclair's foreign operations. All crude purchases by Sinclair were made thereafter through International.

On September 28, 1961, Sinclair caused Sinven to contract with International whereby Sinven agreed to sell all of its crude oil and refined products to International at specified prices. The contract provided for minimum and maximum quantities and prices. The plaintiff contends that Sinclair caused this contract to be breached in two respects. Although the contract called for payment on receipt, International's payments lagged as much as 30 days after receipt. Also, the contract required International to purchase at least a fixed minimum amount of crude and refined products from Sinven. International did not comply with this requirement.

Clearly, Sinclair's act of contracting with its dominated subsidiary was self-dealing. Under the contract Sinclair received the products produced by Sinven, and of course the minority shareholders of Sinven were not able to share in the receipt of these products. If the contract was breached, then Sinclair received these products to the detriment of Sinven's minority shareholders. We agree with the Chancellor's finding that the contract was breached by Sinclair, both as to the time of payments and the amounts purchased.

Although a parent need not bind itself by a contract with its dominated subsidiary, Sinclair chose to operate in this manner. As Sinclair has received the benefits of this contract, so must it comply with the contractual duties.

Under the intrinsic fairness standard, Sinclair must prove that its causing Sinven not to enforce the contract was intrinsically fair to the minority shareholders of Sinven. Sinclair has failed to meet this burden. Late payments were clearly breaches for which Sinven should have sought and received adequate damages. As to the quantities purchased, Sinclair argues that it purchased all the products produced by Sinven. This, however, does not satisfy the standard of intrinsic fairness. Sinclair has failed to prove that Sinven could not possibly have produced or some way have obtained the contract minimums. As such, Sinclair must account on this claim.

...

We will therefore reverse that part of the Chancellor's order that requires Sinclair to account to Sinven for damages sustained as a result of dividends paid between 1960 and 1966, and by reason of the denial to Sinven of expansion during that period. We will affirm the remaining portion of that order and remand the cause for further proceedings.

In this chapter as well as in Chapter 3, we focus on the principle that minority shareholders in closely-held corporations may be entitled to have their "reasonable expectations" met. Actions by the majority that frustrate these reasonable expectations (which may include officer and director positions, employment with reasonable salary and adequate dividend payouts) may be deemed oppressive. Such oppressive conduct may entitle the minority shareholders to procure significant relief, including a buyout of such shareholder's stock at fair value. The case that follows provides a very recent example.

RITCHIE V. RUPE
COURT OF APPEALS OF TEXAS
339 S.W. 3D 275 (2011)

[THIS CASE IS CONTAINED IN THE CHAPTER 3 CASE STUDIES OF THIS BOOK, PAGES 94–109.]

SCENARIO

Josh DeLoach is the chief operating officer (COO) of Marathon Business Corporation (Marathon) and also is a Marathon director. Marathon's business is the purchase of real estate, construction of single family residences on these properties, and subsequent sale of these homes principally to families. Marathon's current operations are conducted solely in Maryland and Pennsylvania.

DeLoach believes he can make way more money than he currently is earning and incorporates his own real estate company (DeLoach Real Estate Corporation). Without Marathon's knowledge, DeLoach commences operations of his own Company (with the same functions as Marathon) situated solely in Virginia. He continues working a 40 hour week for Marathon, devoting his off-duty time to DeLoach Real Estate Corporation. Based upon his relationships with Marathon's bankers, DeLoach obtains significant financing from these bankers for his Company to purchase real estate and build houses in Virginia.

CASE STUDIES

Through the years, DeLoach has become very knowledgeable of Marathon's business strategy, including construction design, products used, pricing, consumer profiles, and marketing techniques. Six months after DeLoach Real Estate Corporation sells its first house to a buyer, DeLoach resigns from Marathon (again without informing Marathon of the existence of DeLoach Real Estate Corporation). Three months thereafter Marathon finds out about DeLoach's "outside" activities and sues him for breach of fiduciary duty. What result and why? If you were advising DeLoach prior to his starting of another business, what would you advise?

Chapter 7

SHAREHOLDER LITIGATION: DERIVATIVE AND DIRECT SUITS

WHEN SHAREHOLDERS BELIEVE they have been injured by the perceived misconduct of corporate directors or officers, they may opt to bring a legal action. These actions frequently seek money damages and improved standards of corporate governance. They also may serve as a deterrent to future misconduct with respect to the individual defendants as well as directors and officers in other corporations. Thus, these actions may serve both compensatory and deterrent objectives. At the outset, the two different types of suits that shareholders may bring should be distinguished—direct and derivative actions.

DIRECT SUITS VERSUS DERIVATIVE SUITS

Let's first distinguish direct from derivative suits. In a direct action, shareholders bring suit in their individual capacity, seeking recovery for an alleged individual harm. Consequently, any damages in a direct action will be awarded directly to the individual plaintiffs rather than to the corporation. Plaintiffs in direct suits must incur some separate or special injury. In other words, the alleged misconduct must impact most directly shareholders in their individual capacity—such as their ownership or voting roles—rather than more directly harming the corporate enterprise as a whole.[1] Examples of direct actions include alleged improper declaration of dividends (or wrongful refusal to declare dividends), impairment of shareholder voting rights, and misrepresentations made in the purchase or sale of securities.[2]

From a plaintiff's perspective, a direct suit has key advantages. For example, after payment of attorneys' fees and costs, any money recovery in a direct action goes to the plaintiffs rather than to the corporation. Second, certain procedural obstacles that must be hurdled in derivative litigation are not present in direct actions.[3] Foremost, the demand (on the board of directors) requirement and the ability of a special litigation committee (SLC) to procure dismissal of actions are huge drawbacks for shareholder-plaintiffs in derivative litigation. From a creditor's viewpoint, derivative actions are favored. Unlike a direct action where recovery goes to the individual plaintiffs, damages in derivative suits are paid to the corporation.[4] Thus, creditors much prefer money coming into the corporation rather than going out.

Direct shareholder suits nonetheless may be problematic. One issue arises in that only those shareholders who sue directly are likely to recover damages for the wrongs incurred. Other similarly situated shareholders who were injured but who elect not to sue are unlikely to receive any compensation. Additionally, individual settlements may ultimately lead to disparate treatment among multiple individual plaintiff shareholders. The use of class actions and the requirements applying to these actions significantly lessen these concerns.[5]

Conversely, when the corporation is the entity most directly harmed, then a derivative suit normally is the appropriate route. Such actions arise, for example, in the context of usurpation of a corporate opportunity, interested director transactions, excessive executive compensation, and general corporate mismanagement.[6]

The term *derivative* has many different meanings depending upon the context in which it is applied. In the financial market context, the term describes financial instruments like futures or options.[7] In the corporate law context, it indicates that a shareholder's power to bring an action on behalf of the corporation comes from her ownership interest in the corporation. Such suits are not brought with the specific goal of financially benefitting individual shareholders, but rather, the corporation as a whole. Consequently, a derivative action is one in which shareholders initiate an action on behalf of, and in the name of, the corporation in which they hold shares.[8]

Derivative actions also may be brought by creditors when a corporation becomes insolvent. As with shareholder-initiated actions, creditor-initiated derivative suits seek to benefit the corporation itself, or specifically, the estate of the corporation in bankruptcy.[9] Additionally, in a closely-held corporation by virtue of being comprised of few shareholders (e.g., often less than ten), a derivative action may be treated the same as a direct action.[10] This chapter focuses on shareholder derivative suits in the publicly-held corporation context, such as those companies whose stock is listed on the New York Stock Exchange.

Ordinarily, shareholders are limited in the scope of their influence over the operations of the company in which they own stock. This power is typically limited to shareholder proposals, specific votes requiring shareholder approval (such as an amendment of the articles of incorporation or approval of a merger), and electing (or removing) members of the board of directors.[11] When perceived harm happens to the corporation and the corporation (acting through its board of directors) declines to take action to rectify the harm, a derivative suit may be appropriate. Thus, the term *derivative* merely indicates the sort of authority shareholders have when they bring suit in the name of the corporation.

Meritorious shareholder derivative actions enhance corporate governance. First, these actions reinforce the role of shareholders as equitable owners of the company in question. Second, they provide an avenue whereby shareholders may hold directors accountable for their conduct, particularly when such conduct may raise concerns as to whether legitimate business judgment was exercised.[12] Since a board of directors ordinarily is granted broad discretion in its decisionmaking process via the business judgment rule,[13] the bringing of derivative actions at least theoretically enables the shareholders to keep this largely discretionary power somewhat in check.

Unlike a direct suit in which the plaintiff-shareholder may directly sue the corporation and its directors and officers, the bringing of a derivative suit entails a more complex set of requirements in order to proceed. One of the key challenges facing would-be derivative plaintiffs is that, since any suit will be taken in the corporation's name with any award (after the payment of attorneys' fees and expenses) going to the corporation, shareholders normally must overcome difficult procedural hurdles before their derivative filing will survive dismissal by the court. Most important of the hurdles that a plaintiff must overcome is the so-called *demand requirement*. This requirement will be discussed after a brief discussion of the *ownership requirements*.

DERIVATIVE LITIGATION

OWNERSHIP REQUIREMENTS

The concept of *clean hands* is a critical one in the process of initiating a derivative action. Put another way, it is important for the plaintiff-shareholder to have the "moral high ground" throughout the derivative action process. This begins with the nature of stock ownership. The shares must be owned by the plaintiff prior to the event at issue in order to bring a derivative suit.[14]

Additionally, with certain exceptions, the shares must be held (or conveyed by bequest or inheritance) during the entirety of the lawsuit (continuous ownership requirement).[15] Nonetheless, if the shares were acquired in anticipation of fiduciary wrongdoing with the objective of attaining shareholder status for bringing a derivative action or were acquired from a wrongdoer, such maneuvering may be deemed an improper purpose precluding such shareholder from pursuing the derivative action.[16]

DEMAND

In a derivative suit against a corporation, demand normally must be made on the board of directors.[17] A principal purpose of the demand requirement is to alert the corporation through its board of directors of the alleged wrongdoing, thereby providing an opportunity for the board to take corrective action or to have the corporation directly pursue the litigation.[18] Since the board of directors is duly elected by the shareholders, the ultimate decision to bring a lawsuit in the corporation's name, like other business decisions, ordinarily rests with the board.[19]

Generally, there are numerous potential outcomes once demand on the board of directors has been made. First, the board may take corrective action (such as cancelling the improper stock options).[20] Second, the board may authorize the corporation to undertake and control the litigation.[21] Third, demand may be refused, which will end the analysis and the shareholders' ability to bring a derivative suit, so long as the board of directors complied with the business judgment rule.[22] And, fourth, in some jurisdictions (like Delaware), demand may be excused as futile if there is a sufficient showing that a majority of the directors have a disabling conflict of interest.[23]

An increasing number of states adhere to requiring a shareholder seeking to bring a derivative action to make ***universal demand*** on the board of directors. Demand is excused under this standard only if irreparable injury is threatened, such as ongoing misappropriation or looting by the fiduciary.[24]

The policy behind the demand requirement is that the board of directors should have the first opportunity to assess the situation. One source provides three reasons supporting this approach:

> [F]irst, to relieve the courts of the necessity of interfering in the management of routine, internal, corporate business affairs; second, to afford a measure of protection to corporate directors against harassment by dissident minority shareholders who may disagree with such directors on matters involving business judgment; and third,

> to discourage so-called "strike" suits in which stockholders make charges, without regard to their truth, for the purpose of coercing corporate management into settling worthless claims in order to get rid of them.[25]

Importantly, the demand requirement also enables the board of directors to remediate the problem without the need for litigation (such as rescinding the improperly granted stock options).

The failure by a shareholder-plaintiff to make a demand when demand is required ordinarily will result in dismissal of the action. From a policy perspective on good corporate governance, this is sound: Although the stockholders collectively are the equitable owners of the corporation, authority to make litigation decisions ordinarily is vested in the board of directors. Therefore, this elected board should have the first opportunity to address the situation and to determine what, if any, action should be taken to serve the corporation's best interests.[26]

With this background in focus, we will next examine the board's response to a shareholder demand. Once a demand has been received, the board will evaluate the perceived merits of the allegations made therein and determine what, if any, steps are appropriate. That assessment may be that: the allegations lack merit; there is a need for more extensive fact-finding that calls for the undertaking of an internal corporation investigation; or that certain conduct or transactions were improper and should be remedied.[27] In this regard, the board may appoint a committee to make these determinations, with such committee being granted the same authority as the board itself.[28]

From the perspective of the corporation's best interests, there are a number of reasons why pursuing an action to redress an injury may not be worthwhile: for example, perhaps the enforceability of the subject contract is very uncertain, or the dispute involves a long-term important and loyal customer, or the wrongdoer is judgment-proof, namely, is unable to pay the amount owed.[29]

Alternatively, from a plaintiff-shareholder's perspective, there may be indications of impropriety by a corporate executive. In such circumstances, those responsible for assessing whether an action should be brought may be reluctant to sue a leadership peer, which may thereby implicate themselves in the unsavory litigation process that ensues.[30]

Derivative litigation often entails accusations that at least some directors acted improperly. Particularly, if these directors financially benefitted from a challenged transaction, they cannot be reasonably expected to exercise objective independence when ascertaining an appropriate response to these allegations.[31] In such instances, a board of directors will frequently appoint a special litigation committee (SLC), comprised of two or more independent and disinterested directors.[32] This SLC is granted the full authority of the board itself concerning the litigation issues presented. Fundamentally, it is the SLC's task to evaluate the merits of the allegations, investigate the pertinent facts and circumstances, and make a decision therefrom. In theory, the delegation of authority to the SLC facilitates an impartial review of the situation at hand.[33]

To illustrate, suppose a director is alleged to have usurped a corporate opportunity.[34] Upon investigating the allegations, the SLC concludes that the opportunity in fact may not have been a corporate opportunity under the applicable state law and that there is uncertainty as to whether the accused board member in fact had previously disclosed the opportunity. With these findings, the SLC will consider not only if there is sufficient evidence of wrongdoing to warrant initiating a suit, but the likelihood that such a suit will be successful for the corporation and the likely amount of recovery and costs (such as attorneys' fees) involved. Also, that the corporation may be obliged to indemnify the defendant-director—such as reimbursing the costs of the accused director's defense—is a relevant variable. Economically speaking, if a corporation were to pursue litigation at great expense where the amount of potential recovery is trivial and the certainty of such recovery in serious doubt, the question of how this endeavor benefits the corporation becomes rhetorical.

The decision reached by the SLC receives judicial deference—the extent of such deference varying with the applicable law. Nearly always, the SLC determines that pursuing such litigation is not in the corporation's best interest. As outlined by one court:

> The defendants assert several grounds for affirmance. ... Principally, they argue that the Special Litigation Committee's determination that [the plaintiff-shareholder's] derivative suit is not in the best interests of the corporation bars the prosecution of this suit. The defendants emphasize that the directors who comprised that Committee were not part of inside management and had not served as directors when the questionable events occurred, thereby guaranteeing the independence of their determination. Moreover, the Committee acted in good faith and with the full authority of the Board of Directors. Accordingly, the defendants claim, that [the] Committee's determination was a business judgment ... that the derivative suit should not proceed ... which is insulated from judicial review and which bars the maintenance of the derivative suit.[35]

DEMAND: REQUIRED OR EXCUSED

Thus, when either the SLC or the board itself determines that pursuing the claims set forth in the shareholder demand are not in the corporation's best interests, that decision may be coined as "demand refused." In this situation, as stated by the Delaware Supreme Court, "a board's decision to cause a derivative suit to be dismissed as detrimental to the company, after demand has been made and refused, will be respected [by the court] unless it was wrongful."[36]

Irrespective of whether demand is required or excused, the board of director's or SLC's determination declining to pursue the litigation is generally protected by the business judgment rule or some variation of that rule. If certain conditions are met, the "business judgment" rule presumes propriety in a board or SLC's decision.[37] In order for the business judgment rule to apply, the following generally must be satisfied: First, the decision must have been deliberative. This factor looks to whether the board or SLC focused on the decision at hand and made a determination. In this regard, decisions to affirmatively act as well as decisions to refrain from acting come within the rule.[38] Second, the decision must be sufficiently informed. To overcome this requirement, a plaintiff must show that the board (or SLC) was so inadequately informed that its determination to base the decision on the information possessed was grossly negligent.[39] Third, those making the decision must not have a disabling conflict of interest. This requirement signifies that the directors making the decision in question are not financially interested in the matter of the alleged wrongdoing and are independent of outside influence or control (such as the domination that may by used by a controlling shareholder).[40] Finally, at least according to some courts, the decision itself must have a rational basis. Here, the threshold for satisfying this requirement is quite low. In order for a plaintiff to surmount the presumption that the decision is rational, the standard for rebutting this presumption is that of gross negligence.[41]

SIGNIFICANCE OF DEMAND EXCUSED

In some jurisdictions, most prominently Delaware, demand on the board of directors in derivative actions may be excused under certain circumstances.[42] Demand most frequently is excused when sufficient question is raised that either a majority of the directors participated (or were complicit) in the wrongdoing, or that a majority of the directors are not otherwise independent or disinterested.[43] When this is the case, then demand upon the board may be regarded as futile.[44]

The difficulty that a plaintiff-shareholder may experience in seeking to excuse demand on the board of directors as futile is illustrated by a case decided over 25 years ago by the Delaware Supreme Court. Specifically, the lawsuit alleged that Leo Fink (who owned 47% of the company) improperly received several lucrative benefits. The court stated:

> [T]he defendants approved an employment agreement between Meyers [Meyers Parking—the Company] and Fink for a five year term with provision for automatic renewal each year thereafter, indefinitely. Meyers agreed to pay Fink $150,000 per year, plus a bonus of 5% of its pre-tax profits over $2,400,000 [a "Reggie Jackson" clause—Signing as a free agent with the New York Yankees, Mr. Jackson's contract provided a percentage bonus if attendance at Yankee Stadium exceeded a specified number]. Fink could terminate the contract at any time, but Meyers could do so only upon six months' notice. At termination, Fink was to become a consultant to Meyers and be paid $150,000 per year for the first three years, $125,000 for the next three years, and $100,000 thereafter for life. Death benefits were also included. Fink agreed to devote his best efforts and substantially his entire business time to advancing Meyers' interests. The agreement also provided that Fink's compensation was not to be affected by any inability to perform services on Meyers' behalf. Fink was 75 years old when his employment agreement with Meyers was approved by the directors. There is no claim that he was, or is, in poor health. ... Additionally, the Meyers board approved and made interest-free loans to Fink totaling $225,000. These loans were unpaid and outstanding ... when the complaint was filed. ...
>
> The complaint charges that these transaction had "no valid business purpose," and were a "waste of corporate assets" because the amounts to be paid are "grossly excessive," that Fink performs "no or little services," and because of his "advanced age" cannot be "expected to perform any such services." The plaintiff also charges that the existence of the Prudential consulting agreement with Fink prevents him from providing his "best efforts" on Meyers' behalf. Finally, it is alleged that the loans to Fink were in reality "additional compensation" without any "consideration" or "benefit" to Meyers.[45]

Here, the position forwarded by the plaintiff was that, because of Fink's relationship with the directors and his 47% stock holdings, the board was incapable of acting in an impartial and disinterested manner. After all, through his stock ownership, Fink was able to elect (and remove) in his sole discretion each and every director. A lower court had agreed with this position, but upon appeal, the Delaware Supreme Court ultimately determined that the plaintiffs failed to show with sufficient specificity how either Fink's relationships or the fact that Fink owned 47% of the stock impaired the ability of the board to act impartially.[46]

With respect to the plaintiff-shareholder's pleading burden, the following standard applies:

> [F]or a plaintiff to plead facts which permit a court to draw a reasonable inference that the impartiality of the directors is in doubt, a plaintiff must do more than merely make conclusory allegations. If the transaction is one which appears to be protected by the presumption of propriety of the business judgment rule, he must, with particularity, allege facts which, if true, show that the business judgment rule would not protect the challenged transaction from judicial scrutiny—at least for the purpose of considering the demand requirement. ...[47]

Thus, the burden for a plaintiff is substantial. When alleging that board members are not independent, facts demonstrating that at least a majority of directors are interested must be sufficiently alleged. This will most likely be the situation where a majority of the directors have a financial interest in the subject transaction(s).

The other generally accepted exception to the demand requirement is when the act of making a demand on the board of directors would result in irreparable harm to the corporation. This exception is even available in jurisdictions which otherwise call for "universal demand."[48] Needless to say, this exception is rarely invoked. A situation of ongoing embezzlement and looting of the corporation serves as an example.

In cases where demand on the board of directors is excused, a special litigation committee (SLC) normally will be appointed by the board of directors to conduct an investigation and thereafter make a determination whether the litigation should proceed. During the time of the SLC's investigation, a stay of discovery normally is ordered by the court. After conducting its investigation, the SLC usually recommends that the stockholder derivative suit should be terminated. At the same time, the SLC may take certain steps to remedy the perceived misconduct. This may include rescinding some of the problematic contracts, having the defendants repay to the corporation a specific amount, and/or instituting improved standards of corporate accountability (such as retention of an independent consultant on environmental standards when the alleged misconduct involved a pollution-related matter).[49]

Although a number of courts apply the "plain vanilla" business judgment rule to the SLC's decision that the litigation should be terminated (just like in the demand required context),[50] some courts apply a more rigorous standard. For example, when demand is excused, a number of courts require the defendants to prove the SLC's independence, good faith, adequacy of its investigation, and the reasonable bases for its determination.[51] Limited discovery is provided to plaintiff-shareholders to procure appropriate documents and to take the testimony of ("depose") the SLC members and perhaps other key players.[52] Under this framework, plaintiff-shareholders instituting a derivative suit have a much better chance (than in the demand required situation) to fend off the SLC's motion to terminate and thereby be able to prosecute the action.

COMMON EXAMPLES OF DERIVATIVE ACTIONS

Directors and officers have fiduciary duties of care and loyalty to the corporation. The examples provided here illustrate instances in which officers or directors have been implicated in allegedly breaching these duties, thus opening the door to shareholder derivative litigation.

"SELF-DEALING" TRANSACTIONS: STOCK OPTION BACKDATING

During the past decade, improper self-dealing in the form of stock option backdating occurred with some frequency. Stock option backdating "involves a company issuing stock options to an executive on one date while providing [false] documentation asserting that the options were actually issued earlier [at a lower price]. Such timing reduces the strike prices and inflates the value of stock options, thereby increasing management compensation."[53] A variant of this practice, called "springloading," occurs when executives are granted stock options shortly prior to the public disclosure of "positive" information. This information is likely to cause an increase in the price of the company's stock.[54] Stock option backdating thus is a form of self-dealing. Generally, self-dealing occurs when a corporate officer or director receives a disproportionate benefit to the detriment of the corporation and its shareholders.[55] A CEO's sale of personal real estate to the corporation at an inflated price over fair market value serves as an example.[56]

When improperly employed, backdating constitutes "secret" excessive executive compensation and skews the financial reports of the corporation in such a way as to underreport the costs associated with those options as compared to the actual stock price. Knowingly improper backdating is fraudulent and a breach of fiduciary duty. As one court asserted: "Any directors engaging in self-dealing and making misrepresentations to shareholders cannot be said to act in the corporation's best interest. Backdating is a form of fraud. In the face of such allegations, defendants simply cannot be said to have acted in the company's best interest."[57]

Corporate Waste

Conduct by directors or officers, which allegedly "wastes" corporate assets, normally will result in a stockholder derivative action. Waste is proven by "showing that no person of ordinary sound business judgment could view the benefits received in the transaction as a fair exchange for the consideration paid by the corporation."[58] This was one of the key issues at play in the *Disney* litigation wherein Disney CEO Michael Eisner as well as other Disney directors were alleged to have engaged in corporate waste due to the employment contract entered into between Disney and Disney President Michael Ovitz. Within months after the commencement of this contract, it became clear that Ovitz was not a good fit for Disney; he was ultimately terminated without cause. Because of this no-fault termination, he was entitled to an enormous $130 million severance payment.[59]

Although the size of the payment was unusual, the specific facts of the case—including the expectation that Ovitz would serve a lengthy period with Disney, the opportunities he had foregone in order to join Disney, and the advice of compensation specialists—all supported the ultimate conclusion that no waste existed in this instance.[60] As a general proposition, however, large corporate gifts conferred upon an executive without any benefit to the corporation are susceptible to being held wasteful.[61]

Usurpation of Corporate Opportunity

Usurpation of a corporate opportunity occurs when a director or executive takes for her own benefit an opportunity which properly belongs to the corporation. As with other fiduciary wrongdoing, the key to understanding why this is wrongful is that it represents a breach of the duty owed by that fiduciary—namely, depriving the corporation of the ability to procure a beneficial opportunity.

For example, in *Brandt v. Somerville*, the corporate opportunity at play involved the acquisition of certain manufacturing rights for a component utilized by the Posilock Company in its products. Instead of having Posilock manufacture this component itself, the defendant created a separate entity, Dynamics 360. Although Dynamics 360 sold to both Posilock and others, Posilock constituted half of its sales.[62] The court held that it was within Posilock's interest to have made use of this opportunity. Since Dynamics 360 supplied half of its capacity to other customers, it followed that Posilock, had it enjoyed the opportunity here usurped, would have similarly found buyers for the remaining half of the output of its manufacturing capacity. Here, Posilock was denied the entry to capitalize on these manufacturing opportunities and thus was improperly deprived of a corporate opportunity.[63]

ACTS INVITING REGULATORY ACTION/SCRUTINY

Action or inaction by corporate officers and directors, resulting in derivative litigation, may be based on negative regulatory scrutiny of the corporation and the adverse consequences arising therefrom. In the *Abbott* case, for example, the striking detail was a $100 million fine levied against the company, Abbott Laboratories, a New York Stock Exchange listed company. This "record" fine, ordered by the Food and Drug Administration based on violative conduct during a six-year period, had a negative impact on the corporation's earnings as well as its reputation. The plaintiff-shareholders alleged that Abbott's injury was preventable and had resulted from the directors' misconduct.[64] Thus, pertinent issues in *Abbott* involved the propriety of director inaction and the levying of personal liability premised on the directors' alleged breach of the duty of care and their failure to act in good faith. Under such circumstances, the court held that demand on the board of directors was excused.[65]

CONCLUSION

Aggrieved shareholders may seek to bring either a direct or a derivative action. If the injury suffered is unique to them in their shareholder capacity, then a direct suit is more likely the appropriate route. In a direct suit, shareholders sue the corporate fiduciaries for the alleged injuries where an award of damages will flow personally to them. If, however, the corporation is most directly harmed, then a derivative suit normally is the appropriate recourse. In a derivative suit, any recovery will go to the corporation for the benefit of all shareholders.

In bringing a derivative suit, the shareholder normally must first make a demand on the board of directors. The board will then decide whether to accept or refuse the demand. Only in the limited circumstances where a shareholder can show that a majority of the directors were involved or complicit in the alleged wrongdoing may demand be excused (and then only in those States that do not have "universal demand"). After examining the alleged misconduct set forth by shareholders, the board (or the SLC) will make its determination. That determination most often is that the litigation is not in the corporation's best interests and should be terminated. This decision by the board (or the SLC) normally will be protected by the business judgment rule or some variation of the rule. Thus, the reality is that frequently only in instances where there is sufficient reason to doubt the independence of board members (such as the SLC) or the thoroughness of its investigation will a shareholder derivative suit be allowed to proceed.[66]

NOTES

1. See *Grimes v. Donald*, 673 A.2d 1207, 1213 (Del. 1996).
2. See *Tooley v. Donaldson, Lufkin & Jenrette, Inc.*, 845 A.2d 1031 (Del. 2004); *Smith v. Van Gorkom*, 488 A.2d 858 (Del. 1985); *Weinberger v. UOP, Inc.*, 457 A.2d 701 (Del. 1983).
3. See, e.g., Model Bus. Corp. Act § 7.41 (contemporaneous ownership requirement); *Shoen v. SAC Holding Co.*, 137 P.3d 1171 (Nev. 2006) (demand on board of directors).
4. See *North American Educational Programming Foundation, Inc. v. Gheewalla*, 930 A. 2d 92 (Del. 2007).
5. See Rule 23 of the Federal Rules of Civil Procedure.
6. See, e.g., *In re Walt Disney Company Derivative Litigation*, 906 A.2d 27 (Del. 2006).
7. See generally W. Klein, J. Coffee, and F. Partnoy, *Business Organization and Finance* 298-299 (11th ed. 2010).
8. See Rule 23.1 of the Federal Rules of Civil Procedure.
9. See *North American Educational Programming Foundation, Inc. v. Gheewalla*, 930 A. 2d 93 (Del. 2007).
10. See § 21.563(c) of the Texas Business Organization Code.
11. See SEC Rule 14a-9 (shareholder proposal rule); Model Bus. Corp. Act §§ 8.08, 10.03, 11.04.
12. See *Ryan v. Gifford*, 918 A.2d 341 (Del. Ch. 2007).
13. See *Smith v. Van Gorkom*, 488 A.2d 858 (Del. 1985).
14. See Model Bus. Corp. Act § 7.41; *Home Fire Insurance Co. v. Barber*, 93 N.W. 1024 (Neb. 1903).

15. See *Strategic Asset Management, Inc. v. Nicholson*, 2004 Del. Ch. LEXIS 178 (Del. Ch. 2004). A number of states have abandoned the continuous ownership requirement. See, e.g., *Brown v. Brown*, 731 A.2d 1212, 1215 (N.J. 1999).
16. See *Bangor Punta Operations, Inc. v. Bangor & A & R Co.*, 417 U.S. 703 (1974).
17. See Rule 23.1 of the Delaware Rules of Civil Procedure; *Aronson v. Lewis*, 473 A.2d 805 (Del. 1984).
18. See American Law Institute (ALI), Principles of Corporate Governance: Analysis and Recommendations § 7.08 cmt. c. (1994).
19. See *Aronson,* 473 A.2d at 811–813.
20. See ALI Restatement, *supra* note 18, at § 7.08 cmt. c.
21. See *Valeant Pharmaceutical International v. Jerney*, 921 A.2d 732 (Del. Ch. 2007).
22. See *Aronson,* 473 A.2d at 813.
23. See *id.* at 814–817; *Zapata Corp. v. Maldonado*, 430 A.2d 779 (Del. 1981).
24. See, e.g., Model Bus. Corp. Act § 7.42; Ariz. Rev. Stat. Ann. § 10-742; Tex. Bus. Org. Code Ann. § 21.553.
25. E. Brodsky and M. Adanski, *Law of Corporate Officers and Directors: Rights, Duties and Liabilities* § 9:6 (2010).
26. See *Aronson*, 473 A.2d at 811–812.
27. See M. Steinberg, *Securities Regulation: Liabilities and Remedies* § 14.03 (2010).
28. See *Houle v. Low*, 556 N.E. 2d 51 (Mass. 1990); *Alford v. Shaw*, 358 S.E.2d 323 (N.C. 1987).
29. See *Desigoudar v. Meyercord*, 133 Cal. Rptr. 2d 408 (Cal. App. 2003).
30. See *Beam v. Martha Stewart,* 845 A.2d 1040 (Del. 2004).
31. *Id.* at 1050–1054.
32. See *Joy v. North*, 692 F.2d 880 (2d Cir. 1982).
33. See *Cuker v. Mikalauskas*, 692 A.2d 1042 (Pa. 1997).
34. See, e.g., *Today Homes, Inc. v. Williams*, 634 S.E.2d 737 (Va. 2006); *infra* notes 64–65 and accompanying text; discussion in Chapter 6.
35. *Cramer v. General Telephone & Electronics Corporation,* 582 F.2d 259, 273–274 (3d Cir. 1978).
36. *Zapata*, 430 A.2d at 784.
37. See *Smith v. Van Gorkom*, 488 A.2d at 872-873; discussion in Chapter 6.
38. *Id*. at 872. Cf. *Brane v. Roth*. 590 N.E.2d 587 (Ind. App. 1992).
39. *Van Gorkom,* 488 A.2d at 873.
40. See *Clark v. Nettleton Financial Corporation*, 581 F.2d 516 (5th Cir. 1978).
41. See *Gimbal v. Signal Companies*, 316 A.2d 599 (Del. Ch.), *aff'd*, 316 A.2d 619 (Del. 1974).
42. See *Shoen v. SAC Holding Co.*, 137 P.3d 1171 (Nev. 2006).
43. See *Rales v. Blasband*, 634 A.2d 927 (Del. 1993).
44. See *Heineman v. Datapoint Corp*., 611 A.2d 950 (Del. 1992). See also, *Beam v. Martha Stewart*, 845 A.2d 1040 (Del. 2004) (addressing professional or personal friendship as ground for conflict of interest).

45. *Lewis v. Aronson*, 473 A.2d at 808–809.
46. *Id.* at 815–818. See *Lewis v. Graves*, 701 F.2d 245 (2d Cir. 1983).
47. *Lewis v. Aronson*, 466 A.2d 375, 385 (Del. Ch. 1983), reversed, 473 A.2d 805 (Del. 1984).
48. See statutes cited note 24 *supra*. See *Boland v. Engle*, 113 F.3d 706 (7th Cir. 1997); *Kubik v. Kubik*, 683 N.W. 2d 330 (Neb. 2004).
49. See *Joy v. North*, 692 F.2d 880 (2d Cir. 1982);
50. See *Auerbach v. Bennett*, 419 N.Y.S. 2d 920, 393 N.E. 2d 994 (N.Y. 1979).
51. See *In re PSE&G Shareholder Litigation*, 801 A.2d 295 (N.J. 2002).
52. *Id.* at 312. See *Kaplan v. Wyatt*, 499 A.2d 1184 (Del. 1985).
53. *Ryan v. Gifford*, 918 A.2d 341, 345 (Del. Ch. 2007).
54. See *In re Tyson Foods Inc. Consolidated Shareholder Litigation*, 919 A.2d 563, 592 (Del. Ch. 2007).
55. See *Sinclair Oil Corp. v. Levien*, 280 A.2d 717 (Del. 1971).
56. Such conduct would be an interested director or related party transaction. See *infra* notes 62-63 and accompanying text; Del. Gen. Corp. Law. § 144; *Fliegler v. Lawrence*, 361 A.2d 218 (Del. 1976).
57. *In re Zoran Corporation Derivative Litigation,* 511 F. Supp. 2d 986 (N.D. Cal. 2007).
58. *Harbor Financial Partners v. Huizenga,* 751 A.2d 543, 554 (Del. 2001). See Morrissey, *The Path of Corporate Law: Of Options Backdating, Derivative Suits, and the Business Judgment Rule,* 86 Oregon L. Rev. 973 (2008).
59. See *In re Walt Disney Company Derivative Litigation*, 906 A.2d 27, 36–46 (Del. 2006).
60. *Id.* at 73–75.
61. See *Zoran,* 511 Supp. 2d at 1019; ALI Restatement, *supra* note 18, at § 1.72.
62. 692 N.W. 2d 144, 147–148 (N.D. 2005).
63. *Id.* at 150–151. For discussion of the corporate opportunity doctrine, see Chapter 6.
64. *In re Abbott Laboratories Derivative Shareholders Litigation*, 325 F.3d 795 (7th Cir. 2003).
65. *Id.* at 807–810. See *McCall v. Scott,* 239 F.3d 808 (6th Cir. 2001), amended, 250 F.3d 997 (6th Cir. 2008).
66. As stated by Professor Morrissey:

    > [W]ho is the appropriate advocate to prosecute the corporation's grievances against its internal malefactors? In theory, of course, management of a corporation is vested in its board of directors, and that responsibility also includes the decision whether to pursue legal action against those who have harmed it. But the driving presumption of a derivative suit is that those in control of the corporation have either committed the wrongful act themselves or have effectively condoned it. Such officials are unlikely to sue themselves. Yet considerable skepticism exists about the bona fide motivations of shareholder-plaintiffs or more

> particularly about the motivations of their counsel. Corporate defendants are quick to claim that these are "strike suits," frivolous litigation brought without merit by lawyers hungry for big, quick settlements.

Morrissey, *supra* note 58, at 996.

ARONSON V. LEWIS
DELAWARE SUPREME COURT
475 A. 2D 805 (1984)

Moore, Justice:

[The issue to be decided in this case is as follows:] when is a stockholder's demand upon a board of directors, to redress an alleged wrong to the corporation, excused as futile prior to the filing of a derivative suit? We granted this interlocutory appeal to the defendants, Meyers Parking System, Inc. (Meyers), a Delaware corporation, and its directors, to review the Court of Chancery's denial of their motion to dismiss this action, pursuant to Chancery Rule 23.1, for the plaintiff's failure to make such a demand or otherwise demonstrate its futility. The Vice Chancellor ruled that plaintiff's allegations raised a "reasonable inference" that the directors' action was unprotected by the business judgment rule. Thus, the board could not have impartially considered and acted upon the demand. See *Lewis v. Aronson*, Del. Ch., 466 A.2d 375, 381 (1983).

We cannot agree with this formulation of the concept of demand futility. In our view demand can only be excused where facts are alleged with particularity which create a reasonable doubt that the directors' action was entitled to the protections of the business judgment rule. Because the plaintiff failed to make a demand, and to allege facts with particularity indicating that such demand would be futile, we reverse the Court of Chancery and remand with instructions that plaintiff be granted leave to amend the complaint.

I.

The issues of demand futility rest upon the allegations of the complaint. The plaintiff, Harry Lewis, is a stockholder of Meyers. The defendants are Meyers and its ten directors, some of whom are also company officers.

In 1979, Prudential Building Maintenance Corp. (Prudential) spun off its shares of Meyers to Prudential's stockholders[, thereby enabling Meyers to become a publicly-traded company]. Prior thereto Meyers was a wholly owned subsidiary of Prudential. Meyers provides parking lot facilities and related services throughout the country. Its stock is actively traded over-the-counter.

This suit challenges certain transactions between Meyers and one of its directors, Leo Fink, who owns 47% of its outstanding stock. Plaintiff claims that these transactions were approved only because Fink personally selected each director and officer of Meyers.

...

On January 1, 1981, the defendants approved an employment agreement between Meyers and Fink for a five year term with provision for automatic renewal each year thereafter, indefinitely. Meyers agreed to pay Fink $150,000 per year, plus a bonus of 5% of its pre-tax profits over $2,400,000. Fink could terminate the contract at any time, but Meyers could do so only upon six months' notice. At termination, Fink was to become a consultant to Meyers and be paid $150,000 per year for the first three years, $125,000 for the next three years, and $100,000 thereafter for life. Death benefits were also included. Fink agreed to devote his best efforts and substantially his entire business time to advancing Meyers' interests. The agreement also provided that Fink's compensation was not to be affected by any inability to perform services on Meyers' behalf. Fink was 75 years old when his employment agreement with Meyers was approved by the directors. There is no claim that he was, or is, in poor health.

Additionally, the Meyers board approved and made interest-free loans to Fink totaling $225,000. [Such loans today are illegal under the Sarbanes-Oxley Act of 2002.] These loans were unpaid and outstanding as of August 1982 when the complaint was filed. At oral argument defendants' counsel represented that these loans had been repaid in full.

The complaint charges that these transactions had "no valid business purpose", and were a "waste of corporate assets" because the amounts to be paid are "grossly excessive", that Fink performs "no or little services", and because of his "advanced age" cannot be "expected to perform any such services". ... Finally, it is alleged that the loans to Fink were in reality "additional compensation" without any "consideration" or "benefit" to Meyers.

The complaint alleged that no demand had been made on the Meyers board because:

> ... such attempt would be futile for the following reasons:
>
> (a) All of the directors in office are named as defendants herein and they have participated in, expressly approved and/or acquiesced in, and are personally liable for, the wrongs complained of herein.

(b) Defendant Fink, having selected each director, controls and dominates every member of the Board and every officer of Meyers.

(c) Institution of this action by present directors would require the defendant-directors to sue themselves, thereby placing the conduct of this action in hostile hands and preventing its effective prosecution.

The relief sought included the cancellation of the Meyers-Fink employment contract and an accounting by the directors, including Fink, for all damage sustained by Meyers and for all profits derived by the directors and Fink.

II.

Defendants moved to dismiss for plaintiff's failure to make demand on the Meyers board prior to suit, or to allege with factual particularity why demand is excused.

...

III.

The defendants make two arguments, one policy-oriented and the other, factual. First, they assert that the demand requirement embraces the policy that directors, rather than stockholders, manage the affairs of the corporation. They contend that this fundamental principle requires the strict construction and enforcement of Chancery Rule 23.1. Second, the defendants point to four of plaintiff's basic allegations and argue that they lack the factual particularity necessary to excuse demand. Concerning the allegation that Fink dominated and controlled the Meyers board, the defendants point to the absence of any facts explaining how he "selected each director". With respect to Fink's 47% stock interest, the defendants say that absent other facts this is insufficient to indicate domination and control. Regarding the claim of hostility to the plaintiff's suit, because defendants would have to sue themselves, the latter assert that this bootstrap argument ignores the possibility that the directors have other alternatives, such as cancelling the challenged agreement. As for the allegation that directorial approval of the agreement excused demand, the defendants reply that such a claim is insufficient, because it would obviate the demand requirement in almost every case. The effect would be to subvert the managerial power of a board of directors. Finally, as to the provision guaranteeing Fink's compensation, even if he is unable to perform any services, the defendants contend that the trial court read this out of context. Based upon the foregoing, the defendants conclude that the plaintiff's allegations fall far short of the factual particularity required by Rule 23.1.

IV.

A.

A cardinal precept of the General Corporation Law of the State of Delaware is that directors, rather than shareholders, manage the business and affairs of the corporation. 8 *Del.C.* § 141(a). Section 141(a) states in pertinent part:

> "The *business and affairs* of a corporation organized under this chapter *shall be managed by or under the direction* of a board of directors except as may be otherwise provided in this chapter or in its certificate of incorporation."

8 *Del.C.* § 141(a) (Emphasis added). The existence and exercise of this power carries with it certain fundamental fiduciary obligations to the corporation and its shareholders. Moreover, a stockholder is not powerless to challenge director action which results in harm to the corporation. The machinery of corporate democracy and the derivative suit are potent tools to redress the conduct of a torpid or unfaithful management. The derivative action developed in equity to enable shareholders to sue in the corporation's name where those in control of the company refused to assert a claim belonging to it. The nature of the action is two-fold. First, it is the equivalent of a suit by the shareholders to compel the corporation to sue. Second, it is a suit by the corporation, asserted by the shareholders on its behalf, against those liable to it.

By its very nature the derivative action impinges on the managerial freedom of directors. Hence, the demand requirement of Chancery Rule 23.1 exists at the threshold, first to insure that a stockholder exhausts his intracorporate remedies, and then to provide a safeguard against strike suits. [A "strike" suit is one that is slightly better than frivolous but where the plaintiff would not win on the merits. To avoid the expense and annoyance of such litigation, the defendants settle the case at relatively modern levels. The winner in such litigation ordinarily is plaintiff's counsel who receives his/her attorney's fees.] Thus, by promoting this form of alternate dispute resolution, rather than immediate recourse to litigation, the demand requirement is a recognition of the fundamental precept that directors manage the business and affairs of corporations.

In our view the entire question of demand futility is inextricably bound to issues of business judgment and the standards of that doctrine's applicability. The business judgment rule is an acknowledgment of the managerial prerogatives of Delaware directors under Section 141(a). It is a presumption that in making a business decision the directors of a corporation acted on an informed basis, in good faith and in the honest belief that the action taken was in the best interests of the company. Absent an abuse of discretion, that judgment will be respected by the courts. The burden is on the party challenging the decision to establish facts rebutting the presumption.

The function of the business judgment rule is of paramount significance in the context of a derivative action. It comes into play in several ways—in addressing a demand, in the determination of demand futility, in efforts by independent disinterested directors to dismiss the action as inimical to the corporation's best interests, and generally, as a defense to the merits of the suit. However, in each of these circumstances there are certain common principles governing the application and operation of the rule.

First, its protections can only be claimed by disinterested directors whose conduct otherwise meets the tests of business judgment. From the standpoint of interest, this means that directors can neither appear on both sides of a transaction nor expect to derive any personal financial benefit from it in the sense of self-dealing, as opposed to a benefit which devolves upon the corporation or all stockholders generally. Thus, if such director interest is present, and the transaction is not approved by a majority consisting of the disinterested directors, then the business judgment rule has no application whatever in determining demand futility.

Second, to invoke the rule's protection directors have a duty to inform themselves, prior to making a business decision, of all material information reasonably available to them. Having become so informed, they must then act with requisite care in the discharge of their duties. While the Delaware cases use a variety of terms to describe the applicable standard of care, our analysis satisfies us that under the business judgment rule director liability is predicated upon concepts of gross negligence.

However, it should be noted that the business judgment rule operates only in the context of director action. Technically speaking, it has no role where directors have either abdicated their functions, or absent a conscious decision, failed to act. But it also follows that under applicable principles, a conscious decision to refrain from acting may nonetheless be a valid exercise of business judgment and enjoy the protections of the rule.

The gap in our law, which we address today, arises from this Court's decision in *Zapata Corp. v. Maldonado*. There, the Court defined the limits of a board's managerial power granted by Section 141(a) and restricted application of the business judgment rule in a factual context similar to this action. *Zapata Corp. v. Maldonado*, 430 A.2d 779, 782–86 (Del. 1981), *rev'g, Maldonado v. Flynn*, Del.Ch., 413 A.2d 1251 (1980).

By way of background, this Court's review in *Zapata* was limited to whether an independent investigation committee of disinterested directors had the *power* to cause the derivative action to be dismissed. Preliminarily, it was noted in *Zapata* that "[d]irectors of Delaware corporations derive their managerial decision making power, which encompasses decisions whether to initiate, or refrain from entering, litigation, from 8 *Del.C.* § 141(a)". … In that context, this Court observed that the business judgment rule has no relevance to corporate decision making until *after a decision has been made*. In *Zapata*, we stated that a shareholder does not possess an independent individual right to continue a derivative action. Moreover, where demand on a board has been made and refused, we apply the business judgment rule in reviewing the board's refusal to act pursuant to a stockholder's demand. Unless the business judgment rule does not protect the refusal to sue, the shareholder lacks the legal managerial power to continue the derivative action, since that power is terminated by the refusal. We also concluded that where demand is excused a shareholder possesses the ability to initiate a derivative action, but the right to prosecute it may be terminated upon the exercise of applicable standards of business judgment. The thrust of *Zapata* is that in either the demand-refused or the demand-excused case, the board still retains its Section 141(a) managerial authority to make decisions regarding corporate litigation. Moreover, the board may delegate its managerial authority to a committee of independent disinterested directors. Thus, even in a demand-excused case, a board has the power to appoint a committee of one or more independent disinterested directors to determine whether the derivative action should be pursued or dismissal sought. Under *Zapata*, the Court of Chancery, in passing on a committee's motion to dismiss a derivative action in a demand excused case, must apply a two-step test. First, the court must inquire into the independence and good faith of the committee and review the reasonableness and good faith of the committee's investigation. Second, the court must apply its own independent business judgment to decide whether the motion to dismiss should be granted.

After *Zapata* numerous derivative suits were filed without prior demand upon boards of directors. The complaints in such actions all alleged that demand was excused because of board interest, approval or acquiescence in the wrongdoing. In any event, the *Zapata* demand-excused/demand-refused bifurcation, has left a crucial issue unanswered: when is demand futile and, therefore, excused?

Delaware courts have addressed the issue of demand futility on several earlier occasions. ... The rule emerging from these decisions is that where officers and directors are under an influence which sterilizes their discretion, they cannot be considered proper persons to conduct litigation on behalf of the corporation. Thus, demand would be futile. ...

However, those cases cannot be taken to mean that any board approval of a challenged transaction automatically connotes "hostile interest" and "guilty participation" by directors, or some other form of sterilizing influence upon them. Were that so, the demand requirements of our law would be meaningless, leaving the clear mandate of Chancery Rule 23.1 devoid of its purpose and substance.

The trial court correctly recognized that demand futility is inextricably bound to issues of business judgment, but stated the test to be based on allegations of fact, which, if true, "show that there is a reasonable inference" the business judgment rule is not applicable for purposes of a pre-suit demand.

The problem with this formulation is the concept of reasonable inferences to be drawn against a board of directors based on allegations in a complaint. As is clear from this case, and the conclusory allegations upon which the Vice Chancellor relied, demand futility becomes virtually automatic under such a test. Bearing in mind the presumptions with which director action is cloaked, we believe that the matter must be approached in a more balanced way.

Our view is that in determining demand futility the Court of Chancery in the proper exercise of its discretion must decide whether, under the particularized facts alleged, a reasonable doubt is created that: (1) the directors are disinterested and independent and (2) the challenged transaction was otherwise the product of a valid exercise of business judgment. Hence, the Court of Chancery must make two inquiries, one into the independence and disinterestedness of the directors and the other into the substantive nature of the challenged transaction and the board's approval thereof. As to the latter inquiry the court does not assume that the transaction is a wrong to the corporation requiring corrective steps by the board. Rather, the alleged wrong is substantively reviewed against the factual background alleged in the complaint. As to the former inquiry, directorial independence and disinterestedness, the court reviews the factual allegations to decide whether they raise a reasonable doubt, as a threshold matter, that the protections of the business judgment rule are available to the board. Certainly, if this is an "interested" director transaction, such that the business judgment rule is inapplicable to the board majority approving the transaction, then the inquiry ceases. In that event futility of demand has been established by any objective or subjective standard. We recognize that drawing the line at a majority of the board may be an arguably arbitrary dividing point. Critics will charge that we are ignoring the structural bias common to corporate boards throughout America, as well as the other unseen socialization processes cutting against independent discussion and decisionmaking in the boardroom. The difficulty with structural bias in a demand futile case is simply one of establishing it in the complaint for purposes of Rule 23.1. We are satisfied that discretionary review by the Court of Chancery of complaints alleging specific facts pointing to bias on a particular board will be sufficient for determining demand futility. [This discussion is taken from footnote 8 of the opinion.]

However, the mere threat of personal liability for approving a questioned transaction, standing alone, is insufficient to challenge either the independence or disinterestedness of directors, although in rare cases a transaction may be so egregious on its face that board approval cannot meet the test of business judgment, and a substantial likelihood of director liability therefore exists. In sum the entire review is factual in nature. The Court of Chancery in the exercise of its sound discretion must be satisfied that a plaintiff has alleged facts with particularity which, taken as true, support a reasonable doubt that the challenged transaction was the product of a valid exercise of business judgment. Only in that context is demand excused.

B.

Having outlined the legal framework within which these issues are to be determined, we consider plaintiff's claims of futility here: Fink's domination and control of the directors, board approval of the Fink-Meyers employment agreement, and board hostility to the plaintiff's derivative action due to the directors' status as defendants.

Plaintiff's claim that Fink dominates and controls the Meyers' board is based on: (1) Fink's 47% ownership of Meyers' outstanding stock, and (2) that he "personally selected" each Meyers director. Plaintiff also alleges that mere approval of the employment agreement illustrates Fink's domination and control of the board. In addition, plaintiff argued on appeal that 47% stock ownership, though less than a majority, constituted control given the large number of shares outstanding, 1,245,745.

Such contentions do not support any claim under Delaware law that these directors lack independence. In *Kaplan v. Centex Corp.*, Del. Ch., 284 A.2d 119 (1971), the Court of Chancery stated that "[s]tock ownership alone, at least when it amounts to less than a majority, is not sufficient proof of domination or control". [Yet, here note that Fink owned 47% of Meyers' stock and was thereby able in practical effect to elect (and remove) each director of the company.] Moreover, in the demand context even proof of majority ownership of a company does not strip the directors of the presumptions of independence, and that their acts have been taken in good faith and in the best interests of the corporation. There must be coupled with the allegation of control such facts as would demonstrate that through personal or other relationships the directors are beholden to the controlling person. [Hence, the power of the majority shareholder to remove a director at his/her whim is not sufficient by itself under Delaware law.]

The requirement of director independence inhers in the conception and rationale of the business judgment rule. The presumption of propriety that flows from an exercise of business judgment is based in part on this unyielding precept. Independence means that a director's decision is based on the corporate merits of the subject before the board rather than extraneous considerations or influences. While directors may confer, debate, and resolve their differences through compromise, or by reasonable reliance upon the expertise of their colleagues and other qualified persons, the end result, nonetheless, must be that each director has brought his or her own informed business judgment to bear with specificity upon the corporate merits of the issues without regard for or succumbing to influences which convert an otherwise valid business decision into a faithless act.

Thus, it is not enough to charge that a director was nominated by or elected at the behest of those controlling the outcome of a corporate election. That is the usual way a person becomes a corporate director. It is the care, attention and sense of individual responsibility to the performance of one's duties, not the method of election, that generally touches on independence.

We conclude that in the demand-futile context a plaintiff charging domination and control of one or more directors must allege particularized facts manifesting "a direction of corporate conduct in such a way as to comport with the wishes or interests of the corporation (or persons) doing the controlling". The shorthand shibboleth of "dominated and controlled directors" is insufficient. ... [W]e stress that the plaintiff need only allege specific facts; he need not plead evidence. ...

Here, plaintiff has not alleged any facts sufficient to support a claim of control. The personal-selection-of-directors allegation stands alone, unsupported. At best it is a conclusion devoid of factual support. The causal link between Fink's control and approval of the employment agreement is alluded to, but nowhere specified. The director's approval, alone, does not establish control, even in the face of Fink's 47% stock ownership. The claim that Fink is unlikely to perform any services under the agreement, because of his age, and his conflicting consultant work with Prudential, adds nothing to the control claim. Therefore, we cannot conclude that the complaint factually particularizes any circumstances of control and domination to overcome the presumption of board independence, and thus render the demand futile.

C.

Turning to the board's approval of the Meyers-Fink employment agreement, plaintiff's argument is simple: all of the Meyers directors are named defendants, because they approved the wasteful agreement; if plaintiff prevails on the merits all the directors will be jointly and severally liable; therefore, the directors' interest in avoiding personal liability automatically and absolutely disqualifies them from passing on a shareholder's demand.

Such allegations are conclusory at best. In Delaware mere directorial approval of a transaction, absent particularized facts supporting a breach of fiduciary duty claim, or otherwise establishing the lack of independence or disinterestedness of a majority of the directors, is insufficient to excuse demand. Here, plaintiff's suit is premised on the notion that the Meyers-Fink employment agreement was a waste of corporate assets. So, the argument goes, by approving such waste the directors now face potential personal liability, thereby rendering futile any demand on them to bring suit. Unfortunately, plaintiff's claim falls in its initial premise. The complaint does not allege particularized facts indicating that the agreement is a waste of corporate assets. Indeed, the complaint as now drafted may not even state a cause of action, given the directors' broad corporate power to fix the compensation of officers.

As for Meyers' loans to Fink, beyond the bare allegation that they were made, the complaint does not allege facts indicating the wastefulness of such arrangements. Again, the mere existence of such loans, given the broad corporate powers conferred by Delaware law, does not even state a claim.

...

D.

Plaintiff's final argument is the incantation that demand is excused because the directors otherwise would have to sue themselves, thereby placing the conduct of the litigation in hostile hands and preventing its effective prosecution. This bootstrap argument has been made to and dismissed by other courts. ... Its acceptance would effectively abrogate Rule 23.1 and weaken the managerial power of directors. Unless facts are alleged with particularity to overcome the presumptions of independence and a proper exercise of business judgment, in which case the directors could not be expected to sue themselves, a bare claim of this sort raises no legally cognizable issue under Delaware corporate law.

V.

In sum, we conclude that the plaintiff has failed to allege facts with particularity indicating that the Meyers directors were tainted by interest, lacked independence, or took action contrary to Meyers' best interests in order to create a reasonable doubt as to the applicability of the business judgment rule. Only in the presence of such a reasonable doubt may a demand be deemed futile. Hence, we reverse the Court of Chancery's denial of the motion to dismiss, and remand with instructions that plaintiff be granted leave to amend his complaint to bring it into compliance with Rule 23.1 based on the principles we have announced today.

In re Oracle Corp. Derivative Litigation
Delaware Court of Chancery
824 A. 2d 917 (2003)

Strine, Vice Chancellor:

In this opinion, [in a case where demand on the board of directors was excused,] I address the motion of the special litigation committee ("SLC") of Oracle Corporation to terminate this action, "the Delaware Derivative Action," and other such actions pending in the name of Oracle against certain Oracle directors and officers. These actions allege that these Oracle directors engaged in insider trading while in possession of material, non-public information showing that Oracle would not meet the earnings guidance it gave to the market for the third quarter of Oracle's fiscal year 2001. The SLC bears the burden of persuasion on this motion and must convince me that there is no material issue of fact calling into doubt its independence. ...

The question of independence "turns on whether a director is, for *any substantial reason*, incapable of making a decision with only the best interests of the corporation in mind." That is, the independence test ultimately "focus[es] on impartiality and objectivity." In this case, the SLC has failed to demonstrate that no material factual question exists regarding its independence.

During discovery, it emerged that the two SLC members—both of whom are professors at Stanford University—are being asked to investigate fellow Oracle directors who have important ties to Stanford, too. Among the directors who are accused by the derivative plaintiffs of insider trading are: (1) another Stanford professor, who taught one of the SLC members when the SLC member was a Ph.D. candidate and who serves as a senior fellow and a steering committee member alongside that SLC member at the Stanford Institute for Economic Policy Research or "SIEPR"; (2) a Stanford alumnus who has directed millions of dollars of contributions to Stanford during recent years, serves as Chair of SIEPR's Advisory Board and has a conference center named for him at SIEPR's facility, and has contributed nearly $600,000 to SIEPR and the Stanford Law School, both parts of Stanford with which one of the SLC members is closely affiliated; and (3) Oracle's CEO, who has made millions of dollars in donations to Stanford through a personal foundation and large donations indirectly through Oracle, and who was considering making donations of his $100 million house and $170 million for a scholarship program as late as August 2001, at around the same time period the SLC members were added to the Oracle board. Taken together, these and other facts cause me to harbor a reasonable doubt about the impartiality of the SLC.

It is no easy task to decide whether to accuse a fellow director of insider trading. For Oracle to compound that difficulty by requiring SLC members to consider accusing a fellow professor and two large benefactors of their university of conduct that is rightly considered a violation of criminal law was unnecessary and inconsistent with the concept of independence recognized by our law. The possibility that these extraneous considerations biased the inquiry of the SLC is too substantial for this court to ignore. I therefore deny the SLC's motion to terminate.

...

The SLC's Investigation and Report

The SLC's investigation was, by any objective measure, extensive. The SLC reviewed an enormous amount of paper and electronic records. SLC counsel interviewed seventy witnesses, some of them twice. SLC members participated in several key interviews, including the interviews of the Trading Defendants.

...

In the end, the SLC produced an extremely lengthy Report totaling 1,110 pages (excluding appendices and exhibits) that concluded that Oracle should not pursue the plaintiffs' claims against the Trading Defendants or any of the other Oracle directors. ...

The SLC Moves to Terminate

Consistent with its Report, the SLC moved to terminate this litigation. The plaintiffs were granted discovery focusing on three primary topics: the independence of the SLC, the good faith of its investigative efforts, and the reasonableness of the bases for its conclusion that the lawsuit should be terminated. Additionally, the plaintiffs received a large volume of documents comprising the materials that the SLC relied upon in preparing its Report.

The Applicable Procedural Standard

In order to prevail on its motion to terminate the Delaware Derivative Action, the SLC must persuade me that: (1) its members were independent; (2) that they acted in good faith; and (3) that they had reasonable bases for their recommendations. If the SLC meets that burden, I am free to grant its motion or may, in my discretion, undertake my own examination of whether Oracle should terminate and permit the suit to proceed if I, in my oxymoronic judicial "business judgment," conclude that procession is in the best interests of the company. This two-step analysis comes, of course, from [the Delaware Supreme Court's decision in] *Zapata*.

...

In this case, the plaintiffs principally challenge the SLC's independence and the reasonableness of its recommendation. For reasons I next explain, I need examine only the more difficult question, which relates to the SLC's independence.

...

The Court's Analysis of the SLC's Independence

...

I begin with an important reminder: the SLC bears the burden of proving its independence. It must convince me.

But of what? According to the SLC, its members are independent unless they are essentially subservient to the Trading Defendants—i.e., they are under the "domination and control" of the interested parties. If the SLC is correct and this is the central inquiry in the independence determination, they would win. Nothing in the record suggests to me that either [SLC member is] dominated and controlled by any of the Trading Defendants, by Oracle, or even by Stanford [University].

But, in my view, an emphasis on "domination and control" would serve only to fetishize much-parroted language, at the cost of denuding the independence inquiry of its intellectual integrity. Take an easy example. Imagine if two brothers were on a corporate board, each successful in different businesses and not dependent in any way on the other's beneficence in order to be wealthy. The brothers are brothers, they stay in touch and consider each other family, but each is opinionated and strong-willed. A derivative action is filed targeting a transaction involving one of the brothers. The other brother is put on a special litigation committee to investigate the case. If the test is domination and control, then one brother could investigate the other. Does any sensible person think that is our law? I do not think it is.

And it should not be our law. Delaware law should not be based on a reductionist view of human nature that simplifies human motivations on the lines of the least sophisticated notions of the law and economics movement. *Homo sapiens* is not merely *homo economicus.* We may be thankful that an array of other motivations exist that influence human behavior; not all are any better than greed or avarice; think of envy, to name just one. But also think of motives like love, friendship, and collegiality; think of those among us who direct their behavior as best they can on a guiding creed or set of moral values.

Nor should our law ignore the social nature of humans. To be direct, corporate directors are generally the sort of people deeply enmeshed in social institutions. Such institutions have norms, expectations that, explicitly and implicitly, influence and channel the behavior of those who participate in their operation. Some things are "just not done," or only at a cost, which might not be so severe as a loss of position, but may involve a loss of standing in the institution. In being appropriately sensitive to this factor, our law also cannot assume—absent some proof of the point—that corporate directors are, as a general matter, persons of unusual social bravery, who operate heedless to the inhibitions that social norms generate for ordinary folk.

For all these reasons, this court has previously held that the Delaware Supreme Court's teachings on independence can be summarized thusly:

> At bottom, the question of independence turns on whether a director is, *for any substantial reason*, incapable of making a decision with only the best interests of the corporation in mind. That is, the Supreme Court cases ultimately focus on impartiality and objectivity.

This formulation is wholly consistent with the teaching of [the Delaware Supreme Court in] *Aronson*, which defines independence as meaning that "a director's decision is based on the corporate merits of the subject before the board rather than extraneous considerations or influences."

The Contextual Nature of the Independence Inquiry Under Delaware Law

In examining whether the SLC has met its burden to demonstrate that there is no material dispute of fact regarding its independence, the court must bear in mind the function of special litigation committees under our jurisprudence. Under Delaware law, the primary means by which corporate defendants may obtain a dismissal of a derivative suit is by showing that the plaintiffs have not met their pleading burden under the test of *Aronson v. Lewis*, or the related standard set forth in *Rales v. Blasband* [634 A. 2d 927 (Del. 1993)]. In simple terms, these tests permit a corporation to terminate a derivative suit if its board is comprised of directors who can impartially consider a demand.

Special litigation committees are permitted as a last chance for a corporation to control a derivative claim in circumstances when a majority of its directors cannot impartially consider a demand. By vesting the power of the board to determine what to do with the suit in a committee of independent directors, a corporation may retain control over whether the suit will proceed, so long as the committee meets the standard set forth in *Zapata*.

In evaluating the independence of a special litigation committee, this court must take into account the extraordinary importance and difficulty of such a committee's responsibility. It is, I daresay, easier to say no to a friend, relative, colleague, or boss who seeks assent for an act (*e.g.*, a transaction) that has not yet occurred than it would be to cause a corporation to sue that person. This is admittedly a determination of so-called "legislative fact," but one that can be rather safely made. Denying a fellow director the ability to proceed on a matter important to him may not be easy, but it must, as a general matter, be less difficult than finding that there is reason to believe that the fellow director has committed serious wrongdoing and that a derivative suit should proceed against him.

The difficulty of making this decision is compounded in the special litigation committee context because the weight of making the moral judgment necessarily falls on less than the full board. A small number of directors feels the moral gravity—and social pressures—of this duty alone.

For all these reasons, the independence inquiry is critically important if the special litigation committee process is to retain its integrity, a quality that is, in turn, essential to the utility of that process. …

Thus, in assessing the independence of the Oracle SLC, I necessarily examine the question of whether the SLC can independently make the difficult decision entrusted to it: to determine whether the Trading Defendants should face suit for insider trading-based allegations of breach of fiduciary duty. An affirmative answer by the SLC to that question would have potentially huge negative consequences for the Trading Defendants, not only by exposing them to the possibility of a large damage award but also by subjecting them to great reputational harm. To have [the SLC members who are Professors at Stanford University] declare that Oracle should press insider trading claims against the Trading Defendants would have been, to put it mildly, "news." Relatedly, it is reasonable to think that an SLC determination that the Trading Defendants had likely engaged in insider trading would have been accompanied by a recommendation that they step down as fiduciaries until their ultimate culpability was decided.

The importance and special sensitivity of the SLC's task is also relevant for another obvious reason: investigations do not follow a scientific process like an old-fashioned assembly line. The investigators' mindset and talent influence, for good or ill, the course of an investigation. Just as there are obvious dangers from investigators suffering from too much zeal, so too are dangers posed by investigators who harbor reasons not to pursue the investigation's targets with full vigor.

The nature of the investigation is important, too. Here, for example, the SLC was required to undertake an investigation that could not avoid a consideration of the subjective state of mind of the Trading Defendants. Their credibility was important, and the SLC could not escape making judgments about that, no matter how objective the criteria the SLC attempted to use.

Therefore, I necessarily measure the SLC's independence contextually, and my ruling confronts the SLC's ability to decide impartially whether the Trading Defendants should be pursued for insider trading. This contextual approach is a strength of our law, as even the best minds have yet to devise across-the-board definitions that capture all the circumstances in which the independence of directors might reasonably be questioned. By taking into account all circumstances, the Delaware approach undoubtedly results in some level of indeterminacy, but with the compensating benefit that independence determinations are tailored to the precise situation at issue.

...

The SLC Has Not Met Its Burden to Demonstrate the Absence of a Material Dispute of Fact About Its Independence

Using the contextual approach I have described, I conclude that the SLC has not met its burden to show the absence of a material factual question about its independence. I find this to be the case because the ties among the SLC, the Trading Defendants, and Stanford are so substantial that they cause reasonable doubt about the SLC's ability to impartially consider whether the Trading Defendants should face suit. ...

As SLC members, [the Professors] were already being asked to consider whether the company should level extremely serious accusations of wrongdoing against fellow board members. As to [one of the directors], both SLC members faced another layer of complexity: the determination of whether to have Oracle press insider trading claims against a fellow professor at their university. Even though [he] was in a different academic department from either SLC member, it is reasonable to assume that the fact that [he] was also on faculty would—to persons possessing typical sensibilities and institutional loyalty—be a matter of more than trivial concern. Universities are obviously places of at times intense debate, but they also see themselves as communities. In fact, Stanford refers to itself as a "community of scholars." To accuse a fellow professor—whom one might see at the faculty club or at interdisciplinary presentations of academic papers—of insider trading cannot be a small thing—even for the most callous of academics.

...

And, for both [SLC members], service on the SLC demanded that they consider whether an extremely generous and influential Stanford alumnus should be sued by Oracle for insider trading. Although they were not responsible for fundraising, as sophisticated professors they undoubtedly are aware of how important large contributors are to Stanford, and they share in the benefits that come from serving at a university with a rich endowment. A reasonable professor giving any thought to the matter would obviously consider the effect his decision might have on the University's relationship with [the subject director], it being (one hopes) sensible to infer that a professor of reasonable collegiality and loyalty cares about the well-being of the institution he serves.

...

Before closing, it is necessary to address two concerns. The first is the undeniable awkwardness of opinions like this one. By finding that there exists too much doubt about the SLC's independence for the SLC to meet its *Zapata* burden, I make no finding about the subjective good faith of the SLC members, both of whom are distinguished academics at one of this nation's most prestigious institutions of higher learning. Nothing in this record leads me to conclude that either of the SLC members acted out of any conscious desire to favor the Trading Defendants or to do anything other than discharge their duties with fidelity. But that is not the purpose of the independence inquiry.

That inquiry recognizes that persons of integrity and reputation can be compromised in their ability to act without bias when they must make a decision adverse to others with whom they share material affiliations. To conclude that the Oracle SLC was not independent is not a conclusion that the two accomplished professors who comprise it are not persons of good faith and moral probity, it is solely to conclude that they were not situated to act with the required degree of impartiality. *Zapata* requires independence to ensure that stockholders do not have to rely upon special litigation committee members who must put aside personal considerations that are ordinarily influential in daily behavior in making the already difficult decision to accuse fellow directors of serious wrongdoing.

Finally, the SLC has made the argument that a ruling against it will chill the ability of corporations to locate qualified independent directors in the academy. This is overwrought. If there are 1,700 professors at Stanford alone, as the SLC says, how many must there be on the west coast of the United States, at institutions without ties to Oracle and the Trading Defendants as substantial as Stanford's? Undoubtedly, a corporation of Oracle's market capitalization could have found prominent academics willing to serve as SLC members, about whom no reasonable question of independence could have been asserted.

Rather than form an SLC whose membership was free from bias-creating relationships, Oracle formed a committee fraught with them. As a result, the SLC has failed to meet its *Zapata* burden, and its motion to terminate must be denied. ...

BOOTH FAMILY TRUST V. ABERCROMBIE & FITCH CO. UNITED STATES COURT OF APPEALS 640 F. 3D 134 (6TH CIR. 2011)

Boyce F. Martin, Jr., Circuit Judge:

Plaintiffs-appellants are shareholders of Abercrombie & Fitch Co. The Shareholders filed a derivative suit on behalf of Abercrombie against several officers and directors alleging that defendants caused Abercrombie to make misleading public statements between June 2 and August 18, 2005, which caused the stock price to rise and then fall once the falsity of these statements was revealed. An investigation by the Securities Exchange Commission and securities fraud lawsuits followed, which the Shareholders allege damaged Abercrombie.

Upon the filing of the lawsuit, Abercrombie invoked a procedural option available under Delaware law by forming a special litigation committee to investigate the claims made by the Shareholders.

The special litigation committee subsequently recommended that Abercrombie seek dismissal of the lawsuit, which Abercrombie did by filing a motion to dismiss. The district court granted the motion, holding that Abercrombie's special litigation committee was independent under Delaware law, it conducted its investigation in good faith, and its decision not to pursue the derivative suit was reasonable. However, we hold that there are serious questions as to Abercrombie's special litigation committee's independence, and therefore reverse the district court's decision, deny the motion to dismiss, and remand for further proceedings.

I.

The Shareholders generally allege that certain officers and directors caused Abercrombie to issue misleading public statements regarding the success of its business model in early 2005, which resulted in the stock price rising and then falling after the falsity of these statements was revealed later that year. Essentially, according to the complaint, Abercrombie adopted a business model of selling products with a low manufacturing cost at high retail prices, resulting in a high per-unit margin. The company sought to create such a desired brand so that it could "train" its customers to not expect a sale or markdowns and instead just pay the high price. This approach manifested itself most particularly in Abercrombie's denim products, which were apparently made cheaply but sold expensively.

Beginning in early 2005 and continuing through the summer, Abercrombie issued reports indicating that its denim sales were strong and that its high gross margin business strategy was working. The Shareholders allege that these statements were misleading because company insiders knew that Abercrombie was amassing a large surplus of inventory such that there would have to be dramatic markdowns to clear out the inventory. The Shareholders further allege that the officers and directors knew that this corrective action would result in a decrease in per-unit profit and cast doubt on the viability of Abercrombie's business model, causing a negative correction in the company's stock price. The stock price eventually did fall, which kicked off a spate of lawsuits and regulatory investigations.

During this time, when the insiders are alleged to have known that the price would soon fall, five of the defendants—Singer, Jeffries, Bachmann, Kessler, and Griffin—sold a large number of their personally owned shares of Abercrombie stock. The Shareholders claim that this amounts to insider trading, and they level additional allegations against this group of defendants.

In response to this lawsuit, in October 2005, Abercrombie's Board of Directors formed a special litigation committee. The board resolution creating the special litigation committee called for it to have two members. Initially, Abercrombie's special litigation committee was comprised of Daniel Brestle and Allan Tuttle, both members of Abercrombie's Board. Although Tuttle is now a defendant, he was not named when Abercrombie formed the special litigation committee. Brestle later resigned, but did so before the special litigation committee issued its report, and was replaced by Lauren Brisky. Brisky is also a Board member, and was a named defendant at the time of her appointment to the special litigation committee. The Board gave the special litigation committee complete authority to investigate the Shareholders' claims and to direct the company on whether to proceed with the lawsuit on its own behalf or to seek its dismissal as being against the interests of the company.

Abercrombie's special litigation committee retained the law firm of Cahill Gordon & Reindell LLP, a national law firm that had no prior relationship with Abercrombie. Cahill Gordon did the bulk of the work in interviewing witnesses and reviewing documents and records, advised the two special litigation committee members on the progress and results of the investigation, and made recommendations on how to proceed. Because of their prior relationship, Tuttle abstained from considering the claims against Singer. The record indicates that Tuttle did not attend the interview with Singer but does not otherwise explain how he was screened from considering the claims against Singer.

Approximately sixteen months after its formation, the special litigation committee produced a 144-page report detailing its investigation and concluding that there was no evidence to support the Shareholders' claims. The special litigation committee therefore directed Abercrombie to seek dismissal of the case. Abercrombie filed its motion to dismiss pursuant to Federal Rule of Civil Procedure 41(a)(2) on September 10, 2007 under the framework set out by the Delaware Supreme Court in *Zapata Corp. v. Maldonado*, 430 A.2d 779 (Del. 1981). Under *Zapata*, as explained more fully below, a corporation may appoint a special litigation committee to investigate claims presented in a derivative action. If a court finds that a corporation's special litigation committee was independent, conducted its investigation in good faith, had reasonable bases for its conclusion and the decision to dismiss the lawsuit is not inconsistent with business judgment, the court will dismiss the derivative action.

...

II.

...

... [W]e will review de novo the district court's decisions under the first prong of the *Zapata* inquiry as to whether the special litigation committee was independent, carried out the investigation in good faith, and had reasonable bases supporting its conclusions.

III.

Abercrombie is a Delaware corporation and [under the internal affairs doctrine] Delaware law governs the substantive issues of this action. The Delaware Supreme Court established a unique procedure for determining whether a special litigation committee's motion to dismiss a shareholder derivative action should be granted. Under this procedure, "[f]irst, the Court should inquire into the independence and good faith of the committee and the bases supporting its conclusions." *Zapata*, 430 A.2d at 788. The corporation has the burden of proving that its special litigation committee was independent, carried out its investigation in good faith, and reached a reasonable conclusion. If the court has doubts about the committee's independence or whether it has shown reasonable bases for its conclusions, the court shall deny the corporation's motion. *Id.* at 789.

If a court is satisfied with the committee's conduct under the first step, the court may apply its own independent business judgment, and determine whether the motion should be granted. "This means, of course, that instances could arise where a committee can establish its independence and sound bases for its good faith decisions and still have the corporation's motion denied." [*Zapata,* 430 A. 2d at 789]

Subject to the court's independent business judgment, this procedure grants a properly formed special litigation committee a tremendous amount of leeway to decide whether a derivative action should be maintained. Maintaining a derivative action can implicate many complex, non-legal concerns. This procedure endeavors to give courts a means to supervise corporations such that they cannot use the special litigation committee procedure to "consistently wrest bona fide derivative actions away from well-meaning derivative plaintiffs," and plaintiffs cannot incapacitate corporations with "meritless or harmful litigation." *Id.* at 787. Therefore, one of the primary concerns becomes whether Abercrombie's special litigation committee was independent.

A. Zapata Independence

Under Delaware law, "[t]he question of independence 'turns on whether a director is, *for any substantial reason*, incapable of making a decision with only the best interests of the corporation in mind.' That is, the independence test ultimately 'focus[es] on impartiality and objectivity.'" ... The special litigation committee bears the burden of proving that there is no material issue of fact as to its independence. If the facts combine to give rise to a perception of an inability to proceed independently, the shareholder need not show that the committee was in fact not independent. ... We need not conclude that any committee member "actually acted improperly" in order to conclude that the moving party failed to meet its burden of showing the absence of any possible issue of material fact regarding the special litigation committee's independence.

Thus, a finding of lack of independence in the special litigation committee context is not a finding that its members "are not persons of good faith and moral probity; it is solely to conclude that they were not situated to act with the required degree of impartiality." ... Concluding that a committee member is not independent merely recognizes that his or her connection to the alleged wrongdoers or the alleged wrongdoing "would be on the mind of the [special litigation committee] member in a way that generates an unacceptable risk of bias." ...

In considering the makeup of a special litigation committee, we look to see if the facts create a "reasonable doubt" as to the committee's impartiality. If a reasonable doubt exists as to the special litigation committee's independence, the special litigation committee's conclusions are rejected then and there; no further resolution is required on the independence question. The case then proceeds to the merits of the claims against the defendants.

A corporation forms a special litigation committee after being presented with either a demand from shareholders, or, in cases where demand may be excused. ... In either case, the corporation is fully aware of the charges that the special litigation committee will be tasked with investigating before it forms the committee. Delaware law does not impose any restrictions on the number of members a special litigation committee must have or which board members must be on the committee. ... Consequently, in a special litigation committee case, there is no presumption of independence and the special litigation committee bears the burden of "establishing its own independence. ... Because the corporation has every opportunity to form a perfectly independent special litigation committee, we require that it do so.

B. Independence of Special Litigation Committee Member Tuttle

Tuttle's decision to recuse himself from considering the allegations against Singer, a named defendant and a central player in the Shareholders' allegations, demonstrates that Tuttle, and therefore the special litigation committee, was not independent. At the time of the events in question, Singer was Abercrombie's Chief Operating Officer and appears to have been involved heavily in the strategy of touting the success of Abercrombie's business model to the market. He is also one of the defendants alleged to have engaged in insider trading while the stock price was allegedly artificially high. Singer had previously been associated with the Gucci Company, where he worked with Tuttle. Singer spearheaded the effort to have Tuttle join the Abercrombie board, and he described Tuttle as "my close personal friend who worked with me at Gucci who I brought to the board." Discovery also revealed that Tuttle was planning a trip to Italy to visit Singer and his wife.

We note at the outset that other areas of Delaware corporate law are relatively flexible and will not find that directors are incapable of exercising independent judgment even if they are friends, and have personal relationships with a board member allegedly responsible for some wrongdoing. ... This is understandable in light of how business is conducted and board positions are filled. However, when considering a special litigation committee's independence, which, unlike a board, can be crafted to be perfectly independent with respect to its charge, it is unclear if Delaware law would be quite as accepting.

In any event, we need not determine precisely where Delaware draws the line between permissible and impermissible relationships in order to resolve this case. Had Tuttle not recused himself from considering the claims against Singer, we might agree with the district court's conclusion that he was independent. However, because Tuttle, for whatever reason or no reason at all, recused himself from considering the claims against Singer he effectively admitted that he was not independent. At the very least, his recusal creates a perception that Tuttle was not independent. Even if Tuttle's relationship with Singer was not so close that it would get caught by the net established in Delaware case law, he cannot now use that to show his independence. When Tuttle recused himself from considering the claims against Singer, he essentially launched a signal flare that he was not independent.

This is not to say that Tuttle is a bad person or did anything wrong. Quite to the contrary, Tuttle appears to have attempted to discharge his duties in good faith by taking action which he believed would preserve his independence with respect to the other members. However, because of Singer's relationship to the other members and implication in the alleged wrongdoing due to his position as Abercrombie's President, Chief Operating Officer and Chief Financial Officer, the recusal was not effective. Abercrombie has not met its burden of showing that Tuttle was able to independently consider the claims against the other directors because in the context of the misleading statement claims, Tuttle's purported abstention from considering claims against Singer was mere formalism. The claims were, generally, that the Board endorsed the issuing of misleading statements as to Abercrombie's profitability. These claims are not individual in nature, and a conclusion that one director engaged in wrongdoing would imply that the other directors did as well. Furthermore, as the Shareholders point out, Singer is alleged to have been at the very center of the allegedly improper activity. Therefore, if Tuttle, as a member of Abercrombie's special litigation committee, had concluded that the claims against *any* of the directors regarding the public statements were meritorious, he would necessarily be concluding that the claims against Singer had merit, even if he did not say so explicitly. Stated differently, Tuttle could not explicitly conclude that any claim against any other defendant had merit without implicitly concluding that the claims against Singer also had merit. It follows, then, that if Tuttle's relationship with Singer was sufficiently close to make him question his ability to pass judgment on Singer, that same relationship would necessarily infect his judgment regarding other defendants. Even if Abercrombie could theoretically establish that Tuttle came to his conclusions regarding the other directors free of any taint caused by his relationship with Singer, the mere appearance of the special litigation committee's lack of independence is enough to deny Abercrombie's motion based on the special litigation committee's recommendation and allow the derivative suit to proceed.

Moreover, Abercrombie did not establish that Tuttle effectively recused himself from considering the claims against Singer. While we do not hold that a recusal can preserve a special litigation committee member's independence, the record in this case does not suggest that Tuttle's recusal was effective. The burden is on Abercrombie to show that its special litigation committee was independent. The extent of Tuttle's recusal appears to have been not attending Singer's interview. None of the affidavits in support of this motion detail the steps the special litigation committee took to keep Tuttle removed from considering the claims against Singer, and Abercrombie did not even establish that Tuttle was screened from considering the parts of the report discussing Singer's involvement. Therefore, the record does not indicate that Abercrombie met its burden of establishing the special litigation committee's independence.

Even if we were to accept the premise that Tuttle's decision to abstain from considering claims against Singer preserved Tuttle's independence with respect to the other defendants—a premise that Abercrombie does not identify support for in any decisions applying Delaware law—the decision to abstain materially altered the special litigation committee as an entity. The Board created a special litigation committee composed of two members to investigate the claims. Tuttle's decision to abstain as to Singer resulted in a committee of one. Abercrombie points to several decisions that indicate that a one-member special litigation committee is not necessarily problematic, and we agree. However, the problem is not that the special litigation committee only had one member as to Singer. The problem is that the special litigation committee only had one member when the [board of directors] resolution that created it called for a two-member committee. If Abercrombie had wanted a special litigation committee with just one member, it could have so chosen. But, instead, it appointed two members, and we assume that Abercrombie saw some value in having two members.

Furthermore, it is not clear from the record that the special litigation committee was even authorized to operate with only one member. The Board's resolution forming the special litigation committee is silent on this point, so it is quite possible that the committee was acting *ultra vires* when it considered the claims against Singer with less than its full complement of members. As special litigation committees derive their power and legitimacy from the board resolutions that create them, any action that runs contrary to the resolution casts doubt on the legitimacy of a special litigation committee's conclusions. Though this point also potentially bears upon the good faith of Abercrombie's special litigation committee and the reasonableness of its conclusions, the problem was born by Tuttle's lack of independence as to Singer, so it seems proper to treat it as an independence issue.

While Tuttle is now a named defendant, it does not appear that Tuttle was named as a defendant at the time that Abercrombie formed its special litigation committee. Furthermore, there is reason to doubt the strength of the claim against him—he became a director only three months prior to the derivative suit being filed and long after the events that are the focus of the Shareholders' claims. Therefore, it seems that he is a defendant solely because he happens to be on the Board. While his current status as a named defendant does not necessarily demonstrate his lack of independence, Tuttle's decision to recuse himself from considering claims against Singer, combined with Singer's central role in the alleged wrongdoing, leave us with serious doubts as to his independence.

C. Independence of Special Litigation Committee Member Brisky

The other member on Abercrombie's special litigation committee with Tuttle, Brisky, is the Vice Chancellor for Administration and Chief Financial Officer of Vanderbilt University. She was also a member of the Board and, specifically, a member of its Audit Committee. Brisky was not originally a member of the special litigation committee, but she replaced Brestle after he resigned.

The Shareholders do not claim that Brisky is particularly beholden to any of the other members of the Board. Instead, they point out that (1) Brisky was a named defendant, and thus theoretically facing liability, and (2) that as a member of the Audit Committee she played a role in the actions being challenged. While both of these factors arguably cast some doubt on her ability to independently consider the Shareholders' claims against the directors, we need not analyze her conduct in detail because it is heavily dependent on Delaware law and unnecessary in light of Tuttle's taint on the special litigation committee.

D. Was the SLC Independent?

Although *Zapata* allows courts to use their business judgment and independently determine whether the special litigation committee's motion to dismiss is actually in the best interests of the corporation, courts put the most weight on *Zapata*'s first prong and, specifically, whether the committee was independent. ... In accordance with this, Delaware courts hold special litigation committees to a very high standard of independence. Special litigation committees are not presumed to be independent, and the special litigation committee must prove its independence. ... In light of Tuttle's recusal, we are left with strong doubts as to the special litigation committee's independence and cannot conclude that Abercrombie has clearly demonstrated its special litigation committee's independence.

While the allegations of Brisky's lack of independence may not, standing alone, compel a finding of lack of independence, we cannot conclude that the special litigation committee was independent in light of Tuttle's recusal. We look not only to the fact of objectivity and validity when reviewing special litigation committee determinations, but also the appearance of objectivity and validity. "The composition and conduct of a special litigation committee therefore must be such as to instill confidence in the judiciary and, as important, the stockholders of the company that the committee can act with integrity and objectivity." ... Tuttle's decision to recuse himself from considering claims against Singer, and Singer's central role in the alleged wrongdoing, casts serious doubt on Tuttle's objectivity as to the claims as a whole and does not instill confidence in us. While not dispositive, Brisky's status as a named defendant adds to the doubt regarding this special litigation committee's independence. Particularly where Abercrombie had the opportunity to work with competent counsel and cherry pick who would serve on its special litigation committee, it cannot now rely on the recommendation of a special litigation committee with such dubious independence.

This is one of those rare situations where Abercrombie had every opportunity to create an independent special litigation committee but nonetheless failed to do so. Delaware law gives an independent special litigation committee extremely wide latitude to conclude that a derivative suit is not in the best interests of the corporation, but the committee must be independent. In light of the tremendous discretion and power that special litigation committees are afforded under the *Zapata* procedure, it is not unreasonable to require that corporations comply with the protocols set out by the Delaware Supreme Court and staff their special litigation committees with individuals who can exercise independent judgment.

Because we conclude that there are serious doubts as to Abercrombie's special litigation committee's independence, we need not consider whether the committee carried out its investigation in good faith or whether its conclusions are reasonable. Without a demonstration that its special litigation committee was independent, Abercrombie's motion to dismiss based on the committee's recommendation cannot be granted.

IV.

Abercrombie contends that this lawsuit is a classic example of a strike suit and, because we are not considering the merits of the suit at this time, that may very well be the case. However, at this stage, because Abercrombie failed to adequately demonstrate its special litigation committee's independence, we cannot dismiss the suit based on its recommendation. Therefore, we reverse the decision of the district court, deny the motion to dismiss this action, and remand for further proceedings.

Griffin, Circuit Judge, Dissenting:

In reversing the district court, the majority holds that the Special Litigation Committee ("SLC") lacked independence because "serious doubts" regarding its independence arise based upon committee member Alan Tuttle's partial recusal as to the claims against defendant Robert Singer. According to the majority:

> Had Tuttle not recused himself from considering the claims against Singer, we might agree with the district court's conclusion that he was independent. However, because Tuttle, for whatever reason or no reason at all, recused himself from considering the claims against Singer he effectively admitted that he was not independent.

From this inference, the majority holds that the SLC lacked independence regarding the claims against the corporation and other directors and officers: "Tuttle's decision to recuse himself from considering the allegations against Singer, a named defendant and a central player in the Shareholders' allegations, demonstrates that Tuttle, and therefore the special litigation committee, was not independent."

The majority fails to cite any authority for its holding and, because its conclusion is inconsistent with Delaware law, I respectfully dissent.

I.

Delaware law controls the substantive issues in this matter. In holding that the SLC did not meet its burden in establishing its independence, the majority relies almost exclusively on Tuttle's partial recusal, asserting that it constitutes an admission of bias. I respectfully disagree.

In my view, Tuttle's partial recusal regarding Singer does not impute bias to the SLC. As the Supreme Court of Delaware has noted, "it is the care, attention and sense of individual responsibility to the performance of one's duties that touch on independence." ... This is exactly what Tuttle demonstrated here. Indeed, through his partial recusal, Tuttle attempted to expel any doubt regarding the independence of the SLC.

Upon detailed review, I have found only one case directly addressing whether a recusal may serve as an admission of bias. In *Buchwald v. University of Minnesota*, 573 N.W.2d 723 (Minn. Ct. App. 1998), the president of the University of Minnesota recused himself from making a determination regarding a professor's alleged misconduct. Later, when the professor sought indemnification for the costs in defending against the allegations, the president denied the request. In challenging this denial, the professor asserted that the president's recusal admitted his bias against the professor. The Minnesota Court of Appeals disagreed, holding that a recusal does not, in and of itself, admit bias.

While it is the SLC's ultimate burden of persuasion to establish its independence, *Zapata Corp. v. Maldonado*, 430 A.2d 779, 788 (Del. 1981), it is the plaintiff who must demonstrate *how* the facts presented rise to the level necessary to demonstrate a lack of independence. …

Significantly, had Tuttle not recused himself and fully addressed all issues presented to the SLC, there would be little doubt regarding the committee's independence. In my view, Tuttle's partial recusal does not alter this result.

"The question of independence turns on whether a director is, *for any substantial reason*, incapable of making a decision with only the best interests of the corporation in mind." … Delaware courts have consistently held that "[n]either mere personal friendship alone, nor mere outside business relationships alone, are sufficient to raise reasonable doubt regarding a director's independence." … Indeed, "business dealings seldom take place between complete strangers and it would be a strained and artificial rule which required a director to be unacquainted or uninvolved with fellow directors in order to be regarded as independent." … Accordingly, Tuttle's friendship with Singer is not a "substantial reason" indicating that he was incapable of making decisions in the best interests of the corporation.

II.

Without directly resolving the question of Lauren Brisky's independence, the majority notes that her status as a named defendant and as a member of the Audit Committee "cast some doubt on her ability to independently consider the Shareholders' claims against the directors." Again, I disagree.

Status as a defendant, in and of itself, does not disqualify a person from serving on an SLC. … Moreover, Brisky's Audit Committee membership does not demonstrate a lack of independence. First, there is no evidence that Brisky, while serving on the Audit Committee, actually reviewed any of the releases relevant to the current lawsuit. Moreover, even if Brisky had approved the releases at issue, such approval would not destroy her independence. *See Kaplan*, 499 A.2d at 1189 ("Even a director's approval of the transaction in question does not establish a lack of independence."). Accordingly, the SLC has met its burden in establishing the independence of Brisky.

III.

Finally, the majority intimates that the SLC may have acted without authority because Tuttle's partial recusal created a one-member SLC. Once again, this assertion is inconsistent with Delaware law and unsupported by any authority. Indeed, Delaware expressly authorizes committees containing one member. ...

Moreover, the doctrine of *ultra vires* is not applicable. *See Black's Law Dictionary* 730 (2d pocket ed. 2001) (defining "ultra vires" as "Unauthorized; beyond the scope of power allowed or granted by a corporate charter or by law"). While the Abercrombie board created an SLC with two members, the majority cites no bylaws or other corporate documents requiring that the members act jointly on all committee business, nor does the majority point to any corporate restrictions forbidding partial recusals. ... There simply is no basis in the record to hold that the SLC acted *ultra vires* and therefore lacked independence.

IV.

In sum, I disagree with the majority's holding that the SLC failed to meet its burden of establishing its independence. Tuttle's partial recusal is not an admission of bias imputed to the SLC.

Because the majority holds that the SLC did not meet its burden in establishing independence, it does address the second and third prongs of the *Zapata* analysis. For the reasons well-stated by the district court, I would hold that the SLC also met its burdens of establishing its good faith and an adequate basis for its conclusions. ...

Accordingly, I respectfully dissent. I would affirm the order of the district court granting defendants' motion to dismiss.

SCENARIO

Daniel and Donna Streetman began American Consolidated Products, Inc. (American Consolidated) in 1985 as a two-person duly incorporated company. Over the next few years, their business and family grew. By 1993, the Streetmans were raising five children (Alice, Bernard, Carl, Drew, Eddy) and American Consolidated had nearly fifty full-time employees. By the end of 2003, the company had continued to flourish, enjoying sales of more that $25 million, specializing in industrial lubricants and bearing products. Donna served as CEO, Daniel as CFO, with Alice and Bernard serving as vice-presidents.

By the end of 2006, American Consolidated had undergone additional rounds of financing. At that time, the Streetman family retained control over 52% of American Consolidated's voting stock. In 2008, Carl and Eddy, who were enjoying their own personal successes, agreed to serve as directors. Drew, never much caring for the family business, struck out on his own. In 2009, he started a small manufacturing firm, Drew's Bearings Corp., that produces specialty bearings for pinball machines. He is managing to make his payroll and a modest profit.

At the end of 2009, a compensation committee for American Consolidated was formed. Eddy was appointed to chair the three-person committee. In short order, the committee approved a compensation package for all "principal" level executives that increased their compensation by more than 300%, totaling near 20% of the company's gross income.

In 2010, while attending a lubricant tradeshow in Milwaukee, Donna and Daniel made the rounds to check out the competition and solicit new business. Their son Drew was also supposed to attend on behalf of his own firm but never arrived because of a business emergency. While at the conference, Daniel met with Steve Sheldon, CEO of Pinball Express LLC, a firm specializing in custom-made pinball machines for top entertainment venues and A-list clientele. After an hour of conversation, Daniel knows that, while American Consolidated currently does not manufacture a product that "exactly" meets what Pinball Express is looking for, it could produce such a product with relative minor modification of its existing facilities.

Without coming to any agreement, Daniel takes Steve's card and the bearing specifications, and sends them to his son Drew. Daniel never mentions the meeting to any one at American Consolidated, nor submits a bid. When Drew receives the information from Daniel, he quickly contacts Steve and negotiates a deal for 100,000 bearings. This order dramatically improves business for Drew's Bearings, and helps to ensure the company's financial security for the next few years.

Several American Consolidated shareholders, who are angry about the amount of compensation paid to the company's executives, subsequently learn of the dialogue between Daniel and Steve, and the subsequent deal with Drew. Incensed, they bring a shareholder derivative action against the directors who are members of the Streetman family for breach of fiduciary duty related to executive compensation and for usurpation of corporate opportunity related to the Pinball Express deal. American Consolidated appoints a special litigation committee (SLC) headed by Luis Salazar and Sylvia Schwartz. Salazar owns a bank which has supplied $20 million of loans to American Consolidated, all of which have been repaid. Schwartz is a business professor at a local college who has a consulting relationship with the company, with fees from this arrangement being $45,000 annually. Upon retaining legal counsel and conducting an investigation, the SLC members determine that the derivative action should be dismissed.

You are a shareholder of American Consolidated who brought this action or, alternatively, you represent such a shareholder. What facts are important for you to uncover during discovery? What arguments do you make in an effort to defeat the defendants' efforts to have the action dismissed? How likely are you to succeed?

Chapter 8

So, It's a Security—What Is the Big Deal?!

Whether one is an entrepreneur, investor, financial intermediary (such as a banker) or attorney, a key question frequently presented is whether the investment vehicle at issue is a "security" under federal and state law. For example, this inquiry arises with respect to corporate stock, limited liability company (LLC) membership interests, limited partnership interests, and debt instruments (such as long-term bonds and debentures as well as notes that are mass marketed).

If the instrument is a security, then the federal and state securities laws apply. These statutes (and regulations adopted thereunder by the U.S. Securities and Exchange Commission (SEC) and state regulators) set forth registration and disclosure requirements. They also outlaw fraud, provide for investor remedies, and set forth civil and criminal sanctions. Noncompliance with the securities laws, therefore, has significant adverse ramifications.[1]

A general principle underlying the securities laws is that, absent an exemption from registration, each offer or sale of a security must be registered with the SEC and applicable state authority. Registration of a securities offering is an arduous process, particularly in the case of a company "going public" and thereby conducting an initial public offering (IPO). Generally, the enterprise must have an established "track" record of impressive earnings, must find receptive investment bankers (such as UBS, Merrill Lynch, or Goldman Sachs) to serve as underwriters and market the offering, must undergo rigorous SEC and perhaps state regulator review, and must launch the IPO process during a period in which the financial markets are receptive (e.g., during "market windows").[2]

Due to these hurdles, enterprises frequently elect to seek an exemption from registration which itself is often a detailed and complex undertaking. One such exemption, for example, is the "private offering" exemption. Generally, to meet this exemption, the company (called the "issuer") must not engage in general solicitation or advertising, must take precautions to ensure that the securities sold are not publicly distributed by purchasers (called "restrictions against resales"), must qualify each purchaser as financially sophisticated (or such purchaser must be advised by one who has the requisite sophistication), and must provide comprehensive and meaningful written disclosure about the enterprise and the securities that are being offered (unless the issuer establishes that the purchaser has access to obtaining such information whereby delivery of the written information may be avoided). As a final point, the issuer and others who seek an exemption from registration have the burden of proof (rather than the plaintiff) in establishing that an exemption indeed was met.[3]

This general overview illustrates the challenges posed when securities are offered and sold. Note that both federal and state law must be obeyed; otherwise, private damages suits and government enforcement actions may ensue. This brings us back to the "larger" question—So what is the "big deal?" What if the securities are offered in violation of the registration requirements (such as by selling a security without satisfying an exemption from registration) or if significant misrepresentations are contained in the offering materials? The answer is frightening. Violation of the securities registration requirements is one of strict liability. No mental culpability, such as negligence or intent, is relevant. A purchaser of the security can bring suit for rescission and receive back the money paid for the security (along with prejudgment interest) against a seller of the subject security. Even if the defendant shows that it received advice from the best lawyers and investment bankers in the USA and completely followed that advice, liability still will be imposed (as a registration violation is one of strict liability). Even more anxiety-provoking is that in many states a securities registration violation is a strict liability offense under the criminal law. Viewed as a public offense, within the discretion of the prosecuting authority, violation of the applicable state's registration requirements may result in criminal fines and time spent in the "slammer." *Succinctly put, that is the "big deal."*[4]

The consequences of a violation based on misrepresentation are also serious. If an offering document or other communication (whether verbal or written) contains a significant misstatement, both the government and private parties can bring lawsuits. Criminal prosecution is a distinct possibility if the violator acted with reckless or intentional misconduct. Private damages actions also are available, with relief being available if the plaintiff proves the requisite elements. In such a case, the plaintiff may be required to prove the materiality (or importance) of the misstatement, that he/she relied on the contents of the communication, that the misrepresentation caused the financial loss, and that the defendant acted with an improper mental frame of mind (such as negligence or intent). What must be proven by a private party ordinarily will depend upon the particular statute invoked by the plaintiff.[5]

Hence the ramifications of an instrument being a "security" are significant. We will next turn to discussion of the types of instruments that come within securities law coverage.

Stock

Stock in the financial world, if it has the ordinary characteristics normally associated with the instrument, is a security. With respect to common stock, these characteristics are "the right to receive dividends contingent upon the apportionment of profits; negotiability; the ability to be pledged; the conferring of voting rights in proportion to the number of shares owned; and the capacity to appreciate in value."[6] As the U.S. Supreme Court has stated: "stock is, as a practical matter, always an investment if it has the economic characteristics traditionally associated with stock."[7] Hence, stock is a security regardless whether such stock represents ownership interests in a closely-held one-person corporation or in a multibillion dollar Fortune 100 publicly-held company whose shares of common stock are listed on the New York Stock Exchange.

On the other hand, where an ownership interest is labeled stock but does not have the attributes of stock in the financial world, it is not a security. For example, stock issued to tenants in a low income government-assisted housing development, where, among other characteristics, the stock could not appreciate in value, could not be pledged, and was required to be redeemed at its purchase price when the tenant vacated the apartment, was held by the Supreme Court not to be a security.[8] As another example, stock issued as membership interests in a golf country club where the members were motivated by the personal benefits (e.g., golf, dining, socializing) that the club had to offer, was ruled not to be a security.[9] Hence, these cases stand for the general proposition that, when one's principal motivation is to use or consume the prospective benefits offered (such as to purchase affordable housing), the subject transaction does not involve the purchase or sale of a security.

DEBT INSTRUMENTS: BONDS, NOTES, AND DEBENTURES

Bonds and debentures generally are long-term obligations. The subject debtor (such as a corporation or municipality) agrees to repay the principal owed by a specified date with interest being paid to the debt holder at a fixed rate. For example, consider a bond or debenture issued to a purchaser on June 1, 2010 in the amount of $100,000 for a ten year term paying annual interest of five percent and maturing on June 1, 2020. In this example, the debt holder would receive an interest payment of $5,000 per year with payment of the $100,000 principal amount due on June 1, 2020. Generally, the difference between a bond and a debenture is that a bond is secured by specified assets of the business (such as real estate owned by the corporation) while a debenture is an unsecured debt instrument.[10] As we will see below, bonds and debentures normally are securities.

Notes, however, may or may not be securities. Notes are used with regularity in the commercial setting. For example, notes executed in connection with home and automobile purchases are not investments and not deemed to be securities. On the other hand, notes frequently are issued in the investment context. Unlike bonds and debentures, notes frequently are short-term debt obligations, often less than twelve months. They generally are unsecured.[11] Notes marketed, for example, to scores of investors paying an attractive interest rate where the business intends to use the proceeds for capital expansion purposes likely are securities.

The Supreme Court looked to the following factors to determine whether a note is a security[12]: First, whether the motivations of the purchaser and seller in entering into the transaction were commercial or investment oriented. For example, as stated by the Court, "[i]f the seller's purpose is to raise money for the general use of a business enterprise or to finance substantial investments and the buyer is interested primarily in the profit the note is expected to generate, the instrument is likely a 'security.'"[13] On the contrary, if the note is transacted for a consumer or commercial purpose, it is unlikely to be a security. Second, notes are more likely to be a security if the plan of distribution is widespread so that common trading of the notes ensues. Third, if the notes are marketed as investments, reasonable persons justifiably assume that the securities laws apply, thereby favoring application of the securities laws. And fourth, determining whether a risk reducing feature exists, such as the presence of other regulation or the collateralization of the notes. The presence of such other regulation or that the notes are collateralized may significantly reduce the risk of loss and make invocation of the securities laws unnecessary.[14]

Based on the foregoing, notes that are broadly marketed as investments that pay a higher rate of interest than insured instruments (such as certificates of deposit) normally are securities. If there is an effective non-securities regulator (such as a banking regulator) or the notes are adequately collateralized, then the notes may not be securities. The four factors set forth above frequently are weighed by the courts, resulting to some degree in commercial uncertainty when determining for planning purposes whether certain notes come within the securities laws.[15]

With respect to bonds and debentures, application of the four factor test signifies that these instruments normally are securities. They generally are broadly marketed, seeking to raise capital for the business enterprise with the investor entering into the transaction with the expectation of earning a profit—namely, an attractive financial return that is not available from insured instruments.

Investment Contracts

Investments contracts are securities. The applicable test under federal law and prevailing state law (called the *Howey* test) asks whether there has been (1) an investment of something of value (normally of money) (2) in a common enterprise (3) with the expectation of profit (4) to be derived essentially from the efforts of others.[16] As discussed earlier, an investment means parting with one's contribution (such as money) with the motivation of receiving a meaningful financial return. Using or consuming the product is not an investment. For example, entering into a venture with the motivation to enjoy the venture's golf course, swimming pool, bar, dining room, and/or sauna is not the making of an investment. Second, the term "common enterprise" referred to above simply means that there is a shared unity of interest in the venture among the investors (called horizontal commonality) and/or the investors and the promoter (called vertical commonality). All courts deem horizontal verticality (that investors share a common interest in the success of the venture) to be sufficient while the courts are divided whether vertical commonality alone (a shared interest among the investors and the promoter) may suffice for deeming an instrument to be a security.[17] Third, there must be an expectation of profit. Of course, this profit may not be realized; it need only be reasonably anticipated. Profit generally means capital appreciation of the value of the investment, participation in earnings (such as through dividends), or periodic payments that are valuable (namely, greater than can be obtained from an insured investment like a certificate of deposit).[18] And, fourth, these profits must be generated essentially from the efforts of others. Those others may be the promoter, a party who is associated with the promoter, or any third party, even one who is entirely independent of the promoter. Significantly, if the purchaser exercises meaningful managerial or entrepreneurial efforts, then the instrument will not be an investment contract.[19]

Observe the distinction between stock and investment contracts. A person who acquires 100% of the stock of a business who intends to manage that enterprise has purchased a security (assuming that the stock acquired has the ordinary attributes of stock as discussed earlier in this chapter). However, a person who acquires that very same business as a majority interest holder of a limited liability company (LLC) and who intends to manage the operations of that enterprise is unlikely to have purchased a security. Thus, the choice of business form (e.g., corporation versus LLC), depending on the circumstances, can determine whether the securities laws apply.

Let's look at a few types of business forms in this context. First, *general partnerships* normally are not investment contracts. The reason is that general partners traditionally have the power to exercise ultimate control. Therefore, they are not relying on the efforts of others to generate the profits of the general partnership.[20]

On the other hand, *limited partnerships* traditionally have been viewed as investment contracts and, hence, securities.[21] In this investment, the limited partners have horizontal commonality with one another, anticipate a profit, and expect to derive that profit from the essential efforts of the general partner (or its designees). Note that limited partners can participate to some degree in the business (such as advising the general partner, voting on certain specified matters set forth in the partnership agreement, and being an employee of the business) and retain their status as limited partners.[22] Nonetheless, for purposes of the securities laws, a limited partner may exercise such a degree of managerial efforts that, although retaining his/her limited liability, nonetheless will not have purchased a security due to the exercise of these essential managerial efforts. For example, a limited partner who serves as the sole director and as chief executive officer of the corporate general partner of the limited partnership may well be deemed to be exercising essential managerial efforts. In this example, the limited partnership interests would not be an investment contract. This is the case even though the limited partner under the state limited partnership statutes is allowed to engage in this extensive activity yet retain his/her limited liability.[23]

In certain limited contexts, general partnership interests may be investment contracts. This is most often the situation where the general partnership agreement vests control authority in the managing general partner(s), leaving the other general partner(s) with no essential managerial efforts to be exercised.[24] One may question why a person sensibly would divest him/herself of the power to exercise control, vest that power in others, yet still be subject to personal unlimited liability. Simply said, it is a bad idea.

Interests in *limited liability companies (LLCs)* may or may not be investment contracts. If the LLC is managed by a board of managers, then the LLC interests purchased by members who are not managers are more likely to be investment contracts because these non-manager members normally are relying essentially upon the efforts of the board of managers. On the other hand, if the LLC is member-managed, then the question arises whether these interests should be treated more like general partnerships or more like limited partnerships.[25] Although such LLC members theoretically may have the power to manage, there may be scores of members having individual influence of relatively small significance. Moreover, unlike a general partnership, LLC members enjoy limited liability. Therefore, the incentive to monitor one's investment is far less. In other words, investors in LLCs, like limited partnerships, are frequently passive. They do not exercise significant managerial efforts and have no desire to do so. The motive is to earn an attractive return as a passive investor. In light of these considerations, many courts treat such LLC members in LLCs that have a significant number of members (such as 25 or more) like limited partners and permit securities law coverage.[26]

The same can be said for *limited liability partnerships (LLPs)*. LLPs are general partnerships that by state statute are permitted to file for LLP status. A partner in a LLP generally enjoys limited liability unless he/she is the tortfeasor, supervises the violator, is otherwise deemed responsible for the violator's conduct, or personally guarantees the debt.[27] In such circumstances, like the LLC member and the limited partner in a limited partnership, the incentive to monitor for a partner in a LLP is significantly lessened because the specter of personal liability has been greatly diminished. Accordingly, a number of courts treat LLPs similarly to limited partnerships and hold that passive LLP partners, depending on the underlying facts and circumstances, have acquired an investment contract and, hence, a security.[28]

Risk Capital Test

Note that some states apply a more expansive test, called the "risk capital test," in order to determine whether an investment contract is present. Generally, this is a broader standard than the prevailing *Howey* test, signifying that an instrument may not be a security under the *Howey* test but may be a security under the risk capital test. Generally, under the risk capital test, the investor contributes initial value of some type which is subject to the risks of the enterprise. This contribution is made by the investor with the reasonable understanding that a valuable benefit of some kind will accrue to the investor as a consequence of the enterprise's operation. And, lastly, the investor does not exercise meaningful control over the managerial or entrepreneurial aspects of the business.[29] Applying the risk capital test, the California Supreme Court held that memberships in a for-profit country club were securities under California law. The California Supreme Court stated:

> We have here nothing like the ordinary sale of a right to use existing facilities. [The promoter-defendants] are soliciting the *risk capital* with which to develop a business for profit. The purchaser's risk is not lessened merely because the interest he purchased is labeled a membership. Only because he risks his capital along with other purchasers can there be any chance that the benefit of club membership will materialize.[30]

Nonetheless, it is important to emphasize that the risk capital test is a minority approach. The applicable test in the U.S. federal courts and the vast majority of state courts is the *Howey* test.

THE AGGREGATION APPROACH

The aggregation approach posits that a transaction that is not a securities transaction when viewed in isolation may become an investment contract and, hence, a security if there are other aspects of the venture that are central to a purchaser's decision to invest. Thus, if the economic substance of the venture is promoted in such a way that the investor reasonably anticipates that profits will be generated through the efforts of others, then the investment may well be deemed a security. For example, in the famous U.S. Supreme Court case *SEC v. Howey*, the promoter sold citrus groves coupled with service contracts. The business plan was for the promoter (or its designee) to plant, tend to, harvest, and take to market the citrus crop. The investors and promoter would receive a percentage of the revenue earned from the crop. The investors lived all over the United States and nearly all had no interest in overseeing their crops. They were induced to invest by the expectation of profits earned from the efforts of the promoter (or its designee) in overseeing and selling the citrus crop. Applying the four-factor test, the Supreme Court held that the economic reality of the transaction signified that the interests purchased were securities—namely, that the purchasers made an investment in a common enterprise with the expectation of profit to be derived from the efforts of others.[31] Note that the *Howey* test, when interpreted in the context of the aggregation approach, has been invoked in a myriad of factual contexts. For example, the sale of condominium units coupled with emphasis on the rental proceeds to be generated through the efforts of the promoter (or its designee), thereby reasonably causing investors to believe that they will earn a profit on the investment due to the revenues earned, has been held to be an investment contract and, hence, a security.[32]

CONCLUSION

The entrepreneur and his/her financial and legal advisers should be cognizant of the existence of a security when seeking to raise capital from others. Security status not only occurs with respect to stock, bonds, debentures and notes, but also when the instrument is an investment contract. Investment contract coverage encompasses a variety of factual situations and enterprises, including, for example, ownership-interests in limited partnerships, limited liability companies, and limited liability partnerships. The failure to recognize the presence of a security can be disastrous. It can result in ruin for the business enterprise, require the promoters who sold the securities to pay damages to aggrieved investors based on strict liability, result in government enforcement actions (including criminal prosecution), and subject the attorney to malpractice liability. In fact, in the case study that follows, a law firm paid hefty damages to its client for its failure to advise the client that the client's issuance of stock to investors was a security.

NOTES

1. See M. Steinberg, *Understanding Securities Law* 39–42 (5th ed. 2009).
2. See Schneider, Manko & Kant, *Going Public: Practice Procedures, and Consequences*, 27 Villanova L. Rev. 1 (1981).
3. See Section 4(2) of the Securities Act of 1933, SEC Rule 506 of Regulation D; *Securities and Exchange Commission v. Ralston Purina Co.*, 346 U.S. 199 (1953). Note that under SEC Regulation D a specified level of net worth or income renders a person an accredited investor. For example, an individual who has $1 million in net worth (exclusive of the value of his/her principal residence) is an accredited investor. As a matter of SEC rule, an accredited investor is deemed irrefutably to be financially sophisticated and to have access to registration-type information.

4. See Sections 5, 12(a)(1) of the Securities Act; *Pinter v. Dahl*, 486 U.S. 622 (1988); *Cox v. Garvin*, 278 Ga. 903, 607 S.E. 2d 549 (2005); Sargent, *A Blue Sky State of Mind: The Meaning of "Willfully" in Blue Sky Criminal Cases*, 20 Sec. Reg. L.J. 96 (1992).
5. See Sections 10(b), 32(a) of the Securities Exchange Act of 1934; *Erica P. John Fund, Inc. v. Halliburton Co.*, 131 S. Ct. 2179 (2011); *Dura Pharmaceuticals v. Broudo*, 544 U.S. 336 (2005); A. Bromberg & L. Lowenfels, *Securities Fraud & Commodities Fraud* (2d ed. 2011); J. Long, *Blue Sky Law* (2010).
6. *Landreth Timber Co. v. Landreth*, 471 U.S. 681, 690 (1985). Accord, *Gould v. Ruefenacht*, 471 U.S. 701 (1985).
7. *Reves v. Ernst & Young*, 494 U.S. 56, 62 (1990).
8. *United Housing Foundation, Inc. v. Forman*, 421 U.S. 837 (1975).
9. *Rice v. Branigar Organization, Inc.*, 922 F.2d 788 (11th Cir. 1991).
10. See D. Branson, J. Heminway, M. Loewenstein, M. Steinberg & M. Warren, *Business Enterprises: Legal Structures, Governance and Policy* 189–195 (2009).
11. *Id.* at 190.
12. *Reves v. Ernst & Young*, 494 U.S. 56 (1996).
13. *Id.* at 67.
14. *Id.* at 66–68.
15. See *McNabb v. SEC*, 298 F. 3d 1126 (9th Cir. 2002); *Resolution Trust Corporation v. Stone*, 998 F. 2d 1534 (10th Cir. 1993); Kerr & Eisenhauer, *Reves Revisited*, 19 Pepperdine L. Rev. 1123 (1992).
16. See *SEC v. Edwards*, 540 U.S. 389 (2004); *SEC v. W.J. Howey Co.*, 328 U.S. 293 (1946).
17. Compare *Salcer v. Merrill Lynch, Pierce, Fenner & Smith, Inc.*, 682 F. 2d 459 (3d Cir. 1982) (only horizontal commonality suffices), *with Long v. Shultz Cattle Co.*, 881 F. 2d 129 (5th Cir. 1989 (vertical as well as horizontal commonality meets common enterprise requirement).
18. See *SEC v. Edwards*, 540 U.S. 389 (2004).
19. See *SEC v. Koscot Interplanetary, Inc.*, 497 F. 2d 473 (5th Cir. 1974).
20. See *Goodwin v. Elkins & Co.*, 730 F. 2d 99 (2d Cir. 1984).
21. See *L & B Hospital Ventures, Inc. V. Healthcare International, Inc.*, 894 F. 2d 150 (5th Cir. 1990); *Mayer v. Oil Field Systems Corp.*,721 F. 2d 59 (2d Cir. 1983).
22. See Section 303 of the Revised Uniform Limited Partnership Act; discussion in chapter 2 *supra*.
23. See *Steinhardt Group, Inc., v. Citicorp*, 126 F. 3d 144 (3d Cir. 1997); *Gordon v. Terry*, 684 F. 2d 736 (11th Cir. 1981).
24. See *Williams v. Tucker*, 645 F. 2d 404 (5th Cir. 1981).
25. See *Robinson v. Glynn*, 349 F. 3d 166 (4th Cir. 2003).
26. See *Leonard v. United States*, 529 F. 2d 83 (2d Cir. 2008); *SEC v. Friendly Power Company*, 49 F. Supp. 2d 1363 (S.D. Fla. 1999).
27. See discussion in chapter 2 *supra*.

28. See *SEC v. Merchant Capital,* 483 F. 3d 747 (11th Cir. 2007); Welle, *Where Are Limited Liability Partnership Interests Securities?,* 27 J. Corp. L. 63 (2001).
29. See *State, Commission of Securities v. Hawaii Market Center, Inc.,* 485 P. 2d 105 (Haw. 1971); Coffey, *The Economic Realities of a "Security": Is There a More Meaningful Formula?,* 18 Case Western L. Rev. 367 (1967).
30. *Silver Hills Country Club v. Sobieski,* 55 Cal. 2d 811, 361 P. 2d 906, 908 (1961).
31. 328 U.S. 293 (1946).
32. See *Hocking v. Dubois,* 885 F. 2d 1449 (9th Cir. 1989) (en banc); *SEC v. Kirkland,* 521 F. Supp. 2d 1281 (M.D. Fla. 2007); SEC Securities Act Release No. 5347 (1973).

WARTZMAN V. HIGHTOWER PRODUCTIONS, LTD. MARYLAND COURT OF SPECIAL APPEALS 456 A.2D 82 (1983)

James S. Getty, Judge:

Woody Hightower did not succeed in breaking the Guinness World Record for flagpole sitting; his failure to accomplish this seemingly nebulous feat, however, did generate protracted litigation. …

Hightower Productions Ltd. (Hightower) … came into being in 1974 as a promotional venture conceived by Ira Adler, Frank Billitz and J. Daniel Quinn. The principals intended to employ a singer-entertainer who would live in a specially constructed mobile flagpole perch from April 1, 1975, until New Year's Eve at which time he would descend in Times Square in New York before a nationwide television audience having established a new world record for flagpole sitting.

The young man selected to perform this feat was to be known as "Woody Hightower." The venture was to be publicized by radio and television exposure, by adopting a theme song and by having the uncrowned champion make appearances from his perch throughout the country at concerts, state fairs and shopping centers.

In November, 1974, the three principals approached Michael Kaminkow of the law firm of Wartzman, Rombro, Rudd and Omansky, P.A., for the specific purpose of incorporating their venture. Mr. Kaminkow, a trial attorney, referred them to his partner, Paul Wartzman.

The three principals met with Mr. Wartzman at his home and reviewed the promotional scheme with him. They indicated that they needed to sell stock to the public in order to raise the $250,000 necessary to finance the project. Shortly thereafter, the law firm prepared and filed the articles of incorporation and Hightower Productions Ltd. came into existence on November 6, 1974. The Articles of Incorporation authorized the issuance of one million shares of stock. …

Following incorporation, the three principals began developing the project. With an initial investment of $20,000, they opened a corporate account at Maryland National Bank and an office in the Pikesville Plaza Building. Then began the search for "Woody Hightower." After numerous interviews, twenty-three year old John Jordan emerged as "Woody Hightower."

After selecting the flagpole tenant, the corporation then sought a company to construct the premises to house him. This consisted of a seven foot wide perch that was to include a bed, toilet, water, refrigerator and heat. The accommodations were atop an hydraulic lift system mounted upon a flat bed tractor trailer.

...

Hightower employed two public relations specialists to coordinate press and public relations efforts and to obtain major corporate backers. "Woody" received a proclamation from the Mayor and City Council of Baltimore and after a press breakfast at the Hilton Hotel on "All Fools Day" ascended to his home in the sky.

Within ten days, Hightower obtained a live appearance for "Woody" on the Mike Douglas Show, and a commitment for an appearance on the Wonderama television program. The principals anticipated a "snow-balling" effect from commercial enterprises as the project progressed with no substantial monetary commitments for approximately six months.

Hightower raised $43,000.00 by selling stock in the corporation. Within two weeks of "Woody's" ascension, another stockholders' meeting was scheduled, because the corporation was low on funds. At that time, Mr. Wartzman informed the principals that no further stock could be sold, because the corporation was "structured wrong," and it would be necessary to obtain the services of a securities attorney to correct the problem. Mr. Wartzman had acquired this information in a casual conversation with a friend who recommended that the corporation should consult with a securities specialist.

The problem was that the law firm had failed to prepare an offering memorandum and failed to assure that the corporation had made the required disclosures to prospective investors in accordance with the provisions of the Maryland Securities Act. ... Mr. Wartzman advised Hightower that the cost of the specialist would be between $10,000.00 and $15,000.00. Hightower asked the firm to pay for the required services and the request was rejected.

Hightower then employed substitute counsel and scheduled a shareholders' meeting on April 28, 1975. At that meeting, the stockholders were advised that Hightower was not in compliance with the securities laws; that $43,000.00, the amount investors had paid for issued stock, had to be ... placed in escrow; that the fee of a securities specialist would be $10,000.00 to $15,000.00; and that the additional work would require between six and eight weeks. In the interim, additional stock could not be sold, nor could "Woody" be exhibited across state lines. Faced with these problems, the shareholders decided to discontinue the entire project.

On October 8, 1975, Hightower filed suit [against the law firm] alleging breach of contract and negligence. …

…

The jury returned a verdict in favor of Hightower in the amount of $170,508.43.

…

In conclusion, the final comment of Judge Lowe is equally apposite here.

The unfortunate oversight on which this case was based was a costly one, but it was made by one who was hired precisely for the purpose of averting the consequent losses. It is he, and his firm, who must bear them.

Judgment affirmed.

In the two cases that follow, we look at LLC interests. Analyzing the attributes of the respective LLC interests as well as the underlying facts and circumstances, the courts reach different conclusions as to whether these interests were securities.

ROBINSON V. GLYNN
UNITED STATES COURT OF APPEALS
349 F. 3D 166 (FOURTH CIRCUIT 2003)

Wilkinson, Circuit Judge:

Plaintiff James Robinson filed suit against Thomas Glynn, Glynn Scientific, Inc., and GeoPhone Company, LLC, alleging that Glynn committed federal securities fraud when he sold Robinson a partial interest in Geophone Company. The district court found that Robinson's membership interest in GeoPhone was not a security within the meaning of the federal securities laws, and it dismissed Robinson's securities fraud claim. Because Robinson was an active and knowledgeable executive at GeoPhone, rather than a mere passive investor in the company, we affirm. To do otherwise would unjustifiably expand the scope of the federal securities laws by treating an ordinary commercial venture as an investment contract.

I.

Robinson appeals from a grant of summary judgment to Glynn, and accordingly we take the facts in the light most favorable to Robinson. In 1995, Glynn organized GeoPhone Corporation to develop and commercially market the GeoPhone telecommunications system. The GeoPhone system was designed around a signal processing technology, Convolutional Ambiguity Multiple Access (CAMA), that Glynn purportedly designed. Glynn was GeoPhone Corporation's majority shareholder and chairman. In September 1995, GeoPhone Corporation became a limited liability company, GeoPhone Company, LLC. LLCs are noncorporate business entities that offer their members limited liability, tax benefits, and organizational flexibility.

In March 1995, Glynn and his associates contacted James Robinson, a businessman with no prior telecommunications experience, in an effort to raise capital for GeoPhone. Over the next several months, Glynn met and corresponded with Robinson, attempting to convince Robinson to invest in GeoPhone. Glynn described to Robinson the CAMA technology, its centrality to the GeoPhone system, and GeoPhone's business plan. In July 1995, Robinson agreed to loan Glynn $1 million so that Glynn could perform a field test of the GeoPhone system and the CAMA technology.

In addition to Robinson's loan, in August 1995 Robinson and Glynn executed a "Letter of Intent," in which Robinson pledged to invest up to $25 million in GeoPhone, LLC if the field test indicated that CAMA worked in the GeoPhone system. Robinson's $25 million investment was to be comprised of his initial $1 million loan, an immediate $14 million investment upon successful completion of the field test, and a later $10 million investment. In October 1995, engineers hired by Glynn performed the field test, but, apparently with Glynn's knowledge, they did not use CAMA in the test. Nevertheless, Glynn allegedly told Robinson that the field test had been a success.

Consistent with the Letter of Intent, in December 1995 Robinson and Glynn executed an "Agreement to Purchase Membership Interests in GeoPhone" (APMIG). Under the APMIG, Robinson agreed to convert his $1 million loan and his $14 million investment into equity and subsequently to invest the additional $10 million. Robinson and Glynn also entered into an "Amended and Restated GeoPhone Operating Agreement" (ARGOA), which detailed the capital contribution, share ownership, and management structure of GeoPhone.

Pursuant to the ARGOA, Robinson received 33,333 of GeoPhone's 133,333 shares. On the back of the share certificates that Robinson received, the restrictive legend referred to the certificates as "shares" and "securities." It also specified that the certificates were exempt from registration under the Securities Act of 1933, and stated that the certificates could not be transferred without proper registration under the federal and state securities laws. *[Note that whether a security exists is a matter of subject matter jurisdiction—it cannot be a matter agreed to by the promoter and/or investors.]*

In addition, the ARGOA established a seven-person board of managers that was authorized to manage GeoPhone's affairs. Two of the managers were to be appointed by Robinson with the remaining five appointed by Glynn and his brother. Finally, the ARGOA vested management of GeoPhone in Robinson and Glynn based on each member's ownership share. Robinson was named GeoPhone's treasurer, and he was appointed to the board of managers and the company's executive committee. Glynn served as GeoPhone's chairman and was intimately involved in the company's operations and technical development.

Trouble first surfaced only a few months later in April 1996, when Robinson sued Glynn in Maryland state court. Robinson alleged breach of fiduciary duty, fraud, and conversion, all due to Glynn's purported mismanagement of GeoPhone funds. In October 1997, Robinson and Glynn settled the state court action, and as part of the settlement in November 1997 they entered into a "Membership Interest Purchase Agreement" (MIPA). Under the MIPA, Robinson purchased all of Glynn's shares in GeoPhone.

Yet in 1998 Robinson allegedly learned for the first time that the CAMA technology had never been implemented in the GeoPhone system—not even in the field test that had provided the basis for Robinson's investment. Robinson then filed suit in federal court, claiming violation of the federal securities laws, specifically § 10(b) of the Securities Exchange Act of 1934 and Rule 10b-5. The district court, however, granted summary judgment to Glynn, because it found that Robinson's membership interest in GeoPhone, LLC did not constitute a security under the federal securities laws. Robinson now challenges the district court's dismissal of his federal securities law claim.

II.

In order to establish a claim under Rule 10b-5, Robinson must prove fraud in connection with the purchase of securities. The Securities Act of 1933 and the Securities Exchange Act of 1934 define a "security" broadly as "any note, stock, treasury stock, security future, bond, debenture, ... , investment contract, ... , or, in general, any interest or instrument commonly known as a 'security.'" In this case, Robinson claims that his membership interest in GeoPhone, a limited liability company (LLC), qualifies as either an "investment contract" or "stock" under the Securities Acts.

A.

The district court determined that Robinson's interest in GeoPhone was not an investment contract, a question of law that we review de novo. The Supreme Court has defined an investment contract as "a contract, transaction or scheme whereby a person invests his money in a common enterprise and is led to expect profits solely from the efforts of the promoter or a third party." *S.E.C. v. W.J. Howey, Co.*, 328 U.S. 293, 298–99 (1946). The parties agree that Robinson invested his money in a common enterprise with an expectation of profits. Their disagreement concerns whether Robinson expected profits "solely from the efforts" of others, most notably Glynn.

Since *Howey*, however, the Supreme Court has endorsed relaxation of the requirement that an investor rely only on others' efforts, by omitting the word "solely" from its restatements of the *Howey* test. ... And neither our court nor our sister circuits have required that an investor like Robinson expect profits "solely" from the efforts of others. ... Requiring investors to rely wholly on the efforts of others would exclude from the protection of the securities laws any agreement that involved even slight efforts from investors themselves. It would also exclude any agreement that offered investors control in theory, but denied it to them in fact. Agreements do not annul the securities laws by retaining nominal powers for investors unable to exercise them.

What matters more than the form of an investment scheme is the "economic reality" that it represents. The question is whether an investor, as a result of the investment agreement itself or the factual circumstances that surround it, is left unable to exercise meaningful control over his investment. Elevating substance over form in this way ensures that the term "investment contract" embodies "a flexible rather than a static principle, one that is capable of adaptation to meet the countless and variable schemes devised by those who seek the use of the money of others on the promise of profits."

B.

In looking at the powers accorded Robinson under GeoPhone's operating agreement, as well as Robinson's activity as an executive at GeoPhone, it is clear that Robinson was no passive investor heavily dependent on the efforts of others like Glynn. Under the ARGOA, management authority for GeoPhone resided in a board of managers. Robinson not only had the power to appoint two of the board members, but he himself assumed one of the board seats and was named as the board's vice-chairman. The board, in turn, delegated extensive responsibility to a four-person executive committee of which Robinson was also a member.

In addition, Robinson served as GeoPhone's Treasurer. Among his powers were the ability to select external financial and legal consultants; to consult with GeoPhone's Chief Financial Officer on all financial matters relating to the company; to review status reports from the President and other officers; and to assemble the executive committee in order to discuss variations from GeoPhone's operating plan. Beyond even these fairly extensive powers, the ARGOA forbade GeoPhone from either incurring any indebtedness outside the normal course of business without Robinson's approval or diluting his interest in GeoPhone without first consulting him. In short, Robinson carefully negotiated for a level of control "antithetical to the notion of member passivity" required to find an investment contract under the federal securities laws.

None of this, of course, establishes that Robinson could entirely direct the affairs of GeoPhone. He controlled neither the board nor the executive committee, and he lacked the technological expertise of Glynn and others at the company. But Robinson was not interested in sole managerial control of GeoPhone; he was interested instead in sufficient managerial control to ensure that other managers like Glynn could neither harm nor dilute his investment. Through his positions as Treasurer, Vice-Chairman of the Board, and member of GeoPhone's executive committee, Robinson may have lacked "decisive control over major decisions," but he preserved "the sort of influence which generally provide[d] [him] with access to important information and protection against a dependence on others." ...

Robinson argues, however, that his lack of technological expertise relative to Glynn prevented him from meaningfully exercising his rights. [This argument] assume[s] too much. ... To the extent that Robinson needed assistance in understanding any particular aspect of the CAMA technology, nothing prevented him from seeking it from outside parties or others at GeoPhone. In fact, prior to purchasing all of Glynn's shares in GeoPhone, Robinson asked his accountant to scrutinize the company's financial records, and he hired an outside engineer to study the company's technology and market potential.

Indeed, the record amply supports the district court's conclusion that Robinson exercised his management rights despite his lack of technical expertise. For instance, Robinson reviewed GeoPhone's technology and financial records, as well as weekly status reports from GeoPhone's President, Chief Operating Officer, and Chief Financial Officer covering numerous aspects of GeoPhone's operation. He disapproved disbursements and proposed licenses of the GeoPhone technology. Robinson even expressed to the board of managers problems he perceived with GeoPhone, including the company's technological development, its management, and marketability. In the end, Robinson generally asserts that he lacked technical sophistication, without explaining in any detail what was beyond his ken or why it left him powerless to exercise his management rights.

Moreover, Robinson's argument would work a fundamental and unjustifiable expansion in the securities laws by bringing innumerable commercial ventures within their purview. *[Note, however, if GeoPhone were a corporation, then the stock Robinson purchased clearly would be a security.]* Business ventures often find their genesis in the different contributions of diverse individuals—for instance, as here, where one contributes his technical expertise and another his capital and business acumen. Yet the securities laws do not extend to every person who lacks the specialized knowledge of his partners or colleagues, without a showing that this lack of knowledge prevents him from meaningfully controlling his investment. Here, Robinson concedes that "nothing of consequence that would affect [his] position adversely could be done without [his] prior expressed approval," thus undermining his claim that his lack of technical expertise left him powerless over his investment. In essence, Robinson was a savvy and experienced businessman who negotiated for formal management rights and actively exercised those rights, only now relying on his lack of technical sophistication to claim the cover of the federal securities laws.

...

Finally, Robinson argues that he and Glynn considered his interest in GeoPhone a security, based on language in the APMIG, in the ARGOA, and on the back of Robinson's GeoPhone certificates. For instance, the restrictive legend on the back of Robinson's certificates refers to the certificates as "shares" and "securities." While this may be persuasive evidence that Robinson and Glynn believed the securities laws to apply, it does not indicate that their understanding was well-founded. Just as agreements cannot evade the securities laws by reserving powers to members unable to exercise them, neither can agreements invoke those same laws simply by labeling commercial ventures as securities. It is the "economic reality" of a particular instrument, rather than the label attached to it, that ultimately determines whether it falls within the reach of the securities laws. The "economic reality" here is that Robinson was not a passive investor relying on the efforts of others, but a knowledgeable executive actively protecting his interest and position in the company.

III.

Robinson further claims that his membership interest in GeoPhone was not only an "investment contract" within the meaning of the federal securities laws, but "stock" as well. Congress intended catch-all terms like "investment contract" to encompass the range of novel and unusual instruments whose economic realities invite application of the securities laws; but the term "stock" refers to a narrower set of instruments with a common name and characteristics. *See Landreth*

Timber Co. v. Landreth, 471 U.S. 681, 686 (1985). Thus the securities laws apply "when an instrument is both called 'stock' and bears stock's usual characteristics." ... Yet Robinson's membership interest was neither denominated stock by the parties, nor did it possess all the usual characteristics of stock.

The characteristics typically associated with common stock are (i) the right to receive dividends contingent upon an apportionment of profits; (ii) negotiability; (iii) the ability to be pledged or hypothecated; (iv) the conferring of voting rights in proportion to the number of shares owned; and (v) the capacity to appreciate in value. Robinson's membership interest in GeoPhone lacked several of these characteristics.

First, as is common with interests in LLCs, GeoPhone's members did not share in the profits in proportion to the number of their shares. ... Pursuant to the ARGOA, Robinson was to receive 100 percent of GeoPhone's net profits up to a certain amount, only after which were funds to be distributed pro rata to the members in proportion to their relative shares.

Second, like interests in LLCs more generally, Robinson's membership interests were not freely negotiable. According to the ARGOA, Robinson could only transfer his interests if he first offered other members the opportunity to purchase his interests on similar terms. Moreover, unlike with stock (except some stock in close corporations), anyone to whom Robinson or other members transferred their interests would not have thereby acquired any of the control or management rights that normally attend a stock transfer. ... Rather, the ARGOA requires that transferees satisfy several conditions to become members, in addition to receiving the approval of a majority of GeoPhone's managers.

Similarly, Robinson could pledge his interest, but the pledgee would acquire only distribution rights and not control rights. ... As for the apportionment of voting rights, the parties dispute whether voting rights were conferred in proportion to members' interests in GeoPhone. Even resolving this dispute in Robinson's favor, it remains clear that Robinson's membership interest lacked the ordinary attributes of stock.

Finally, from the very beginning Robinson and Glynn consistently viewed Robinson's investment as a "membership interest," and never as "stock." The purchase and operating agreements that Robinson and Glynn executed, as well as the agreement in which Robinson bought out Glynn's interest in GeoPhone, all termed Robinson's investment as a "membership interest" rather than "stock." Even the shares that Robinson received as a result of his investments declared Robinson the holder of "membership interests in GeoPhone Company, L.L.C., within the meaning of the Delaware Limited Liability Company Act." Robinson thus cannot argue that he was misled into believing that his membership interests were stock whose purchases were governed by the securities laws. ... And it would do violence to the statutory language of the securities laws to include within the term "stock" an instrument that was neither labeled stock nor like stock. *[Question whether the provisions at issue in this LLC resemble those entered into by shareholders in a close corporation.]*

IV.

The parties have vigorously urged us to rule broadly in this case, asking that we generally classify interests in limited liability companies, or LLCs, as investment contracts (Robinson's view) or non-securities (Glynn's view). LLCs are particularly difficult to categorize under the securities laws, however, because they are hybrid business entities that combine features of corporations, general partnerships, and limited partnerships. As their name indicates, LLCs can limit the liability of their members, which may mean that LLC members are more likely to be passive investors who need the protection of the securities laws. However, LLC members are also able to actively participate in management without piercing the veil of their liability, which would suggest that LLC members are more likely than limited partners ... to be active investors not in need of the securities statutes.

Precisely because LLCs lack standardized membership rights or organizational structures, they can assume an almost unlimited variety of forms. It becomes, then, exceedingly difficult to declare that LLCs, whatever their form, either possess or lack the economic characteristics associated with investment contracts. Even drawing firm lines between member-managed and manager-managed LLCs threatens impermissibly to elevate form over substance. Certainly the members in a member-managed LLC will often have powers too significant to be considered passive investors under the securities laws. And yet even members in a member-managed LLC may be unable as a practical matter to exercise any meaningful control, perhaps because they are too numerous, inexperienced, or geographically disparate. By the same token, while interests in manager-managed LLCs may often be securities, their members need not necessarily be reliant on the efforts of their managers.

We decline, therefore, the parties' invitation for a broader holding. On the facts of this case, it is clear that Robinson did not lack the ability to meaningfully exercise the rights granted him under GeoPhone's operating agreement. To the contrary, Robinson had a significant say in GeoPhone's management. If Robinson, despite his own managerial efforts, was misled by Glynn about his investment, his remedy belongs to another forum. The federal securities laws were not intended to be a substitute for state fraud and breach of contract actions. ... We therefore affirm the district court's dismissal of the action in this case.

United States v. Leonard
United States Court of Appeals
529 F. 3d 83 (Second Circuit 2008)

Katzmann, Circuit Judge:

Over sixty years ago, the Supreme Court established the test for whether a given financial instrument or transaction constitutes an "investment contract"—and, therefore, a security-for purposes of the federal securities laws. *SEC v. W.J. Howey Co.*, 328 U.S. 293 (1946). We write today to underscore that, in applying the *Howey* factors, courts can (and should) look beyond the formal terms of a relationship to the reality of the parties' positions to evaluate whether "the reasonable expectation was one of significant investor control." ...

Appellants Dickau and Silverstein were two of twenty-five individuals Indicted for criminal fraud for their role in marketing investment interests in film companies. Following a jury trial, they were each convicted of securities fraud and conspiracy to commit securities and mail fraud. On appeal, they challenge their convictions, claiming, inter alia, that insufficient evidence supported the determination that the interests at issue were securities. ... We find the various objections to the conviction to be without merit. ...

Background

Appellants Paul C. Dickau and Nanci Silverstein each operated an independent sales office ("ISO") selling interests in companies formed to finance the production and distribution of motion pictures. Dickau's ISO sold interests in Little Giant, LLC, an entity created to produce the film Carlo's Wake. Both appellants' ISOs sold interests in Heritage Film Group, LLC, which was established to produce the film The Amati Girls. As their names suggest, Little Giant and Heritage are limited liability companies ("LLCs"), and the interests in the companies took the form of investment "units," priced at $10,000 each.

The ISOs solicited investments in Little Giant and Heritage over the phone, calling potential investors to generate interest in the film projects. The film's promoters would then mail potential investors offering materials, including a brochure, operating agreement, subscription agreement, risk disclosure sheet, and instruction sheet. If the potential investor decided to participate in the investment, he or she would send the subscription agreement, along with a check, directly to the film's promoters.

When an ISO succeeded in selling an interest in Little Giant or Heritage, it would receive a commission. Dickau's company received a 42% and 45% commission on sales of Little Giant and Heritage units, respectively. Silverstein's company received a 45% commission on sales of Heritage units. The offering memoranda did not reflect these hefty commission rates. Read liberally, the offering materials might be said to indicate that no more than 20% of the unit price would go toward sales commissions.

Dickau's company sold a combined total of $520,000 worth of Little Giant and Heritage units and retained $210,376 in commissions. Silverstein's company sold $90,000 in interests in Heritage, pocketing $32,939 in commissions.

The government charged Dickau with four counts: one count of conspiracy to commit securities and mail fraud in relation to each of Little Giant and Heritage, see 18 U.S.C. § 371, and one count of securities fraud in relation to each of Little Giant and Heritage, see 15 U.S.C. §§ 78j, 78ff. The government charged Silverstein with one conspiracy count and one fraud count in relation to Heritage. All counts centered around the failure to disclose accurately the sales commission that the ISOs would be taking on the investment units. Following a trial in the Eastern District of New York, the jury returned a verdict of guilty on all counts against Dickau and Silverstein. Judge Wexler sentenced Dickau to forty-three months' imprisonment and ordered him to pay $499,989.64 in restitution. Judge Wexler sentenced Silverstein to six months' imprisonment, ordering her to pay $14,490 in restitution.

Discussion

I. Whether Sufficient Evidence Supported the Finding that the Units Were Securities

...

Section 10(b) of the Securities Exchange Act of 1934 (the "1934 Act") makes it unlawful "[t]o use or employ, in connection with the purchase or sale of any security ... any manipulative or deceptive device." ... Section 32 of the 1934 Act creates criminal penalties for willful violations of the provisions of the 1934 Act, including violations of Section 10(b). Thus, for the convictions of securities fraud and conspiracy to commit securities fraud to stand, there must be sufficient record evidence for the jury to have concluded that the interests in Little Giant and Heritage were "securities" within the meaning of the 1934 Act.

Although federal statutes enumerate many different instruments that fit the definition of security, the parties agree that the only category that potentially applies to this case is "investment contract." In the seminal case, *SEC v. W.J. Howey Co.*, 328 U.S. 293 (1946), the Supreme Court provided the following definition of investment contract:

> an investment contract for purposes of the Securities Act means a contract, transaction or scheme whereby a person invests his money in a common enterprise and is led to expect profits solely from the efforts of the promoter or a third party. ...

... Appellants suggest that the Little Giant and Heritage units cannot constitute securities because investors never expected profits "solely from the efforts" of the promoters or others.

Following the Ninth Circuit's lead, see *SEC v. Glenn W. Turner Enterprises*, 474 F.2d 476, 482 (9th Cir.1973), we have held that the word "solely" should not be construed as a literal limitation; rather, we "consider whether, under all the circumstances, the scheme was being promoted primarily as an investment or as a means whereby participants could pool their own activities, their money and the promoter's contribution in a meaningful way." *SEC v. Aqua-Sonic Prods. Corp.*, 687 F.2d 577, 582 (2d Cir.1982). Thus, in Aqua-Sonic we distinguished between companies that seek the "passive investor" and situations where there is a "reasonable expectation of significant investor control." ... It is the passive investor "for whose benefit the securities laws were enacted"; where there is a reasonable expectation of significant investor control, "the protection of the 1933 and 1934 Acts would be unnecessary." ...

Our consideration of whether the investors in Little Giant and Heritage viewed the units primarily as a passive investment is complicated by the fact that Little Giant and Heritage were each structured as an LLC—a relatively new, hybrid vehicle that combines elements of the traditional corporation with elements of the general partnership while retaining flexibility for federal tax purposes. ... Although "common stock is the quintessence of a security," *Reves v. Ernst & Young*, 494 U.S. 56, 62 (1990), and "[n]ormally, a general partnership interest is not considered a 'security,'" *Odom v. Slavik*, 703 F.2d 212, 215 (6th Cir.1983), because of the sheer diversity of LLCs, membership interests therein resist categorical classification. Thus, an interest in an LLC is the sort of instrument that requires "case-by-case analysis" into the "economic realities" of the underlying transaction. ...

One of the original promoters of Little Giant and Heritage, Russell Finnegan, testified at trial that the LLCs were structured so as to minimize the possibility that the investment units would constitute securities—"to get into ... the gray areas of the securities law." Indeed, were we to confine ourselves to a review of the organizational documents, we would likely conclude that the interests in Little Giant and Heritage could not constitute securities because the documents would lead us to believe that members were expected to play an active role in the management of the companies. For example, the sheet titled "Summary of Business Opportunity: Heritage Film Group, LLC" explains:

> Each Member is required to participate in the management of the Company retaining one (1) vote for each Unit acquired. Each important decision relating to the business of the Company must be submitted to a vote of the Members.

> The purchase of interests in the Company is not a passive investment. While specific knowledge and expertise in the day to day operation of a film producing and distributing company is not required, Members should have such knowledge and experience in general business, investment and/or financial affairs as to intelligently exercise their management and voting rights. Further, each Member is required to participate in the management of the Company by serving on one or more committees established by the Members.

The summary further states that a manager may be chosen to perform certain "ministerial functions," such as keeping books and records, keeping the members informed, and circulating ballots to members, but the members retain the right to replace the manager and appoint his successor upon majority vote. Likewise, the operating agreement for Heritage provides that the "Company shall be managed by the Members. [E]ach Member shall have the right to act for and bind the Company in the ordinary course of its business." Thus, on the face of the documents, Heritage and Little Giant appear to provide for too much investor control to allow the jury to conclude that the units were securities.

In actuality, however, the Little Giant and Heritage members played an extremely passive role in the management and operation of the companies. At trial, members testified that they voted, at most, "a couple of times." Although the organizational documents provided for the formation of a number of committees, only two committees were formed for each of Heritage and Little Giant—a financial committee and a management committee. Of the 250–300 investors in Little Giant, five served on the management committee and seven served on the financial committee. Of the 350–400 investors in Heritage, ten served on the management committee and seven served on the financial committee. Thus, the vast majority of investors in both companies did not actively participate in the venture, exercising almost no control.

Record evidence allowed the jury to conclude that—notwithstanding the language in the organizational documents suggesting otherwise—from the start there could be no "reasonable expectation" of investor control. ... Such consideration of the reality of the transaction is consistent with the Supreme Court's repeated instruction to prize

substance over form in our evaluation of what constitutes a security.
...

For one, under the organizational documents, the members' managerial rights and obligations did not accrue until the LLCs were "fully organized." As promoter James Alex testified, so-called "interim managers" initially held legal control rights, and they decided almost every significant issue prior to the completion of fundraising: "The script, the director, the cast, the crew, scoring of it, editing. The entire picture was pretty well preproduced." Thus, the jury could reasonably have found the managerial rights contained in the organizational documents were hollow and illusory.

The jury was also entitled to consider the fact that the members appear not to have negotiated any terms of the LLC agreements. Rather, they were presented with the subscription agreements on a take-it-or-leave-it basis. That they played no role in shaping the organizational agreements themselves raises doubts as to whether the members were expected to have significant control over the enterprise.

Moreover, the members had no particular experience in film or entertainment and therefore would have had difficulty exercising their formal right to take over management of the companies after they were fully organized. ... And their number and geographic dispersion left investors particularly dependent on centralized management. We echo the Fifth Circuit in finding that investors may be so lacking in requisite expertise, so numerous, or so dispersed that they become utterly dependent on centralized management, counteracting a legal right of control. ... "What matters more than the form of an investment scheme is the 'economic reality' that it represents. The question is whether an investor, as a result of the investment agreement itself *or the factual circumstances that surround it*, is left unable to exercise meaningful control over his investment." ...

In sum, upon consideration of the totality of the circumstances, we conclude that the jury could have determined that, notwithstanding the organizational documents drafted to suggest active participation by members, the defendants sought and expected passive investors for Little Giant and Heritage, and therefore the interests that they marketed constituted securities.

...

SCENARIO

Anchor Marina is situated in Annapolis, Maryland. Part of its business is to rent out its boat slips to sailboat owners when the sailboats are docked. Peter McGee, the sole owner of Anchor Marina, comes up with what he perceives as a brilliant idea: Rather than simply renting out the boat slips, he will sell thirty of his slips for $25,000 each to boat owners. Once this amount is paid (as well as a modest maintenance fee), the slip owner will be entitled to use the slips whenever he/she so desires if at least seven days notice is given to Anchor Marina. In the event that boat slips are vacant, they will be rented out by Anchor Marina to other sailboat owners. The proceeds from the rentals will be split—50% to Anchor Marina and 50% to the slip owners. When McGee meets with potential purchasers, he states that this is a "no lose" proposition. With the income generated from the rental of the boat slips, the boat owners will be able to recoup the $25,000 paid for their respective slips within three years. Even better, within a ten year period, McGee tells the potential purchasers that they may be able to triple their money. Assume that McGee's projections are honestly believed by him and that they are within the range of being reasonable. Is McGee, on behalf of Anchor Marina, offering for sale a "security" to these prospective purchasers?

Chapter 9

INSIDER TRADING

As evidenced by the enactment of the Sarbanes-Oxley Act in 2002[1] and the Dodd-Frank legislation in 2010,[2] the focus on corporate accountability and standards of conduct has become magnified.[3] Related to this development is the continued emphasis on insider trading regulation.[4] Tales of alleged insider trading abuse highlight this scrutiny in the United States.[5] To an increasing degree, other developed markets also are becoming more sensitized.[6] The following discussion focuses on the U.S. law on insider trading as well as addressing insider trading from an international perspective.

U.S. LAW: INSIDER TRADING

In this area, federal law is the fundamental source of regulation.[7] Although a number of states, such as New York, permit derivative suits against alleged inside traders premised on unjust enrichment[8] and perceived harm to the corporation,[9] state law frequently is unavailable in this setting.[10] For example, some state courts decline to recognize that an insider has a disclosure obligation when the trade is executed on an impersonal securities market.[11] Similarly, in the derivative suit context, these courts find no requisite injury to the corporation.[12] The effect of these state court decisions is that aggrieved investors must resort to federal law.[13]

Federal law principally addresses the scope of insider trading regulation. The SEC and the federal courts are the leading actors. Prior to the U.S. Supreme Court handing down its restrictive decisions in the 1980s, lower

Litigación

courts adopted the parity of information[14] and equal access theories[15] when construing the "disclose or abstain" mandate of the federal securities laws' broad antifraud provisions—Section 10(b)[16] and SEC Rule 10b-5[17]—in the insider trading setting. Under the parity of information approach, as set forth by the U.S. Court of Appeals for the Second Circuit, "anyone in possession of material inside information must either disclose it to the investing public, or ... must abstain from trading in or recommending the securities concerned while such information remains undisclosed."[18] The equal access approach, embodying a more narrow concept, holds that "[a]nyone—corporate insider or not—who regularly receives material nonpublic information may not use this information to trade in securities without incurring an affirmative duty to disclose."[19] With respect to tipper-tippee liability exposure, lower courts posited that a tippee stood in the shoes of her tipper. Hence, a tippee, who knowingly received material nonpublic information from a tipper when the tipper could not legally trade on that information, likewise could not legally trade or tip.[20] As will be explored later in this chapter, several countries by statute follow a number of the foregoing principles.

Today, the parity of information and equal access theories under Section 10(b) are "dead." Rather, as interpreted by the U.S. Supreme Court, the scope of the insider trading prohibition under Section 10(b) is based on fiduciary duty and trust and confidence principles.[21] Other key elements in this setting include whether the subject information is deemed "material"[22] and whether that information is "nonpublic" (namely, whether such information has been adequately communicated to and absorbed by the investment community).[23]

Thus, as construed by the U.S. Supreme Court, trading in possession of material confidential information by an officer, director, or other insider (such as a controlling shareholder) in the subject enterprise's securities is illegal under Section 10(b) because, by so trading, such person breaches a fiduciary duty owed to the enterprise and to the trader(s) on the opposite side of the transaction(s), namely, the corporation's shareholders.[24] Accordingly, a disclosure obligation exists in this context due to a relationship of confidence and trust between the transacting parties.[25] Similarly, the subject enterprise's consultants, including its attorneys, bankers and accountants, who become privy to material inside information having the understanding that such information must remain confidential, are viewed as quasi-insiders and thereby are held to have a relationship of confidence and trust with the corporation and its shareholders.[26] Such persons thereby are subject to the disclose or abstain mandate, thus being obligated to adequately disseminate the material information to the securities markets or abstain from trading (and tipping) until such dissemination is successfully completed.[27] However, any insider, who seeks to make sufficient disclosure prior to the subject trade(s) (or tip(s)), violates the company's need for confidentiality concerning such information and incurs liability exposure under state law.[28]

With respect to "outsiders," to wit, those persons who do not have a fiduciary duty to those who are on the opposite side of the subject transaction(s), the misappropriation theory may be available.[29] Under this approach, Section 10(b) is violated when the pertinent individual misappropriates material confidential information for securities trading purposes, thereby effecting the breach of a relationship of trust and confidence to the source of the information, regardless whether such source is (or is not) a party to the transaction.[30] For example, an employee who misappropriates material nonpublic information entrusted to his employer and who uses this information for trading in the subject securities breaches the trust and confidence owed to her employer and perhaps to the clients of her employer.[31]

The legality of "tipping" is treated in a similar fashion. Ascertaining whether "tipping" is permissible under Section 10(b), the critical determinants are whether the tipper breached her fiduciary duty (or a relationship of trust and confidence) by conveying the inside information to her tippee(s) and whether the tippee(s) knew or should have known of such breach.[32] Without the existence of a breach, a tippee may trade and tip in compliance with Section 10(b).[33] Under the Supreme Court's rationale, an insider breaches her fiduciary duty by tipping the material nonpublic information with the motivation of obtaining a personal benefit. Such personal benefit ordinarily is of a pecuniary nature, such as cash or enhancement of status impacting one's employment situation that will redound in future financial benefits.[34] The conveyance of a gift likewise is a sufficient personal benefit: The communication of the material confidential information is equated to trading by the insider herself with the presentation of the gift to the tippee-recipient of the profits gained from the trades.[35]

Turning to another statute, Section 16 of the Securities Exchange Act of 1934 focuses on "short-swing" reporting and trading by officers, directors, and ten percent equity holders of publicly-held enterprises. Under Section 16(b), these persons are held strictly liable, requiring disgorgement of all their gains, if they purchase and sell (or sell and purchase) an equity security (such as common stock) within a six-month period.[36] Section 16 raises several challenging issues,[37] including whether the provision has served its historical purposes and should be repealed.[38]

Yet, another federal provision—SEC Rule 14e-3—applies only in the tender offer context.[39] [Generally, a tender offer is an offer by the bidder to purchase the shares of the target corporation that is made directly to the shareholders of the target corporation, thereby bypassing approval of the target's board of directors.] In this limited setting, the prohibitions against trading on and tipping of material inside information are much broader than those applicable under Section 10(b). Under Rule 14e-3, a person who procures material non-public information concerning a tender offer directly or indirectly from the offeror (bidder), target company, or an intermediary cannot trade or tip until there is sufficient public disclosure (and absorption) of this information.[40] Moreover, a tippee of material nonpublic information concerning a tender offer who knows or should know that the applicable information comes directly or indirectly from an offeror, target company or intermediary likewise can neither trade nor tip prior to sufficient public dissemination (and absorption) of the information.[41] Rule 14e-3 sets forth an exception to this broad disclose or abstain mandate for multi-service financial firms that adopt and institute adequate screening mechanisms that effectively prevent the communication of nonpublic information to those persons who execute or recommend transactions in the subject corporation's securities.[42]

CRITIQUE OF THE U.S. INSIDER TRADING PROHIBITION

U.S. law on insider trading is subject to criticism. Today, due to Supreme Court decisions, principles focusing on fiduciary duty, financial benefit and misappropriation define the legality of transactions effected or contemplated. The goal that ordinary investors play on a level playing field with market professionals, having equal access to material nonpublic information, no longer survives under Section 10(b) insider trading jurisprudence.[43] Irrespective that Congress designed the federal securities acts to provide greater investor safeguards than state law, the Supreme Court's heavy reliance on state law-based principles of fiduciary duty minimizes that congressional objective.[44]

Perhaps not surprisingly, the SEC, acting purportedly within its rulemaking authority, has expanded restrictive Supreme Court law. For example the SEC's adoption of Rule 14e-3 sets forth broad parity of information and anti-tipping prescriptions in the tender offer setting.[45] In the Section 10(b) context, the Commission has advanced a "flexible" construction of Supreme Court precedent,[46] even promulgating new rules that in practice "overturn" lower court authority.[47] In another regulatory development, the SEC's embracement of Regulation FD (standing for "Fair Disclosure") seeks to terminate the practice of selective disclosure of material nonpublic information by company insiders to market professionals, institutional shareholders, and other favored constituents.[48] While such selective disclosure is illegal insider tipping under the laws of several countries[49] and indeed was outlawed in this country before the Supreme Court's decision in *Dirks*,[50] this conduct currently is prohibited under Section 10(b) jurisprudence only if the tipper seeks to gain personally from the selective disclosure.[51]

Some specific examples demonstrate the inconsistent treatment of U.S. insider trading law. One striking illustration involves the different treatment accorded to tender offers because of SEC Rule 14e-3. Literally, a person can legally keep profits by trading on material inside information or be found liable solely due to the fortuity of whether the transaction involves a tender offer. For instance, Barry Switzer, who served as the football coach for the Dallas Cowboys and the University of Oklahoma, inadvertently was the recipient of material confidential information that derived from a reputable corporate executive concerning a forthcoming merger.[52] Aware that the information was reliable because of his relationship with the executive, Switzer (along with his friends) traded on the basis of such information, making a handsome profit. Because the executive did not know that Switzer was privy to the subject communications, no unlawful tipping occurred under Section 10(b). In that a tippee's liability pursuant to Section 10(b) is derivative (namely, dependent on whether the tipper is itself liable),[53] the holding that the insider-tipper had not breached his fiduciary duty meant that Switzer as the tippee had lawfully traded, and, accordingly, was entitled to retain his profits.[54]

The result in *Switzer* would have been otherwise if the contemplated transaction was structured as a tender offer (and not a merger). In such event, Rule 14e-3 would have been invoked (as well as Section 10(b)). Although Switzer would have escaped liability under Section 10(b), he would have breached Rule 14e-3 by trading on material confidential information that he knew came from a reliable inside source. Thus, pursuant to Rule 14e-3, regardless of the tipper's liability, a tippee has liability by knowingly trading on material confidential information that directly or indirectly comes from a subject corporation.[55] Hence, Switzer's avoidance of liability and permissible retention of large profits were due to the manner in which the subject transaction was structured.

This inconsistency becomes more pronounced when the *Chestman*[56] case, involving a criminal prosecution, is examined. There, the Second Circuit en banc ruled that Chestman avoided liability under Section 10(b) because his tipper did not breach a fiduciary duty by communicating material nonpublic information concerning a forthcoming tender offer.[57] Nonetheless, Chestman's criminal conviction that he violated Rule 14e-3 was affirmed due to the fact that he knowingly traded while having material inside information regarding a tender offer that derived, directly or indirectly, from the bidder or target corporation.[58] Hence, although Chestman (like Switzer) escaped Section 10(b) liability because the subject tipper did not unlawfully tip under that statute, Chestman (unlike Switzer) was found liable under Rule 14e-3 because, unfortunately for Chestman, the "deal" was structured as a tender offer rather than another viable acquisition alternative, such as a merger, exchange of shares or sale of assets. Such disparate treatment cannot be reconciled with investor protection, market integrity, or fundamental concepts of fair treatment among similarly-situated market participants.[59]

The *Chestman* decision has another troubling issue. In determining whether a fiduciary duty was present giving rise to the disclose or abstain mandate, the court ruled that marriage, considered alone, does not constitute a fiduciary relationship.[60] For such a relationship of trust and confidence to exist, other attributes must be present, such as an understanding to maintain the confidentiality of the material information or a pre-existing status of being a recipient of family business secrets.[61] Not only does the court's rationale minimize "family values," it also in effect gives greater sanctity to a stockholder's relationship with a director of a publicly-held corporation (with whom such stockholder has never spoken or met) than to his/her spouse, child, parent, or sibling. This result is due to the U.S. Supreme Court's focus on the presence of a fiduciary duty (or a relationship of trust and confidence) premised on state law principles. Without a concept based on equal access, state law principles of fiduciary duty can cause, as it did in *Chestman*, an illogical result.

By more recently promulgating Rule 10b5-2,[62] the SEC in practical effect has nullified this part of *Chestman*. The rule invokes the Section 10(b) misappropriation theory when a person is the recipient of material confidential information from a spouse, child, parent, or sibling unless such person can show that, in light of the particular family relationship, no reasonable expectation of confidentiality existed.[63] In adopting Rule 10b5-2, the Commission in all practicality "overturned" a decision handed down by the U.S. Court of Appeals.

The foregoing evidences that U.S. law with respect to insider trading is deficient. Statutes generally are silent on insider trading, thus leaving this area largely to the courts. The U.S. Supreme Court, in declining to embrace the parity of information and equal access rationales, has adhered to traditional state law concepts of fiduciary duty. This approach, in turn, as illustrated by the *Chestman* and *Switzer* decisions, has led to absurd lower court precedent. On another level, the SEC, seeking to combat narrow Supreme Court decisions regarding the Section 10(b) law of insider trading, has enunciated expansive interpretations of those decisions.[64] Thus, the U.S. framework on insider trading should not be emulated. Other countries apparently agree.[65]

A COMPARISON TO OTHER DEVELOPED MARKETS

Contrasted with the United States where insider trading law generally has been formulated by the judiciary, countries abroad have adopted detailed and specific legislation defining the parameters of the insider trading proscription.[66]

GENERAL ADHERENCE TO THE "ACCESS" STANDARD

For example, other countries have rejected the U.S. fiduciary duty (or relationship of trust and confidence) standard to define the contours of illegal insider trading and tipping.[67] The U.S. approach is problematic. For example, the U.S. rationale focuses on the existence (or absence) of relatively difficult inquiries to determine whether the insider trading prohibition prevails in a specific setting: Does a fiduciary relationship exist? What type of relationship is viewed as fiduciary or one of trust and confidence? Which individuals are deemed quasi-insiders and under what circumstances? What facts establish misappropriation of the subject information? Must an "insider" indeed "use" or merely be "in possession of" the pertinent information at the time of the trade(s)?[68] What must be shown for proving that a tipper conveyed the subject information for "personal benefit"? What is deemed an "improper personal benefit"? To leave these questions to ad hoc adjudication and SEC rulemaking may be acceptable to the United States with its abundance of litigation and its plethora of lawyers, regulators, and judges. This approach, arguably representing the antithesis of cost-effectiveness, understandably garners little support elsewhere.

Moreover, from a fairness perspective, the U.S. framework contains significant loopholes. For example, should the loose-lip executive and his tippees escape insider trading liability when those tippees intentionally trade on material inside information?[69] Should a person be criminally convicted or be entirely exonerated based on the distinction that the confidential information concerned a tender offer rather than a merger? Should a relative or friend be able to trade legally on material inside information when she inadvertently learns of this information when visiting the insider's home or office? By adopting a fiduciary relationship–like model (that is rejected by the SEC in the tender offer context), the U.S. insider trading regime complicates an already confusing area and at times unfairly treats similarly situated market participants. Contrasted with the United States, many countries opt for an insider trading prohibition based on the "access" doctrine.[70] Generally, this standard proscribes insider trading by those persons who have unequal access to the material confidential information. This standard may extend the insider trading proscription to tippees who receive the material information from traditional insiders or others who, because of their employment, office or profession, have access to this information.[71] This general approach is followed in several jurisdictions, including the United Kingdom,[72] France,[73] Germany,[74] Italy,[75] (Ontario) Canada,[76] and Mexico.[77]

Significantly fewer jurisdictions elect a more expansive approach based on the parity of information principle.[78] For instance, Australia's prohibition against insider trading generally encompasses any person or entity who possesses nonpublic price sensitive information.[79]

TIPPING LIABILITY

In regard to "tipping," as with liability of insiders and access persons for trading, the U.S. standard has been rejected elsewhere. Adhering to an expansive approach, Australia, for example, prohibits any tippee (regardless how remote), who knowingly has material inside information from trading on or tipping that information.[80] Similarly, the United Kingdom has a broad proscription against trading and tipping for those persons who knowingly have obtained material confidential information, directly or indirectly, from an insider.[81]

A number of other nations adhere to approaches that are more straightforward than the U.S. standard but that may not be as encompassing. Under German law, for example, primary insiders are prohibited from trading and tipping. However, recipients of material confidential information from a primary insider, while subject to the prohibition against trading, permissibly may tip the subject information to others.[82] France,[83] Italy,[84] and Japan[85] have adopted similar standards.

SOME ADDITIONAL THOUGHTS

U.S. regulation of insider trading is far from perfect. Without sufficient justification, ambiguity, complexity, and disparate treatment of similarly situated market participants at times prevails. Perhaps cognizant of these shortcomings, nations with developed securities markets have declined to follow U.S. standards in the insider trading context. The approaches endorsed by these other countries seek to set forth clear statutory direction in regard to the insider trading prohibition.

However, because of insufficient funding, resources, personnel and surveillance, inadequate enforcement generally has been prevalent in markets abroad. Laws ordinarily are as potent as their effective implementation. The deterrent effect of rigorous statutes lessens drastically as the likelihood of successful usage decreases. Hence, statutes designed to promote market integrity and investor protection have relatively minor impact if widespread noncompliance persists. The lack of successful enforcement accordingly may induce disobedience by market participants with applicable statutory mandates.[86]

This scenario helps to explain why the U.S. markets, although generating significant criticism in light of recent regulatory failures and financial frauds, are viewed as preeminent. As addressed above, the legal prescriptions concerning insider trading have their shortcomings. Although far from perfect, the standards adopted are viewed as acceptable and are embedded in the ethos of the U.S. capital markets. As significant, these standards are adequately enforced by the U.S. SEC, the U.S. Department of Justice in criminal prosecutions, and private parties who seek damages from alleged violators. Thus, reasonably effective enforcement of judicial, statutory, and regulatory pronouncements that define specified conduct as being illegal promotes compliance with the rule of law as well as investor confidence in market integrity.

Several countries, including those that are members of the European Community, are expending greater resources toward successful implementation of their statutory mandates proscribing abusive practices such as insider trading. Sufficient allocation of resources, of course, entails successfully procuring adequate personnel, funding, and technological surveillance mechanisms. Agendas also should address educational or "enlightenment" missions to emphasize the importance of these statutory mandates to affected constituencies, such as corporate insiders, bankers, brokers, judges, legislators, and the investing public.

NOTES

This chapter is derived from an article written by Professor Steinberg entitled *Insider Trading Regulation: A Comparative Perspective*, 37 The International Lawyer 153 (2003).

1. Sarbanes—Oxley Act of 2002, 107th Congress, Public Law No. 107-204 (2002). See generally H. Bloomenthal, *Sarbanes-Oxley Act in Perspective* (2002); J. Hamilton & T. Trautmann, *Sarbanes-Oxley Act of 2002: Law and Explanation* (2002).
2. The Dodd-Frank Wall Street Reform and Consumer Protection Act, 111th Congress, Public Law 111-203 (2010). See generally *Dodd-Frank Wall Street Reform and Consumer Protection Act—Law Explanation and Analysis* (CCH 2010).

3. See Bostelman et al., *Enactment of Broad Accounting, Corporate Governance Reform Act Brings New Prohibitions, Requirements for Executives and Auditors,* 34 Sec. Reg. & L. Rep. (BNA) 1281 (2002); Cooper, *Governments Go to Extremes as the Downturn Wears On*, N.Y. Times, Aug. 7, 2010, at A8.
4. See generally M. Steinberg & W. Wang, *Insider Trading* (Oxford University Press) (3d edition 2010).
5. See *Insider Trading 'Rampant,' Becoming Harder to Detect,* 42 Sec. Reg. & L. Rep. (BNA) 2046 (2010); Editorial, *Martha, Martha, Martha,* Wall St. J., Oct. 24, 2002, at A16; Pulliam, *U.S. in Vast Insider Trading Probe,* Wall St. J., Nov. 20, 2010, at A1; Stanley & Hays, *Martha Stewart's To-Do List May Include Image Polishing*, N.Y. Times, June 23, 2002, at § 1, p. 1; Strasburg & Eaglesham, *Insider Case Alleges Doctor's Tips,* Wall St. J., Nov. 3, 2010, at C1.
6. See Wrighton, *Soros Awaits Verdict In Case In France On Insider Trading*, Wall St. J., Dec. 5, 2002, at C8.
7. See generally M. Steinberg & W. Wang, note 4 *supra.*
8. See, e.g., *Diamond v. Oreanumo*, 24 N.Y.2d 494, 498–499, 248 N.E.2d, 910, 912, 301 N.Y.S.2d 78, 81 (1969).
9. *Id.* at 500–503, 248 N.E.2d at 913–915, 301 N.Y.S.2d at 82–85.
10. See, e.g., *Freeman v. Decio*, 584 F.2d 186, 187–196 (7th Cir. 1978) (applying Indiana law); *Schein v. Chasen*, 313 So.2d 739, 746 (Fla. 1975); M. Steinberg & W. Wang, *supra* note 4 at §16.1 ("State law is rarely applied to stock market insider trading.").
11. See, e.g., *Van Shaack Holdings, Ltd. v. Van Shaack*, 867 P.2d 892 (Colo. 1994); *Bailey v. Vaughan,* 178 W.Va. 371, 359 N.E.2d 599 (1987); *Hotchkiss v. Fischer*, 136 Kan. 530, 16 P.2d 531 (1932).
12. Sources cited note 11 *supra.* See Branson, *Choosing the Appropriate Default Rule—Insider Trading Under State Law,* 45 Ala. L. Rev. 753 (1994); Hazen, *Corporate Insider Trading: Reawakening the Common Law,* 39 Wash. & Lee L. Rev. 845 (1982).
13. Note that certain state securities laws may allow government and/or private actions based on alleged insider trading violations. See generally M. Steinberg & R. Ferrara, *Securities Practice: Federal and State Enforcement* §§ 12:01–12:29 (2d ed. 2001 & 2011 supp).
14. See, e.g., *SEC v. Texas Gulf Sulphur Co.*, 401 F.2d 833, 849 (2d Cir. 1968) (en banc).
15. See, e.g., *United States v. Chiarella*, 588 F.2d 1358, 1365 (2d Cir. 1978), *rev'd*, 445 U.S. 222 (1980).
16. 15 U.S.C. § 78j(b). Section 10(b) prohibits any person, in connection with the purchase or sale of a security, from engaging in deceptive or manipulative conduct. The interstate commerce requirement, such as use of the mails or telephone, must be met in order for the statute to apply.
17. 17 C.F.R. § 240.10b-5. Rule 10b-5, adopted by the SEC, provides:

    It shall be unlawful for any person, directly or indirectly, by the use of any means or instrumentality of interstate commerce, or of the mails or of any facility of any national securities exchange,

    (a) To employ any device, scheme, or artifice to defraud,

(b) To make any untrue statement of a material fact or to omit to state a material fact necessary in order to make the statements made, in the light of the circumstances under which they were made, not misleading, or

(c) To engage in any act, practice, or course of business which operates or would operate as a fraud or deceit upon any person, in connection with the purchase or sale of any security.

See generally Ferrara & Steinberg, *A Reappraisal of Santa Fe: Rule 10b-5 and the New Federalism,* 129 U. Pa. L. Rev. 263 (1980).

18. *SEC v. Texas Gulf Sulphur Co.*, 401 F.2d 833, 849 (2d Cir. 1968) (en banc).
19. *United States v. Chiarella*, 588 F.2d 1358, 1365 (2d Cir. 1978), *rev'd*, 445 U.S. 222 (1980).
20. See, e.g., *Elkind v. Liggett & Myers, Inc.*, 635 F.2d 156 (2d Cir. 1980); *Shapiro v. Merrill Lynch, Pierce, Fenner & Smith, Inc.,* 495 F.2d 228 (2d Cir. 1974).
21. See e.g., *Chiarella*, 445 U.S. at 230 (opining that such liability "is premised upon a duty to disclose arising from a relationship of trust and confidence").
22. See, e.g., *Basic, Inc. v. Levinson*, 485 U.S. 224, 232, 240 n. 18 (1988); *Ganino v. Citizens Utilities Company*, 228 F.3d 154 (2d Cir. 2000); *SEC v. Mayhew*, 121 F.3d 44 (2d Cir. 1997).
23. See, e.g., *United States v. Libera*, 989 F.2d 596, 601 (2d Cir. 1993); *In re Faberge, Inc.*, 45 S.E.C. 244, 256 (1973). From a general perspective:

    [M]aterial information becomes public in either of two ways. The first view is that information that is disseminated and absorbed by the investment community is public. The second view is premised on the efficient market theory, and under this view, information is deemed public when the active investment community is aware of such information. Under the efficient market theory, information that is known by the investment community will be reflected in the price of an efficiently traded security.

    M. Steinberg, *Securities Regulation: Liabilities and Remedies* § 3.03 (2010). As used in this chapter, the words nonpublic, inside, and confidential have an identical meaning.
24. See, e.g., *Chiarella*, 445 U.S. at 230.
25. *Id.*
26. *Dirks*, 463 U.S. 646, 655 n. 14 (1983).
27. *Id.* ("The basis for recognizing this fiduciary duty is not simply that such persons acquired nonpublic corporate information, but rather that they have entered into a special confidential relationship in the conduct of the business of the enterprise and are given access to information solely for corporate purposes.").
28. See M. Steinberg & W. Wang, *supra* note 4, at § 5.2.
29. See, e.g., *United States v. O'Hagan,* 521 U.S. 642 (1997).
30. *Id.* at 654–656.
31. *Id.* at 661–663. See *SEC v. Dorozhko,* 574 F. 3d 42 (2d Cir. 2009); *SEC v. Talbot,* 530 F.3d 1085 (9th Cir. 2008); *United States v. Newman*, 664 F.2d 12 (2d Cir. 1981). See generally M. Steinberg & W. Wang, *supra* note 4, at § 5.4; Nagy, *Reframing the*

Misappropriation Theory of Insider Trading Liability: A Post-O'Hagan Suggestion, 59 Ohio St. L. J. 1223 (1998); Ramirez & Gilbert, *The Misappropriation Theory of Insider Trading Under United States v. O'Hagan: Why Its Bark Is Worse Than Its Bite*, 26 Sec. Reg. L.J. 162 (1998).

32. *Dirks v. SEC*, 463 U.S. 646 (1983).
33. *Id.* at 662.
34. *Id.* at 662–664.
35. *Id.* at 664 (opining that "[t]he tip and trade resemble trading by the insider followed by a gift of the profits to the recipient"). See *SEC v. Ginsburg*, 362 F.3d 1292 (11th Cir. 2004); Hiler, *Dirks v. SEC—A Study in Cause and Effect*, 43 Md. L. Rev. 292 (1984).
36. See, e.g., *Whittaker v. Whittaker Corp.*, 639 F.2d 516 (9th Cir. 1981); *Smolowe v. Delendo Corp.*, 136 F.2d 231 (2d Cir. 1943). See generally P. Romeo & A. Dye, *Section 16 Reporting Guide* (2010).
37. For example, these issues include the concepts of beneficial ownership and attribution, identifying which persons may be officers, and applying the objective versus the pragmatic approach. See, e.g., *Kern County Land Co. v. Occidental Petroleum Corp.*, 411 U.S. 582 (1973); *CBI Industries, Inc. v. Horton*, 682 F.2d 643 (7th Cir. 1982); *Merrill Lynch, Pierce, Fenner and Smith v. Livingston*, 566 F.2d 1119 (9th Cir. 1978); Securities Exchange Act Release No. 25234, [1990–1991 Transfer Binder] Fed. Sec. L. Rep. (CCH) ¶ 84,709 (SEC 1991).
38. See O'Conner, *Toward a More Efficient Deterrence of Insider Trading: The Repeal of Section 16(b)*, 58 Fordham L. Rev. 309 (1989). But see Thel, *The Genius of Section 16: Regulating the Management of Publicly Held Companies*, 42 Hastings L.J. 391 (1991). See generally Steinberg & Lansdale, *The Judicial and Regulatory Constriction of Section 16(b) of the Securities Exchange Act of 1934*, 68 Notre Dame L. Rev. 33 (1992).
39. 17 C.F.R. § 240.14e-3. Rule 14e-3 was adopted in Securities Exchange Act Release No. 17120, [1980 Transfer Binder] Fed. Sec. L. Rep. (CCH) ¶ 82,646 (1980).
40. See Rule 14e-3(a), (d), 17 C.F.R. § 240.14e-3(a), (d). The Supreme Court upheld Rule 14e-3's validity in *United States v. O'Hagan*, 521 U.S. 642 (1997).
41. Rule 14e-3(d), 17 C.F.R. § 240.14e-3(d).
42. Rule 14e-3(b). See SEC Division of Market Regulation, "Broker-Dealer Policies and Procedures Designed to Segment the Flow and Prevent the Misuse of Material Nonpublic Information," [1989–1990 Transfer Binder] Fed. Sec. L. Rep. (CCH) ¶ 84,520 (1990); Levine, Gardiner & Swanson, *Multiservice Securities Firms: Coping With Conflicts in a Tender Offer Context*, 23 Wake Forest L. Rev. 41 (1988); Steinberg & Fletcher, *Compliance Programs for Insider Trading*, 47 SMU L. Rev. 1783 (1994).
43. See *supra* notes 14–35 and accompanying text.
44. See *Chiarella*, 445 U.S. at 245–252 (Blackmun, J., dissenting). As Justice Blackmun opined:

    By its narrow construction of § 10(b) and Rule 10b-5, the Court places the federal securities laws in the rearguard of this movement, a position

> opposite to the expectations of Congress at the time the securities laws were enacted. … I cannot agree that the statute and Rule are so limited. The Court has observed that the securities laws were not intended to replicate the law of fiduciary relations. Rather, their purpose is to ensure the fair and honest functioning of impersonal national securities markets where common-law protections have proved inadequate. As Congress itself has recognized, it is integral to this purpose to assure that dealing in securities is fair and without undue preferences or advantages among investors.

Id. at 248. See also, Anderson, *Fraud, Fiduciaries, and Insider Trading*, 10 Hofstra L. Rev. 341 (1982); Bainbridge, *Incorporating State Law Fiduciary Duties Into the Federal Insider Trading Prohibition*, 52 Wash. & Lee L. Rev. 1189 (1995).

45. See *supra* notes 39–42 and accompanying text.
46. Two such examples are the SEC's assertion that applicable Supreme Court decisions allow for broad interpretations of trading "on the basis of" inside information and the requisite "benefit" for tipping purposes. See, e.g., *SEC v. Adler*, 137 F.3d 1325 (11th Cir. 1998) (rejecting SEC's assertion but adopting a presumption of use when one trades while knowingly possessing material nonpublic information); *SEC v. Stevens*, SEC Litigation Release No. 12813 (March 19, 1991) (settlement where SEC alleged that insider received personal benefit under *Dirks* test by "tipping" inside information to securities analysts).
47. See SEC Rules 10b5-1, 10b5-2, 17 C.F.R. §§ 240.10b5-1, 240.10b5-2, adopted in, Securities Exchange Act Release No. 43154, [2000 Transfer Binder] Fed. Sec. L. Rep.(CCH) ¶ 86,319 (2000). By adopting in Rule 10b5-1 a broad "awareness" test rather than a "use" standard for determining when trading is "on the basis" of material nonpublic information, the SEC rejected the standards set forth in at least two appellate court decisions. See *United States v. Smith*, 55 F.3d 1051 (9th Cir. 1998); *SEC v. Adler*, 37 F.3d 1325 (11th Cir. 1998); Sinai, *Rumors, Possession v. Use, Fiduciary Duty and Other Current Insider Trading Considerations,* 55 Bus. Law. 743 (2000). Moreover, by its promulgation of Rule 10b5-2, the SEC has "overturned" the Second Circuit's decision in *United States v. Chestman*, 947 F.2d 551 (2d Cir. 1991) (en banc) (discussed *infra* notes 56–63 and accompanying text).
48. See Securities Exchange Act Release No. 43154, [2000 Transfer Binder] Fed. Sec. L. Rep. (CCH) ¶ 86,319 (2000). Generally, Regulation FD

> prohibits issuers or individuals acting on their behalf from selectively disclosing material nonpublic information to certain enumerated persons (generally securities market professionals and holders of the issuer's securities who may well trade on the basis of the information) without disclosing the information publicly. If the selective disclosure is intentional, then the issuer must publicly disclose the information simultaneously by filing or furnishing a Form 8-K to the SEC or in a manner reasonably designed to provide broad distribution of the information. If the selective disclosure is unintentional, then the issuer must disclose the information to the public promptly, but in no event after the later of 24 hours or the opening of the next day's trading on the New York Stock Exchange. Violating Regulation FD exposes the issuer to SEC administrative and civil enforcement action, but does not by itself

> impose any Rule 10b-5 antifraud liability on the issuer or establish a private right of action.

M. Steinberg, *Understanding Securities Law* (5th ed. 2009). See generally Steinberg & Myers, *Lurking in the Shadows: The Hidden Issues of the Securities and Exchange Commission's Regulation FD*, 27 J. Corp. L. 173 (2002).

49. See *infra* notes 80–85 and accompanying text.
50. See, e.g., *Elkind v. Liggett & Myers, Inc.*, 635 F.2d 156 (2d Cir. 1980).
51. See *supra* notes 32–35 and accompanying text.
52. *SEC v. Switzer*, 590 F. Supp. 756, 758, 762 (W.D. Okla. 1984).
53. *Dirks*, 463 U.S. at 660–664.
54. *Switzer*, 590 F. Supp. at 758, 762–766.
55. Rule 14e-3(a).
56. *United States v. Chestman*, 947 F.2d 551 (2d Cir. 1991) (en banc).
57. *Id.* at 570–571.
58. *Id.* at 556–564. Note, moreover, that "Rule 14e-3 does not require that a person charged with violating the rule have knowledge that the nonpublic information in his possession relates to a tender offer." *SEC v. Sargent*, 229 F.3d 68, 79 (1st Cir. 2000). Accord, *United States v. O'Hagan* 139 F.3d 641, 650 (8th Cir. 1998); Securities Exchange Act Release No. 17120 (1980).
59. See, e.g., *United States v. Naftalin*, 441 U.S. 768 (1979) (stating that purposes of Securities Act include "investor protection," achieving "a high standard of business ethics ... in every facet of the securities industry," and observing that "the welfare of investors and financial intermediaries are inextricably linked—frauds perpetrated upon either business or investors can redound to the detriment of the other and to the economy as a whole").
60. *Chestman*, 947 F.2d at 571 (stating that "Keith's status as Susan's husband could not itself establish fiduciary status").
61. *Id.* at 568–571. In a separate opinion in *Chestman*, Judge Winter reasoned:

> [F]amily members who have benefitted from the family's control of the corporation are under a duty not to disclose confidential corporate information that comes to them in the ordinary course of family affairs. In the case of family-controlled corporations, family and business affairs are necessarily intertwined, and it is inevitable that from time to time normal familial interactions will lead to the revelation of confidential corporate matters to various family members. Indeed, the very nature of familial relationships may cause the disclosure of corporate matters to avoid misunderstandings among family members or suggestions that a family member is unworthy of trust.

Id. at 579 (Winter, J., concurring in part and dissenting in part). In a subsequent decision, the Eleventh Circuit agreed with Judge Winter's position. See *SEC v. Yun*, 327 F.3d 1263, 1272–1273 (11th Cir. 2003).

62. 17 C.F.R. § 240.10b5-2.
63. *Id.* See Securities Exchange Act Release No. 43154, [2000 Transfer Binder] Fed. Sec. L. Rep. (CCH) ¶ 86,319 (2000).

64. Note that statutory treatment exists for certain insider trading aspects, such as "short-swing" trading, option traders, insider trades during specified "blackout" periods, the ability of contemporaneous traders to bring a private right of action, the levying of money penalties, and the adoption of specific mechanisms to be implemented by broker-dealers and investment advisers. See, e.g., Sections 16, 20(d), 20A, 21A of the Securities Exchange Act.
65. See *infra* notes 66–85 and accompanying text.
66. See M. Steinberg, *International Securities Law—A Contemporary and Comparative Analysis* 105–148 (1999).

    In 1989, the Council of the European Communities promulgated the European Economic Community Directive Coordinating Regulation on Insider Trading. Council Directive 89/592 of November 13, 1989 Coordinating Regulations on Insider Dealing 1989 OJ (L 344) 30 (the Directive). The Directive, for example, sets forth minimum standards for defining the concepts "inside information" and "insider" with respect to which Member States of the European Union must comply. Directive art. 5. Nonetheless, significant details regarding methods of enforcement are left principally to the Member States. Directive art. 8. See Pingel, "The EC Directive of 1989," in *Insider Trading" The Laws of Europe, the United States and Japan* 5, 5–6 (E. Gaillard ed. 1992).
67. See *infra* notes 70–85 and accompanying text.
68. See SEC Rule 10b5-1, 17 C.F.R. § 240.10b5-1; *supra* notes 46–47.
69. Such conduct today is governed by Regulation FD. See *supra* note 48 and accompanying text.
70. EC Directive on Insider Trading, note 66 *supra*.
71. See *infra* notes 72–77 and accompanying text.
72. See Criminal Justice Act §§ 52, 57.
73. Hence, under Regulation 90-08, the following are defined as insiders:

    > (a) [P]ersons holding privileged information by reason of their capacity as members of management, board of directors of an issuer, or by reason of their functions which they exercise with respect to an issuer; (b) [p]ersons holding privileged information by reason of the planning and execution of a financial operation; (c) [p]ersons to whom privileged information is disclosed during the exercise of their professional activities or functions; and (d) [p]ersons who, with full knowledge of the facts, possess privileged information originating directly or indirectly from [any of the foregoing insiders].

    Id. See Steinberg, *supra* note 66, at 138.
74. Securities Act § 13(1). See generally Krause, *The German Securities Trading Act (1994): A Ban on Insider Trading and an Issuer's Affirmative Duty to Disclose Material Nonpublic Information,* 30 Int'l Law. 555 (1996); von Dryander, *The German Securities Trading Act: Insider Trading and Other Secondary Market Regulation,* 9 Insights No. 1, at 26 (1995).
75. Consolidated Act on Financial Intermediation, art. 180, para. 3. See Steinberg, *supra* note 66, at 132.

76. OSA § 76(5).
77. See "Amendments to the Mexican Securities Law," 465 Int'l Fin. L. Rev. 83 (2001).
78. Cf. *SEC v. Texas Gulf Sulfur Co.*, 401 F.2d 833, 849 (2d Cir. 1968) (en banc).
79. See Corporations Law § 1002G. Under the Australian regimen, one is deemed an insider, hence becoming subject to the insider trading and tipping prohibitions, by "(a) possess[ing] information that is not generally available but, if the information were generally available, a reasonable person would expect it to have a material effect on the price or value of securities of a body corporate; and (b) ... know[ing], or ought reasonably know[ing] that (i) the information is not generally available; and (ii) if it were generally available, it might have a material effect on the price or value of those securities."
80. Corporations Law § 1002E. See R. Tomasic & S. Bottomley, *Corporations Law in Australia* 698–699 (1995). See generally P. Redmond, *Companies and Securities Law* (2d ed. 1992).
81. Criminal Justice Act §§ 52, 57. See Herrington & Glover, "The United Kingdom" in *Insider Trading in Western Europe: Current Status* 33, 43 (G. Wegen & H. Assmann eds. 1994); Stamp & Welsh, "United Kingdom," in *International Insider Dealing*, 95, 109 (M. Stamp & C. Welsh eds. 1996).
82. Securities Act § 14(1)–(2). See Steinberg, *supra* note 66, at 128–129: Primary insiders are prohibited from trading on inside information for their own account or for the account of others, conveying inside information to others without proper authorization, and making recommendations to a third party to trade based upon inside information (tipping). Secondary insiders are prohibited from trading for their own account or for the account of others. Unlike primary insiders, secondary insiders are neither prohibited from disclosing information to other people nor from tipping. However, the recipients of such information would then become secondary insiders (tippees) and thus would be prohibited from trading on the inside information for their own account or for the account of others. Nonetheless, tippees can continue to pass along inside information provided that they do not trade on it themselves or for the account of others. This result may be explained as a means of facilitating the free flow of information in order to more expeditiously transform non-public inside information into public information. *Id.*
83. Commission des Opérations de Bourse Regulation 90-08 arts. 2–5; art. 10-1 of Ordinance No. 67-833. See Borde, "France" in *Insider Trading in Western Europe: Current Status* 59, 66–69 (G. Wegen & H. Assmann eds. 1994).
84. Consolidated Act on Financial Intermediation No. 58, art. 180, paras. 1, 2, discussed in Steinberg, *supra* note 66, at 132–133.
85. Securities and Exchange Law art. 166, paras, 1, 3. See Kobayashi, Mihara & Sugimoto, "Japan" in *International Insider Dealing* 321, 334–335 (M. Stamp & C. Welsh eds. 1996).
86. See Black, *The Core Institutions That Support Strong Securities Markets,* 55 Bus. Law. 1565, 1576–1578 (2000); Steinberg, *Emerging Capital Markets: Proposals and Recommendations for Implementation,* 30 Int'l Law. 715, 723–725 (1996).

THE TWO CASES that follow focus on key problematic issues with respect to potential insider trading liability. The individuals involved in these cases are well known in "sports" circles.

SECURITIES AND EXCHANGE COMMISSION V. CUBAN UNITED STATES COURT OF APPEALS 620 F.3D 551 (FIFTH CIRCUIT 2010)

Higginbotham, Circuit Judge:

This case raises questions of the scope of liability under the misappropriation theory of insider trading. Taking a different view from our able district court brother of the allegations of the complaint, we are persuaded that the case should not have been dismissed ... and must proceed to discovery.

Mark Cuban is a well known entrepreneur and current owner of the Dallas Mavericks and Landmark theaters, among other businesses. The SEC brought this suit against Cuban alleging he violated [the federal securities laws] by trading in Mamma.com stock in breach of his duty to the CEO and Mamma.com—amounting to insider trading under the misappropriation theory of liability. The core allegation is that Cuban received confidential information from the CEO of Mamma.com, a Canadian search engine company in which Cuban was a large minority stakeholder, agreed to keep the information confidential, and acknowledged he could not trade on the information. The SEC alleges that, armed with the inside information regarding a private investment of public equity (PIPE) offering, Cuban sold his stake in the company in an effort to avoid losses from the inevitable fall in Mamma.com's share price when the offering was announced.

Cuban moved to dismiss the action. The district court found that, at most, the complaint alleged an agreement to keep the information confidential, but did not include an agreement not to trade. Finding a simple confidentiality agreement to be insufficient to create a duty to disclose or abstain from trading under the securities laws, the court granted Cuban's motion to dismiss. The SEC appeals, arguing that a confidentiality agreement creates a duty to disclose or abstain and that, regardless, the confidentiality agreement alleged in the complaint also contained an agreement not to trade on the information and that agreement would create such a duty.

...

The SEC alleges that Cuban's trading constituted insider trading. ... The Supreme Court has interpreted section 10(b) [of the Securities Exchange Act] to prohibit insider trading under two complementary theories, the "classical theory" and the "misappropriation theory."

The classical theory of insider trading prohibits a "corporate insider" from trading on material nonpublic information obtained from his position within the corporation without disclosing the information. According to this theory, there exists "a relationship of trust and confidence between the shareholders of a corporation and those insiders who have obtained confidential information by reason of their position with that corporation." Trading on such confidential information qualifies as a "deceptive device" under section 10(b) because by using that information for his own personal benefit, the corporate insider breaches his duty to the shareholders. The corporate insider is under a duty to "disclose or abstain"—he must tell the shareholders of his knowledge and intention to trade or abstain from trading altogether.

There are at least two important variations of the classical theory of insider trading. The first is that even an individual who does not qualify as a traditional insider may become a "temporary insider" if by entering "into a special confidential relationship in the conduct of the business of the enterprise [he/she is] given access to information solely for corporate purposes." Thus underwriters, accountants, lawyers, or consultants are all considered corporate insiders when by virtue of their professional relationship with the corporation they are given access to confidential information. The second variation is that an individual who receives information from a corporate insider may be, but is not always, prohibited from trading on that information as a tippee. "[T]he tippee's duty to disclose or abstain is derivative from that of the insider's duty" and the tippee's obligation arises "from his role as a participant after the fact in the insider's breach of a fiduciary duty." Crucially, "a tippee assumes a fiduciary duty to the shareholders of a corporation not to trade on material nonpublic information only when the insider has breached his fiduciary duty to the shareholders by disclosing the information to the tippee and the tippee knows or should know there has been a breach." The insider breaches his fiduciary duty when he receives a "direct or indirect personal benefit from the disclosure."

Both the temporary-insider and tippee twists on the classical theory retain its core principle that the duty to disclose or abstain is derived from the corporate insider's duty to his shareholders. The misappropriation theory does not rest on this duty. It rather holds that a person violates section 10(b) "when he misappropriates confidential information for securities trading purposes, in breach of a duty owed to the source of the information." The Supreme Court first adopted this theory in *United States v. O'Hagan.* There, a lawyer traded the securities of a company his client was targeting for a takeover. O'Hagan could not be liable under the classical theory as he owed no duty to the shareholders of the target company. Nevertheless, the court found O'Hagan violated section 10(b). The Court held that in trading the target company's securities, O'Hagan misappropriated the confidential information regarding the planned corporate takeover, breaching "a duty of trust and confidence" he owed to his law firm and client. Trading on such information "involves feigning fidelity to the source of information and thus utilizes a 'deceptive device' as required by section 10(b)." The Court stated that while there is "no general duty between all participants in market transactions to forgo actions based on material nonpublic information," the breach of a duty to the source of the information is sufficient to give rise to insider trading liability. ... Because the duty flows to the source of the information and not to shareholders "if the fiduciary discloses to the source that he plans to trade on the nonpublic information, there is no 'deceptive device' and thus no § 10(b) violation."

While *O'Hagan* did not set the contours of a relationship of "trust and confidence" giving rise to the duty to disclose or abstain and misappropriation liability, we are tasked to determine whether Cuban had such a relationship with Mamma.com. The SEC seeks to rely on Rule 10b5-2(b)(1), which states that a person has "a duty of trust and confidence" for purposes of misappropriation liability when that person "agrees to maintain information in confidence." In dismissing the case, the district court read the complaint to allege that Cuban agreed not to disclose any confidential information but did not agree not to trade, that such a confidentiality agreement was insufficient to create a duty to disclose or abstain from trading under the misappropriation theory, and that the SEC overstepped its authority under section 10(b) in issuing Rule 10b5-2(b)(1). We differ from the district court in reading the complaint and need not reach the latter issues.

The complaint alleges that, in March 2004, Cuban acquired 600,000 shares, a 6.3% stake, of Mamma.com. Later that spring, Mamma.com decided to raise capital through a PIPE offering on the advice of the investment bank Merriman Curhan Ford & Co. At the end of June, at Merriman's suggestion, Mamma.com decided to invite Cuban to participate in the PIPE offering. "The CEO was instructed to contact Cuban and to preface the conversation by informing Cuban that he had confidential information to convey to him in order to make sure that Cuban understood—before the information was conveyed to him—that he would have to keep the information confidential." [SEC Complaint at Paragraph 12]

After getting in touch with Cuban on June 28, Mamma.com's CEO told Cuban he had confidential information for him and Cuban agreed to keep whatever information the CEO shared confidential. The CEO then told Cuban about the PIPE offering. Cuban became very upset "and said, among other things, that he did not like PIPEs because they dilute the existing shareholders." "At the end of the call, Cuban told the CEO 'Well, now I'm screwed. I can't sell.'" [SEC Complaint at Paragraph 14]

The CEO told the company's executive chairman about the conversation with Cuban. The executive chairman sent an email to the other Mamma.com board members updating them on the PIPE offering, [stating:]

> Today, after much discussion, [the CEO] spoke to Mark Cuban about this equity raise [the PIPE offering] and whether or not he would be interested in participating. As anticipated he initially "flew off the handle" and said he would sell his shares (recognizing that he was not able to do anything until we announce the [offering]) but then asked to see the terms and conditions which we have arranged for him to receive from one of the participating investor groups with which he has dealt in the past.

The CEO then sent Cuban a follow up email, writing "'[i]f you want more details about the private placement please contact ... [Merriman].'"

Cuban called the Merriman representative and they spoke for eight minutes. "During that call, the salesman supplied Cuban with additional confidential details about the PIPE. In response to

Cuban's questions, the salesman told him that the PIPE was being sold at a discount to the market price and that the offering included other incentives for the PIPE investors." It is a plausible inference that Cuban learned the off-market prices available to him and other PIPE participants.

With that information and one minute after speaking with the Merriman representative, Cuban called his broker and instructed him to sell his entire stake in the company. Cuban sold 10,000 shares during the evening of June 28, 2004, and the remainder during regular trading the next day.

That day, the executive chairman sent another email to the board, updating them on the previous day's discussions with Cuban, stating, "'we did speak to Mark Cuban ([, the CEO,] and, subsequently, our investment banker) to find out if he had any interest in participating to the extent of maintaining his interest. His answers were: he would not invest, he does not want the company to make acquisitions, he will sell his shares which he can not do until after we announce [the PIPE offering].'"

After the markets closed on June 29, Mamma.com announced the PIPE offering. The next day, Mamma.com's stock price fell 8.5% and continued to decline over the next week, eventually closing down 39% from the June 29 closing price. By selling his shares when he did, Cuban avoided over $750,000 in losses. Cuban notified the SEC that he had sold his stake in the company and publically stated that he sold his shares because Mamma.com "was conducting a PIPE, which issued shares at a discount to the prevailing market price and also would have caused his ownership position to be diluted."

In reading the complaint to allege only an agreement of confidentiality, the [district] court held that Cuban's statement that he was "screwed" because he "[could not] sell" "appears to express his belief, at least at that time, that it would be illegal for him to sell his Mamma.com shares based on the information the CEO provided." But the court stated that this statement "cannot reasonably be understood as an agreement not to sell based on the information." The court found "the complaint asserts no facts that reasonably suggest that the CEO intended to obtain from Cuban an agreement to refrain from trading on the information as opposed to an agreement merely to keep it confidential." Finally, the court stated that "the CEO's expectation that Cuban would not sell was also insufficient" to allege any further agreement.

Reading the complaint in the light most favorable to the SEC, we reach a different conclusion. In isolation, the statement "Well, now I'm screwed. I can't sell" can plausibly be read to express Cuban's view that learning the confidences regarding the PIPE forbade his selling his stock before the offering but to express no agreement not to do so. However, after Cuban expressed to the CEO the view that he could not sell, he gained access to the confidences of the PIPE offering. According to the complaint's recounting of the executive chairman's email to the board, during his short conversation with the CEO regarding the planned PIPE offering, Cuban requested the terms and conditions of the offering. Based on this request, the CEO sent Cuban a follow up email providing the contact information for Merriman. Cuban called the salesman, who told Cuban "that the PIPE was being sold at a discount to the market price and that the offering included other incentives for the PIPE investors." Only after Cuban reached out to obtain this additional information, following the statement of his understanding that he could not sell, did Cuban contact his broker and sell his stake in the company.

The allegations, taken in their entirety, provide more than a plausible basis to find that the understanding between the CEO and Cuban was that he was not to trade, that it was more than a simple confidentiality agreement. By contacting the sales representative to obtain the pricing information, Cuban was able to evaluate his potential losses or gains from his decision to either participate or refrain from participating in the PIPE offering. It is at least plausible that each of the parties understood, if only implicitly, that Mamma.com would only provide the terms and conditions of the offering to Cuban for the purpose of evaluating whether he would participate in the offering, and that Cuban could not use the information for his own personal benefit.[1] It would require additional facts that have not been put before us for us to conclude that the parties could not plausibly have reached this shared understanding. Under Cuban's reading, he was allowed to trade on the information but prohibited from telling others—in effect

1 The parties dispute Mamma.com's motive in providing the information to Cuban. Cuban contends that the offering was already oversubscribed and that this demonstrates the sole purpose of the phone call was to prevent Cuban from trading ahead of the offering. We express no opinion on this factual dispute or the potential implications of Cuban's allegations if they are true. At the motion-to-dismiss stage we must view all the facts in light most favorable to the SEC and assume that Mamma.com had a legitimate reason for contacting Cuban.

providing him an exclusive license to trade on the material nonpublic information. Perhaps this was the understanding, or perhaps Cuban mislead the CEO regarding the timing of his sale in order to obtain a confidential look at the details of the PIPE. We say only that on this factually sparse record, it is at least equally plausible that all sides understood there was to be no trading before the PIPE.[2] That both Cuban and the CEO expressed the belief that Cuban could not trade appears to reinforce the plausibility of this reading.

Given the paucity of jurisprudence on the question of what constitutes a relationship of "trust and confidence" and the inherently fact-bound nature of determining whether such a duty exists, we decline to first determine or place our thumb on the scale in the district court's determination of its presence or to now draw the contours of any liability that it might bring, including the force of Rule 10b5-2(b)(1). Rather, we VACATE the judgment dismissing the case and REMAND to the court of first instance for further proceedings including discovery, consideration of summary judgment, and trial, if reached.

---

2 Such an arrangement would raise serious tipper/tippee liability concerns were it explicit. If the CEO knowingly gave Cuban material nonpublic information and arranged so he could trade on it, it would not be difficult for a court to infer that the CEO must have done so for some personal benefit—e.g., goodwill from a wealthy investor and large minority stakeholder. "A reputational benefit that translates into future earnings, a quid pro quo, or a gift to a trading friend or relative all could suffice to show the tipper personally benefitted." *SEC v. Yun*, 327 F.3d 1263, 1277 (11th Cir. 2003). This of course is not to suggest any such improprieties occurred; rather, it simply reinforces the plausibility of the interpretation of the alleged facts as evidencing an understanding that the agreement included an agreement by Cuban not to trade.

SECURITIES AND EXCHANGE COMMISSION V. SWITZER UNITED STATES DISTRICT COURT 590 F. SUPP. 756 (WESTERN DISTRICT OF OKLAHOMA 1984)

Saffels, District Judge, Sitting by Designation:

This action brought by the Securities and Exchange Commission [hereinafter SEC] was tried to the court on March 19–22, 1984. It involved allegations of violations of Section 10(b) of the Securities Exchange Act of 1934 and violations of Commission Rule 10b-5. On the basis of the following findings of fact and conclusions of law, the court shall enter judgment on behalf of the defendants.

Findings of Fact

The following findings of fact have been stipulated to by all parties and accepted by the court and are set forth as follows.

...

6. Barry L. Switzer resides at 2811 Castlewood Drive, Norman, Oklahoma (73070). At all times mentioned in the complaint, Switzer was the head football coach at the University of Oklahoma ["Sooners"] in Norman, Oklahoma.

...

13. Texas International Company [hereinafter TIC] is a Delaware corporation with principal offices located in Oklahoma City, Oklahoma. At all times mentioned in the complaint, TIC was engaged in, among other things, exploration for and development of oil and natural gas properties. ... On or about June 18, 1982, a wholly-owned subsidiary of TIC merged with Phoenix Resources Company [hereinafter Phoenix] and Phoenix became a wholly-owned subsidiary of TIC. At all times mentioned in the complaint prior to the merger, TIC owned in excess of fifty percent (50%) of the common stock of Phoenix, and, by reason of such ownership position, controlled Phoenix through election of three of the five members of the Phoenix Board of Directors.

14. Prior to the merger, Phoenix, the successor to King Resources Company, was a Maine corporation with principal offices located in Oklahoma City, Oklahoma. At all times mentioned in the complaint prior to the merger, Phoenix engaged in, among other things, exploration for and development of oil and natural gas properties. ...

...

18. On or about Wednesday, June 10, 1981, after the public announcement [of the merger, defendant] Hoover sold all sixteen thousand five hundred (16,500) shares of Phoenix at prices between Fifty-Nine Dollars ($59) and Sixty-Three and 50/100 Dollars ($63.50) per share; the pre-tax profits realized on the basis of trading over this three-day period [June 8–10] amounted to approximately Two Hundred Sixty-Seven Thousand Seven Hundred Twenty-Eight Dollars ($267,728); and the pre-tax profits paid to and divided by [defendants] Switzer and Smith amounted to approximately One Hundred Ten Thousand Four Hundred Ninety-One Dollars ($110,491).

19. [Defendants] Hodges and Amyx agreed to purchase Phoenix stock through the Hodges, Amyx, Cross and Hodges investment partnership account.

20. On or about Monday, June 8, and Tuesday, June 9, 1981, Amyx, on behalf of the Hodges, Amyx, Cross and Hodges investment partnership, purchased thirteen thousand (13,000) shares of Phoenix at prices between Forty-Three and 50/100 Dollars ($43.50) and Forty-Eight and 50/100 Dollars ($48.50) per share.

21. On or about Wednesday, June 10, and Thursday, June 11, 1981, the Hodges, Amyx, Cross and Hodges investment partnership sold all thirteen thousand (13,000) shares of Phoenix at prices between Fifty-Nine Dollars ($59) and Sixty-Five Dollars ($65) per share; the pre-tax profits realized by the investment partnership on the basis of trading over a four-day period amounted to approximately Two Hundred Five Thousand Fifty-Five Dollars ($205,055); and the pre-tax profits from such trading paid to and divided by [defendants] Switzer and Smith amounted to approximately Eighty-Five Thousand Three Hundred Ten Dollars ($85,310).

...

The following additional facts are found by the court:

...

32. Barry Switzer is a well-recognized "celebrity" in Oklahoma and elsewhere. He has an interest in the oil and gas industry, as he is personally involved in various ventures within the industry.

33. Over the past several years, defendants Switzer, Kennedy, Deem, Smith, Hodges, Amyx and Hoover have acted together in varying combinations of persons (or in various groups of persons) in making investments. They have formed partnerships such as S & H Investments, Waverly Ltd., and Hodges, Amyx, Cross and Hodges,

to assist them in their investment ventures. Oftentimes, they trade on rumors or gossip they hear within the investing community. Profits and losses occurring as a result of stock investments made through these partnerships are shared by the members of the partnerships.

34. TIC had been considering various options for either consolidating or separating TIC and Phoenix for some time prior to its approaching Morgan Stanley on June 4 or 5, 1981. Rumors concerning these various options were circulating within the investing oil and gas community prior to June 4 or 5, 1981.

35. On June 6, 1981, four days prior to the public announcement concerning Phoenix, a state invitational secondary school track meet was held at John Jacobs Field on the University of Oklahoma campus. The track meet was a day long event. Several hundred spectators attended, including Barry Switzer, who arrived at the meet between 10:00 and 10:30 a.m. to watch his son compete, and George and Linda Platt, who arrived between 9:00 and 10:00 a.m. to watch their son compete. [G. Platt was Chairman of the Board and the Chief Executive Officer of TIC and served as a director on the Phoenix Board of Directors.] Soon after Switzer's arrival at the track meet, he and G. Platt recognized and greeted each other. Neither Switzer nor G. Platt knew that the other would be attending the meet.

36. G. Platt was a supporter of Oklahoma University football and had met Switzer at a few social engagements prior to June of 1981. TIC was a sponsor of Switzer's football show, "Play Back." G. Platt had had season tickets to the OU football games for approximately five years. G. Platt had obtained autographs from Switzer for G. Platt's minor children, and had had his secretary telephone Switzer to request that his season tickets be upgraded. Upgrading of tickets was extended as a courtesy by Switzer to many season ticket holders. On at least two occasions Switzer had phoned G. Platt requesting continued sponsorship by TIC of Switzer's football television program. These calls were made at the urging of Tom Goodgame, General Manager of the television station which then produced "Play Back." As of June 5, 1981, Switzer knew that G. Platt was Chairman of the Board of TIC and further knew that TIC was a substantial shareholder of Phoenix because Switzer was a stockholder in TIC and thereby knew Phoenix was a subsidiary.

37. Neither G. Platt nor his wife Linda are particularly impressed by Switzer. They view him as "just a nice fellow."

38. Upon first greeting each other at the track meet, G. Platt and Switzer exchanged pleasantries. Switzer then departed and continued on through the bleachers.

39. Throughout the course of the day, G. Platt and Linda Platt generally remained in one place in the bleachers. Switzer, however, throughout the day moved around a great deal, at times speaking with his son or other participants and their families, signing autographs and watching the different events on the field. While moving about, Switzer joined the Platts to visit with them about three to five times. During these visits Switzer and the Platts talked about their sons' participation in the meet, the oil and gas business, the economy, football and their respective personal investments.

40. G. Platt and Switzer did not have any conversations regarding Phoenix or Morgan Stanley, nor did they have any conversations regarding any mergers, acquisitions, take-overs or possible liquidations of Phoenix in which Morgan Stanley would play a part. G. Platt did not make any stock recommendations to Switzer, nor did he intentionally communicate material, non-public corporate information to Switzer about Phoenix during their conversations at the track meet. The information that Switzer heard at the track meet about Phoenix was overheard and was not the result of an intentional disclosure by G. Platt.

41. Sometime in the afternoon, after his last conversation with G. Platt, Switzer laid down on a row of bleachers behind the Platts to sunbathe while waiting for his son's next event. While Switzer was sunbathing, he overheard G. Platt talking to his wife about his trip to New York the prior day. In that conversation, G. Platt mentioned Morgan Stanley and his desire to dispose of or liquidate Phoenix. G. Platt further talked about several companies bidding on Phoenix. Switzer also overheard that an announcement of a "possible" liquidation of Phoenix might occur the following Thursday. Switzer remained on the bleachers behind the Platts for approximately twenty minutes then got up and continued to move about.

42. At this time Switzer had no knowledge as to whether the information he had overheard was confidential.

43. G. Platt was not conscious of Switzer's presence on the bleachers behind him that day, nor that Switzer had overheard any conversation.

44. G. Platt had returned home late the previous day from his meetings in New York, and his wife was to leave town for an entire week on the following day. Having minor children, it is the Platts' common

practice to try to arrange for G. Platt to be at home when his wife is out of town. The day of the track meet provided the Platts with an opportunity to discuss their respective plans for the up-coming week. During this discussion, G. Platt's prior business activities in New York and his resultant obligations and appointments were mentioned. In addition, when G. Platt appears distracted, it is not uncommon for his wife to inquire of him what is on his mind. On these occasions, he will talk to her about his problems, even though she does not have an understanding of nor interest in business matters. On the day of the track meet, Phoenix was weighing upon the mind of G. Platt, as it had been for the past several years, prompting G. Platt to talk to his wife about it.

45. On June 6, 1981, after the track meet, Switzer returned home and looked up the price of Phoenix in the paper. He then had dinner with [defendant] Sedwyn Kennedy, a close friend of both his and defendant Lee Allan Smith. In the past, they had all made investments through their partnership, SKS. Switzer told Kennedy he had overheard a conversation about the possible liquidation of Phoenix and that it would probably occur or be announced the next Thursday. Switzer told him the source was a gentleman who was an executive with TIC. Switzer did not tell Kennedy the man was G. Platt. Switzer and Kennedy are close friends and have known each other since 1966.

46. By the end of the evening, Switzer and Kennedy had each expressed an intention to purchase Phoenix stock.

47. On Sunday, June 7, 1981, Kennedy telephoned [defendant] Deem, his partner in S&H Investments, to discuss the possible purchase of Phoenix stock. Kennedy told Deem that Barry Switzer had talked to him about Phoenix, but did not give him any other details. As a result, Kennedy and Deem agreed to purchase shares of Phoenix through their partnership, S&H Investments.

48. On or about Monday, June 8, 1981, Kennedy purchased five thousand (5,000) shares of Phoenix stock at Forty-Two and 75/100 Dollars ($42.75) per share through the S&H Investments account; and on or about Tuesday, June 9, 1981, after further discussions with Deem, Kennedy purchased an additional one thousand (1,000) shares of Phoenix at Forty-Nine Dollars ($49) per share.

49. On Sunday, June 7, 1981, Switzer called Lee Allan Smith, a close friend with whom he had previously entered joint investments. Switzer told Smith that he had been at a track meet on Saturday and had overheard some information regarding the possible liquidation

or buy-out of Phoenix. Switzer attributed the information to "someone who should know," and said that he had overheard that Morgan Stanley was involved and that something could happen by Thursday of the following week. Switzer and Smith decided to approach Harold Hodges and Robert Hoover about providing the capital for buying some Phoenix stock with them because Smith and Switzer had insufficient available cash at that time to purchase a significant number of shares on their own. Hodges, Smith and Switzer were personal friends through participation in community and charitable activities in Oklahoma City. Hoover has known Smith for thirty years and has been a personal friend of both Smith and Switzer.

50. On Sunday, June 7, 1981, Switzer and Smith met with Hodges at the latter's offices. At this meeting, Switzer told Hodges that he had overheard some information that Phoenix stock was going to go up. Switzer did not state the source of the information, and Hodges did not inquire, because Switzer and Smith are good friends of his, and he often invests on information of this nature. During most of this meeting, Smith was occupied in making telephone calls on other matters in another area of the room.

51. At the conclusion of the meeting, it was agreed that Hodges would supply the capital and purchase the stock, and that any profits or losses would be split, fifty percent (50%) to Hodges and fifty percent (50%) to be divided between Smith and Switzer.

52. On Monday, June 8, 1981, Hodges told Robert Amyx that he had visited with Smith and Switzer the previous day and that they had told him they had heard a rumor that something favorable was going to happen regarding TIC or Phoenix, and instructed him to make stock purchases in both companies.

53. On Monday, June 8, and Tuesday, June 9, 1981, Robert Amyx, on behalf of the Hodges, Amyx, Cross and Hodges investment partnership, purchased thirteen thousand (13,000) shares of Phoenix, at prices between Forty-Three and 50/100 Dollars ($43.50) and Forty-Eight and 50/100 Dollars ($48.50) per share.

54. Because Hodges did not know which company was going to have a stock price rise, he requested Amyx not only to purchase Phoenix stock, but also stock of TIC, through the Hodges, Amyx, Cross and Hodges investment partnership account.

55. At the same time that he made the Phoenix purchases, Amyx purchased twenty thousand (20,000) shares of TIC stock at Twenty-Seven Dollars ($27) and Twenty-Seven and 1/8 Dollars ($27-1/8) per share.

56. On Sunday, June 7, 1981, after their meeting with Hodges, Switzer and Smith met with Robert Hoover at his home, where he was having a party. Switzer and Smith arrived separately. Smith first discussed the matter with Hoover and did not mention where he had received the information. Switzer also told Hoover something was going to happen with Phoenix, but did not say from whom he had heard the information.

57. Hoover agreed to purchase Phoenix stock jointly with Smith and Switzer. Hoover advanced the capital and purchased the stock for his account, based on an understanding that any losses or profits would be split, fifty percent (50%) to Hoover, and the remaining fifty percent (50%) to be divided between Smith and Switzer.

58. Hoover purchased sixteen thousand (16,000) shares of Phoenix stock on or about Monday, June 8, or Tuesday, June 9, 1981.

59. G. Platt did not learn of Switzer's purchase or sale of Phoenix stock, or of the conversation Switzer had overheard, until on or about March 10 or 11, 1982. On or about March 10 or 11, 1982, Switzer called G. Platt at Platt's condominium in Snow Mass, Colorado, and asked to meet with him because Switzer said something he had inadvertently done would affect Platt. At the time Switzer was also staying in Snow Mass, Colorado. During this meeting, Switzer told G. Platt, for the first time, that Switzer had been sitting behind G. Platt and his wife at the track meet on June 6, 1981, and had overheard G. Platt's conversation with his wife regarding Phoenix, and that as a result of that overheard conversation, Switzer and other friends of his had subsequently purchased and sold Phoenix stock. G. Platt had heard as early as February of 1982 that Phoenix was under investigation by the SEC. …

…

61. G. Platt did not share in the profits made through the transactions in Phoenix stock by Switzer, Kennedy, Deem, Smith, Hodges, Amyx and Hoover, nor did he receive any other financial benefit as a result of those transactions.

62. G. Platt did not receive any direct or indirect pecuniary gain nor any reputational benefit likely to translate into future earnings due to Switzer's inadvertent receipt of the information regarding Phoenix.

63. G. Platt did not make any gift to Switzer at this time, nor has he ever made a gift to Switzer.

64. Neither Switzer, Kennedy, Smith, Deem, Hodges, Amyx nor Hoover has ever been employed by or been an officer or director of Phoenix or TIC, nor have any of these defendants ever had any business relationship with Phoenix or with G. Platt personally. None of these defendants is a relative or personal friend of G. Platt.

65. None of the defendants had a relationship of trust and confidence with Phoenix, its shareholders or G. Platt.

66. In June, 1981, neither Switzer, Smith, Kennedy, Deem, Hodges, Amyx nor Hoover had any information from any source as to whether there was in fact any prospective purchaser of the stock or assets of Phoenix, nor whether a liquidation of the company would actually take place.

67. Smith, Hodges, Amyx, Kennedy, Deem and Hoover did not know nor did they act in reckless disregard of circumstances through which they could have had a reason to believe that the information received by Switzer came from other than an overheard conversation. None of these defendants knew or acted in reckless disregard of circumstances through which they could have had a reason to believe that the information they received was disclosed by an insider of Phoenix for an improper purpose.

Conclusions of Law

Based upon the foregoing findings of fact, the court makes the following conclusions of law.

...

7. [O]nly when a disclosure is made for an "improper purpose" will such a "tip" constitute a breach of an insider's duty, and only when there has been a breach of an insider's duty which the "tippee" knew or should have known constituted such a breach will there be "tippee" liability sufficient to constitute a violation of § 10(b) and Commission Rule 10b-5.

8. In *Dirks*, the court held that a disclosure is made for an "improper purpose" when an insider personally will benefit, directly or indirectly, from his disclosure. That court stated: "Absent some personal gain, there has been no breach of duty to stockholders. And absent a breach by the insider [to his stockholders], there is no derivative breach [by the tippee]."

9. G. Platt did not breach a fiduciary duty to stockholders of Phoenix for purposes of Rule 10b-5 liability nor § 10(b) liability, when he disclosed to his wife at the track meet of June 6, 1981, that there was going to be a possible liquidation of Phoenix.

10. This information was given to Mrs. Platt by G. Platt for the purpose of informing her of his up-coming business schedule so that arrangements for child care could be made.

11. The information was inadvertently overheard by Switzer at the track meet.

12. Rule 10b-5 does not bar trading on the basis of information inadvertently revealed by an insider.

13. The information was not intentionally imparted to Switzer by G. Platt, nor was the disclosure made for an improper purpose.

14. G. Platt did not personally benefit, directly or indirectly, monetarily or otherwise from the inadvertent disclosure.

15. As noted above, *Dirks* set forth a two-prong test for purposes of determining whether a tippee has acquired a fiduciary duty. First, it must be shown that an insider breached a fiduciary duty to the shareholders by disclosing inside information; and, second, it must be shown that the tippee knew or should have known that there had been a breach by the insider.

16. G. Platt did not breach a duty to the shareholders of Phoenix, and thus plaintiff failed to meet its burden of proof as to the first prong established in *Dirks*. Since G. Platt did not breach a fiduciary duty to Phoenix shareholders, Switzer did not acquire nor assume a fiduciary duty to Phoenix's shareholders, and because Switzer did not acquire a fiduciary duty to Phoenix shareholders, any information he passed on to defendants Smith, Hodges, Amyx, Hoover, Kennedy and Deem was not in violation of Rule 10b-5.

17. Since plaintiff did not meet its burden of proof as to the first prong of the two-prong *Dirks* test, i.e., it was not proved that G. Platt breached a fiduciary duty to the shareholders of Phoenix, tippee liability cannot result from G. Platt's inadvertent disclosure to Switzer.

...

SCENARIO

The SEC has filed the following Complaint. Upon review of the Complaint, what are the SEC's theories? If the SEC can prove the facts as alleged in its Complaint, can the defendants nonetheless prevail? Note that the names in this Complaint are fictitious.

IN THE UNITED STATES DISTRICT COURT
FOR THE NORTHERN DISTRICT OF OHIO

SECURITIES AND EXCHANGE COMMISSION,

Plaintiff

vs.

DAVID Q. LOCKNER and
CONRAD P. DILLARD

Defendants.

COMPLAINT FOR INJUNCTIVE AND OTHER RELIEF

1. The Securities and Exchange Commission ("Commission" or "SEC") hereby files its complaint, and alleges the following:

SUMMARY

2. This matter involves insider trading in the securities of Littler Products Corporation ("Littler Products") by defendant Dillard, who received tips directly or indirectly from defendant Lockner. Defendant Lockner was, at the time, in possession of material nonpublic information by virtue of his status as a member of Littler Products board of directors.

3. Lockner had knowledge of pending merger talks between Littler Products and QP Synergy, Inc. ("QP Synergy") as early as the latter part of August 2010. In fact, the merger was discussed extensively at a board meeting the day before Lockner left for a hunting trip in Michigan in September 2010.

4. Lockner tipped Dillard about the pending merger between Littler Products and QP Synergy during the Michigan hunting trip that Lockner and Dillard both attended.

5. On September 18, 2010, the day Dillard returned from the hunting trip, he purchased 7,000 shares of Littler Products stock for approximately $165,000.

6. Dillard, who had no prior history of trading Littler Products shares, sold the only five stock holdings he held in his portfolio in order to purchase the Littler Products shares.

7. On September 25, 2010, Littler Products announced a definitive merger agreement with QP Synergy. Littler Products shares, which were then traded on the American Stock Exchange, increased in price by almost 60% on the news that day.

8. On October 3, 2010, Dillard sold all of his Littler Synergy stock for a profit of approximately $130,000.

9. Defendants Lockner and Dillard have engaged, and unless restrained and enjoined by this Court, will continue to engage in acts and practices which constitute and will constitute violations of Section 10(b) of the Securities Exchange Act of 1934 ("Exchange Act") [15 U.S.C. 78j(b)] and Rule 10b-5 thereunder [17 C.F.R. 240.10b-5].

JURISDICTION AND VENUE

10. The SEC brings this action pursuant to Sections 21(d) and 21(e) of the Exchange Act [15 U.S.C. §§ 78u(d) and 78u(e)] to enjoin the defendants from engaging in transactions, acts, practices and courses of business alleged in this complaint, and transactions, acts, practices, and courses of business of similar purport and object, for disgorgement of illegally obtained funds and other equitable relief, and for civil money penalties. This Court has jurisdiction of this action pursuant to Sections 21(d), 21(e), and 27 of the Exchange Act [15 U.S.C. §§ 78u(d), 78u(e) and 78aa].

11. The defendants, directly and indirectly, have made use of the mails, the means and instruments of transportation and communication in interstate commerce, and the means and instrumentalities of interstate commerce, in connection with the transactions, acts, practices and courses of business alleged in this Complaint.

12. Venue lies in this Court pursuant to Section 27 of the Exchange Act [15 U.S.C. § 78aa] because the defendants reside within this

district, and certain of the actions set forth herein occurred within the Northern District of Ohio.

THE DEFENDANTS

13. David Q. Lockner, 47, resides in Beechwood, Ohio. Lockner served as a member of Littler Products' board of directors from April 2005 until December 2010, when Littler Products merged with QP Synergy.

14. Conrad P. Dillard, 43, resides in Shaker Heights, Ohio. Dillard, a college friend of Lockner's, works for a steel company based in Allentown, Pennsylvania. Dillard holds a B.A. degree in history.

FACTS

A. Lockner Learns about the Merger

15. Lockner joined Littler Products' board of directors in April 2005, three years after Littler Products completed its initial public offering.

16. In early August 2010, Lockner learned from Littler Products' CEO that the company was in negotiations with QP Synergy, a "potential buyer" of Littler Products.

17. On August 28, 2010, Lockner attended the first in a series of Littler Products board meetings at which senior management updated the board on the company's negotiations with QP Synergy. According to the minutes of that meeting, management reported that QP Synergy had "expressed an interest in a business combination," but had not specified a price range for purchasing Littler Products' shares. The "bottom line issue" for Littler Products management was whether QP Synergy "would make an offer in the high \$30 to low \$40 price range, which would be a significant premium over current market." At that time, Littler Products stock traded in the range of \$27 per share. Moreover, the board encouraged management to continue the discussions with QP Synergy.

18. On August 31, 2010, QP Synergy's CEO sent a letter to Littler Products' CEO proposing a cash and stock transaction that valued Littler Products at \$39 per share. Shortly thereafter, Lockner attended follow-up board meetings on September 1 and 2, 2010, at which QP Synergy's proposal was discussed at length. Minutes of the September

2 meeting state: "The Board discussed the offer and after reflection felt that it was a good offer which should be pursued." At this meeting, Lockner was appointed to a committee of independent directors to "consider the transaction as it progressed."

19. On September 12, 2010, the day before he left for the hunting trip with Dillard, Lockner attended a Littler Products board meeting, at which the board was advised that an offer was imminent. Specifically, the meeting minutes reflect that QP Synergy's due diligence process was essentially complete and that "QP Synergy had said it now has 90% to 95% of the information which is needed."

20. According to the minutes of the September 12, 2010 board meeting, Littler Products board was told that QP Synergy's chairman "has been pressing for his people to end their analysis today or tomorrow, so that he can get authorization from his Board to move forward with the deal on September 13, 2010."

21. Because of a small delay in providing the written merger agreement to Littler Products, however, the board was told that its "consideration of the deal will need to slide a few days." The board tentatively planned to meet on September 18, 2010, to consider the anticipated merger agreement.

22. Although there was some concern raised at the September 12, 2010 board meeting about how the recent decline in stock price for Littler Products and QP Synergy might impact the deal (Littler Products' share price had declined by approximately six percent from late August 2010 to September 12, 2010, and QP Synergy's share price had declined by approximately 12 percent during the same period), one board member noted that the underlying values of both companies were "still strong," and that, "from a deal perspective there were a number of ways to handle market fluctuation."

23. Thus, by the fourth such board meeting, held on September 12, 2010, the day before Lockner left for the hunting trip with Dillard, management had reported that (a) QP Synergy contemplated paying a significant premium over the market price for Littler Products shares, (b) both parties had substantially completed the due diligence process, and (c) the board's consideration of a definitive merger agreement was imminent.

24. Upon returning from the trip, Lockner attended a series of Littler Products board meetings held between September 20–22, 2010, at which the board discussed extensively, and ultimately approved, a

definitive merger agreement with QP Synergy. Littler Products shares were ultimately valued at approximately $36 per share.

25. Littler Products and QP Synergy announced the merger agreement on September 25, 2010. On that day, Littler Products' shares closed at $34.85 per share, representing an increase of nearly 60 percent over the prior day's closing price.

B. Lockner Viewed the Merger as Confidential Material Information

26. As a director of a public company, Lockner was aware "that insiders are to keep information that isn't generally available to the public confidential to the organization." As of September 12, 2010, when he left for the hunting trip, Lockner viewed the merger as a "potentially material event that was to be kept confidential."

27. Additionally, Lockner was aware that, starting in August 2010, in connection with the negotiation of the merger agreement, Littler Products had instituted a blackout period restricting employees from trading the company's shares.

28. In fact, Lockner was himself a Littler Products shareholder having acquired at least 12,000 shares of Littler Products through the company's IPO. Littler held those shares until they were converted to cash and QP Synergy stock when the merger closed in December 2010.

C. The Hunting Trip

29. Lockner and Dillard have maintained a close friendship dating back to college, where they played together on the lacrosse team. Lockner and Dillard talk two to three times per month on the phone, and meet in person six to ten times per year. They live within 25 miles from each other.

30. From September 13 to September 17, 2010, Lockner and Dillard attended a hunting trip near Escanaba, Michigan. The hunting party consisted of about six men in total, all of whom were friends or relatives of Lockner's. The hunters spent their days hunting "in the field," and their nights relaxing in a lodge provided by the tour organizer, where they had cocktails, smoked cigars, and talked about various subjects, including the hunt.

31. During the hunting trip, Lockner and Dillard discussed the merger agreement between Littler Products and QP Synergy.

32. During the hunting trip, Lockner advised some men on his hunting trip one evening after dinner and "a couple of cocktails," when asked by one of the men what was "wrong" with Littler Products (in apparent reference to the company's declining share price), that "fundamentally, there was nothing wrong with the stock."

33. Lockner's conversation about Littler Products' stock price with the men on the hunting trip was not an extended conversation, but one that took only a few minutes.

34. Dillard overheard the conversation about Littler Products and asked, "What company are you talking about?" to which Lockner replied, "Littler Products."

35. In addition to the general conversation about the performance of Littler Products stock, Lockner also discussed with Dillard, prior to Dillard's stock purchase of Littler Products stock, whether Littler Products "was a good stock."

36. Lockner and Dillard clearly discussed Littler Products during the hunting trip.

37. At some point, most likely during the hunting trip, Dillard directly asked Lockner whether Littler Products represented a "good buy," and Lockner's confirmation in response thereto influenced Dillard's purchase of Littler Products.

D. Dillard's Trading in Littler Products Shares

38. On September 18, 2010, the first business day after returning from the hunting trip, Dillard purchased 7,000 shares of Littler Products.

39. Dillard entered the order himself on-line at 5:17 p.m., after the market closed, and the transactions posted to his account the next day.

40. To come up with cash for the purchase, Dillard sold his entire positions in the only five stocks held in his investment portfolio (each of which resulted in a long-term loss), and also cashed out of a money market fund.

41. Unfamiliar with the mechanics of on-line stock trading, Dillard called a brokerage helpline earlier that day for assistance in selling those stocks.

42. Dillard sold all his Littler Products shares on October 2, 2010, one week after the merger was publicly announced, at a profit of approximately $130,000. Dillard placed this order himself on-line after the market closed.

43. Dillard, who maintained both an individual investment account and an IRA, had no prior history trading Littler Products shares.

44. Preceding his purchase of Littler Products stock, Dillard did not engage in frequent stock trades.

45. In fact, Dillard had adopted a conservative approach to investing after losing money investing in the 1990s.

46. Dillard's stock trading history establishes that he was essentially a long-term investor who looked for capital appreciation.

47. Dillard's quick purchase and quick sale of Littler Products stock in 2010 was inconsistent with his stock trading history.

48. Prior to his purchase of Littler Products stock in 2010, Dillard had never bought shares in any companies with which Lockner had an affiliation.

49. When Dillard bought Littler Products shares, he was aware of the contemplated merger and expected the price of Littler Products shares to increase on the news, when the announcement was made.

CLAIM FOR RELIEF

COUNT I—FRAUD

Violations of Section 10(b) of the Exchange Act [15 U.S.C. § 78j(b) and Rule 10b-5 thereunder [17 C.F.R. § 240.10b-5]

50. Paragraphs 1 through 49 are hereby realleged and are incorporated herein by reference.

51. Defendants Lockner and Dillard, in the latter half of 2010, singly or in concert, in connection with the purchase and sale of securities described herein, by the use of the means and instrumentalities of interstate commerce and by use of the mails, directly and indirectly:

a) employed devices, schemes, and artifices to defraud;

b) made untrue statements of material facts and omitted to state material facts necessary in order to make the statements made, in light of the circumstances under which they were made, not misleading; and

c) engaged in acts, practices, and courses of business which would and did operate as a fraud and deceit upon the purchasers of such securities, all as more particularly described above.

52. The Defendants knowingly, intentionally, and/or recklessly engaged in the aforementioned devices, schemes and artifices to defraud, made untrue statements of material facts and omitted to state material facts, and engaged in fraudulent acts, practices and courses of business. In engaging in such conduct, the Defendants acted with scienter, that is, with an intent to deceive, manipulate or defraud or with a severe reckless disregard for the truth.

53. By reason of the foregoing, the Defendants, directly and indirectly, have violated and, unless enjoined, will continue to violate Section 10(b) of the Exchange Act [15 U.S.C. § 17j(b)] and Rule 10b-5 thereunder [17 C.F.R. § 240.10b-5].

PRAYER FOR RELIEF

WHEREFORE, Plaintiff Commission, respectfully prays that the Court:

I.

Make findings of fact and conclusions of law in accordance with Rule 52 of the Federal Rules of Civil Procedure.

II.

Issue a permanent injunction enjoining defendants Lockner, Dillard and their agents, servants, employees, attorneys, and all other persons in active concert or participation with them who receive actual notice of the order by personal service or otherwise, and each of them from violating Section 10(b) of the Exchange Act [15 U.S.C. 78j(b)] and Rule 10b-5 thereunder [17 C.F.R. 240.10b-5].

III.

Issue an Order requiring defendants Lockner and Dillard to disgorge all ill-gotten gains as alleged in the Commission's Complaint, plus pay prejudgment interest thereon.

IV.

Issue an Order requiring defendants Lockner and Dillard, pursuant to Sections 21(d)(3) and 21A of the Exchange Act [15 U.S.C. 78u(d)(3) and 78u-1], to pay civil monetary penalties.

V.

Issue an Order that retains jurisdiction over this action in order to implement and carry out the terms of all orders and decrees that may have been entered or to entertain any suitable application or motion by the Commission for additional relief within the jurisdiction of this Court.

VI.

Grant such other and further relief as may be necessary and appropriate.

Respectfully Submitted,

Sylvia O'Davis
Senior Trial Counsel
Counsel for Plaintiff
U.S. Securities and Exchange Commission

Chapter 10

MERGERS AND ACQUISITIONS

THE GLOBAL VOLUME of mergers and acquisitions (M&A) annually totals over $2 trillion.[1] This figure represents the U.S. dollar value of assets sold or exchanged between business enterprises. Stated generally, a merger normally occurs where one corporation is "merged" into another corporation, with the surviving company assuming all of the assets and liabilities.[2] By comparison, an acquisition occurs when one company buys another company's assets (in whole or in part).[3]

Mergers and acquisitions are often front page news. For example, in 2011, AT&T announced plans to acquire mobile services competitor T-Mobile for $39 billion.[4] United and Continental Airlines merged in 2010 to create the world's largest airline.[5] And Microsoft announced in 2011 that it intends to spend $8.5 billion to purchase Skype—software that allows users to make video and voice calls over the internet.[6]

Acquisitions thus enable an enterprise to purchase preferred assets from another corporation, or even to acquire an entire corporation. Enterprises elect to engage in M&A transactions for a variety of reasons. For instance, an acquirer may believe that it can operate the purchased company on a more efficient basis. Or, an acquirer may seek to bolster its business by purchasing another enterprise's product line or attractive division. As another example, the acquirer may conclude that the target corporation's stock price is depressed, thereby providing an opportunity to purchase the target's assets at a relatively bargain price.[7]

Corporations may choose among several different structures to effectuate a merger or acquisition. The basic merger and acquisition structures include the following: sale of all or substantially all of a corporation's assets, merger (including triangular merger, two-step merger, and a short-form merger), proxy contest, and tender offer.

Structures and Methods for Obtaining Control of a Corporation

Sale of All or Substantially All of a Corporation's Assets

With regularity, business enterprises sell assets to other enterprises in regular commercial transactions. Regular asset transactions of significance normally receive board of director approval (with no requirement of shareholder approval). However, a sale of "substantially all" of a company's assets ordinarily requires the corporation's board as well as its shareholders to approve the transaction.[8]

Defining what constitutes "substantially all" of a company's assets is murky. In Delaware, for example, a company sells "substantially all" of its assets when the sale is "quantitatively vital to the operation of the corporation and is out of the ordinary and substantially affects the existence and purpose of the corporation."[9] In other words, "substantially all" is determined by both quantitative and qualitative criteria. Quantitative factors encompass the company's assets, revenues, and earnings. Qualitative factors focus on the extent to which the asset sale would impact the corporation's existence or purpose.[10]

A flexible interpretation of the meaning of "substantially all" assets is seen in *Katz v. Bregman.*[11] In that case, the company's board of directors determined to sell its steel division (that made steel drums) and start a new venture to manufacture plastic drums. Upon shareholder challenge, the court reasoned that the company's principal business was that of a steel drum manufacturer. Thus, the court found that selling the steel division was a departure from the corporation's historically profitable business. In this respect, the steel division comprised over 51% of the assets and generated approximately 45% of its revenues. Therefore, the court held that the sale of the steel division was a sale of "substantially all" of the corporation's assets.[12]

Under prevailing company law, including that of Delaware, a board of directors must obtain shareholder approval to sell substantially all of a corporation's assets. A sale is generally approved when the majority of the outstanding shares vote in favor of the asset sale.[13] Remedies for shareholders who object to the asset sale vary by state. Some states provide shareholders with appraisal rights (the entitlement to be paid "fair value" for one's stock).[14] Delaware, however, does not provide appraisal rights in this context.[15] Nevertheless, an allegedly aggrieved shareholder may file suit asserting that a director or officer breached his/her fiduciary duty.[16]

MERGERS

Generally a merger occurs when two or more companies combine their businesses into one company.[17] The board of directors of each company normally approves the merger. In addition, with certain exceptions, the shareholders of each company must vote to approve the merger.[18] Note, however, that in certain situations, such as where there is only a nominal change to the acquirer, the acquirer's shareholders do not vote on the merger.[19]

When shareholders vote on a merger, the companies must follow Securities and Exchange Commission (SEC) regulations. These regulations largely focus on disclosure to help enable shareholders to make an informed voting decision.[20] In this regard, SEC regulations prohibit proxy materials that contain materially false or misleading statements.[21] Note that conducting a shareholder vote at a duly called meeting takes time. Consequently, use of a merger structure incurs the risk that other prospective acquirers may enter the fray and make offers to purchase the target company. This could eventuate a bidding war between the original acquirer and another suitor—thereby driving up the acquisition price.[22]

Shareholders who object to a merger may elect to invoke their appraisal rights under state law.[23] Appraisal rights entitle dissenting shareholders to have their shares purchased for "fair value."[24] A tribunal determines "fair value" of the stock by considering relevant financial factors such as assets, revenues, earnings, and premiums paid in other similar "deals."[25] Moreover, many states do not provide an appraisal remedy if the acquired company's stock is listed on a national securities exchange (such as the New York Stock Exchange).[26] In such states, shareholders who are dissatisfied with an acquirer's offer may seek to sue for breach of fiduciary duty or simply sell their stock before the merger is consummated.[27]

TRIANGULAR MERGERS

A triangular merger involves three or more corporations. In a basic triangular merger the acquiring corporation first creates a subsidiary (which conducts no business and will become a party to the merger). The acquiring corporation is the sole shareholder of the subsidiary. Next, the acquiring corporation transfers the consideration to be paid in the merger—stock or cash—to the subsidiary. These funds will be used by the subsidiary to acquire the target. After the subsidiary is funded, the subsidiary merges with the target corporation. Thus, the merger is between the target and the subsidiary, not the target and the acquiring corporation.[28]

An acquiring corporation obtains significant benefits by utilizing a triangular merger. First, because the subsidiary merged with the target, the acquiring company's shareholders ordinarily do not vote on the merger. This allows the acquiring corporation's board to complete a merger with fewer impediments. But note that, if at least twenty percent of the acquiring corporation's stock is to be issued pursuant to the merger, then the New York Stock Exchange requires that the shareholders of the acquiring corporation be entitled to vote.[29] A second benefit is that the shareholders of the acquiring corporation do not have appraisal rights. On the other hand, the target corporation's shareholders still vote on the merger and may invoke appraisal rights as provided by applicable state law. And another key benefit is that the acquiring company is not burdened by the target's liabilities. Since the subsidiary merged with the target, the subsidiary (and not the parent) assumes the target's assets and liabilities.[30]

Proxy Contests

A potential acquirer may also launch a proxy contest in an effort to obtain control of a target company's board of directors. A proxy contest enables a potential insurgent or shareholders with other objectives to nominate directors to the target's board. Assuming the insurgent's nominees receive a sufficient number of votes, those nominees become directors of the board. Depending on the number of directors standing for election, the insurgent's nominees (if elected) may become a majority of the directors of the board.[31] However, in cases of a staggered board of directors, procuring control of the target's board could take two proxy fights. For example, if only three vacancies are open each year on a nine-person board, it would take two years before an insurgent obtains a majority of seats on the target's board.[32]

Carl Icahn's efforts to oust Yahoo!'s board of directors in 2008 provides an illustration of a high-profile proxy contest. Early in 2008 Microsoft made an unsolicited bid to acquire Yahoo! for over $44 billion. The offer was a 62% premium over Yahoo!'s stock price.[33] Nonetheless, Yahoo!'s board of directors opted to reject Microsoft's offer.[34] Thereafter, Carl Icahn, a well known corporate activist, announced a proxy contest seeking to replace Yahoo!'s board of directors.[35] Subsequently, Yahoo! settled with Icahn prior to the shareholder vote. Pursuant to the settlement, although eight of the nine incumbent directors were retained, Icahn was appointed to the board. In addition, the Yahoo! board agreed to expand the size of its board to eleven members, appointing two of Icahn's nominees to fill these positions.[36]

TENDER OFFERS

A prospective acquirer may launch a tender offer in its efforts to acquire control of a corporation. Generally, a tender offer is an offer that bypasses the target's board of directors and is made directly to the target company's shareholders. To induce target shareholders to tender their shares, ordinarily the prospective bidder makes its offer at a substantial premium above the then current stock price.

Many rules govern tender offers. For example, federal law governs the procedural process as well as disclosures that must be made during the tender offer process.[37] For instance, a tender offer for a publicly-held company must be open to all shareholders of the class of securities subject to the tender offer, thereby prohibiting exclusionary bids.[38] Regulations require that the bidder's offer remain open for at least 20 business days[39] and that all shares tendered during the entire period that the offer remains open be accepted on a pro rata basis.[40] This statutory period allows shareholders to make an informed decision whether to tender their shares. Moreover, federal regulations require a prospective bidder to disclose its identity within ten days after it acquires more than 5% of the subject company's shares.[41] During the takeover battle, the bidder may increase its price to outbid a competing suitor or to persuade reluctant shareholders to tender their shares. Such an increase in price must be available to all selling shareholders.[42]

TWO-STEP MERGERS

The term "two-step merger" generally consists of a tender offer whereby the bidder acquires a majority of the target company's common stock followed by a merger in which the minority shareholders receive cash as consideration for their shares. The two-step merger is referred to by critics as a "squeeze-out" because shareholders who decline to tender their stock during the takeover bid are forced to relinquish their shares in the subsequent cash-out merger.

Hence, the first acquisition in a two-step merger is the consummation of a tender offer. The bidder's objective in making the tender offer ordinarily is to acquire a majority of the target company's stock. The second transaction is where a bidder, after acquiring over fifty percent of the target's stock in the tender offer, launches a back-end merger to purchase 100% of the target's stock. Having acquired a majority of the target's stock during the tender offer, the bidder thus has the necessary votes for approval. In this way, the bidder invokes its voting control to effectuate the acquisition of the target company.[43]

A key issue that typically arises in a two-step merger is the available remedies that may be invoked by a target shareholder who objects to the back-end merger.[44] Under state law, a dissenting shareholder may perfect the appraisal remedy in order to receive "fair value" for his/her stock.[45] In addition, in a number of jurisdictions, a minority shareholder may sue a majority shareholder (namely, the bidder corporation) for breach of the duty of loyalty. In Delaware, the minority shareholder's suit must allege specific acts of fraud, misrepresentation, or other palpable overreaching to show that the merger is unfair to the minority shareholders.[46]

SHORT-FORM MERGERS

A short-form merger allows a shareholder who owns at least 90% of the subject company's stock to effectuate a merger with relatively little hassle. For instance, a takeover bidder who acquired at least 90% of a subject company's stock, may subsequently employ a short-form merger to own 100 percent of that company.[47] The purpose of the short-form merger is to provide an expeditious process for effectuating a merger where a shareholder has at least 90% ownership. State law provides that the subsidiary's shareholders who object to the merger have the right to seek payment of "fair value" for their shares by means of the appraisal process.[48] Nonetheless, absent the commission of fraud or illegality by the majority shareholder (or its representatives), appraisal ordinarily is the only remedy that may be invoked by minority shareholders who object to a short-form merger.[49]

TAKEOVER DEFENSES

A target company's board of directors may determine that it is in the corporation's best interest to remain an independent enterprise rather than being purchased by the bidder. To thwart the takeover bid, a board may implement defensive tactics. As a matter of good practice, these tactics should be adopted (and thereby be ready to be deployed) prior to the time that an unwanted suitor emerges. A company's takeover defense arsenal may include, for example, a poison pill, supermajority shareholder voting, a staggered board of directors, and the "just say no" defense. In addition, a "white knight" may emerge to make a competing offer.

Poison Pill

A shareholder rights plan, pejoratively known as a "poison pill," is a common takeover defense. The purpose of a poison pill is to make an acquisition significantly more costly to the bidder. A poison pill, if triggered, greatly increases the price a bidder has to pay to procure control of the target. Typically, a poison pill is triggered when a prospective bidder purchases a specified percentage of the target company's outstanding stock (such as 15%). A poison pill, for example, through the use of stock warrants, could give the target's shareholders (with the bidder excluded) the right to purchase additional shares of stock at a greatly reduced price. As shareholders exercise their warrants to buy the shares, the bidder's ownership interest in the target is diluted, thereby rendering it more expensive for the bidder to gain control of the target.[50]

State law generally allows a company's board of directors to adopt a poison pill.[51] For instance, under Delaware law, a board of directors may unilaterally adopt a poison pill without receiving shareholder approval, if the board believes that there is a threat to corporate policy and effectiveness and the poison pill is reasonable in relation to the risk posed.[52] Notably, however, a number of states permit shareholders to adopt bylaws that confine (or eliminate) the board's authority to unilaterally employ a poison pill.[53]

Supermajority Voting

In most states, a merger's approval requires a majority of the shares outstanding.[54] Nonetheless, this "bare" majority requirement may be enhanced through an amendment to the articles of incorporation.[55] For instance, under a supermajority voting provision, the required shareholder vote may be increased to 75%. Such a provision would make it more onerous for a bidder to gain control of the target corporation.[56]

Staggered Board of Directors

Directors on a board normally all stand for election at the same time. Some corporations, however, have a staggered board whereby only a minority of directors are elected each year.[57] For instance, assume a nine-person board of directors has directors who serve three-year terms, with three board seats filled on an annual basis. Under this framework, an insurgent would have to win two proxy contests in order to obtain control of the board of directors. This is particularly the case if removal of directors is only "for cause."[58]

Hence, to provide further "defensive" protection, a corporation's articles of incorporation may stipulate that directors may be removed only "for cause."[59] Generally, "for cause" means conduct that constitutes gross negligence or malfeasance.[60] State law requires that a director who is sought to be removed "for cause" be provided sufficient notice of the charges and an adequate opportunity to respond to the accusations.[61]

White Knight

A white knight is a bidder that emerges to make a competing offer or other strategic acquisition. When a determined bidder is viewed by the target's board of directors as posing a significant threat to the target company, the board may seek out a suitor deemed more friendly to the target. The white knight's entry into the fray frequently will increase the bidding price. This will make a hostile bidder's potential acquisition of the target more costly and likely more difficult to complete.[62] Notably, if the tender offer is consummated, target shareholders frequently benefit by receiving the increased price. And this is the case irrespective whether the hostile bidder or the white knight emerges victorious.[63]

"Just Say No" Defense

An important takeover defense is a board's ability to "just say no" to a bidder's offer.[64] A board uses this defense coupled with a "poison pill." Normally, fearful of the consequences, a prospective bidder will not reach the ownership percentage threshold to trigger the poison pill. Triggering the pill would inflict significant financial harm on the bidder. Accordingly, faced with what it views as an inadequate offer, the target's board says "no" to the offer while keeping the poison pill intact. Of course, the board's decision to reject the bidder's offer must be sufficiently informed.

In this setting, the board of directors must assess whether the bidder's offer is in the best interests of the corporation and its shareholders. Ascertaining whether an offer is in the corporation's best interests typically requires several steps, including the target board's assessment of the target's assets, strategic plans, and earnings potential; its analysis of the potential combined enterprise comprised of the prospective acquirer and the target; and the hiring by the board of a reputable investment bank to help ascertain the target's value. After conducting these analyses, a board often determines that the takeover bid is not in the company's best interests and that the company should remain independent.[65]

Although the target's board may reject a bidder's offer, a number of maneuvers remain available to a potential acquirer. For example, a potential acquirer could seek to restrict the board's authority to trigger a poison pill. Assume that when a potential acquirer buys 10% of the target's stock, the target's bylaws (along with state law) authorize the shareholder to call a special shareholder meeting.[66] During this shareholder meeting, the potential acquirer may propose for adoption new bylaws that restrict the board's ability to implement a poison pill.[67] Alternatively, the suitor could mount a proxy contest seeking to elect directors who are friendly to its cause. Once a sufficient number of directors friendly to the suitor are elected to the target's board, these directors would amend the target's bylaws to remove the poison pill.[68]

Fiduciary Duties in Takeover Defenses

A board of directors institutes takeover defenses in order to help protect the corporation from an acquisition that is deemed contrary to the corporation's and its shareholders' best interests. Directors, however, may implement defensive maneuvers while having a conflict of interest, such as seeking to preserve their own positions of power and accompanying generous compensation.[69] As one Delaware court explained, where the "board has acted solely or primarily because of the desire to perpetuate themselves in office, the use of corporate funds for such purposes is improper."[70] Therefore, many courts do not apply the traditional or "plain vanilla" business judgment rule when analyzing a board's determination to adopt and implement takeover defenses. Rather, several courts impose more rigorous standards, such as the "*Unocal* test."[71]

Unocal Standard

Under the *Unocal* test, defensive maneuvers, undertaken by a board of directors to fend off a takeover bid, must satisfy two requirements. First, the target's board must show that the board has "reasonable grounds for believing" that the prospective acquirer's offer constituted a "danger to corporate policy and effectiveness."[72] A board ordinarily satisfies this requirement by establishing that it acted in good faith and conducted a reasonable investigation regarding the offer's attributes.[73]

In addition to conducting a reasonable investigation, the *Unocal* test contains a second requirement: The target's board of directors must show that any defensive tactic adopted (and implemented) must be reasonable in relation to the threat posed.[74] A defense tactic passes judicial scrutiny under this standard when it is deemed proportionate, and neither coercive nor preclusive.[75] To illustrate, the Delaware Supreme Court has opined that a poison pill was not preclusive because the pill still permitted the suitor to launch a proxy contest. In addition, the court ruled that the poison pill was not preclusive because it did not unduly limit the target's shareholders from receiving tender offers from other bidders.[76]

Revlon Duties

The *Unocal* test applies when a court considers actions taken by a target's board of directors that is fending off a takeover bid in order for the target to remain an independent enterprise. By contrast, *Revlon* duties apply when a board abandons the corporation's strategy to remain independent and determines to sell or break-up the corporation.[77] In this setting—involving the sale or break-up of the corporate enterprise—the board of directors under *Revlon* must seek to achieve for shareholders, within such directors' good faith business judgment, the highest share price practicable.[78]

CONCLUSION

Mergers and acquisitions are critical to the U.S. economy and when implementing corporate strategy. Business enterprises merge with or acquire assets from other companies as a means, for example, to generate earnings growth, expand into new markets, and/or cut operating costs. The following cases focus on M&A transactions in three settings: sales of substantially all assets, cash-out mergers, and takeover bids.

NOTES

1. See Investment Banking Scorecard, *M&A Volume*, Wall St. J. (May 21, 2011), *available at* http://graphicsweb.wsj.com/documents/INVESTMENT/InvestmentBankQuarterly_1007.html.
2. See Black's Law Dictionary 1078 (9th ed. 2009).
3. See *id.* at 26.
4. See Press release, AT&T, *AT&T to Acquire T-Mobile USA from Deutsche Telekom* (March 20, 2011), *available at* http://www.att.com/gen/press-room?pid=19358&cdvn=news&newsarticleid=31703&mapcode=corporate/financial. This proposed merger was challenged by the U.S. Department of Justice. See *U.S. Sues*

to Stop AT&T Deal, Wall St. J. Sept. 1, 2011, at A1. The proposed deal is now dead. See "AT&T, T-Mobile Kill Merger," Deal Journal, WSJ Blogs, Dec. 19, 2011.

5. See Press release, *United and Continental Close Merger*, United, (Oct. 1, 2010) *available at* http://www.united.com/press/detail/0,7056,67936-1,00.html.
6. See Press Release, Microsoft, *Microsoft to Acquire Skype* (May 10, 2011), *available at* http://www.microsoft.com/presspass/2011/may11/05-10corpnewspr.mspx.
7. See K. Davidson, *Megamergers: Corporate America's Billion-Dollar Takeovers* (1985).
8. See § 271 of the Delaware General Corporation Law.
9. *Gimbel v. Signal Companies, Inc.*, 316 A. 2d 599, 606 (Del. Ch. 1974).
10. See *id.*
11. 431 A. 2d 1274 (Del. Ch. 1981).
12. See *id.* at 1275–1276.
13. § 271 of the Delaware General Corporation Law.
14. See, e.g., § 13.02(a)(3) of the Model Business Corporation Act.
15. See *Hariton v. Arco Elecs., Inc.*, 182 A. 2d 22, 24 (Del. Ch. 1962).
16. See *Gimbel v. Signal Companies, Inc.*, 316 A. 2d 599 (Del. Ch. 1974); materials in Chapters 6, 7 herein.
17. See D. Branson, J. Heminway, M. Loewenstein, M. Steinberg, & M. Warren, *Business Enterprises: Legal Structures, Governance, and Policy* 625–626 (2009).
18. See § 251 of the Delaware General Corporation Law; § 11.04 of the Model Business Corporation Act.
19. See § 251(f) of the Delaware General Corporation Law; § 11.04(g) of the Model Business Corporation Act.
20. See Marc I. Steinberg, *Securities Regulation* 517–537 (revised 5th ed. 2009).
21. SEC Rule 14a-9, 17 C.F.R. § 240.14a-9 (2011).
22. See, e.g., *Omnicare, Inc. v. NCS Healthcare, Inc.*, 818 A. 2d 914 (Del. 2003); *Paramount Communications, Inc. v. Time, Inc.*, 571 A. 2d 1140 (Del. 1990).
23. See, e.g., § 251(c) of the Delaware General Corporation Law.
24. *Id.*
25. See, e.g., *Weinberger v. UOP, Inc.*, 457 A. 2d 701 (Del. 1983).
26. See, e.g., § 262(b)(1) of the Delaware General Corporation Law. Other states that do not permit appraisal in this context include, for example, Arizona, California, Florida, Maryland, Michigan, New Jersey, Pennsylvania, Tennessee, Virginia, and Wisconsin.
27. See, e.g., *Kahn v. Tremont Corp.*, 694 A. 2d 422 (Del. 1997).
28. See Branson et al., *supra* note 17, at 620-621.
29. See *Paramount Communications, Inc. v. Time, Inc.*, 571 A. 2d 1140, 1146 (Del. 1990).
30. See Branson et al., *supra* note 17, at 621.
31. See, e.g., *GAF Corp. v. Heyman*, 724 F. 2d 727 (2d Cir. 1983).
32. See, e.g., *Air Products and Chemicals, Inc. v. Airgas, Inc.*, 16 A. 3d 48 (Del. Ch. 2011).
33. Press release, Microsoft, *Microsoft Proposes Acquisition of Yahoo! For $31 Per Share* (Feb. 1, 2008), *available at* http://www.microsoft.com/presspass/press/2008/feb08/02-01CorpNewsPR.mspx.

34. Press release, Yahoo!, *Yahoo! Board of Directors Says Microsoft's Proposal Substantially Undervalues Yahoo!* (Feb. 10, 2008), *available at* http://pressroom.yahoo.net/pr/ycorp/293129.aspx.
35. Zuckerman and Delaney, *Icahn Pushing Yahoo! Back to Microsoft,* Wall. St. J. (May 15, 2008), *available at* http://online.wsj.com/article/SB121080418563993117.html.
36. Press release, Yahoo!, *Yahoo! Announces Settlement with Carl Icahn* (July 21, 2008), *available at* http://pressroom.yahoo.net/pr/ycorp/323246/aspx.
37. See §§ 13(d), (e), 14(d), (e) of the Securities Exchange Act of 1934, and SEC rules thereafter; SEC Schedules TO and 14D-9.
38. See SEC Rules 13e-4, 14d-10, 17 C.F.R. § 240.13e-4, 14d-10. The SEC action in adopting these rules nullifies the Delaware Supreme Court's decision in *Unocal Corp. v. Mesa Petroleum Company*, 498 A. 2d 946 (Del. 1985), that permitted certain shareholders to be excluded if sufficient justification were shown.
39. See § 14(d)(1) of the Securities Exchange Act.
40. Section 14(d)(6) of the Securities Exchange Act; Rule 14d-8, 17 C.F.R. § 240.14d-8.
41. See § 13(d)(1) of the Securities Exchange Act; Rule 13d-1, 17 C.F.R. § 240.13d-1.
42. SEC Rule 14d-10, 17 C.F.R. § 240.14d-10; Securities Exchange Act Release No. 54684 (2006).
43. See Branson et al., *supra* note 17, at 656.
44. See M. Steinberg, *Securities Regulation: Liabilities and Remedies* §§ 8.04–8.06 (2011).
45. See § 262 of the Delaware General Corporation Law; § 13.02 of the Model Business Corporation Act.
46. See *Weinberger v. UOP, Inc.*, 457 A. 2d 701, 703 (Del. 1983).
47. See § 253 of the Delaware General Corporation Law.
48. *Id.* § 253(d).
49. See *Glassman v. Unocal Exploration Corp.*, 777 A. 2d 242 (Del. 2001); Steinberg, *Short-Form Mergers in Delaware*, 27 Del. J. Corp. L. 489 (2002).
50. See, e.g., *Yucaipa American Alliance Fund II, L.P. v. Riggio,* 1 A. 3d 310 (Del. Ch. 2010).
51. See, e.g., *Int'l Bhd. Of Teamsters Gen. Fund v. Fleming Cos.*, 975 P. 2d 907 (Okla. 1999).
52. See, e.g., *Versata Enterprises, Inc. v. Selectica, Inc.*, 5 A. 3d 586 (Del. 2010); *Account v. Hilton Hotels Corp.*, 780 A. 2d 245 (Del. 2001).
53. See *Fleming*, 975 P. 2d at 908.
54. See, e.g., § 251(c) of the Delaware General Corporation Law.
55. See, e.g., § 7.27 of the Model Business Corporation Act.
56. See Branson et al., *supra* note 17, at 672.
57. See, e.g., § 8.06 of the Model Business Corporation Act.
58. See, e.g., *Air Products and Chemicals, Inc. v. Airgas, Inc.*, 16 A. 3d 48 (Del. Ch. 2011).
59. See § 141(k) of the Delaware General Corporation Law.

60. *In re Walt Disney Co. Derivative Litigation,* 906 A. 2d 27, 71 (2006).
61. See *Superwire.com, Inc. v. Hampton,* 805 A 2d 904, 912 (Del. 2002).
62. See, e.g., *MacAndrews & Forbes Holdings v. Revlon, Inc.,* 506 A. 2d 173 (Del. 1986).
63. See M. Steinberg, *Understanding Securities Law* 482 (5th Cir. 2009) (stating that "[a]ction taken by a white knight may include purchasing a large block of the target company's stock or making a competing tender offer").
64. See, e.g., *Moore Corp. v. Wallace Computer Services, Inc.,* 907 F. Supp. 1545 (Del 1995); *Air Products and Chemicals, Inc. v. Airgas, Inc.,* 16 A. 3d 48 (Del. Ch. 2011).
65. See, e.g., *Unitrin v. American General Corp.,* 651 A. 2d 1361 (Del. 1995).
66. See § 7.02 of the Model Business Corporation Act.
67. See *Int'l Bhd. Of Teamsters Gen. Fund v. Fleming Cos.,* 975 P. 2d 907, 913 (Okla. 1999).
68. See *Air Products and Chemicals Inc. v. Airgas, Inc.,* 16 A. 3d 48 (Del. Ch. 2011); Branson, et al., *supra* note 17, at 672–673.
69. See *Unocal Corp. v. Mesa Petroleum Co.,* 493 A. 2d 946, 954 (Del. 1985).
70. *Cheff v. Mathes,* 199 A. 2d 548, 554 (Del. 1964).
71. See, e.g., *Unocal Corp.,* 493 A. 2d at 954–955.
72. *Id.* at 955.
73. See *id.*
74. See *id.* at 955.
75. See *Unitrin, Inc., v. American General Corporation* 651 A. 2d 1361, 1387 (Del. 1995).
76. See cases cited in notes 52, 64, 75 *supra.*
77. See *Paramount Communications, Inc. v. Time, Inc.,* 571 A. 2d 1140, 1150 (Del. 1989).
78. See, e.g., *Paramount Communications, Inc. v. QVC Network, Inc.,* 637 A. 2d 34 (Del. 1994); *Revlon, Inc. v. MacAndrews & Forbes Holdings, Inc.,* 506 A. 2d 173 (Del. 1986).

SALES OF "SUBSTANTIALLY ALL" ASSETS

GIMBEL V. SIGNAL COMPANIES, INC.
COURT OF CHANCERY OF DELAWARE
316 A. 2D 599 (1974)

Quillen, Chancellor:

This action was commenced on December 24, 1973 by plaintiff, a stockholder of the Signal Companies, Inc. ("Signal"). The complaint seeks, among other things, injunctive relief to prevent the consummation of the pending sale by Signal to Burmah Oil Incorporated ("Burmah") of all of the outstanding capital stock of Signal Oil and Gas Company ("Signal Oil"), a wholly-owned subsidiary of Signal. The effective sale price exceeds 480 million dollars. The sale was approved at a special meeting of the Board of Directors of Signal. …

… This is the Court's decision on plaintiff's application for a preliminary injunction to prevent the sale of Signal Oil to Burmah pending trial on the merits of plaintiff's contentions. …

I turn first to the question of 8 Del. C. § 271(a) which requires majority stockholder approval for the sale of "all or substantially all" of the assets of a Delaware corporation. A sale of less than all or substantially all assets is not covered by negative implication from the statute. …

It is important to note in the first instance that the statute does not speak of a requirement of shareholder approval simply because an independent, important branch of a corporate business is being sold. … Similarly, it is not our law that shareholder approval is required upon every "major" restructuring of the corporation. Again, it is not necessary to go beyond the statute. The statute requires shareholder approval upon the sale of "all or substantially all" of the corporation's assets. That is the sole test to be applied. While it is true that test does not lend itself to a strict mathematical standard to be applied in every case, the qualitative factor can be defined to some degree notwithstanding the limited Delaware authority. But the definition must begin with and ultimately necessarily relate to our statutory language.

In interpreting the statute the plaintiff relies on *Philadelphia National Bank v. B.S.F. Co.*, 199 A.2d 557 (Ch.1964), rev'd on other grounds, 204 A.2d 746 (Supr. Ct. 1964). In that case, B.S.F. Company owned stock in two corporations. It sold its stock in one of the corporations, and retained the stock in the other corporation. The Court found that the stock sold was the principal asset B.S.F. Company had available for sale and that the value of the stock retained was declining. The Court rejected the defendant's contention that the stock sold represented only 47.4% of consolidated assets, and looked to the actual value of the stock sold. On this basis, the Court held that the stock constituted at least 75% of the total assets and the sale of the stock was a sale of substantially all assets.

But two things must be noted about the *Philadelphia National Bank* case. First, even though shareholder approval was obtained under § 271, the case did not arise under § 271 but under an Indenture [Agreement] limiting the activities of B.S.F. for creditor financial security purposes. On appeal, Chief Justice Wolcott was careful to state the following:

> "We are of the opinion that this question is not necessarily to be answered by references to the general law concerning the sale of assets by a corporation. The question before us is the narrow one of what particular language of a contract means and is to be answered in terms of what the parties were intending to guard against or to insure."

...

Secondly, the *Philadelphia National Bank* case dealt with the sale of the company's only substantial income producing asset.

The key language in the Court of Chancery opinion in *Philadelphia National Bank* is the suggestion that "the critical factor in determining the character of a sale of assets is generally considered not the amount of property sold but whether the sale is in fact an unusual transaction or one made in the regular course of business of the seller." ...

But any "ordinary and regular course of the business" test in this context obviously is not intended to limit the directors to customary daily business activities. Indeed, a question concerning the statute would not arise unless the transaction was somewhat out of the ordinary. While it is true that a transaction in the ordinary course of business does not require shareholder approval, the converse is not true. Every transaction out of normal routine does not necessarily require shareholder approval. The unusual nature of the transaction must strike at the heart of the corporate existence and purpose. As it is written at 6A Fletcher, Cyclopedia Corporations:

> "The purpose of the consent statutes is to protect the shareholders from fundamental change, or more specifically to protect the shareholder from the destruction of the means to accomplish the purposes or objects for which the corporation was incorporated and actually performs."

It is in this sense that the "unusual transaction" judgment is to be made and the statute's applicability determined. If the sale is of assets quantitatively vital to the operation of the corporation and is out of the ordinary and substantially affects the existence and purpose of the corporation, then it is beyond the power of the Board of Directors. With these guidelines, I turn to Signal and the transaction in this case. Signal or its predecessor was incorporated in the oil business in 1922. But, beginning in 1952, Signal diversified its interests. In 1952, Signal acquired a substantial stock interest in American President lines. From 1957 to 1962 Signal was the sole owner of Laura Scudders, a nationwide snack food business. In 1964, Signal acquired Garrett Corporation which is engaged in the aircraft, aerospace, and uranium enrichment business. In 1967, Signal acquired Mack Trucks, Inc., which is engaged in the manufacture and sale of trucks and related equipment. Also in 1968, the oil and gas business was transferred to a separate division and later in 1970 to the Signal Oil subsidiary. Since 1967, Signal has made acquisitions of or formed substantial companies, none of which are involved or related with the oil and gas industry. As indicated previously, the oil and gas production development of Signal's business is now carried on by Signal Oil, the sale of the stock of which is an issue in this lawsuit.

...

Based on the company's figures, Signal Oil represents only about 26% of the total assets of Signal. While Signal Oil represents 41% of Signal's total net worth, it produces only about 15% of Signal's revenues and earnings. Moreover, [a] ... low rate of return ... has been realized recently from the oil and gas operation.

...

While it is true, based on the experience of the Signal-Burmah transaction and the record in this lawsuit, that Signal Oil is more valuable than shown by the company's books, even if, as plaintiff suggests in his brief, the $761,000,000 value attached to Signal Oil's properties by the plaintiff's expert were substituted as the asset figure, the oil and gas properties would still constitute less than half the value of Signal's total assets. Thus, from a straight quantative approach, I agree with Signal's position that the sale to Burmah does not constitute a sale of "all or substantially all" of Signal's assets.

In addition, if the character of the transaction is examined, the plaintiff's position is also weak. While it is true that Signal's original purpose was oil and gas and while oil and gas is still listed first in the certificate of incorporation, the simple fact is that Signal is now a conglomerate engaged in the aircraft and aerospace business, the manufacture and sale of trucks and related equipment, and other businesses besides oil and gas. The very nature of its business, as it now in fact exists, contemplates the acquisition and disposal of independent branches of its corporate business. Indeed, given the operations since 1952, it can be said that such acquisitions and dispositions have become part of the ordinary course of business. The facts that the oil and gas business was historically first and that authorization for such operations are listed first in the certificate do not prohibit disposal of such interest. As Director Harold M. Williams [who subsequently became Dean of the UCLA School of Management, Chairman of the SEC, and Director of the J.P. Getty Museum] testified, business history is not "compelling" and "many companies go down the drain because they try to be historic." ...

It is perhaps true, as plaintiff has argued, that the advent of multi-business corporations has in one sense emasculated § 271 since one business may be sold without shareholder approval when other substantial businesses are retained. But it is one thing for a corporation to evolve over a period of years into a multi-business corporation, the operations of which include the purchase and sale of whole businesses, and another for a single business corporation by a one transaction revolution to sell the entire means of operating its business in exchange for money or a separate business. In the former situation, the processes of corporate democracy customarily have had the opportunity to restrain or otherwise control over a period of years. Thus, there is a chance for some shareholder participation. The Signal development illustrates the difference. For example, when Signal, itself formerly called Signal Oil and Gas Company, changed its name in 1968, it was for the announced "need for a new name appropriate to the broadly diversified activities of Signal's multi-industry complex."

The situation is also dramatically illustrated financially in this very case. Independent of the contract with Burmah, the affidavit of Signal's Board Chairman shows that over $200,000,000 of Signal Oil's refining and marketing assets have been sold in the past five years. This activity, prior to the sale at issue here, in itself constitutes a major restructuring of the corporate structure.

I conclude that measured quantatively and qualitatively, the sale of the stock of Signal Oil by Signal to Burmah does not constitute a sale of "all or substantially all" of Signal's assets. ...

Cash-Out Mergers

Weinberger v. UOP, Inc.
Supreme Court of Delaware
457 A.2d 701 (1983)

Moore, Justice:

This post-trial appeal was reheard en banc from a decision of the Court of Chancery. It was brought by the class action plaintiff below, a former shareholder of UOP, Inc., who challenged the elimination of UOP's minority shareholders by a cash-out merger between UOP and its majority owner, The Signal Companies, Inc. Originally, the defendants in this action were Signal, UOP, certain officers and directors of those companies, and UOP's investment banker, Lehman Brothers Kuhn Loeb, Inc. [Lehman was dismissed from the case by the plaintiffs.] The present Chancellor held that the terms of the merger were fair to the plaintiff and the other minority shareholders of UOP. Accordingly, he entered judgment in favor of the defendants.

Numerous points were raised by the parties, but we address only the following questions presented by the trial court's opinion:

1. The plaintiff's duty to plead sufficient facts demonstrating the unfairness of the challenged merger;
2. The burden of proof upon the parties where the merger has been approved by the purportedly informed vote of a majority of the minority shareholders;
3. The fairness of the merger in terms of adequacy of the defendants' disclosures to the minority shareholders;
4. The fairness of the merger in terms of adequacy of the price paid for the minority shares and the remedy appropriate to that issue; and
5. The continued force and effect of *Singer v. Magnavox Co.*, Del. Supr., 380 A.2d 969, 980 (1977), and its progeny.

In ruling for the defendants, the Chancellor re-stated his earlier conclusion that the plaintiff in a suit challenging a cash-out merger must allege specific acts of fraud, misrepresentation, or other items of misconduct to demonstrate the unfairness of the merger terms to the minority. We approve this rule and affirm it.

The Chancellor also held that even though the ultimate burden of proof is on the majority shareholder to show by a preponderance of the evidence that the transaction is fair, it is first the burden of the plaintiff attacking the merger to demonstrate some basis for invoking the fairness obligation. We agree with that principle. However, where corporate action has been approved by an informed vote of a majority of the minority shareholders, we conclude that the burden entirely shifts to the plaintiff to show that the transaction was unfair to the minority. But in all this, the burden clearly remains on those relying on the vote to show that they completely disclosed all material facts relevant to the transaction.

Here, the record does not support a conclusion that the minority stockholder vote was an informed one. Material information, necessary to acquaint those shareholders with the bargaining positions of Signal and UOP, was withheld under circumstances amounting to a breach of fiduciary duty. We therefore conclude that this merger does not meet the test of fairness, at least as we address that concept, and no burden thus shifted to the plaintiff by reason of the minority shareholder vote. Accordingly, we reverse and remand for further proceedings consistent herewith.

In considering the nature of the remedy available under our law to minority shareholders in a cash-out merger, we believe that it is, and hereafter should be, an appraisal under 8 Del.C. § 262 as hereinafter construed. We therefore overrule *Lynch v. Vickers Energy Corp.*, Del. Supr., 429 A.2d 497 (1981), to the extent that it purports to limit a stockholder's monetary relief to a specific damage formula. But to give full effect to section 262 within the framework of the General Corporation Law we adopt a more liberal, less rigid and stylized, approach to the valuation process than has heretofore been permitted by our courts. While the present state of these proceedings does not admit the plaintiff to the appraisal remedy per se, the practical effect of the remedy we do grant him will be co-extensive with the liberalized valuation and appraisal methods we herein approve for cases coming after this decision.

Our treatment of these matters has necessarily led us to a reconsideration of the business purpose rule announced in the trilogy of *Singer v. Magnavox Co.*, [Del. Supr., 380 A.2d 969 (1977)]; *Tanzer v. International General Industries, Inc.,* Del. Supr., 379 A.2d 1121 (1977); and *Roland International Corp. v. Najjar*, Del. Supr., 407 A.2d 1032 (1979). For the reasons hereafter set forth we consider that the business purpose requirement of these cases is no longer the law of Delaware.

I.

The facts found by the trial court, pertinent to the issues before us, are supported by the record, and we draw from them as set out in the Chancellor's opinion.

Signal is a diversified, technically based company operating through various subsidiaries. Its stock is publicly traded on the New York, Philadelphia and Pacific Stock Exchanges. UOP, formerly known as Universal Oil Products Company, was a diversified industrial company engaged in various lines of business, including petroleum and petro-chemical services and related products, construction, fabricated metal products, transportation equipment products, chemicals and plastics, and other products and services including land development, lumber products and waste disposal. Its stock was publicly held and listed on the New York Stock Exchange.

In 1974 Signal sold one of its wholly-owned subsidiaries for $420,000,000 in cash. *See Gimbel v. Signal Companies, Inc.,* Del. Ch., 316 A.2d 599, *aff'd*, Del. Supr., 316 A.2d 619 (1974). While looking to invest this cash surplus, Signal became interested in UOP as a possible acquisition. Friendly negotiations ensued, and Signal proposed to acquire a controlling interest in UOP at a price of $19 per share. UOP's representatives sought $25 per share. In the arm's length bargaining that followed, an understanding was reached whereby Signal agreed to purchase from UOP 1,500,000 shares of UOP's authorized but unissued stock at $21 per share.

This purchase was contingent upon Signal making a successful cash tender offer for 4,300,000 publicly held shares of UOP, also at a price of $21 per share. This combined method of acquisition permitted Signal to acquire 5,800,000 shares of stock, representing 50.5% of UOP's outstanding shares. ...

The negotiations between Signal and UOP occurred during April 1975, and the resulting tender offer was greatly oversubscribed. However, Signal limited its total purchase of the tendered shares so that, when coupled with the stock bought from UOP, it had achieved its goal of becoming a 50.5% shareholder of UOP.

Although UOP's board consisted of thirteen directors, Signal nominated and elected only six. Of these, five were either directors or employees of Signal. The sixth, a partner in the banking firm of Lazard Freres & Co., had been one of Signal's representatives in the negotiations and bargaining with UOP concerning the tender offer and purchase price of the UOP shares.

However, the president and chief executive officer of UOP retired during 1975, and Signal caused him to be replaced by James V. Crawford, a long-time employee and senior executive vice president of one of Signal's wholly-owned subsidiaries. Crawford succeeded his predecessor on UOP's board of directors and also was made a director of Signal.

By the end of 1977 Signal basically was unsuccessful in finding other suitable investment candidates for its excess cash, and by February 1978 considered that it had no other realistic acquisitions available to it on a friendly basis. Once again its attention turned to UOP.

The trial court found that at the instigation of certain Signal management personnel, including William W. Walkup, its board chairman, and Forrest N. Shumway, its president, a feasibility study was made concerning the possible acquisition of the balance of UOP's outstanding shares. This study was performed by two Signal officers, Charles S. Arledge, vice president (director of planning), and Andrew J. Chitiea, senior vice president (chief financial officer). Messrs. Walkup, Shumway, Arledge and Chitiea were all directors of UOP in addition to their membership on the Signal board.

Arledge and Chitiea concluded that it would be a good investment for Signal to acquire the remaining 49.5% of UOP shares at any price up to $24 each. Their report was discussed between Walkup and Shumway who, along with Arledge, Chitiea and Brewster L. Arms, internal counsel for Signal, constituted Signal's senior management. ...

The executive committee meeting was set for February 28, 1978. As a courtesy, UOP's president, Crawford, was invited to attend, although he was not a member of Signal's executive committee. On his arrival, and prior to the meeting, Crawford was asked to meet privately with Walkup and Shumway. He was then told of Signal's plan to acquire full ownership of UOP and was asked for his reaction to the proposed price range of $20 to $21 per share. Crawford said he thought such a price would be "generous," and that it was certainly one which should be submitted to UOP's minority shareholders for their ultimate consideration. He stated, however, that Signal's 100% ownership could cause internal problems at UOP. He believed that employees would have to be given some assurance of their future place in a fully-owned Signal subsidiary. Otherwise, he feared the departure of essential personnel. Also, many of UOP's key employees had stock option incentive programs which would be wiped out by a merger. Crawford therefore urged that some adjustment would have to be made, such as providing a comparable incentive in Signal's shares, if after the merger he was to maintain his quality of personnel and efficiency at UOP.

Thus, Crawford voiced no objection to the $20 to $21 price range, nor did he suggest that Signal should consider paying more than $21 per share for the minority interests. Later, at the executive committee meeting the same factors were discussed, with Crawford repeating the position he earlier took with Walkup and Shumway. ...

Thus, it was the consensus that a price of $20 to $21 per share would be fair to both Signal and the minority shareholders of UOP. Signal's executive committee authorized its management "to negotiate" with UOP "for a cash acquisition of the minority ownership in UOP, Inc.

...

[T]he closing price of UOP's common stock on that day was $14.50 per share.

...

Between Tuesday, February 28, 1978 and Monday, March 6, 1978, a total of four business days, Crawford spoke by telephone with all of UOP's non-Signal, i.e., outside, directors. Also during that period, Crawford retained Lehman Brothers to render a fairness opinion as to the price offered the minority for its stock. He gave two reasons for this choice. First, the time schedule between the announcement and the board meetings was short (by then only three business days) and since Lehman Brothers had been acting as UOP's investment banker for many years, Crawford felt that it would be in the best position to respond on such brief notice. Second, James W. Glanville, a long-time director of UOP and a partner in Lehman Brothers, had acted as a financial advisor to UOP for many years. Crawford believed that Glanville's familiarity with UOP, as a member of its board, would also be of assistance in enabling Lehman Brothers to render a fairness opinion within the existing time constraints.

Crawford telephoned Glanville, who gave his assurance that Lehman Brothers had no conflicts that would prevent it from accepting the task. Glanville's immediate personal reaction was that a price of $20 to $21 would certainly be fair, since it represented almost a 50% premium over UOP's market price. Glanville sought a $250,000 fee for Lehman Brothers' services, but Crawford thought this too much. After further discussions Glanville finally agreed that Lehman Brothers would render its fairness opinion for $150,000.

During this period Crawford also had several telephone contacts with Signal officials. In only one of them, however, was the price of the shares discussed. In a conversation with Walkup, Crawford advised that as a result of his communications with UOP's non-Signal directors, it was his feeling that the price would have to be the top of the proposed range, or $21 per share, if the approval of UOP's outside directors was to be obtained. But again, he did not seek any price higher than $21.

Glanville assembled a three-man Lehman Brothers team to do the work on the fairness opinion. These persons examined relevant documents and information concerning UOP, including its annual reports and its Securities and Exchange Commission filings from 1973 through 1976, as well as its audited financial statements for 1977, its interim reports to shareholders, and its recent and historical market prices and trading volumes. In addition, on Friday, March 3, 1978, two members of the Lehman Brothers team flew to UOP's headquarters in Des Plaines, Illinois, to perform a "due diligence" visit, during the course of which they interviewed Crawford as well as UOP's general counsel, its chief financial officer, and other key executives and personnel.

As a result, the Lehman Brothers team concluded that "the price of either $20 or $21 would be a fair price for the remaining shares of UOP". They telephoned this impression to Glanville, who was spending the weekend in Vermont.

On Monday morning, March 6, 1978, Glanville and the senior member of the Lehman Brothers team flew to Des Plaines to attend the scheduled UOP directors meeting. Glanville looked over the assembled information during the flight. The two had with them the draft of a "fairness opinion letter" in which the price had been left blank. Either during or immediately prior to the directors' meeting, the two-page "fairness opinion letter" was typed in final form and the price of $21 per share was inserted.

On March 6, 1978, both the Signal and UOP boards were convened to consider the proposed merger. Telephone communications were maintained between the two meetings. Walkup, Signal's board chairman, and also a UOP director, attended UOP's meeting with Crawford in order to present Signal's position and answer any questions that UOP's non-Signal directors might have. Arledge and Chitiea, along with Signal's other designees on UOP's board, participated by conference telephone. All of UOP's outside directors attended the meeting either in person or by conference telephone.

First, Signal's board unanimously adopted a resolution authorizing Signal to propose to UOP a cash merger of $21 per share as outlined in a certain merger agreement and other supporting documents. This proposal required that the merger be approved by a majority of UOP's outstanding minority shares voting at the stockholders meeting at which the merger would be considered, and that the minority shares voting in favor of the merger, when coupled with Signal's 50.5% interest would have to comprise at least two-thirds of all UOP shares. Otherwise the proposed merger would be deemed disapproved.

UOP's board then considered the proposal. Copies of the agreement were delivered to the directors in attendance, and other copies had been forwarded earlier to the directors participating by telephone. They also had before them UOP financial data for 1974–1977, UOP's most recent financial statements, market price information, and budget projections for 1978. In addition they had Lehman Brothers' hurriedly prepared fairness opinion letter finding the price of $21 to be fair. Glanville, the Lehman Brothers partner, and UOP director, commented on the information that had gone into preparation of the letter.

Signal also suggests that the Arledge-Chitiea feasibility study, indicating that a price of up to $24 per share would be a "good investment" for Signal, was discussed at the UOP directors' meeting. The Chancellor made no such finding, and our independent review of the record, detailed *infra*, satisfies us by a preponderance of the evidence that there was no discussion of this document at UOP's board meeting. Furthermore, it is clear beyond peradventure that nothing in that report was ever disclosed to UOP's minority shareholders prior to their approval of the merger.

After consideration of Signal's proposal, Walkup and Crawford left the meeting to permit a free and uninhibited exchange between UOP's non-Signal directors. Upon their return a resolution to accept Signal's offer was then proposed and adopted. While Signal's men on UOP's board participated in various aspects of the meeting, they abstained from voting. However, the minutes show that each of them "if voting would have voted yes."

On March 7, 1978, UOP sent a letter to its shareholders advising them of the action taken by UOP's board with respect to Signal's offer. This document pointed out, among other things, that on February 28, 1978, "both companies had announced negotiations were being conducted."

Despite the swift board action of the two companies, the merger was not submitted to UOP's shareholders until their annual meeting on May 26, 1978. In the notice of that meeting and proxy statement sent to shareholders in May, UOP's management and board urged that the merger be approved. The proxy statement also advised:

> The price was determined after *discussions* between James V. Crawford, a director of Signal and Chief Executive Officer of UOP, and officers of Signal which took place during meetings on February 28, 1978, and in the course of several subsequent telephone conversations. (Emphasis added.)

In the original draft of the proxy statement the word "negotiations" had been used rather than "discussions". However, when the Securities and Exchange Commission sought details of the "negotiations" as part of its review of these materials, the term was deleted and the word "discussions" was substituted. The proxy statement indicated that the vote of UOP's board in approving the merger had been unanimous. It also advised the shareholders that Lehman Brothers had given its opinion that the merger prior of $21 per share was fair to UOP's minority. However, it did not disclose the hurried method by which this conclusion was reached. As of the record date of UOP's annual meeting, there were 11,488,302 shares of UOP common stock outstanding, 5,688,302 of which were owned by the minority. At the meeting only 56%, or 3,208,652, of the minority shares were voted. Of these, 2,953,812, or 51.9% of the total minority, voted for the merger, and 254,840 voted against it. When Signal's stock was added to the minority shares voting in favor, a total of 76.2% of UOP's outstanding shares approved the merger while only 2.2% opposed it.

By its terms the merger became effective on May 26, 1978, and each share of UOP's stock held by the minority was automatically converted into a right to receive $21 cash.

II.

A.

A primary issue mandating reversal is the preparation by two UOP directors, Arledge and Chitiea, of their feasibility study for the exclusive use and benefit of Signal. This document was of obvious significance to both Signal and UOP. Using UOP data, it described the advantages to Signal of ousting the minority at a price range of $21–$24 per share. Mr. Arledge, one of the authors, outlined the benefits to Signal:

Purpose of the Merger

(1) Provides an outstanding investment opportunity for Signal—(Better than any recent acquisition we have seen.)
(2) Increases Signal's earnings.
(3) Facilitates the flow of resources between Signal and its subsidiaries—(Big factor—works both ways.)
(4) Provides cost savings potential for Signal and UOP.
(5) Improves the percentage of Signal's "operating earnings" as opposed to "holding company earnings."
(6) Simplifies the understanding of Signal.
(7) Facilitates technological exchange among Signal's subsidiaries.
(8) Eliminates potential conflicts of interest.

Having written those words, solely for the use of Signal, it is clear from the record that neither Arledge nor Chitiea shared this report with their fellow directors of UOP. We are satisfied that no one else did either. This conduct hardly meets the fiduciary standards applicable to such a transaction.

...

The Arledge-Chitiea report speaks for itself in supporting the Chancellor's finding that a price of up to $24 was a "good investment" for Signal. It shows that a return on the investment at $21 would be 15.7% versus 15.5% at $24 per share. This was a difference of only two-tenths of one percent, while it meant over $17,000,000 to the minority. Under such circumstances, paying UOP's minority shareholders $24 would have had relatively little long-term effect on Signal, and the Chancellor's findings concerning the benefit to Signal, even at a price of $24, were obviously correct. ...

Certainly, this was a matter of material significance to UOP and its shareholders. Since the study was prepared by two UOP directors, using UOP information for the exclusive benefit of Signal, and nothing whatever was done to disclose it to the outside UOP directors or the minority shareholders, a question of breach of fiduciary duty arises. This problem occurs because there were common Signal-UOP directors participating, at least to some extent, in the UOP board's decision-making processes without full disclosure of the conflicts they faced.

[[This footnote has been moved to the text:] Although perfection is not possible, or expected, the result here could have been entirely different if UOP had appointed an independent negotiating committee of its outside directors to deal with Signal at arm's length. ... Since fairness in this context can be equated to conduct by a theoretical, wholly independent, board of directors acting upon the matter before them, it is unfortunate that this course apparently was neither considered nor pursued. ... Particularly in a parent-subsidiary context, a showing that the action taken was as though each of the contending parties had in fact exerted its bargaining power against the other at arm's length is strong evidence that the transaction meets the test of fairness. ...]

B.

In assessing this situation, the Court of Chancery was required to examine what information defendants had and to measure it against what they gave to the minority stockholders, in a context in which "complete candor" is required. In other words, the limited function of the Court was to determine whether defendants had disclosed all information in their possession germane to the transaction in issue. And by "germane" we mean, for present purposes, information such as a reasonable shareholder would consider important in deciding whether to sell or retain stock.

...

This is merely stating in another way the long-existing principle of Delaware law that these Signal designated directors on UOP's board still owed UOP and its shareholders an uncompromising duty of loyalty. ...

Given the absence of any attempt to structure this transaction on an arm's length basis, Signal cannot escape the effects of the conflicts it faced, particularly when its designees on UOP's board did not totally abstain from participation in the matter. There is no "safe harbor" for such divided loyalties in Delaware. When directors of a Delaware corporation are on both sides of a transaction, they are required to demonstrate their utmost good faith and the most scrupulous inherent fairness of the bargain. ... The requirement of fairness is unflinching in its demand that where one stands on both sides of a transaction, he has the burden of establishing its entire fairness, sufficient to pass the test of careful scrutiny by the courts. ...

There is no dilution of this obligation where one holds dual or multiple directorships, as in a parent-subsidiary context. ... Thus, individuals who act in a dual capacity as directors of two corporations, one of whom is parent and the other subsidiary, owe the same duty of good management to both corporations, and in the absence of an independent negotiating structure or the directors' total abstention from any participation in the matter, this duty is to be exercised in light of what is best for both companies. ... The record demonstrates that Signal has not met this obligation.

C.

The concept of fairness has two basic aspects: fair dealing and fair price. The former embraces questions of when the transaction was timed, how it was initiated, structured, negotiated, disclosed to the directors, and how the approvals of the directors and the stockholders were obtained. The latter aspect of fairness relates to the economic and financial considerations of the proposed merger, including all relevant factors: assets, market value, earnings, future prospects, and any other elements that affect the intrinsic or inherent value of a company's stock. ... However, the test for fairness is not a bifurcated one as between fair dealing and price. All aspects of the issue must be examined as a whole since the question is one of entire fairness. However, in a non-fraudulent transaction we recognize that price may be the preponderant consideration outweighing other features of the merger. Here, we address the two basic aspects of fairness separately because we find reversible error as to both.

D.

Part of fair dealing is the obvious duty of candor. ... Moreover, one possessing superior knowledge may not mislead any stockholder by use of corporate information to which the latter is not privy. ... Delaware has long imposed this duty even upon persons who are not corporate officers or directors, but who nonetheless are privy to matters of interest or significance to their company. *Brophy v. Cities Service Co.*, Del. Ch., 70 A.2d 5, 7 (1949). With the well-established Delaware law on the subject, and the Court of Chancery's findings of fact here, it is inevitable that the obvious conflicts posed by Arledge and Chitiea's preparation of their "feasibility study," derived from UOP information, for the sole use and benefit of Signal, cannot pass muster.

The Arledge-Chitiea report is but one aspect of the element of fair dealing. How did this merger evolve? It is clear that it was entirely initiated by Signal. The serious time constraints under which the principals acted were all set by Signal. It had not found a suitable outlet for its excess cash and considered UOP a desirable investment, particularly since it was now in a position to acquire the whole company for itself. For whatever reasons, and they were only Signal's, the entire transaction was presented to and approved by UOP's board within four business days. Standing alone, this is not necessarily indicative of any lack of fairness by a majority shareholder. It was what occurred, or more properly, what did not occur, during this brief period that makes the time constraints imposed by Signal relevant to the issue of fairness.

The structure of the transaction, again, was Signal's doing. So far as negotiations were concerned, it is clear that they were modest at best. Crawford, Signal's man at UOP, never really talked price with Signal, except to accede to its management's statements on the subject, and to convey to Signal the UOP outside directors' view that as between the $20–$21 range under consideration, it would have to be $21. The latter is not a surprising outcome, but hardly arm's length negotiations. Only the protection of benefits for UOP's key employees and the issue of Lehman Brothers' fee approached any concept of bargaining.

As we have noted, the matter of disclosure to the UOP directors was wholly flawed by the conflicts of interest raised by the Arledge-Chitiea report. All of those conflicts were resolved by Signal in its own favor without divulging any aspect of them to UOP.

This cannot but undermine a conclusion that this merger meets any reasonable test of fairness. The outside UOP directors lacked one material piece of information generated by two of their colleagues, but shared only with Signal. True, the UOP board had the Lehman Brothers' fairness opinion, but that firm has been blamed by the plaintiff for the hurried task it performed, when more properly the responsibility for this lies with Signal. There was no disclosure of the circumstances surrounding the rather cursory preparation of the Lehman Brothers' fairness opinion. Instead, the impression was given UOP's minority that a careful study had been made, when in fact speed was the hallmark, and Mr. Glanville, Lehman's partner in charge of the matter, and also a UOP director, having spent the weekend in Vermont, brought a draft of the "fairness opinion letter" to the UOP directors' meeting on March 6, 1978 with the price left blank. We can only conclude from the record that the rush imposed on Lehman Brothers by Signal's timetable contributed to the difficulties under which this investment banking firm attempted to perform its responsibilities. Yet, none of this was disclosed to UOP's minority.

Finally, the minority stockholders were denied the critical information that Signal considered a price of $24 to be a good investment. Since this would have meant over $17,000,000 more to the minority, we cannot conclude that the shareholder vote was an informed one. Under the circumstances, an approval by a majority of the minority was meaningless. ...

Given these particulars and the Delaware law on the subject, the record does not establish that this transaction satisfies any reasonable concept of fair dealing, and the Chancellor's findings in that regard must be reversed.

E.

Turning to the matter of price, plaintiff also challenges its fairness. His evidence was that on the date the merger was approved the stock was worth at least $26 per share. In support, he offered the testimony of a chartered investment analyst who used two basic approaches to valuation: a comparative analysis of the premium paid over market in ten other tender offer-merger combinations, and a discounted cash flow analysis.

In this breach of fiduciary duty case, the Chancellor perceived that the approach to valuation was the same as that in an appraisal proceeding. Consistent with precedent, he rejected plaintiff's method of proof and accepted defendants' evidence of value as being in accord with practice under prior case law. This means that the so-called "Delaware block" or weighted average method was employed wherein the elements of value, i.e., assets, market price, earnings, etc., were assigned a particular weight and the resulting amounts added to determine the value per share. This procedure has been in use for decades. ... However, to the extent it excludes other generally accepted techniques used in the financial community and the courts, it is now clearly outmoded. It is time we recognize this in appraisal and other stock valuation proceedings and bring our law current on the subject.

While the Chancellor rejected plaintiff's discounted cash flow method of valuing UOP's stock, as not corresponding with "either logic or the existing law" ... , it is significant that this was essentially the focus, i.e., earnings potential of UOP, of Messrs. Arledge and Chitiea in their evaluation of the merger. Accordingly, the standard "Delaware block" or weighted average method of valuation, formerly employed in appraisal and other stock valuation cases, shall no longer exclusively control such proceedings. We believe that a more liberal approach must include proof of value by any techniques or methods which are generally considered acceptable in the financial community and otherwise admissible in court, subject only to our interpretation of 8 Del.C. § 262(h), *infra.* ... This will obviate the very structured and mechanistic procedure that has heretofore governed such matters. ...

Fair price obviously requires consideration of all relevant factors involving the value of a company. ...

Under 8 Del.C. § 262(h), the Court of Chancery:

> shall appraise the shares, determining their *fair* value exclusive of any element of value arising from the accomplishment or expectation of the merger, together with a fair rate of interest, if any, to be paid upon the amount determined to be the *fair* value. In determining such *fair* value, the Court shall take into account *all relevant factors.* ... (Emphasis added.)

...

It is significant that section 262 now mandates the determination of "fair" value based upon "all relevant factors." Only the speculative elements of value that may arise from the "accomplishment or expectation" of the merger are excluded. We take this to be a very narrow exception to the appraisal process, designed to eliminate use of *pro forma* data and projections of a speculative variety relating to the completion of a merger. But elements of future value, including the nature of the enterprise, which are known or susceptible of proof as of the date of the merger and not the product of speculation, may be considered. When the trial court deems it appropriate, fair value also includes any damages, resulting from the taking, which the stockholders sustain as a class. If that was not the case, then the obligation to consider "all relevant factors" in the valuation process would be eroded. ...

... Clearly, there is a legislative intent to fully compensate shareholders for whatever their loss may be, subject only to the narrow limitation that one cannot take speculative effects of the merger into account.

Although the Chancellor received the plaintiff's evidence, his opinion indicates that the use of it was precluded because of past Delaware practice. While we do not suggest a monetary result one way or the other, we do think the plaintiff's evidence should be part of the factual mix and weighed as such. Until the $21 price is measured on remand by the valuation standards mandated by Delaware law, there can be no finding at the present stage of these proceedings that the price is fair. Given the lack of any candid disclosure of the material facts surrounding establishment of the $21 price, the majority of the minority vote, approving the merger, is meaningless.

The plaintiff has not sought an appraisal, but rescissory damages of the type contemplated by *Lynch v. Vickers Energy Corp.*, Del. Supr., 429 A.2d 497, 505–06 (1981) (*Lynch II*). [Generally, under rescissory damages, the measure of damages is determined at the time of judgment rather than at the time of the merger. Hence, if the value of the stock increases during this period, this benefits the plaintiff. Of course, if the value of the stock decreases during this period, the plaintiff will not seek rescissory damages.] In view of the approach to valuation that we announce today, we see no basis in our law for *Lynch II's* exclusive monetary formula for relief. On remand the plaintiff will be permitted to test the fairness of the $21 price by the standards we herein establish, in conformity with the principle applicable to an appraisal—that fair value be determined by taking "into account all relevant factors" [*see* 8 Del.C. § 262(h), *supra*]. In our view this includes the elements of rescissory damages if the Chancellor considers them susceptible of proof and a remedy appropriate to all the issues of fairness before him. To the extent that *Lynch II* purports to limit the Chancellor's discretion to a single remedial formula for monetary damages in a cash-out merger, it is overruled.

While a plaintiff's monetary remedy ordinarily should be confined to the more liberalized appraisal proceeding herein established, we do not intend any limitation on the historic powers of the Chancellor to grant such other relief as the facts of a particular case may dictate. The appraisal remedy we approve may not be adequate in certain cases, particularly where fraud, misrepresentation, self-dealing, deliberate waste of corporate assets, or gross and palpable overreaching are involved. ... Under such circumstances, the Chancellor's powers are complete to fashion any form of equitable and monetary relief as may be appropriate, including rescissory damages. Since it is apparent that this long completed transaction is too involved to undo, and in view of the Chancellor's discretion, the award, if any, should be in the form of monetary damages based upon entire fairness standards, i.e., fair dealing and fair price. ... [Nonetheless,] we return to the well established principles of *Stauffer v. Standard Brands, Inc.*, Del.Supr., 187 A.2d 78 (1962), and *David J. Greene & Co. v. Schenley Industries, Inc.*, Del.Ch., 281 A.2d 30 (1971), mandating a stockholder's recourse to the basic remedy of an appraisal.

III.

Finally, we address the matter of business purpose. The defendants contend that the purpose of this merger was not a proper subject of inquiry by the trial court. The plaintiff says that no valid purpose existed—the entire transaction was a mere subterfuge designed to eliminate the minority. The Chancellor ruled otherwise, but in so doing he clearly circumscribed the thrust and effect of *Singer*. …

The requirement of a business purpose is new to our law of mergers and was a departure from prior case law. …

In view of the fairness test which has long been applicable to parent-subsidiary mergers[,] … the expanded appraisal remedy now available to shareholders, and the broad discretion of the Chancellor to fashion such relief as the facts of a given case may dictate, we do not believe that any additional meaningful protection is afforded minority shareholders by the business purpose requirement of the trilogy of *Singer*, *Tanzer*, *Najjar*, and their progeny. Accordingly, such requirement shall no longer be of any force or effect.

The judgment of the Court of Chancery, finding both the circumstances of the merger and the price paid the minority shareholders to be fair, is reversed. The matter is remanded for further proceedings consistent herewith. Upon remand the plaintiff's post-trial motion to enlarge the class should be granted.

…

Reversed and Remanded.

TAKEOVER BIDS

VERSATA ENTERPRISES, INC. V. SELECTICA, INC. SUPREME COURT OF DELAWARE 5 A. 3D 586 (2010)

Holland, Justice:

This is an appeal from a final judgment entered by the Court of Chancery. On November 16, 2008 the Board of Directors of Selectica, Inc. ("Selectica") reduced the trigger of its "poison pill" Shareholder Rights Plan from 15% to 4.99% of Selectica's outstanding shares and capped existing shareholders who held a 5% or more interest to a further increase of only 0.5% (the "NOL Poison Pill"). Selectica's reason for taking such action was to protect the company's net operating loss carryforwards ("NOLs"). When Trilogy, Inc. ("Trilogy") subsequently purchased shares above this cap, Selectica filed suit in the Court of Chancery on December 21, 2008, seeking a declaration that the NOL Poison Pill was valid and enforceable. On January 2, 2009, Selectica implemented the dilutive exchange provision (the "Exchange") of the NOL Poison Pill, which reduced Trilogy's interest from 6.7% to 3.3%, and adopted another Rights Plan with a 4.99% trigger (the "Reloaded NOL Poison Pill"). Selectica then amended its complaint to seek a declaration that the Exchange and the Reloaded NOL Poison Pill were valid.

Trilogy and its subsidiary Versata Enterprises, Inc. ("Versata") counterclaimed that the NOL Poison Pill, the Reloaded NOL Poison Pill, and the Exchange were unlawful on the grounds that, before acting, the Board failed to consider that its NOLs were unusable or that the two NOL poison pills were unnecessary given Selectica's unbroken history of losses and doubtful prospects of annual profits. Trilogy and Versata also asserted that the NOL Poison Pill and the Reloaded NOL Poison Pill were impermissibly preclusive of a successful proxy contest for Board control, particularly when combined with Selectica's staggered director terms. After trial, the Court of Chancery held that the NOL Poison Pill, the Reloaded NOL Poison Pill, and the Exchange were all valid under Delaware law.

Trilogy and Versata now appeal and assert two claims of error. First, they contend that the Court of Chancery erred in applying the *Unocal* test for enhanced judicial scrutiny when confronting what they frame as a question of first impression. The issue (as framed by them) is: "what are the minimum requirements for a reasonable investigation before the board of a never-profitable company may adopt a [Rights Plan with a 4.99% trigger] for the ostensible purpose of protecting NOLs from an 'ownership change' under Section 382 of the Internal Revenue Code?" Second, they submit that the Court of Chancery erred in holding that the two NOL poison pills, either individually or in combination with a charter-based classified Board, did not have a preclusive effect on the shareholders' ability to pursue a successful proxy contest for control of the Company's board. We conclude that both arguments are without merit.

...

Facts

The Court of Chancery described this as a case about the value of net operating loss carryforwards ("NOLs") to a currently profitless corporation, and the extent to which such a corporation may fight to preserve those NOLs. The Court of Chancery also provided a helpful overview of the concepts surrounding NOLs, their calculation, and possible impairment.

NOLs are tax losses, realized and accumulated by a corporation, that can be used to shelter future (or immediate past) income from taxation. (NOLs may be carried backward two years and carried forward twenty years.) If taxable profit has been realized, the NOLs operate either to provide a refund of prior taxes paid or to reduce the amount of future income tax owed. Thus, NOLs can be a valuable asset, as a means of lowering tax payments and producing positive cash flow. NOLs are considered a contingent asset, their value being contingent upon the firm's reporting a future profit or having an immediate past profit.

Should the firm fail to realize a profit during the lifetime of the NOL (twenty years), the NOL expires. The precise value of a given NOL is usually impossible to determine since its ultimate use is subject to the timing and amount of recognized profit at the firm. If the firm never realizes taxable income, at dissolution its NOLs, regardless of their amount, would have zero value.

In order to prevent corporate taxpayers from benefitting from NOLs generated by other entities, Internal Revenue Code Section 382 establishes limitations on the use of NOLs in periods following an "ownership change." If Section 382 is triggered, the law restricts the amount of prior NOLs that can be used in subsequent years to reduce the firm's tax obligations. Once NOLs are so impaired, a substantial portion of their value is lost.

The precise definition of an "ownership change" under Section 382 is rather complex. At its most basic, an ownership change occurs when more than 50% of a firm's stock ownership changes over a three-year period. Specific provisions in Section 382 define the precise manner by which this determination is made. Most importantly for purposes of this case, the only shareholders considered when calculating an ownership change under Section 382 are those who hold, or have obtained during the testing period, a 5% or greater block of the corporation's shares outstanding.

The Parties

Selectica, Inc. ("Selectica" or the "Company") is a Delaware corporation, headquartered in California and listed on the NASDAQ Global Market. It provides enterprise software solutions for contract management and sales configuration systems. Selectica is a micro-cap company with a concentrated shareholder base: the Company's seven largest investors own a majority of the stock, while fewer than twenty-five investors hold nearly two-thirds of the stock. (However, because of the Shareholder Rights Plan first instituted in 2003, no stockholder holds more than 15% of the outstanding shares.)

Trilogy, Inc. ("Trilogy") is a Delaware corporation also specializing in enterprise software solutions. Trilogy stock is not publicly traded, and its founder, Joseph Liemandt, holds over 85% of the stock. Versata Enterprises, Inc. ("Versata"), a Delaware corporation and a subsidiary of Trilogy, provides technology powered business services to clients.

Before the events giving rise to this action, Versata and Trilogy beneficially owned 6.7% of Selectica's common stock. After they intentionally triggered Selectica's Shareholder Rights Plan through the purchase of additional shares, Versata's and Trilogy's joint beneficial ownership was diluted from 6.7% to approximately 3.3%.

James Arnold, Alan B. Howe, Lloyd Sems, Jim Thanos, and Brenda Zawatski are members of the Selectica Board of Directors (the "Board"). Zawatski and Thanos also served as Co-Chairs of the Board during the events at issue in the case. In this role, they handled the day-to-day operations of the Company, as Selectica had been without a Chief Executive Officer since June 30, 2008.

Selectica's Historical Operating Difficulties

Since it became a public company in March 2000, Selectica has lost a substantial amount of money and failed to turn an annual profit, despite routinely projecting near-term profitability. Its IPO price of $30 per share has steadily fallen and now languishes below $1 per share, placing Selectica's market capitalization at roughly $23 million as of the end of March 2009. By Selectica's own admission, its value today "consists primarily in its cash reserves, its intellectual property portfolio, its customer and revenue base, and its accumulated NOLs." By consistently failing to achieve positive net income, Selectica has generated an estimated $160 million in NOLs for federal tax purposes over the past several years.

Selectica's Relationship with Trilogy

Selectica has had a complicated and often adversarial relationship with Trilogy, stretching back at least five years. Both companies compete in the relatively narrow market space of contract management and sales configuration. In April 2004, a Trilogy affiliate sued Selectica for patent infringement and secured a judgment that required Selectica, among other things, to pay Trilogy $7.5 million. While their suit was pending, in January 2005 Trilogy made an offer to buy Selectica for $4 per share in cash—a 20% premium above the then-trading price—which Selectica's Board rejected. Nevertheless, during March and April of that year, a Trilogy affiliate acquired nearly 7% of Selectica's common stock through open market trades. In early fall 2005, Trilogy made another offer for Selectica's shares at a 16%–23% premium, which was also rejected.

In September 2006, a Trilogy-affiliated holder of Selectica stock sent a letter to the Board questioning whether certain stock option grants had been backdated.[1] The following month, Trilogy filed another pat-

1 A special committee empanelled by the Board ultimately concluded that certain options had, in fact, been backdated. Consequently, Selectica was required to restate its financial statements to record additional stock-based compensation and related tax effects for past option grants and incurred fees associated with the investigation in excess of $6.2 million. This episode also led to the resignation of

ent infringement lawsuit against Selectica. That action was settled in October 2007, when Selectica agreed to a one-time payment of $10 million, plus an additional amount of not more than $7.5 million in subsequent payments to be made quarterly. In late fall 2006, Trilogy sold down its holdings in Selectica.

Steel Partners

Steel Partners is a private equity fund that has been a Selectica shareholder since at least 2006 and is currently its largest shareholder. One of Steel Partners' apparent investment strategies is to invest in small companies with large NOLs with the intent to pair the failing company with a profitable business in order to reap the tax benefits of the NOLs. Steel Partners has actively worked with Selectica to calculate and monitor the Company's NOLs since the time of its original investment.

By early 2008, Steel Partners was advocating a quick sale of Selectica's assets, leaving a NOL shell that could be merged with a profitable operating company in order to shelter the profits of the operating company. In October 2008, Steel Partners informed members of Selectica's Board that it planned to increase its ownership position to 14.9% just below the 15% trigger of the 2003 Rights Plan, which it later did. Jack Howard, President of Steel Partners, lobbied for a Board seat twice in 2008, citing his experience dealing with NOLs, but was rebuffed.

Selectica Investigates Its NOLs

In 2006, at the urging of Steel Partners, Selectica directed Alan Chinn, its outside tax adviser, to perform a high-level analysis into whether its NOLs were subject to any limitations under Section 382 of the Internal Revenue Code. Chinn concluded that five prior changes in ownership had caused the forfeiture of approximately $24.6 million in NOLs. Selectica provided the results of this study to Steel Partners, although not to any other Selectica shareholder.

Selectica's then-Chairmen and Chief Executive Officer Stephen Bannion (who had been the Company's Chief Financial Officer at the time of the grants of question) and the appointment of then-Director Robert Jurkowski to the Chief Executive and Chair position.

In March 2007, again at Steel Partner's recommendation, Selectica retained a second accountant who specialized in NOL calculations, John Brogan of Burr Pilger & Mayer, LLP, to analyze the Company's NOLs more carefully and report on Chinn's Section 382 analysis. Brogan had previously analyzed the NOLs at other Steel Partners ventures. Brogan ultimately determined that Chinn's conclusions were erroneous.

The Company engaged Brogan to perform additional work on the topic of NOLs in June 2007. One of Steel Partners's employees, Avi Goodman, worked closely with Brogan on the matter, although Brogan was working for and being paid by Selectica and received no compensation from Steel Partners. Brogan's draft letter opinion, concluding that the Company had not undergone an "ownership change" for Section 382 purposes since 1999, was shared with Steel Partners, although again not with any other outside investors.

In the fall of 2007, Brogan proposed a third, more detailed, Section 382 study, which Selectica's then-CEO, Robert Jurkowski, opposed. In February 2008, the Board voted against spending $40,000–$50,000 to fund this Section 382 study. By July, however, the Board asked Brogan to update his study. Brogan delivered the draft opinion that, as of March 31, 2008, the Company had approximately $165 million in NOLs. Brogan was later asked to advise the Board in the fall of 2008 on the updated status of its NOLs when the Board moved to amend its Rights Plan.

Lloyd Sems Elected Director

In April 2008, the Board began interviewing candidates for an open board seat, giving preference to the Company's large stockholders. Selectica investor Lloyd Sems had previously expressed interest in joining the Board and had sought support from certain shareholders, including Steel Partners, through Howard, and Lloyd Miller, another large Selectica shareholder not affiliated with Steel Partners. Both Miller and Howard wrote to the Board in support of Sems's appointment, although Sems was already favored by the Board by that time. In June 2008, Sems was appointed to the Board.

As large shareholders, Sems, Howard, and Miller had periodically discussed Selectica as early as October 2007. At that time, Sems had emailed Howard, stating, "I wanted to get your opinion of how or if you would like me to proceed with [Selectica]." Howard replied,

"Lloyd [Miller] said he would call you about [Selectica]." Both before and after his appointment to the Board, Sems discussed with Howard and Miller a number of the proposals that Sems ultimately advocated as a director, including that Selectica should buy back its stock, that Selectica should consider selling its businesses, that the NOLs were important and should be preserved through the adoption of a Rights Plan with a 5% trigger, and that Jurkowski should be removed as CEO.

Selectica Restructures and Explores Alternatives

In early July 2008, after determining that the Company needed to change course, the Board terminated Jurkowski as CEO and eliminated several management positions in the sales configuration business. Later that month, prompted by the receipt of five unsolicited acquisition offers over the span of a few weeks, the Board announced that it was in the process of selecting an investment banker (ultimately, Jim Reilly of Needham & Company) to evaluate strategic alternatives for the Company and to assist with a process that ultimately might result in the Company's sale. In view of the potential sale, the Board decided to forgo the expense of replacing Jurkowski and, instead, asked Zawatski and Thanos jointly to assume the title of Co-Chair and to perform operational oversight roles on an interim basis.

The Needham Process

Needham has actively carried out its task of evaluating Selectica's strategic options since its selection by the Board. Needham first discussed with the Board the various strategic choices that the Company could take. These included a merger of equals with a public company, a reverse IPO or other going-private transaction, the sale of certain assets, and the use of cash to acquire another company, as well as stock repurchases or the issuance of dividends if Selectica decided to continue as an independent public company in the absence of sufficient market interest for an acquisition.

In October 2008, Needham prepared an Executive Summary of the assets and operations of Selectica and subsequently reached out to potential buyers, keeping in touch with various interested parties throughout the remainder of the year and into the first part of 2009. By February 2009, at least half a dozen parties had come forward with letters of intent and were in the process of meeting with Selectica management and conducting due diligence in the Company, with Needham evaluating their various proposals for the purchase of all or part of Selectica's operations. As of April 2009, Selectica, through Needham, had signed a letter of intent and entered into exclusive negotiations with a potential buyer.

Trilogy's Offers Rejected

On July 15, 2008, Trilogy's President, Joseph Liemandt, called Zawatski to inquire generally about the possibility of an acquisition of Selectica by Trilogy. On July 29, Trilogy Chief Financial Officer Sean Fallon, Trilogy Director of Finance Andrew Price, and Versata Chief Executive Officer Randy Jacops participated in a conference call with Selectica Co-Chairs Zawatski and Thanos on the same topic. During the call, Thanos inquired as to how Trilogy would calculate a value for the Company's NOLs. Fallon replied that Trilogy, "really [did not] pursue them with as much vigor as other[s] might since that is not our core strategy."

The following evening, Fallon contacted Zawatski and outlined two proposals for Trilogy to acquire Selectica's business: (1) Trilogy's purchase of all of the assets of Selectica's sales configuration business in exchange for the cancellation of the $7.1 million in debt Selectica still owed under the October 2007 settlement with Trilogy; or (2) Trilogy's purchase of Selectica's entire operations for the cancellation of the debt plus an additional $6 million in cash. Fallon subsequently followed up with an email reiterating both proposals and suggesting that either proposal would allow Selectica to still make use of its NOLs through the later sale of its corporate entity.

Shortly thereafter, the Board rejected both proposals, made no counterproposal, and there were no follow-up discussions. On October 9, 2008, Trilogy made a second bid to acquire all of the Selectica's assets for $10 million in cash plus the cancellation of the debt, which the Board also rejected. Although Trilogy was invited to participate in the sale process being overseen by Needham, Trilogy was apparently unwilling to sign a non-disclosure agreement, which was a prerequisite for participation. Around this same time, Trilogy had begun making open-market purchases for Selectica stock, although the Board apparently was not aware of this fact at the time.

Trilogy Buys Selectica Stock

On the evening of November 10, Fallon contacted Zawatski and informed her that Trilogy had purchased more than 5% of Selectica's outstanding stock and would be filing a Schedule 13D shortly, which it did on November 13. On a subsequent call with Zawatski and Reilly, Fallon explained that Trilogy had begun buying because it believed that "the company should work quickly to preserve whatever shareholder value remained and that we were interested in seeing this process that they announced with Needham, that we were interested in seeing that accelerate. ..." Within four days of its 13D filing, Trilogy had acquired more than 320,000 additional shares, representing an additional 1% of the Company's outstanding shares.

NOL Poison Pill Adopted

In the wake of Trilogy's decision to begin acquiring Selectica shares, the Board took actions to gauge the impact of these acquisitions, if any, on the Company's NOLs, and to determine whether anything needed to be done to mitigate their effects. Sems immediately asked Brogan to revise his Section 382 analysis—which had not been formally updated since July—to take into account the recent purchases. The revised analysis was delivered to Sems and the Company's new CFO, Richard Heaps, on November 15. It showed that the cumulative acquisition of stock by shareholders over the past three years stood at 40%, which was roughly unchanged from the previous calculation, due to some double counting that occurred in the July analysis.

The Board met on November 16 to discuss the situation and to consider amending Selectica's Shareholder Rights Plan, which had been in place since February 2003. As with many Rights Plans employed as protection devices against hostile takeovers, Selectica's Rights Plan had a 15% trigger. The Board considered an amendment that would reduce that threshold trigger to 4.99% in order to prevent additional 5% owners from emerging and potentially causing a change-in-control event, thereby devaluing Selectica's NOLs. Also present at the meeting were Heaps, Brogan, and Reilly, along with Delaware counsel.

Heaps gave an overview of the Company's existing Shareholder Rights Plan and reviewed the stock price activity since Trilogy had filed its Schedule 13D, noting that shares totaling approximately 2.3% of the Company had changed hands in the two days following the filing. Brogan reviewed the Section 382 ownership analysis that his firm had undertaken on behalf of the Company, noting that additional acquisitions of roughly 10% of the float by new or existing 5% holders would "result in a permanent limitation on use of the Company's net operating loss carryforwards and that, once an ownership change occurred, there would be no way to cure the use limitation on the net operating loss carryforwards." He further advised the Board that "net operating loss carryforwards were a significant asset" and that he generally advises companies to consider steps to protect their NOLs when they experience a 30% or greater change in beneficial ownership. Lastly, Brogan noted that, while he believed that the cumulative ownership change calculations would decline significantly over the next twelve months, "it would decline only modestly, if at all, over the next three to four months," meaning that "the Company would continue to be at risk of an ownership change over the near term."

Reilly discussed the Company's strategic alternatives and noted that Steel Partners and other parties had expressed interest in pursuing a transaction that would realize the value of Selectica's NOLs. He also reviewed potential transaction structures in which the Company might be able to utilize its NOLs. Responding to questions from the Board, Reilly noted that "it is difficult to value the Company's net operating loss carryforwards with greater precision, because their value depends, among other things, on the ability of the Company to generate profits." He confirmed that "existing stockholders may realize significant potential value" from the utilization of the Company's NOLs, which would be "significantly impaired" if a Section 382 ownership change occurred.

At the request of the Board, Delaware counsel reviewed the Delaware law standards that apply for adopting and implementing measures that have an anti-takeover effect. The Board then discussed amending the existing Shareholder Rights Plan, and the possible terms of such an amendment. These included: the pros and cons of providing a cushion for preexisting 5% holders, the appropriate effective date of the new Shareholder Rights Plan, whether the Board should have authority to exclude purchases by specific stockholders from triggering the Rights Plan, and whether a review process should be implemented to determine periodically whether the Rights Plan should remain in effect.

The Board then unanimously passed a resolution amending Selectica's Shareholder Rights Plan, by decreasing the beneficial ownership trigger from 15% to 4.99%, while grandfathering in existing 5% shareholders and permitting them to acquire up to an additional 0.5%

(subject to the original 15% cap) without triggering the NOL Poison Pill.

The Board resolution also established an Independent Director Evaluation Committee (the "Committee") as a standing committee of the Board to review periodically the rights agreement at the behest of the Board and to "determine whether the Rights [Plan] continues to be in the best interest of the Corporation and its stockholders." The Committee was also directed to review "the appropriate trigger percentage" of the Rights Plan based on corporate and shareholder developments, any broader developments relating to rights plans generally—including academic studies of rights plans and contests for corporate control—and any other factors it deems relevant. The Board set April 30, 2009, as the first date that the Committee should report its findings.

Trilogy Triggers NOL Poison Pill

The Board publicly announced the amendment of Selectica's Rights Plan on Monday, November 17. Early the following morning, Fallon emailed Trilogy's broker, saying "[W]e need to stop buying SLTC. They announced a new pill and we need to understand it." Fallon also sent Liemandt a copy of Selectica's 8-K containing the amended language of the NOL Poison Pill. Trilogy immediately sought legal advice about the NOL Poison Pill. The following morning, Liemandt e-mailed Price, with a copy to Fallon, asking, "What percentage of [Selectica] would we need to buy to ruin the tax attributes that [S]teel [P]artners is looking for?" They concluded that they would need to acquire 23% to trigger a change-in-control event.

Later that week, Trilogy sent Selectica a letter asserting that a Selectica contract with Sun Microsystems constituted a breach of the October 2007 settlement and seeking an immediate meeting with Selectica purportedly to discuss the breach, even though members of Trilogy's management had been on notice of the contract as early as July. Fallon, Liemandt, and Jacops from Trilogy, along with Zawatski, Thanos, and Heaps from Selectica met on December 17. The parties' discussions at this meeting are protected by a confidentiality agreement that had been circulated in advance. However, Selectica contends that "based solely on statements and conduct outside that meeting, it is evident that Trilogy threatened to trigger the NOL Poison Pill deliberately unless Selectica agreed to Trilogy's renewed efforts to extract money from the Company."

On December 18, Trilogy purchased an additional 30,000 Selectica shares, and Trilogy management verified with Liemandt his intention to proceed with "buying through" the NOL Poison Pill. The following morning, Trilogy purchased an additional 124,061 shares of Selectica, bringing its ownership share to 6.7% and thereby becoming an "Acquiring Person" under the NOL Poison Pill. Liemandt testified that the rationale behind triggering the pill was to "bring accountability" to the Board and "expose" what Liemandt characterized as "illegal behavior" by the Board in adopting a pill with such a low trigger. Fallon asserted that the reason for triggering the NOL Poison Pill was to "bring some clarity and urgency" to their discussions with Selectica about the two parties' somewhat complicated relationship by "setting a time frame that might help accelerate discussions" on the direction of the business.

Fallon placed a telephone call to Zawatski on December 19 to advise her that Trilogy had bought through the NOL Poison Pill. During a return call by Zawatski later that evening, Fallon indicated that Trilogy felt, based on the conversations from December 17, that Selectica no longer wanted Trilogy as a shareholder or creditor. He then proposed that Selectica repurchase Trilogy's shares, accelerate the payment of its debt, terminate its license with Sun, and make a payment to Trilogy of $5 million "for settlement of basically all outstanding issues between our companies." Zawatski recalled that Fallon told her that Trilogy had triggered the pill "to get our attention and create a sense of urgency;" that, since the Board would have ten days to determine how to react to the pill trigger, "it would force the board to make a decision."

Board Considers Options and Requests a Standstill

The Selectica Board had a telephonic meeting on Saturday, December 20, to discuss Trilogy's demands and an appropriate response. The Board discussed "the desirability of taking steps to ensure the validity of the Shareholder Rights Plan," and ultimately passed a resolution authorizing the filing of this lawsuit, which occurred the following day. On December 22, Trilogy filed an amended Schedule 13D disclosing its ownership percentage and again the Selectica Board met telephonically to discuss the litigation. It eventually agreed to have a representative contact Trilogy to seek a standstill on any additional open market purchases while the Board used the ten-day clock under the NOL Poison Pill to determine whether to consider Trilogy's purchases "exempt" under the Rights Plan, and if not, how Selectica would go about implementing the pill.

The amended Rights Plan allowed the Board to declare Trilogy an "Exempt Person" during the ten-day period following the trigger, if the Board determined that Trilogy would not "jeopardize or endanger the availability to the Company of the NOLs. ..." The Board could also decide during this window to exchange the rights (other than those held by Trilogy) for shares of common stock. If the Board did nothing, then after ten days the rights would "flip in" automatically, becoming exercisable for $36 worth of newly-issued common stock at a price of $18 per right.

The Board met again by telephone the following day, December 23, to discuss the progress of the litigation and to consider the potential impact of the various alternatives under the NOL Poison Pill. The Board agreed to meet in person the following Monday, December 29, along with the Company's financial, legal, and accounting advisors, to evaluate further the available options. The Board also voted to reduce the number of authorized directors from seven to five.

On Wednesday, December 24, the Board met once again by telephone upon learning that the Company's counsel had not succeeded in convincing Trilogy to agree to a standstill. The Board resolved that Zawatski should call Fallon to determine whether Trilogy was willing "to negotiate a standstill agreement that might make triggering the remedies available under the Shareholder Rights Plan, as amended, unnecessary at this time." Zawatski spoke with Fallon on the morning of December 26. Fallon stated that Trilogy did not want to agree to a standstill, that relief from the NOL Poison Pill was not Trilogy's goal, and that Trilogy expected that the NOL Poison Pill would apply to it. Fallon reiterated that the ten-day window would help "speed [the] course" towards a resolution of their claims.

The Board and its advisors met again on December 29. Thanos provided an update on recent developments at the Company, including financial results, management changes, and the Needham Process, as well as an overview of the make-up of the Company's shareholder base. Reilly then provided a more detailed report on the status of the Needham Process. Thereafter, Brogan presented his firm's updated analysis of Selectica's NOLs, which found that the Company had at least $160 million in NOLs and that there had been a roughly 40%

ownership change by 5% holders over the three-year testing period. Since those were not expected to "roll off" in the near term, there was "a significant risk of a Section 382 ownership change."

Brogan subsequently discussed the possible consequences of the two principal mechanisms for implementing the triggered NOL Poison Pill to the change-in-control analysis. He stated that employing a share exchange would not likely have a materially negative impact on the Section 382 analysis. He expressed concern, however, about the uncertain effect of a flip-in pill on subsequent ownership levels (specifically, the possibility that a flip-in pill would, itself, trigger a Section 382 ownership change). Reilly once again addressed the Board to explain the ways he believed the NOLs would be valuable to the Company in its ongoing exploration of strategic alternatives, and reiterated his opinion that an ownership change would "reduce the value of the Company."

The Board also discussed Trilogy's settlement demands. It found them "highly unreasonable" and "lack[ing] any reasonable basis in fact," and that "it [was] not in the best interests of the Company and its stockholders to accept Trilogy/Versata's settlement demands relating to entirely separate intellectual property disputes as a precondition to negotiating a standstill agreement to resolve this dispute." The Board discussed Trilogy's actions at some length, ultimately concluding that they "were very harmful to the Company in a number of respects," and that "implementing the exchange was reasonable in relation to the threat imposed by Trilogy." In particular, that was because (1) the NOLs were seen as "an important corporate asset that could significantly enhance stockholder value," and (2) Trilogy had intentionally triggered the NOL Poison Pill, publicly suggested it might purchase additional stock, and had refused to negotiate a standstill agreement, even though an additional 10% acquisition by a 5% shareholder would likely trigger an ownership change under Section 382.

The Board then authorized Delaware counsel to contact Trilogy in writing, one final time, to seek a standstill agreement. It also passed resolutions delegating the full power of the Board to the Committee to determine whether or not to treat Trilogy or its acquisition as "exempt," and nominating Alan Howe as a new member of the Board. On the evening of December 29, Selectica's Delaware counsel e-mailed Trilogy's trial counsel at the Board's instruction, seeking a standstill agreement "so that the Board could consider either declaring them an 'Exempt Person' under the Rights Plan ... or alternatively, settle the litigation altogether in exchange for a long term agreement relating to your clients' ownership of additional shares." The following afternoon, Trilogy's counsel responded that Trilogy was not willing to agree to the proposed standstill.

Two days later, on December 31, the Board met telephonically and was informed of Trilogy's latest rejection of a standstill agreement. The Board discussed its options with its legal advisors and ultimately concluded that the NOL Poison Pill should go into effect and that an exchange was the best alternative and should be implemented as soon as possible in order to protect the NOLs, even at the risk of disrupting common stock trading. The Board directed advisers to prepare a technical amendment to the NOL Poison Pill to clarify the time at which the exchange would become effective.

Board Adopts Reloaded Pill and Dilutes Trilogy Holdings

On January 2, the Board met telephonically once more, reiterating its delegation of authority to the Committee to make recommendations regarding the implementation of the NOL Poison Pill. The Board also passed a resolution expressly confirming that the Board's delegation of authority to the Committee included the power to effect an exchange of the rights under the NOL Poison Pill and to declare a new dividend of rights under an amended Rights Plan (the "Reloaded NOL Poison Pill"). The Board then adjourned and the Committee—comprised of Sems and Arnold—met with legal and financial advisors, who confirmed that there had been no new agreement with representatives from Trilogy, reiterated that the NOLs remained "a valuable corporate asset of the Company in connection with the Company's ongoing exploration of strategic alternatives," and advised the Committee members of their fiduciary obligations under Delaware law.

Reilly presented information to the Committee about the current takeover environment and the use of Rights Plans (specifically, the types of pills commonly employed and their triggering thresholds), and reviewed the Company's then-current anti-takeover defenses compared with those of other public companies. Reilly stated that "a so-called NOL rights plan with a 4.99% trigger threshold is designed to help protect against stock accumulations that would trigger an 'ownership change,'" and that "implementing appropriate protections of the Company's net operating loss carryforwards was especially important at present," given Trilogy's recent share acquisitions superimposed on the Company's existing Section 382 ownership levels. Finally, Reilly reviewed the proposed terms and conditions of the Reloaded NOL Poison Pill, discussed the methodology for determining the exercise price of the new rights, and made recommendations. The Committee sought and obtained reconfirmed assurances by its financial and legal advisors that the NOLs were a valuable corporate asset and that they remained at a significant risk of being impaired.

The Committee concluded that Trilogy should not be deemed an "Exempt Person," that its purchase of additional shares should not be deemed an "Exempt Transaction," that an exchange of rights for common stock (the "Exchange") should occur, and that a new rights dividend on substantially similar terms should be adopted. The Committee passed resolutions implementing those conclusions, thereby adopting the Reloaded NOL Poison Pill and instituting the Exchange.

The Exchange doubled the number of shares of Selectica common stock owned by each shareholder of record, other than Trilogy or Versata, thereby reducing their beneficial holdings from 6.7% to 3.3%. The implementation of the Exchange led to a freeze in the trading of Selectica stock from January 5, 2009 until February 4, 2009, with the stock price frozen at $0.69. The Reloaded NOL Poison Pill will expire on January 2, 2012, unless the expiration date is advanced or extended, or unless these rights are exchanged or redeemed by the Board some time before.

ANALYSIS

Unocal Standard Applies

In *Unocal* [493 A.2d 946 (Del. 1985)], this Court recognized that "our corporate law is not static. It must grow and develop in response to, indeed in anticipation of, evolving concepts and needs." [In this litigation,] [t]he Court of Chancery concluded that the protection of company NOLs may be an appropriate corporate policy that merits a defensive response when they are threatened. We agree.

The *Unocal* two part test is useful as a judicial analytical tool because of the flexibility of its application in a variety of fact scenarios. Delaware courts have approved the adoption of a Shareholder Rights Plan as an antitakeover device, and have applied the *Unocal* test to analyze a board's response to an actual or potential hostile takeover threat. Any NOL poison pill's principal intent, however, is to prevent the inadvertent forfeiture of potentially valuable assets, not to protect against hostile takeover attempts. Even so, any Shareholder Rights Plan, by its nature, operates as an antitakeover device. Consequently, notwithstanding its primary purpose, a NOL poison pill must also be analyzed under *Unocal* because of its effect and its direct implications for hostile takeovers.

Threat Reasonably Identified

The first part of *Unocal* review requires a board to show that it had reasonable grounds for concluding that a threat to the corporate enterprise existed. The Selectica Board concluded that the NOLs were an asset worth preserving and that their protection was an important corporate objective. Trilogy contends that the Board failed to demonstrate that it conducted a reasonable investigation before determining that the NOLs were an asset worth protecting. We disagree.

The record reflects that the Selectica Board met for more than two and a half hours on November 16. The Court of Chancery heard testimony from all four directors and from Brogan, Reilly, and Heaps, who also attended that meeting and advised the Board. The record shows that the Board first analyzed the NOLs in September 2006, and sought updated Section 382 analyses from Brogan in March 2007, June 2007, and July 2008. At the November 16 meeting, Brogan advised the Board that the NOLs were a "significant asset" based on his recently updated calculations of the NOLs' magnitude. Reilly, an investment banker, similarly advised the Board that the NOLs were worth protecting given the possibility of a sale of Selectica or its assets. Accordingly, the record supports the Court of Chancery's factual finding that the Board acted in good faith reliance on the advice of experts in concluding that "the NOLs were an asset worth protecting and thus, that their preservation was an important corporate objective."

The record also supports the reasonableness of the Board's decision to act promptly by reducing the trigger on Selectica's Rights Plan from 15% to 4.99%. At the November 16 meeting, Brogan advised the Board that the change-of-ownership calculation under Section 382 stood at approximately 40%. Trilogy's ownership had climbed to over 5% in just over a month, and Trilogy intended to continue buying more stock. There was nothing to stop others from acquiring stock up to the 15% trigger in the Company's existing Rights Plan. Once the

Section 382 limitation was tripped, the Board was advised it could not be undone.

At the November 16 meeting, the Board voted to amend Selectica's existing Rights Plan to protect the NOLs against a potential Section 382 "change of ownership." It reduced the trigger of its Shareholders Rights Plan from 15% to 4.99% and provided that existing shareholders who held in excess of 4.99% would be subject to dilutive consequences if they increased their holdings by 0.5%. The Board also created the Review Committee (Arnold and Sems) with a mandate to conduct a periodic review of the continuing appropriateness of the NOL Poison Pill.

The Court of Chancery found the record "replete with evidence" that, based upon the expert advice it received, the Board was reasonable in concluding that Selectica's NOLs were worth preserving and that Trilogy's actions presented a serious threat of their impairment. The Court of Chancery explained those findings, as follows:

> The threat posed by Trilogy was reasonably viewed as qualitatively different from the normal corporate control dispute that leads to the adoption of a shareholder rights plan. In this instance, Trilogy, a competitor with a contentious history, recognized that harm would befall its rival if it purchased sufficient shares of Selectica stock, and Trilogy proceeded to act accordingly. It was reasonable for the Board to respond, and the timing of Trilogy's campaign required the Board to act promptly. Moreover, the 4.99% threshold for the NOL Poison Pill was driven by our tax laws and regulations; the threshold, low as it is, was measured by reference to an external standard, one created neither by the Board nor by the Court [of Chancery]. Within this context, it is not for the Court [of Chancery] to second-guess the Board's efforts to protect Selectica's NOLs.

Those findings are not clearly erroneous. They are supported by the record and the result of a logical deductive reasoning process. Accordingly, we hold that the Selectica directors satisfied the first part of the *Unocal* test by showing "that they had reasonable grounds for believing that a danger to corporate policy and effectiveness existed because of another person's stock ownership."

Selectica Defenses Not Preclusive

The second part of the *Unocal* test requires an initial evaluation of whether a board's defensive response to the threat was preclusive or coercive and, if neither, whether the response was "reasonable in relation to the threat" identified. Under *Unitrin*, a defensive measure is disproportionate and unreasonable *per se* if it is draconian by being either coercive or preclusive. A coercive response is one that is "aimed at 'cramming down' on its shareholders a management-sponsored alternative." A defensive measure is preclusive where it "makes a bidder's ability to wage a successful proxy contest and gain control either 'mathematically impossible' or 'realistically unattainable.'" A successful proxy contest that is mathematically impossible is, *ipso facto*, realistically unattainable. Because the "mathematically impossible" formulation in *Unitrin* is subsumed within the category of preclusivity described as "realistically unattainable," there is, analytically speaking, only one test of preclusivity: "realistically unattainable."

Trilogy claims that a Rights Plan with a 4.99% trigger renders the possibility of an effective proxy contest realistically unattainable. In support of that position, Trilogy argues that, because a proxy contest can only be successful where the challenger has sufficient credibility, the 4.99% pill trigger prevents a potential dissident from signaling its financial commitment to the company so as to establish such credibility. In addition, Professor Ferrell, Trilogy's expert witness, testified that the 5% cap on ownership exacerbates the free rider problem already experienced by investors considering fielding an insurgent slate of directors, and makes initiating a proxy fight an economically unattractive proposition. [[This footnote has been moved to the text:] According to Professor Ferrell, the free rider problem is that, even if an investor believes that replacing the board would result in a material benefit to shareholders, the investor has to bear the full cost of a proxy fight while only receiving her proportionate fraction of the benefit bestowed upon shareholders. Professor Ferrell testified that, along with the reduced likelihood of success at a 5% position, the capped position would mean that the challenger would be unable to internalize more of the benefits by increasing her share ownership.]

This Court first examined the validity of a Shareholder Rights Plan in *Moran v. Household International, Inc.* [500 A.2d 1346 (Del. 1985)] In *Moran* the Rights Plan at issue had a 20% trigger. We recognized that, while a Rights Plan "does deter the formation of proxy efforts of a certain magnitude, it does not limit the voting power of individual shares." In *Moran*, we concluded that the assertion that a Rights Plan would frustrate proxy fights was "highly conjectural" and pointed to "recent corporate takeover battles in which insurgents holding less than 10% stock ownership were able to secure corporate control through a proxy contest or the threat of one."

The 5% trigger that is necessary for a NOL poison pill to serve its primary objective imposes a lower threshold than the Rights Plan thresholds that have traditionally been adopted and upheld as acceptable anti-takeover defenses by Delaware courts. Selectica submits that the distinguishing feature of the NOL Poison Pill and Reloaded NOL Poison Pill—the 5% trigger—is not enough to differentiate them from other Rights Plans previously upheld by Delaware courts, and that there is no evidence that a challenger starting below 5% could not realistically hope to prevail in a proxy contest at Selectica. In support of those arguments Selectica presented expert testimony from Professor John C. Coates IV and Peter C. Harkins.

Professor Coates identified more than fifty publicly held companies that have implemented NOL poison pills with triggers at roughly 5%, including several large, well-known corporations, some among the Fortune 1000. Professor Coates noted that 5% Rights Plans are customarily adopted where issuers have "ownership controlled" assets, such as the NOLs at issue in this case. Professor Coates also testified that Selectica's 5% Rights Plan trigger was narrowly tailored to protect the NOLs because the relevant tax law, Section 382, measures ownership changes based on shareholders who own 5% or more of the outstanding stock.

Moreover, and as the Court of Chancery noted, shareholder advisory firm RiskMetrics Group now supports Rights Plans with a trigger below 5% on a case-by-case basis if adopted for the stated purpose of preserving a company's net operating losses. The factors RiskMetrics will consider in determining whether to support a management proposal to adopt a NOL poison pill are the pill's trigger, the value of the NOLs, the term of the pill, and any corresponding shareholder protection mechanisms in place, such as a sunset provision causing the pill to expire upon exhaustion or expiration of the NOLs.

Selectica expert witness Harkins of the D.F. King & Co. proxy solicitation firm analyzed proxy contests over the three-year period ending December 31, 2008. He found that of the fifteen proxy contests that occurred in micro-cap companies where the challenger controlled less than 5.49% of the outstanding shares, the challenger successfully obtained board seats in ten contests, five of which involved companies with classified boards. Harkins opined that Selectica's unique shareholder profile would considerably reduce the costs associated with a proxy fight, since seven shareholders controlled 55% of Selectica's shares, and twenty-two shareholders controlled 62%. Harkins testified that "if you have a compelling platform, which is critical, it would be easy from a logistical perspective; and from a cost perspective, it would be *de minimis* expense to communicate with those investors, among others." Harkins noted that to win a proxy contest at Selectica, one would need to gain only the support of owners of 43.2% plus one share.

The Court of Chancery concluded that the NOL Poison Pill and Reloaded NOL Poison Pill were not preclusive. For a measure to be preclusive, it must render a successful proxy contest realistically unattainable given the specific factual context. The record supports the Court of Chancery's factual determination and legal conclusion that Selectica's NOL Poison Pill and Reloaded NOL Poison Pill do not meet that preclusivity standard.

Our observation in *Unitrin* is also applicable here: "[I]t is hard to imagine a company more readily susceptible to a proxy contest concerning a pure issue of dollars." The key variable in a proxy contest would be the merit of the bidder's proposal and not the magnitude of its stockholdings. The record reflects that Selectica's adoption of a 4.99% trigger for its Rights Plan would not preclude a hostile bidder's ability to marshal enough shareholder votes to win a proxy contest.

Trilogy argues that, even if a 4.99% shareholder could realistically win a proxy contest "the preclusiveness question focuses on whether a challenger could realistically attain sufficient board control to remove the pill." Here, Trilogy contends, Selectica's charter-based classified board effectively forecloses a bid conditioned upon a redemption of the NOL Poison Pill, because it requires a proxy challenger to launch and complete two successful proxy contests in order to change control. Therefore, Trilogy argues that even if a less than 5% shareholder could win a proxy contest, Selectica's Rights Plan with a 4.99% trigger in combination with Selectica's charter-based classified board, makes a successful proxy contest for control of the board "realistically unattainable."

Trilogy's preclusivity argument conflates two distinct questions: first, is a successful proxy contest realistically attainable; and second, will a successful proxy contest result in gaining control of the board at the next election? Trilogy argues that unless both questions can be answered affirmatively, a Rights Plan and a classified board, viewed collectively, are preclusive. If that preclusivity argument is correct, then it would apply whenever a corporation has both a classified board and a Rights Plan, irrespective whether the trigger is 4.99%, 20%, or anywhere in between those thresholds.

Classified boards are authorized by statute and are adopted for a variety of business purposes. Any classified board also operates as an antitakeover defense by preventing an insurgent from obtaining control of the board in one election. More than a decade ago, in *Carmody* [723 A.2d 1180, 1186 n. 17 (Del. Ch. 1998)], the Court of Chancery noted "because only one third of a classified board would stand for election each year, a classified board would *delay—but not prevent—a hostile acquiror from obtaining control of the board*, since a determined acquiror could wage a proxy contest and obtain control of two thirds of the target board over a two year period, as opposed to seizing control in a single election." The fact that a combination of defensive measures makes it more difficult for an acquirer to obtain control of a board does not make such measures realistically unattainable, i.e., preclusive.

In *Moran*, we rejected the contention "that the Rights Plan strips stockholders of their rights to receive tender offers, and that the Rights Plan fundamentally restricts proxy contests." [500 A.2d at 1357] We explained that "the Rights Plan will not have a severe impact upon proxy contests and it will not *preclude* all hostile acquisitions of Household." In this case, we hold that the combination of a classified board and a Rights Plan do not constitute a preclusive defense.[2]

Range of Reasonableness

If a defensive measure is neither coercive nor preclusive, the *Unocal* proportionality test "requires the focus of enhanced judicial scrutiny to shift to 'the range of reasonableness.'" Where all of the defenses "are inextricably related, the principles of *Unocal* require that such actions be scrutinized collectively as a unitary response to the perceived threat." Trilogy asserts that the NOL Poison Pill, the Exchange, and

2 We note that Selectica no longer has a classified Board. After trial, the Selectica Board amended its charter to eliminate its staggered board structure. On October 15, 2009 the Court of Chancery granted Trilogy's Second Motion for Judicial Notice, which requested the court to take judicial notice of the Selectica proxy statement that referenced the foregoing charter amendment eliminating the staggered board terms.

the Reloaded NOL Poison Pill were not a reasonable collective response to the threat of the impairment of Selectica's NOLs.

The critical facts do not support that assertion. On November 20, within days of learning of the NOL Poison Pill, Trilogy sent Selectica a letter, demanding a conference to discuss an alleged breach of a patent settlement agreement between the parties. The parties met on December 17, and the following day, Trilogy resumed its purchases of Selectica stock.

Fallon testified that he and Liemandt had a discussion wherein Fallon advised Liemandt that Trilogy had purchased additional shares, but not enough to trigger the NOL Poison Pill. Fallon then asked if Liemandt really wanted to trigger the pill, and Liemandt expressly directed Fallon to proceed. On December 19, 2008, Trilogy bought a sufficient number of shares to become an "Acquiring Person" under the NOL Poison Pill. According to Fallon, this was done to "'bring some clarity and urgency' to Trilogy's discussions with Selectica about the two parties' somewhat complicated relationship by 'setting a time frame that might help accelerate discussions' on the direction of the business."

Fallon described Trilogy's relationship with Selectica as a "three-legged stool," referring to Trilogy's status as a competitor, a creditor, and a stockholder of Selectica. The two companies had settled prior patent disputes in 2007 under terms that included a cross-license of intellectual property and quarterly payments from Selectica to Trilogy based on Selectica's revenues from certain products. Selectica argues that Trilogy took the unprecedented step of deliberately triggering the NOL Poison Pill—exposing its equity investment of under $2 million to dilution—primarily to extract substantially more value for the other two "legs" of the stool.

Trilogy's deliberate trigger started a ten business day clock under the terms of the NOL Poison Pill. *If the Board took no action during that time, then the rights (other than those belonging to Trilogy) would "flip-in" and become exercisable for deeply discounted common stock. Alternatively, the Board had the power to exchange the rights (other than those belonging to Trilogy) for newly-issued common stock, or to grant Trilogy an exemption.* Three times in the two weeks following the triggering, Selectica offered Trilogy an exemption in exchange for an agreement to stand still and to withdraw its threat to impair the value and usability of Selectica's NOLs. Three times Trilogy refused and insisted instead that Selectica repurchase its stock, terminate a license agreement with an important client, sign over intellectual property, and pay Trilogy millions of dollars. After three failed attempts to negotiate with Trilogy, it was reasonable for the Board to determine that they had no other option than to implement the NOL Poison Pill.

The Exchange employed by the Board was a more proportionate response than the "flip-in" mechanism traditionally envisioned for a Rights Plan. Because the Board opted to use the Exchange instead of the traditional "flip-in" mechanism, Trilogy experienced less dilution of its position than a Rights Plan is traditionally designed to achieve.

The implementation of the Reloaded NOL Poison Pill was also a reasonable response. The Reloaded NOL Poison Pill was considered a necessary defensive measure because, although the NOL Poison Pill and the Exchange effectively thwarted Trilogy's immediate threat to Selectica's NOLs, they did not eliminate the general threat of a Section 382 change-in-control. Following implementation of the Exchange, Selectica still had a roughly 40% ownership change for Section 382 purposes and there was no longer a Rights Plan in place to discourage additional acquisitions by 5% holders. Selectica argues that the decision to adopt the Reloaded NOL Poison Pill was reasonable under those circumstances. We agree.

The record indicates that the Board was presented with expert advice that supported its ultimate findings that the NOLs were a corporate asset worth protecting, that the NOLs were at risk as a result of Trilogy's actions, and that the steps that the Board ultimately took were reasonable in relation to that threat. Outside experts were present and advised the Board on these matters at both the November 16 meeting at which the NOL Poison Pill was adopted and at the Board's December 29 meeting. The Committee also heard from expert advisers a third time at the January 2 meeting prior to instituting the Exchange and adopting the Reloaded NOL Poison Pill.

Under part two of the *Unocal* test, the Court of Chancery found that the combination of the NOL Poison Pill, the Exchange, and the Reloaded NOL Poison Pill was a proportionate response to the threatened loss of Selectica's NOLs. Those findings are not clearly erroneous. They are supported by the record and the result of a logical deductive reasoning process. Accordingly, we hold that the Selectica directors satisfied the second part of the *Unocal* test by showing that their defensive response was proportionate by being "reasonable in relation to the threat" identified.

Context Determines Reasonableness

Under a *Unocal* analysis, the reasonableness of a board's response is determined in relation to the "specific threat," at the time it was identified. Thus, it is the specific nature of the threat that "sets the parameters for the range of permissible defensive tactics" at any given time. The record demonstrates that a longtime competitor sought to increase the percentage of its stock ownership, not for the purpose of conducting a hostile takeover but, to intentionally impair corporate assets, or else coerce Selectica into meeting certain business demands under the threat of such impairment. Only in relation to that specific threat have the Court of Chancery and this Court considered the reasonableness of Selectica's response.

The Selectica Board carried its burden of proof under both parts of the *Unocal* test. Therefore, at this time, the Selectica Board has withstood the enhanced judicial scrutiny required by the two part *Unocal* test. That does not, however, end the matter.

As we held in *Moran*, the adoption of a Rights Plan is not absolute. In other cases, we have upheld the adoption of Rights Plans in specific defensive circumstances while simultaneously holding that it may be inappropriate for a Rights Plan to remain in place when those specific circumstances change dramatically. The fact that the NOL Poison Pill was reasonable under the specific facts and circumstances of this case, should not be construed as generally approving the reasonableness of a 4.99% trigger in the Rights Plan of a corporation with or without NOLs.

To reiterate *Moran*, "the ultimate response to an actual takeover bid must be judged by the Directors' actions at that time." If and when the Selectica Board "is faced with a tender offer and a request to redeem the [Reloaded NOL Poison Pill], they will not be able to arbitrarily reject the offer. They will be held to the same fiduciary standards any other board of directors would be held to in deciding to adopt a defensive mechanism." The Selectica Board has no more discretion in refusing to redeem the Rights Plan than it does in enacting any defensive mechanism." [*Moran,* 500 A.2d at 1354, 1357] Therefore, the Selectica Board's future use of the Reloaded NOL Poison Pill must be evaluated if and when that issue arises.

...

[Affirmed]

SCENARIO

Target Tuna Corporation (TT) is a publicly traded company whose stock is listed on the New York Stock Exchange. TT's stock was trading at $43 per share when Bidder Buylow Corp. (BB) sought to acquire TT. BB approached TT's board of directors and offered to acquire TT pursuant to a "friendly" merger at $50 per share. TT's board investigated BB's offer. TT's board learned that BB had previously acquired other companies and soon thereafter dismantled those companies and sold off the assets. After TT's board completed its investigation, the board concluded that BB's offer was too low and, in any event, it was in TT's best interests to remain independent under current management. In an effort to fend off BB's overture, TT's board adopted a poison pill that would take effect when any prospective acquirer purchased over 15% of TT's outstanding common stock.

After being rebuffed by TT's board, BB launched a hostile tender offer for $51 per share. Before announcing the tender offer, BB had already acquired 11% of TT's outstanding shares. TT's board responded by approaching a white knight (WK Inc.). WK informed TT's board that it was interested in making a competing bid. But to enter the fray, WK insisted on an option to purchase one of TT's most valuable assets (comprising 20% of TT's total assets) at a very attractive price if another bidder (such as BB) were successful in acquiring a majority of TT's stock.

Consider the following:

1. What other tactics could BB employ to try and acquire TT?
2. What other steps could TT's board have taken to protect itself from unwanted suitors?
3. Assume that BB sues TT's board alleging that TT's board breached its fiduciary duty by entering into the asset option agreement with WK. What would BB argue? What arguments would TT make in its defense? What result and why?

Chapter 11

A Look at the SEC

THE UNITED STATES Securities and Exchange Commission (SEC) is the government agency authorized to regulate and oversee the U.S. securities markets. These responsibilities include, for example, mandating disclosure requirements for companies selling securities in the U.S. securities markets, setting forth specified financial and conduct obligations for financial intermediaries (such as brokers, financial advisers, and licensed representatives), prohibiting fraudulent and other deceptive practices in the offer or sale of securities, protecting the investing public while not unduly impairing capital formation, and instituting enforcement actions when appropriate. The remedies that the SEC can obtain include, for example, the ordering of: an injunction, a civil money penalty, and/or a bar (e.g., prohibiting the violator from working in the brokerage business). Note that criminal proceedings are brought by the U.S. Department of Justice (DOJ), not the SEC.

The following excerpt provides a good initial overview focusing on the "work" of the SEC.

The "Work" of the SEC (available at http://www.sec.gov/about/whatwedo.shtml)

Introduction

The mission of the U.S. Securities and Exchange Commission is to protect investors, maintain fair, orderly, and efficient markets, and facilitate capital formation.

...

The laws and rules that govern the securities industry in the United States derive from a simple and straightforward concept: all investors, whether large institutions or private individuals, should have access to certain basic facts about an investment prior to buying it, and so long as they hold it. To achieve this, the SEC requires public companies to disclose meaningful financial and other information to the public. This provides a common pool of knowledge for all investors to use to judge for themselves whether to buy, sell, or hold a particular security. Only through the steady flow of timely, comprehensive, and accurate information can people make sound investment decisions.

The result of this information flow is a far more active, efficient, and transparent capital market that facilitates the capital formation so important to our nation's economy. To insure that this objective is always being met, the SEC continually works with all major market participants, including especially the investors in our securities markets, to listen to their concerns and to learn from their experience.

The SEC oversees the key participants in the securities world, including securities exchanges, securities brokers and dealers, investment advisors, and mutual funds. Here the SEC is concerned primarily with promoting the disclosure of important market-related information, maintaining fair dealing, and protecting against fraud.

Crucial to the SEC's effectiveness in each of these areas is its enforcement authority. Each year the SEC brings hundreds of civil enforcement actions against individuals and companies for violation of the securities laws. Typical infractions include insider trading, accounting fraud, and providing false or misleading information about securities and the companies that issue them.

...

Though it is the primary overseer and regulator of the U.S. securities markets, the SEC works closely with many other institutions, including Congress, other federal departments and agencies, the self-regulatory organizations (e.g. the stock exchanges), state securities regulators, and various private sector organizations. In particular, the Chairman of the SEC, together with the Chairman of the Federal Reserve, the Secretary of the Treasury, and the Chairman of the Commodity Futures Trading Commission, serves as a member of the President's Working Group on Financial Markets.

This article is an overview of the SEC's history, responsibilities, activities, organization, and operation.

CREATION OF THE SEC

The SEC's foundation was laid in an era that was ripe for reform. Before the Great Crash of 1929, there was little support for federal regulation of the securities markets. This was particularly true during the post–World War I surge of securities activity. Proposals that the federal government require financial disclosure and prevent the fraudulent sale of stock were never seriously pursued.

Tempted by promises of "rags to riches" transformations and easy credit, most investors gave little thought to the systemic risk that arose from widespread abuse of margin financing and unreliable information about the securities in which they were investing. During the 1920s, approximately 20 million large and small shareholders took advantage of post-war prosperity and set out to make their fortunes in the stock market. It is estimated that of the $50 billion in new securities offered during this period, half became worthless.

When the stock market crashed in October 1929, public confidence in the markets plummeted. Investors large and small, as well as the banks who had loaned to these investors, lost great sums of money in the ensuing Great Depression. There was a consensus that for the economy to recover, the public's faith in the capital markets needed to be restored. Congress held hearings to identify the problems and search for solutions.

Based on the findings in these hearings, Congress—during the peak year of the Depression—passed the Securities Act of 1933. This law, together with the Securities Exchange Act of 1934, which created the SEC, was designed to restore investor confidence in our capital markets by providing investors and the markets with more reliable information and clear rules of honest dealing. ...

Monitoring the securities industry requires a highly coordinated effort. Congress established the Securities and Exchange Commission in 1934 to enforce the newly-passed securities laws, to promote stability in the markets and, most importantly, to protect investors. President Franklin Delano Roosevelt appointed Joseph P. Kennedy, President John F. Kennedy's father, to serve as the first Chairman of the SEC.

ORGANIZATION OF THE SEC

The SEC consists of five presidentially-appointed Commissioners, with staggered five-year terms. One of them is designated by the President as Chairman of the Commission—the agency's chief executive. By law, no more than three of the Commissioners may belong to the same political party, ensuring nonpartisanship. The agency's functional responsibilities are organized into five Divisions and 16 Offices, each of which is headquartered in Washington, DC. The Commission's approximately 3,500 staff are located in Washington and in 11 Regional Offices throughout the country.

It is the responsibility of the Commission to:

- interpret federal securities laws;
- issue new rules and amend existing rules;
- oversee the inspection of securities firms, brokers, investment advisers, and ratings agencies;
- oversee private regulatory organizations in the securities, accounting, and auditing fields; and
- coordinate U.S. securities regulation with federal, state, and foreign authorities.

The Commission convenes regularly at meetings that are open to the public and the news media unless the discussion pertains to confidential subjects, such as whether to begin an enforcement investigation.

DIVISIONS

Division of Corporation Finance

The Division of Corporation Finance assists the Commission in executing its responsibility to oversee corporate disclosure of important information to the investing public. Corporations are required to comply with regulations pertaining to disclosure that must be made when stock is initially sold and then on a continuing and periodic basis. The Division's staff routinely reviews the disclosure documents filed by companies. The staff also provides companies with assistance interpreting the Commission's rules and recommends to the Commission new rules for adoption.

The Division of Corporation Finance reviews documents that publicly-held companies are required to file with the Commission. The documents include:

- registration statements for newly-offered securities;
- annual and quarterly filings (Forms 10-K and 10-Q);

- proxy materials sent to shareholders before an annual shareholder meeting;
- annual reports to shareholders;
- documents concerning tender offers (a tender offer is an offer [made by a bidder to shareholders of a target corporation] to buy a large number of shares of [such target] corporation, [normally] at a premium above the current market price); and
- filings related to mergers and acquisitions.

These documents disclose information about the companies' financial condition and business practices to help investors make informed investment decisions. Through the Division's review process, the staff checks to see if publicly-held companies are meeting their disclosure requirements and seeks to improve the quality of the disclosure. To meet the SEC's requirements for disclosure, a company issuing securities or whose securities are publicly traded must make available [specified] information, whether it is positive or negative, that [is significant] to an investor's decision to buy, sell, or hold the security.

...

Division of Trading and Markets

The Division of Trading and Markets assists the Commission in executing its responsibility for maintaining fair, orderly, and efficient markets. The staff of the Division provide day-to-day oversight of the major securities market participants: the securities exchanges; securities firms; self-regulatory organizations (SROs) including the Financial Industry Regulatory Authority (FINRA), the Municipal Securities Rulemaking Board (MSRB), clearing agencies that help facilitate trade settlement; transfer agents (parties that maintain records of securities owners); securities information processors; and credit rating agencies.

The Division also oversees the Securities Investor Protection Corporation (SIPC), which is a private, non-profit corporation that insures the securities and cash in the customer accounts of member brokerage firms against the failure of those firms. Importantly, SIPC insurance does not cover investor losses arising from market declines or fraud.

The Division's additional responsibilities include:

- carrying out the Commission's financial integrity program for broker-dealers;

- reviewing (and in some cases approving, under authority delegated from the Commission) proposed new rules and proposed changes to existing rules filed by the SROs;
- assisting the Commission in establishing rules and issuing interpretations on matters affecting the operation of the securities markets; and
- surveilling the markets.

Division of Investment Management

The Division of Investment Management assists the Commission in executing its responsibility for investor protection and for promoting capital formation through oversight and regulation of America's $26 trillion investment management industry. This important part of the U.S. capital markets includes mutual funds and the professional fund managers who advise them; analysts who research individual assets and asset classes; and investment advisers to individual customers. Because of the high concentration of individual investors in the mutual funds, exchange-traded funds, and other investments that fall within the Division's purview, the Division of Investment Management is focused on ensuring that disclosures about these investments are useful to retail customers, and that the regulatory costs which consumers must bear are not excessive.

The Division's additional responsibilities include:

- assisting the Commission in interpreting laws and regulations for the public and SEC inspection ... ;
- responding to no-action requests and requests for exemptive relief;
- reviewing investment company and investment adviser filings;
- assisting the Commission in enforcement matters involving investment companies and advisers; and
- advising the Commission on adapting SEC rules to new circumstances.

Division of Enforcement

First and foremost, the SEC is a law enforcement agency. The Division of Enforcement assists the Commission in executing its law enforcement function by recommending the commencement of investigations of securities law violations, by recommending that the Commission bring civil actions in federal court or before an administrative law judge, and by prosecuting these cases on behalf of the Commission. As an adjunct to the SEC's civil enforcement authority, the Division works closely with law enforcement agencies in the U.S. and around the world to bring criminal cases when appropriate.

The Division obtains evidence of possible violations of the securities laws from many sources, including market surveillance activities, investor tips and complaints, other Divisions and Offices of the SEC, the self-regulatory organizations and other securities industry sources, and media reports.

All SEC investigations are conducted privately. Facts are developed to the fullest extent possible through informal inquiry, interviewing witnesses, examining brokerage records, reviewing trading data, and other methods. With a formal order of investigation, the Division's staff may compel witnesses by subpoena to testify and produce books, records, and other relevant documents. Following an investigation, SEC staff present their findings to the Commission for its review. The Commission can authorize the staff to file a case in federal court or bring an administrative action. In many cases, the Commission and the party charged decide to settle a matter without trial.

Common violations that may lead to SEC investigations include:

- misrepresentation or omission of important information about securities;
- manipulating the market prices of securities;
- stealing customers' funds or securities;
- violating broker-dealers' responsibility to treat customers fairly;
- insider trading (violating a trust relationship by trading on material, non-public information about a security); and
- selling unregistered securities.

Whether the Commission decides to bring a case in federal court or within the SEC before an administrative law judge may depend upon the type of sanction or relief that is being sought. For example, the Commission may bar someone from the brokerage industry in an administrative proceeding. ... Often, when the misconduct warrants it, the Commission will bring both proceedings.

- *Civil action:* The Commission files a complaint with a U.S. District Court and asks the court for a sanction or remedy. Often the Commission asks for a court order, called an injunction, that prohibits any further acts or practices that violate the law or Commission rules. An injunction can also require audits, accounting for frauds, or special supervisory arrangements. In addition, the SEC can seek civil monetary penalties, or the return of illegal profits (called disgorgement). The court may also bar or suspend an individual from serving as a corporate officer or director [of a publicly-traded company]. A person who violates the court's order may be found in contempt and be subject to additional fines or imprisonment.

- *Administrative action:* The Commission can seek a variety of sanctions through the administrative proceeding process. Administrative proceedings differ from civil court actions in that they are heard by an administrative law judge (ALJ), who is independent of the Commission. The administrative law judge presides over a hearing and considers the evidence presented by the Division staff, as well as any evidence submitted by the subject of the proceeding. Following the hearing, the ALJ issues an initial decision that includes findings of fact and legal conclusions. The initial decision may also contain sanction[s]. Both the Division staff and the defendant may appeal all or any portion of the initial decision to the Commission. The Commission may affirm the decision of the ALJ, reverse the decision, or remand it for additional hearings. Administrative sanctions include cease and desist orders, suspension or revocation of broker-dealer and investment advisor registrations, censures, bars from association with the securities industry, civil monetary penalties, and disgorgement.

Division of Risk, Strategy, and Financial Innovation

The Division of Risk, Strategy, and Financial Innovation was established in 2009 to help further identify developing risks and trends in the financial markets.

This new Division is providing the Commission with sophisticated analysis that integrates economic, financial, and legal disciplines. The Division's responsibilities cover three broad areas: risk and economic analysis; strategic research; and financial innovation.

The emergence of derivatives, hedge funds, new technology, and other factors have transformed both capital markets and corporate governance. The Division of Risk, Strategy, and Financial Innovation is working to advise the Commission through an interdisciplinary approach that is informed by law and modern finance and economics, as well as developments in real world products and practices on Wall Street and Main Street.

Among the functions being performed by the Division are: (1) strategic and long-term analysis; (2) identifying new developments and trends in financial markets and systemic risk; (3) making recommendations as to how these new developments and trends affect the Commission's regulatory activities; (4) conducting research and analysis in furtherance and support of the functions of the Commission and its divisions and offices; and (5) providing training on new developments and trends and other matters.

OFFICES

Office of the General Counsel

The General Counsel is appointed by the Chairman as the chief legal officer of the Commission, with overall responsibility for the establishment of agency policy on legal matters. The General Counsel serves as the chief legal advisor to the Chairman regarding all legal matters and services performed within, or involving, the agency, and provides legal advice to the Commissioners, the Divisions, the Offices, and other SEC components as appropriate.

The General Counsel represents the SEC in civil, private, or appellate proceedings as appropriate, including appeals from the decisions of the federal district courts or the Commission in enforcement matters, and appeals from the denial of requests under the Freedom of Information Act. Through its amicus curiae program, the General Counsel often intervenes in private appellate litigation involving novel or important interpretations of the securities laws, and the Office is responsible for coordinating with the Department of Justice in the preparation of briefs on behalf of the United States involving matters in which the SEC has an interest.

The General Counsel is also responsible for determining the adherence by attorneys in the SEC to appropriate professional standards, as well as for providing advice on standards of conduct to Commissioners and staff, as appropriate. It is responsible for the final drafting of all proposed legislation that the Chairman or the Commission choose to submit for consideration to the Congress or the states, and for coordinating the SEC staff positions on such legislation.

Office of the Chief Accountant

The Chief Accountant is appointed by the Chairman to be the principal adviser to the Commission on accounting and auditing matters. The Office of the Chief Accountant assists the Commission in executing its responsibility under the securities laws to establish accounting principles, and for overseeing the private sector standards-setting process. The Office works closely with the Financial Accounting Standards Board, to which the SEC has delegated authority for accounting standards setting, as well as the International Accounting Standards Board and the American Institute of Certified Public Accountants.

In addition to its responsibility for accounting standards, the Commission is responsible for the approval or disapproval of auditing rules put forward by the Public Company Accounting Oversight Board, a private-sector regulator established by the Sarbanes-Oxley Act to oversee the auditing profession. The Commission also has thorough-going oversight responsibility for all of the activities of the Public Company Accounting Oversight Board (PCAOB), including approval of its annual budget. To assist the Commission in the execution of these responsibilities, the Office of the Chief Accountant is the principal liaison with the PCAOB. The Office also consults with registrants and auditors on a regular basis regarding the application of accounting and auditing standards and financial disclosure requirements.

...

Office of Compliance Inspections and Examinations

The Office of Compliance Inspections and Examinations administers the SEC's nationwide examination and inspection program for registered self-regulatory organizations, broker-dealers, transfer agents, clearing agencies, investment companies, and investment advisers. The Office conducts inspections to foster compliance with the securities laws, to detect violations of the law, and to keep the Commission informed of developments in the regulated community. Among the more important goals of the examination program is the quick and informal correction of compliance problems. When the Office finds deficiencies, it issues a "deficiency letter" identifying the problems that need to be rectified and monitors the situation until compliance is achieved. Violations that appear too serious for informal correction are referred to the Division of Enforcement.

Office of International Affairs

The SEC works extensively in the international arena to promote cooperation among national securities regulatory agencies, and to encourage the maintenance of high regulatory standards worldwide. The Office of International Affairs assists the Chairman and the Commission in the development and implementation of the SEC's international regulatory and enforcement initiatives. The Office negotiates bilateral and multilateral agreements for Commission approval on such subjects as regulatory cooperation and enforcement assistance, and oversees the implementation of such arrangements. It is also responsible for advancing the Commission's agenda in international meetings and organizations. The Office also conducts a technical assistance program for countries with emerging securities markets, which includes training both in the United States and in the requesting country. Over 100 countries currently participate in this program.

Office of Investor Education and Advocacy

The Office of Investor Education and Advocacy has three main functional areas:

The *Office of Policy* has responsibility for reviewing agency action from the perspective of the individual investor, including conducting investor surveys and focus groups. It also plays a role in the Commission's efforts to help ensure that investor disclosures are written in plain English.

The *Office of Investor Advocacy* responds to questions, complaints, and suggestions from the members of the public. Tens of thousands of investors contact the SEC each year using the agency's online forms or our (800) SEC-0330 hotline (toll-free in U.S.) to ask questions on a wide range of securities-related topics, to complain about problems with their investments or their financial professionals, or to suggest improvements to the agency's regulations and procedures.

The *Office of Investor Education* carries out the SEC's investor education program, which includes producing and distributing educational materials, participating in educational seminars and investor-oriented events, and partnering with federal agencies, state regulators, and others on investor literacy initiatives.

Office of Information Technology

The Office of Information Technology supports the Commission and staff of the SEC in all aspects of information technology. The Office has overall management responsibility for the Commission's IT program including application development, infrastructure operations and engineering, user support, IT program management, capital planning, security, and enterprise architecture. The Office operates the Electronic Data Gathering Analysis and Retrieval (EDGAR) system, which electronically receives, processes, and disseminates more than 500,000 financial statements every year. The Office also maintains a very active website that contains a wealth of information about the Commission and the securities industry, and also hosts the EDGAR database for free public access.

Office of the Executive Director

The Office of the Executive Director assists the Chairman in developing and executing the management policies of the SEC. The Office formulates budget and authorization strategies, supervises the allocation and use of SEC resources, promotes management controls and financial integrity, manages the administrative support offices, and oversees the development and implementation of the SEC's automated information systems.

...

Office of Legislative Affairs and Intergovernmental Relations

The Office of Legislative Affairs and Intergovernmental Relations serves as the agency's formal liaison with the Congress, other Executive Branch agencies, and state and local governments. The staff carefully monitors ongoing legislative activities and initiatives on Capitol Hill that affect the Commission and its mission. Through regular communication and consultation with House and Senate members and staff, the Office communicates legislators' goals to the agency, and communicates the agency's own regulatory and management initiatives to the Congress.

The Office is responsible for responding to congressional requests for testimony of SEC officials, as well as requests for documents, technical assistance, and other information. In addition, the Office monitors legislative and oversight hearings that pertain to the securities markets and the protection of investors, even when an SEC witness is not present.

Office of Public Affairs

The Office of Public Affairs assists the Commission in making the work of the SEC open to the public, understandable to investors, and accountable to taxpayers. It helps every other SEC Division and Office accomplish the agency's overall mission—to protect investors, maintain fair, orderly, and efficient markets, and facilitate capital formation. The Office coordinates the agency's relations with the media and the general public, in this country and around the world.

...

Office of the Secretary

The Secretary of the Commission is appointed by the Chairman, and is responsible for the procedural administration of Commission meetings, rulemaking, practice, and procedure. Among the responsibilities of the Office are the scheduling and recording of public and non-public meetings of the Commission; the administration of the process by which the Commission takes action without a meeting (called the seriatim process); the administration of the duty-officer process (by which a single Commissioner is designated to authorize emergency action); the maintenance of records of Commission actions; and the maintenance of records of financial judgments in enforcement proceedings. The Office also provides advice to the Commission and the staff on questions of practice and procedure.

...

Office of Equal Employment Opportunity

Because the SEC's employees are its most important resource, the Office of Equal Employment Opportunity works to ensure that the agency's professional staff come from diverse backgrounds that reflect the diversity of the investing public. Equal employment opportunity at the SEC is a continuing commitment. To maintain neutrality in resolving disputes, the EEO Office is independent of any other SEC office. The EEO Director reports to the Chairman. The primary mission of the EEO Office is to prevent employment discrimination, including discriminatory harassment, so that all SEC employees have the working environment to support them in their efforts to protect investors, maintain healthy markets, and promote capital formation.

Office of the Inspector General

The Office of the Inspector General conducts internal audits and investigations of SEC programs and operations. Through these audits and investigations, the Inspector General seeks to identify and mitigate operational risks, enhance government integrity, and improve the efficiency and effectiveness of SEC programs.

Office of Administrative Law Judges

The Commission's Office of Administrative Law Judges consists of independent judicial officers who conduct hearings and rule on allegations of securities law violations in cases initiated by the Commission. When the Commission initiates a public administrative proceeding, it refers the case to the Office, where it is assigned to an individual Administrative Law Judge (ALJ). The ALJ then conducts a public hearing that is similar to a non-jury trial in the federal courts. Just as a federal judge can do, an ALJ issues subpoenas, rules on motions, and rules on the admissibility of evidence. At the conclusion of the hearing, the parties submit proposed findings of fact and conclusions of law. The ALJ prepares an initial decision that includes factual findings and legal conclusions that are matters of public record. Parties may appeal an initial decision to the Commission, which can affirm, reverse, modify, set aside or remand for further proceedings. Appeals from Commission action are to a United States Court of Appeals.

THE LAWS THAT GOVERN THE SECURITIES INDUSTRY

Securities Act of 1933

Often referred to as the "truth in securities" law, the Securities Act of 1933 has two basic objectives:

- require that investors receive financial and other significant information concerning securities being offered for public sale; and
- prohibit deceit, misrepresentations, and other fraud in the sale of securities.

Purpose of Registration

A primary means of accomplishing these goals is the disclosure of important financial information through the registration of securities. This information enables investors, not the government, to make informed judgments about whether to purchase a company's securities. While the SEC requires that the information provided be accurate, it does not guarantee it. Investors who purchase securities and suffer losses [may] have important recovery rights if they can prove that there was [materially] incomplete or inaccurate disclosure of important information.

The Registration Process

In general, securities sold in the U.S. must be registered. The registration forms companies file provide essential facts while minimizing the burden and expense of complying with the law. In general, registration forms call for:

- a description of the company's properties and business;
- a description of the security to be offered for sale;
- information about the management of the company; and
- financial statements certified by independent accountants.

All companies, both domestic and foreign, must file their registration statements electronically. These statements and the accompanying prospectuses become public shortly after filing, and investors can access them using the Electronic

Data Gathering, Analysis, and Retrieval System (EDGAR). Registration statements are subject to examination for compliance with disclosure requirements.

Not all offerings of securities must be registered with the Commission. Some exemptions from the registration requirement include:

- private offerings to a limited number of persons or institutions;
- offerings of limited size;
- intrastate offerings; and
- securities of municipal, state, and federal governments.

By exempting many small offerings from the registration process, the SEC seeks to foster capital formation by lowering the cost of offering securities to the public.

Securities Exchange Act of 1934

With this Act, Congress created the Securities and Exchange Commission. The Act empowers the SEC with broad authority over all aspects of the securities industry. This includes the power to register, regulate, and oversee brokerage firms, transfer agents, and clearing agencies as well as the nation's securities self-regulatory organizations (SROs). The various stock exchanges, such as the New York Stock Exchange and the American Stock Exchange, are SROs. The Financial Industry Regulatory Authority, which operates the NASDAQ system, is also an SRO.

The Act also identifies and prohibits certain types of conduct in the markets and provides the Commission with disciplinary powers over regulated entities and persons associated with them.

The Act also empowers the SEC to require periodic reporting of information by companies with publicly traded securities. [Under its Securities Exchange Act authority the SEC, for example, engages in regulating the following activities:]

Corporate Reporting

Companies with more than $10 million in assets whose securities are held by more than 500 owners must file annual and other periodic reports. These reports are available to the public through the SEC's EDGAR database.

Proxy Solicitations

The Securities Exchange Act also governs the disclosure in materials used to solicit shareholders' votes in annual or special meetings held for the election of directors and the approval of other corporate action. This information, contained in proxy materials, must be filed with the Commission in advance of any solicitation to ensure compliance with the disclosure rules. Solicitations, whether by management or shareholder groups, must disclose all important facts concerning the issues on which holders are asked to vote.

Tender Offers

The Securities Exchange Act requires disclosure of important information by anyone acquir[ing] more than 5 percent of a company's securities by direct purchase or tender offer. Such an offer often is extended in an effort to gain control of the company. As with the proxy rules, this allows shareholders to make informed decisions on these critical corporate events.

Insider Trading

The securities laws broadly prohibit fraudulent activities of any kind in connection with the offer, purchase, or sale of securities. These provisions are the basis for many types of disciplinary actions, including actions against fraudulent insider trading. Insider trading is illegal when a person trades a security while in possession of material nonpublic information in violation of a duty to withhold the information or refrain from trading.

Registration of Exchanges, Associations, and Others

The Act requires a variety of market participants to register with the Commission, including exchanges, brokers and dealers, transfer agents, and clearing agencies. Registration for these organizations involves filing disclosure documents that are updated on a regular basis.

The exchanges and the National Association of Securities Dealers (NASD) are identified as self-regulatory organizations (SRO). SROs must create rules that allow for disciplining members for improper conduct and for establishing measures to ensure market integrity and investor protection. SRO proposed rules are published for comment before final SEC review and approval.

Trust Indenture Act of 1939

This Act applies to debt securities such as bonds, debentures, and notes that are offered for public sale. Even though such securities may be registered under the Securities Act, they may not be offered for sale to the public unless a formal agreement between the issuer of bonds and the bondholder, known as the trust indenture, conforms to the standards of this Act.

Investment Company Act of 1940

This Act regulates the organization of companies, including mutual funds, that engage primarily in investing, reinvesting, and trading in securities, and whose own securities are offered to the investing public. The regulation is designed to minimize conflicts of interest that arise in these complex operations. The Act requires these companies to disclose their financial condition and investment policies to investors when stock is initially sold and, subsequently, on a regular basis. The focus of this Act is on disclosure to the investing public of information about the fund and its investment objectives, as well as on investment company structure and operations. It is important to remember that the Act does not permit the SEC to directly supervise the investment decisions or activities of these companies or judge the merits of their investments.

Investment Advisers Act of 1940

This law regulates investment advisers. With certain exceptions, this Act requires that firms compensated for advising others about securities investments must register with the SEC and conform to regulations designed to protect investors. ...

Sarbanes-Oxley Act of 2002 [and Dodd-Frank Act of 2010]

On July 30, 2002, President Bush signed into law the Sarbanes-Oxley Act of 2002 [SOX], which he characterized as "the most far reaching reforms of American business practices since the time of Franklin Delano Roosevelt." The Act mandated a number of reforms to enhance corporate responsibility, [improve] financial disclosures, and combat corporate and accounting fraud. [SOX also] created the "Public Company Accounting Oversight Board," also known as the PCAOB, to oversee the activities of the auditing profession. [Similarly, the Dodd-Frank Act of 2010 impacts corporate governance by requiring, for example, a shareholder advisory vote on the level of executive compensation, greater disclosure with respect to executive pay, and compensation committees being comprised entirely of independent directors.]

SOME THOUGHTS ON GOVERNMENT REGULATION

A number of interesting policy questions are raised regarding the presence and powers of a government regulator, like the SEC. These issues also arise in the context of emerging and developing capital markets. The following excerpt (Steinberg, *Emerging Capital Markets: Proposals and Recommendations for Implementation*, 30 The International Lawyer 715 (1996) (citations omitted) (reprinted with permission; all rights reserved)) addresses a number of these issues:

It is clear that some form of oversight or regulation of securities markets is appropriate. The options include, for example, (1) a central government regulator having extensive authority; (2) government regulation by means of regional bodies; (3) self-regulation conducted by stock exchanges and/or other self-regulatory organizations (SROs) established to oversee issuers and financial intermediaries (such as brokers, dealers, investment advisers, and clearing agents); and (4) some combination of the foregoing.

In emerging markets, government regulation along the lines of a United States model Securities and Exchange Commission (SEC) evokes fear of stringent government regulation that impedes capital formation and entrepreneurial creativity. According to such critics, the resulting bureaucratic maze with its accompanying high transaction costs is a burden that emerging and even more developed securities markets can ill afford.

On the other hand, to induce investors to enter these markets, there ordinarily must be in place an oversight authority to help engender much needed confidence in market integrity. Where sharp practices prevail (or are so perceived), mechanisms should be implemented to enforce applicable law and to deter fraud. In such circumstances, much can be said for speaking loudly and carrying a big stick. In those countries where an SRO by custom or law cannot command such presence, a government regulator is the preferable route.

Regardless of whether a U.S.-type SEC is established or self-regulation or some hybrid, adequate powers should be provided. Such powers include, for example, (1) investigatory authority (such as the ability to issue subpoenas demanding the production of relevant documents and the appearance of individuals to testify under oath), (2) enforcement authority enabling the regulator to seek either directly or efficiently through a different regulatory source remedial relief (such as injunctions, disgorgement, and the appointment of a receiver) as well as punitive measures (including civil fines, forfeitures, and criminal prosecution), and (3) the wherewithal to secure judicial relief (such as criminal contempt) in the event of a subject person's noncompliance with an order previously imposed.

Whether a particular capital securities market opts for a government regulator or SRO oversight may depend on such factors as the applicable country's culture, resources, and level of sophistication in this area. There are difficult choices to be made. It may soundly be argued that a country with little expertise that seeks to develop a securities market would be imprudent from both a cost and efficiency perspective to establish a U.S.-type SEC. This putting the cart before the horse approach elevates theory over reality, reflecting waste with little tangible benefit. On the contrary, it may be asserted with some justification that, unless the prospects for economic gain are strikingly encouraging, investors outside of the host country will not enter a market that lacks basic regulatory oversight. Hence, in order to induce the inflow of foreign capital, it may be necessary for a country with an emerging capital securities market to establish a governmental regulatory body.

...

When an alleged violation of the securities laws occurs, should civil and/or criminal enforcement be pursued? For illustration purposes, the U.S. SEC may bring civil enforcement action seeking a wide range of relief, such as the entry of a cease and desist order, ordering of an injunction, appointment of a receiver, levying of money penalties, imposition of an officer and director bar, and ordering of disgorgement of ill-gotten profits. Moreover, the SEC may institute criminal contempt actions against those who have not obeyed injunctions previously issued.

In addition, the U.S. Department of Justice may criminally prosecute accused violators of the federal securities laws. Hefty criminal sentences of up to 25 years imprisonment may be imposed for many violations as well as severe money fines (e.g., for illegal insider trading, stock manipulation, and filing with the SEC materially false statements). Added to the prosecutors' criminal arsenal under U.S. law are statutes that may be invoked in addition to or in lieu of the federal securities laws. These statutes include the federal mail and wire fraud provisions as well as the Racketeer Influenced Corrupt Organizations Act (RICO).

The state securities laws (or "blue sky" laws) enacted by each of the fifty states likewise provide for both government civil and criminal enforcement. Indeed, some of the state securities laws are more onerous than the federal statutes. For example, a number of states authorize criminal liability premised on principles of strict liability.

The SROs in the United States also have significant civil enforcement powers. For example, the stock exchanges may assess censures, bars, and money fines upon broker-dealers and their associated persons who violate the federal securities laws or the respective exchange's rules. An exchange also can delist a security. Moreover, the Financial Industry Regulatory Authority (FINRA) has broad authority to discipline those subject to its regulation.

In contrast to the United States, many countries today, both in emerging and more developed securities markets, rely chiefly (if not solely) on criminal enforcement. It may be questioned whether this is the most effective approach. Today, in a number of these countries such practices as insider trading are made criminal where [not that long before] they were viewed as standard fare or at worst a slap against one's reputation. From current experience, it appears at this time that many judges and juries are reluctant to criminally convict supposedly "reputable" business persons for practices that were [previously] part of the societal mainstream. Indeed, in a number of countries, there have been few if any convictions for illegal insider trading (although the practice continues to occur with some frequency).

Although the climate in the United States points toward increased criminalization of the securities laws, this situation should be viewed from an historical perspective. Insider trading serves as a useful example. Although the major U.S. securities acts were enacted in the 1930s, it was not until the early 1960s that the SEC instituted a key civil enforcement proceeding based on illegal insider trading. A significant appellate court decision based on an SEC civil action was not handed down until the late 1960s. [*SEC v. Texas Gulf Sulphur Co.*, 401 F.2d 833 (2d Cir. 1968).] Some ten years later the U.S. Department of Justice brought the initial criminal prosecutions for insider trading violations. [e.g., *Chiarella v. United States,* 445 U.S. 222 (1980).] Hence, criminal prosecution was initiated only after successful civil enforcement made clear that the practice at issue was illegitimate from a consensual point of view. Although it seems doubtful that such an enforcement policy was part of a grand strategic plan, the U.S. government's current success in the criminal arena underscores the merits of this approach.

To buttress this proposition, the heavier burden of proof in a criminal as compared to a civil proceeding perhaps has prompted judges and juries to refrain from criminally convicting defendants based on circumstantial evidence.

From a prosecutor's viewpoint, financial frauds like insider trading or stock manipulation are not necessarily subject to direct evidence; if a conviction is to be had, circumstantial evidence frequently remains essential. With some exceptions, prosecutors in the United States have been more successful in this respect.

Stated succinctly, it is not suggested that regulators in foreign capital markets abandon criminal enforcement efforts. Rather, the point is that civil regulatory remedies should be made available and should be invoked on a frequent basis. Successful enforcement actions in civil suits will encourage compliance, stimulate securities enforcement efforts in other contexts, and facilitate a consensual understanding of behavior subject to sanction. Criminal enforcement under this scenario would become the "heavy club" to be swung against those deemed sufficiently blameworthy to deserve imprisonment.

SCENARIO

You are a legislative assistant to a United States Senator. The Senator is concerned with the current "work" of the SEC. The Senator requests that you examine the role and functions of the SEC to make your recommendations whether the current framework in effect is appropriate or whether modifications should be made. Based on your recommendations and discussions with other authoritative sources, the Senator intends to introduce a Bill in Congress seeking appropriate changes. Please provide the Senator with your recommendations.

At times, government regulation utterly fails. The recent Madoff scandal represents the most outlandish failure of government oversight. The next chapter focuses on the Madoff scandal.

Chapter 12

WHEN REGULATION FAILS: THE MADOFF DEBACLE

As seen from the discussion in the previous chapter, the Securities and Exchange Commission (SEC) seeks to protect investors by promoting fair, orderly and efficient securities markets. The basic disclosure premise underlying the federal securities laws is that "all investors, whether large institutions or private individuals, should have access to certain basic facts about [a security] investment prior to buying it, and so long as they hold it."[1] Nevertheless, when regulation fails, financial debacles may ensue.[2] Recent scandals, like the Madoff and Stanford frauds, highlight this demise.

For example, in 2009, Allan Stanford was charged with securities fraud for conducting an alleged $8 billion "ponzi" scheme.[3] The lack of effective investigation by federal authorities along with difficulty in obtaining meaningful financial data from a key bank in Antigua kept the SEC from uncovering the fraud.[4] Far too late, the SEC deciphered that the investments held by the Stanford Financial Group were deceptively overvalued.[5] Stanford now awaits trial in a federal prison.[6]

Undoubtedly, the most infamous scandal was that orchestrated by Bernard Madoff, who pled guilty to securities fraud[7] and other criminal charges (including mail fraud, wire fraud and money laundering).[8] Estimated at roughly $65 billion, Madoff committed perhaps the largest securities fraud in history.[9] At the age of 70, he pled guilty and received a sentence of 150 years.[10]

Madoff was "caught" when he told two upper level employees (who happened also to be his sons) that his investment advisory business was "all just one big lie" and "basically, a giant ponzi scheme."[11] Under the seemingly elaborate but surprisingly basic ponzi scheme, Madoff directed payments received from new investors to redeem interests held by other investors.[12] Madoff's scheme "plunged … investors who thought they were wealthy into poverty and forced numerous charities and foundations to close."[13]

Through his firm—Bernard L. Madoff Investment Securities (BMIS)—Madoff projected to investors annual returns as high as 53% (when typical returns were in the four to eight percent range).[14] Madoff directed employees, who purportedly had little knowledge of the securities industry, to provide clients with false monthly account statements and trading confirmations.[15] Astonishingly, "a court appointed trustee found that no trading [had] occurred [in these accounts] for more than a decade."[16]

Investors were attracted by Madoff's proclaimed use of a secret strategy based on a "split-strike conversion" (or "collar" strategy).[17] Employing this proclaimed strategy, Madoff would trade in a basket of stocks and hedge those transactions by buying and selling options contracts (thereby limiting potential losses).[18] A key way Madoff created the appearance that he was engaged in such trading was to move client funds from his U.S. operation to a propriety securities firm that he controlled in London. In reality, this trading was fictitious. Rather, Madoff misappropriated investor money to pay for a lavish lifestyle for himself, his family members, and associates.[19] Among many other extravagant possessions, Madoff owned a penthouse apartment in Manhattan, interests in two private jets, and a yacht moored off the French Riviera.[20]

The victims of Madoff's securities fraud range from ordinary investors (who lost "mere thousands") to sophisticated institutional investors (who lost millions). "Hedge funds were among the main victims, along with well-heeled individual investors, nonprofit endowment funds and foreign financial companies."[21] Some families lost millions of dollars.[22] Powerful investors such as Senator Frank Lautenberg, former Philadelphia Eagles owner Norman Braman, and New York Mets owner Fred Wilpon lost large amounts.[23] To illustrate, Frank Lautenberg, one of the wealthiest Senators, entrusted his family's charity to Madoff.[24] Other distinguished individual victims were the "real estate magnate Moritimer Zuckerman, Nobel Prize winner Elie Wiesel, and film director and producer Steven Spielberg,"[25] as well as actress Zsa Zsa Gabor, actor John Malkovich, former Miss America Phyllis George, talk-show host Larry King, and former Los Angeles Dodger hall of fame pitcher Sandy Koufax.[26] Several global corporations and organizations suffered significant financial losses, including HSBC, Banco Santander, BNP Paribas, Royal Bank of Scotland Group, the pension fund of Royal Dutch Shell,[27] the International Olympic Committee, and New York University.[28] Charitable foundations also were victimized, including the Jewish Community Foundation of Los

Angeles, Hadassah, the Pioneer Foundation, the Elie Wiesel Foundation for Humanity, and the Spielberg charity—the Wunderkinder Foundation.[29]

The precise adverse economic impact resulting from Madoff's fraud is uncertain; but, clearly, scores, if not hundreds, of investors incurred severe losses. In Palm Beach, Florida (where Madoff was a member of the West Palm Beach Country Club), "a number of high-priced Palm Beach homes were put on the market ... by [Madoff] victims who have been nearly financially wiped out."[30] The owner of a pawn shop reported that Madoff victims had been contacting him asking for loans and offering everything from four-carat diamonds to yachts as collateral.[31] Devastatingly, French aristocratic banker Thierry Magon de la Villehuchet apparently committed suicide at his New York office after learning he had lost $1.5 billion on behalf of customers (including the investment bank Rothschild & Cie) and $50 million of his own money.[32]

Even those who believed they had a close relationship with Madoff were victimized by the treachery. For example, former business acquaintance Robert Gettinger first invested with Madoff in 1973 after being introduced to him by a friend. Prior to the uncovering of the ponzi scheme, Gettinger thought his investment was worth more than $10 million (and that the trust for his sons had about $3 million).[33] And Andrew Cohen, a former employee for Madoff's firm BMIS, left most of his money with his former employer because he "trusted him."[34]

Due to his distinguished Wall Street reputation, Madoff enjoyed widespread trust. For instance, Richard Spring, a former securities analyst, because he believed in Madoff, had nearly $11 million—comprising 95% of his net worth—invested with Madoff.[35] Madoff's role with NASDAQ (and its creation of a computerized high-volume, high speed trading system) in the 1970s helped to elevate his status in the securities industry.[36] Additionally, Madoff had the distinction of being a former chairman of the Nasdaq Stock Market.[37] Even SEC regulators respected Madoff. The SEC selected Madoff to serve on an advisory committee on market structure in 2000 and frequently invited him to be a participant at agency round-table discussions.[38] Indeed, former SEC Chairman Arthur Levitt, Jr. "said his reaction after Mr. Madoff confessed ... was 'astonishment.'"[39]

The allure attached to Madoff's "touch" in conjunction with consistent returns seduced investors. Investing with Madoff gave investors a "members only feeling." In this manner, Madoff was able to shift "investors' fears from concerns that they might lose money to the risk they might lose out on making money."[40] The fancy offices, cars, and private jets, and associations with mayors, governors, athletes and movie stars also enabled Madoff to build his "web of deception."[41]

As a generalization, spectacular scandals often occur during investing bubbles—and only become known when they pop. "Bubbles provide the cover the crooked need to perpetrate their scams [because] ... [w]hen the market's heading up, any investment seems possible."[42] Once the securities markets spiraled downward, Madoff's ponzi scheme effectively collapsed when clients opted to pull their money out.[43]

For many years, Madoff's business evidently fell into a regulatory gray zone; the ambiguity of Madoff's investment strategy facilitated the evasion of regulatory oversight.[44] Although he purportedly was deciding how to invest his client's money, he was not registered as an investment advisor with the SEC until 2006. Indeed, his business at times was called a hedge fund even though there was no formal investment fund.[45]

When exercising its investigative functions, due to a finite amount of resources, the SEC generally must focus on complaints by order of severity and likelihood of an actual violation.[46] As stated by a former SEC Director of Enforcement, "[t]he primary consideration in determining whether to pursue any particular tip depends on whether, based on judgment and experience, the tip provides sufficient information to suggest that it might lead to an enforcement action involving a violation of the federal securities law."[47] Among the factors to be considered are:

> [T]he source of the tip; the nature, accuracy and plausibility of the information provided; an assessment of how closely the information relates to a possible violation of federal securities law; the validity and strength of the legal theory on which a potential violation would be based; the nature and type of evidence that would have to be gathered in the course of further investigation; the amount of resources the investigation might consume; and whether there are any obvious impediments that would prevent the information from leading to an enforcement action (for example, the conduct complained of is not securities-related).[48]

Nevertheless, the SEC missed several opportunities to uncover Madoff's illegal scheme. "The inability of the SEC to discover Madoff's fraud ... enabled the fraudster to exploit the government's ineptness as a cover for his ongoing duplicity and contributed to his success."[49] As stated in the Report issued by the SEC's Office of Inspector General:

> The OIG [Office of Inspector General] Investigation found that the SEC received numerous substantive complaints since 1992 that raised

> significant red flags concerning Madoff's hedge fund operations and should have led to questions about whether Madoff was actually engaged in trading and should have led to a thorough examination and/or investigation of the possibility that Madoff was operating a Ponzi scheme. However, the OIG found that although the SEC conducted five examinations and investigations of Madoff based upon these substantive complaints, they never took the necessary and basic steps to determine if Madoff was misrepresenting his trading. We also found that had these efforts been made with appropriate follow-up, the SEC could have uncovered the Ponzi scheme well before Madoff confessed.
>
> The OIG found that the conduct of the examinations and investigations was similar in that they were generally conducted by inexperienced personnel, not planned adequately, and were too limited in scope. While examiners and investigators discovered suspicious information and evidence and caught Madoff in contradictions and inconsistencies, they either disregarded these concerns or relied inappropriately upon Madoff's representations and documentation in dismissing them. Further, the SEC examiners and investigators failed to understand the complexities of Madoff's trading and the importance of verifying his returns with independent third-parties. ...
>
> ...
>
> [W]e found that not only was the SEC unable to uncover Madoff's fraud in the several investigations and examinations it conducted over a period of years, the fact that they had conducted examinations and investigations and did not detect the fraud, lent credibility to Madoff's operations and had the effect of encouraging additional individuals and entities to invest with him.[50]

The Madoff scandal also raises concern regarding the seeming "culture of deference toward the Wall Street elite at the SEC."[51] In response to these criticisms, the SEC has implemented substantial changes as well as appointing a former prosecutor as its enforcement director.[52]

As a result of the Madoff fraud, the Investment Advisers Act was amended in 2010 to require "money managers to keep client assets at a qualified custodian, and by requiring investment funds to be audited by independent public accounting firms that are overseen by the PCAOB [Public Company Accounting Oversight Board]."[53] Thus, "the custodian requirement largely removes the ability of an investment advisor to pay the proceeds invested by new investors to pay old investors."[54]

Madoff investors, nonetheless, have received some good news. The widow of a wealthy investor who enormously profited from investing with Madoff agreed to return $7.2 billion to help recoup the losses suffered by other Madoff investors.[55] Along with other amounts recovered, the customer fund to compensate Madoff investors now totals approximately $10 billion.[56] This amount likely will enable Madoff investors to recover more than fifty percent of their principal investments.[57] Although the losses suffered by the investors remain in the billions, regulators deserve kudos for their successful recoupment of these funds.

Perhaps the underlying focus of the Madoff scandal is that the SEC (due to its shortage of personnel, ineptness at times, and complexity of the securities markets) will not timely detect every fraud. Therefore, it is imperative that, when parting with their funds, investors perform adequate due diligence and effectively diversify their investments.[58]

NOTES

1. U.S. Securities and Exchange Commission, *The Investor's Advocate: How the SEC Protects Investors, Maintains Market Integrity, and Facilitates Capital Formation*, at p. 1, available at http://www.sec.gov/about/whatwedo.shtml.
2. The enactment of the Dodd-Frank Act of 2010, in response to perceived regulatory failures, provides the most recent example.
3. *See* Complaint in *Securities and Exchange Commission v. Stanford International Bank, Ltd., et. al.*, No. 3:09 cv-0298 (N.D Tex. Feb. 27 2009), available at http://www.sec.gov/litigation/complaints/2009/comp20959.pdf. A "ponzi" offers to investors the lure of incredible profits (e.g., double your money in two months). In fact, the scheme is a fraud—funds invested by current investors are used to pay off earlier investors. As long as sufficient amounts continue to flow in, the scheme continues. This type of fraud is named after Charles Ponzi who masterminded an elaborate fraud. See *In re Ponzi*, 268 F. 997 (D. Mass. 1920).
4. See Simpson, *The Stanford Affair: Madoff Case Led SEC to Intensify Stanford Probe,* Wall St. J, Feb. 19, 2009, at A14. See generally Report of Investigation, SEC Office of Inspector General, *Investigation of the SEC's Response to Concerns Regarding Robert Allen Stanford's Alleged Ponzi Scheme*, Case No. OIG-526 (March 31, 2010).
5. See Lake, Federal Criminal Defense Blog, *The SEC's Case Against Sir Robert Allen Stanford—A Case Study in Investigative and Enforcement Failure,* Apr. 20, 2010, available at http://www.federalcriminaldefenseblog.com/2010/04/articles/securities-and-exchange-commis/the-secs-case-against-sir-robert-allen-stanford-a-case-study-in-investigative-and-enforcement-failure/.
6. See Driver, *Judge Postpones Allen Stanford's Trial,* Reuters, Jan. 7, 2011, available at http://www.reuters.com/article/2011/01/07/us-stanford-trial. See also, Calkins & Harris, *Allen Stanford's Trial Set to Start in January 2011*, Bloomberg, http://

www.bloomberg.com/apps/news?pid=newsarchive&sid=aumD.AqRGkYU (Stanford has pled not guilty).

7. See Federal Bureau of Investigation, Department of Justice Press Release, http://newyork.fbi.gov/dojpressrel/pressrel09/nyfo031209.htm.
8. *Id.* See generally E. Arvedlund, *Too Good to be True: The Rise and Fall of Bernie Madoff* (2009); D. Henriques, *The Wizard of Lies* (2011); Rhee, *The Madoff Scandal, Market Regulatory Abuse and the Business Education of Lawyers,* 35 J. Corp. L. 363 (2009).
9. See Efrati and Frank, *Madoff Set to Plead Guilty to 11 Felonies—Accounts Totaled $65 Billion,* Wall St. J., March 11, 2009, at A1.
10. *See* Wechsler and Glovin, *Madoff Life Prison Term Means Inmate Blame for Crash*, http://www.bloomberg.com/apps/news?pid=newsarchive&sid=aZrX3aXsZ4qE.
11. *SEC v. Madoff*, SEC Litigation Release No. 20889 (2009).
12. See Pengelly, *Madoff Fraud Puts Focus on Fund Due Diligence*, 22 London Issue 1, at 8 (Jan. 2009).
13. Efrati and Frank, *supra* note 9, at A1.
14. See Borzykowski, *The Question: How Do I Know that My Advisor Isn't Another Bernie Madoff?*, 82 Canadian Business, Issue 17, Sep. 29, 2009, at 80.
15. Efrati and Frank, *supra* note 9, at A1.
16. *Id.*
17. See Curran, *Traders Say Madoff's Strategy Was Unworkable*, Wall St. J., Dec. 24, 2008, at C5.
18. *Id.* See Tracy, *Madoff Strategy Put to Test—Credit Suisse Sees Gains of 8.6%; Factoring In a Collar,* Wall St. J., Apr. 15, 2009, at C6.
19. See Efrati and Frank, *supra* note 9, at A1.
20. See Creswell & Thomas, *The Talented Mr. Madoff*, Int'l Herald Tribune, Jan. 26, 2009, at 8.
21. *Madoff and Markets*, Wall St. J., Dec. 15, 2008, at A18.
22. See *Not Just Super Rich Caught Up in Madoff Case*, The Associated Pres MSNBC, Dec. 15, 2008, available at http://www.msnbc.msn.com/id/28226910/.
23. *Id.* See also, DeCambre, *Wilpon's Charity Is Targeted*, NY Post, March 15, 2011, at Bus. 1 (stating that the bankruptcy trustee seeks to recover from the Wilpon family trust "fictitious profits" made from the Madoff funds).
24. *Id.*
25. See Mintz, *Madoff: The Pain Runs Deep*, BusinessWeek Online, Dec. 18, 2008, at 7.
26. The Wall Street Journal, *Madoff's Victims*, http://s.wsj.net/public/resources/documents/st_madoff_victims_20081215.html.
27. *Id.*
28. *Id.*
29. *Id.*
30. Mintz, *supra* note 25, at 7.
31. *Id.*

32. Gauthier-Villars, *Financier's Own Fortune Led Investors to Madoff*, Wall St. J., Dec. 29, 2008, at C1 ("relatives say they doubt they will be able to keep Mr. de La Villehuchet's crown jewel: a riverside chateau in the Brittany village of Plouer-sur-Rance, which has belonged to the family since 1695").
33. See Lauricella and Patterson, *With Roots in '70's, Madoff Scheme Takes New Toll—Vienna's Bank Medici Had About $ 2.1 Billion Invested; Earliest Suspicions About Returns Now Date Back to '91*, Wall St. J., Dec. 24, 2008, at A7.
34. Mintz, *supra* note 25, at 7.
35. *Id.*
36. See Lowenfels and Bromberg, *How Did Madoff 'Pull It Off'?*, 43 Sec. Reg. L. Rep. (BNA) 550, 551 (2011).
37. *Id.*
38. See Scannell, *SEC Had Chances for Years to Expose Madoff's Alleged Ponzi Scheme*, Wall St. J., Dec. 15, 2008, at A16.
39. Henriques, *Madoff Says S.E.C. Exams Were a 'Nightmare,'* New York Times Dealbook, Oct. 30, 2009, available at http://dealbook.blogs.nytimes.com/2009/10/30/sec-releases-details-of-madoff-report/.
40. Zweig, *The Intelligent Investor: How Bernie Madoff Made Smart Folks Look Dumb*, Wall St. J., Dec. 13, 2008, at B1. See Gelles and Tett, *Madoff Spins His Story,* Financial Times, April 9–10, 2011, at 1 (Life & Arts).
41. Levisohn, *Madoff: Lessons from a Disaster*, BusinessWeek Online, Mar. 16, 2009, at 13. See Zweig, *supra* note 40, at B1. See Gelles and Tett, *Madoff Spins His Story,* Financial Times, April 9–10, 2011, at 1 (Life & Arts).
42. Levisohn, *How to Make a Madoff*, BusinessWeek Online, Dec. 17, 2008, at 31.
43. See Gandel, *Wall Street's Latest Downfall: Madoff Charged with Fraud*, Time, Dec. 12, 2008, available at http://www.time.com/time/business/article/0,8816,1866154,00.html.
44. See Scannell, *supra* note 38, at A16.
45. *Id.*
46. See M. Steinberg and R. Ferrara, *Securities Practice: Federal and State Enforcement* (2d ed. 2001 and 2011 supp.).
47. Thomsen, *Testimony on Madoff Investment Securities Matter,* 24 Regulatory Register 25 (2009).
48. *Id.*
49. Lowenfels and Bromberg, *supra* note 36, at 551.
50. Report of the Office of Inspector General of the SEC, Case No. OIG-509 at pp. 429, 456–457, 2009 WL 2981882 (FINCRIS) (Aug. 31, 2009).
51. Scannell, *supra* note 38, at A16 (quoting U.S. Senator Charles Grassley).
52. *Id.* See Torbenson, *Chief: SEC Has Learned from Past,* Dallas Morning News, April 9, 2011 at 1D ("Pummeled by congressional critics for missing the biggest financial frauds of our time, the Securities and Exchange Commission has been retooled and re-energized to police a complex financial landscape, its chairman said. ...").

53. Senate Report No. 111-176, Section 411—Custody of Client Assets (April 30, 2010).
54. *Id.* (quoting testimony of Professor John Coffee).
55. See Rothfeld and Bray, *Widow to Return $7.2 Billion*, Wall St. J., Dec. 18–19, 2010, at B1. These funds constituted the largest amount ever recouped through a civil forfeiture proceeding. By opting to settle this proceeding, the widow Mrs. Picower "has acted in contrast to hundreds of others accused by the trustee of ignoring warning signs of the fraud or profiting from the scheme." *Id.*
56. *Madoff Trustee Has Recovered $10 Billion to Repay Customers; $7.2B Now in Escrow*, 43 Sec. Reg. & L. Rep. (BNA) 536 (2011).
57. *Id.* See Rothfeld and Bray, *supra* note 55, at B1.
58. See Zweig, *supra* note 40, at B1. See also, Wyatt, *S.E.C. Hurt by Disarray in Its Books,* N.Y. Times, Business Day, Feb. 2, 2011 (reporting that the General Accounting Office (GAO) had found that the SEC's "books were in such disarray that it had failed at some of the [SEC's] most fundamental tasks").

Sentence Hearing

UNITED STATES DISTRICT COURT
SOUTHERN DISTRICT OF NEW YORK

UNITED STATES OF AMERICA
v. 09 CR 213 (DC)
BERNARD L. MADOFF,

Defendant

New York, N.Y.
June 29, 2009
10:00 a.m.

Before:

HON. DENNY CHIN,

District Judge

THE COURT: Please be seated. Good morning. Mr. Madoff, would you please stand.

Mr. Madoff, you pled guilty on March 12th, 2009 to 11 counts of securities fraud, investment advisor fraud, wire and mail fraud, money laundering, making false statements, perjury, filing false documents with the SEC and theft from employee benefit funds. You are here this morning to be sentenced for those crimes

Have you reviewed the presentence report?

THE DEFENDANT: Yes, I have, your Honor.

THE COURT: Did you discuss it with your lawyers?

THE DEFENDANT: I have.

THE COURT: Mr. Sorkin, have you reviewed the presentence report and discussed it with your client?

MR. SORKIN: Yes, your Honor, we have.

THE COURT: Do you or your client have any objections to the factual recitations or the guidelines calculations?

MR. SORKIN: We do not, your Honor.

THE COURT: Thank you. You can be seated.

Ms. Baroni, does the government have any objections to the presentence report?

MS. BARONI: No, your Honor.

THE COURT: Thank you.

I accept and adopt the factual recitations set forth in the presentence report. I accept and adopt the guidelines calculation set forth in the presentence report with one clarification. ...

[In this matter,] the guideline range is not life imprisonment, but 150 years, the maximum sentences for each of the 11 counts added together. Of course, in light of *Booker* [125 S. Ct. 738 (2005)] and the case law that followed, the guideline range is advisory only. While I must give the guideline range fair and respectful consideration, I am not bound by it. In fact, the Probation Department recommends a sentence of 50 years. Instead I must make an individualized assessment based on all the facts and circumstances, including the factors set forth in the statute. In the end, I must impose a sentence that is reasonable.

We will proceed as follows:

First we will hear from the victims. Then Mr. Sorkin will speak on behalf of Mr. Madoff. Next Mr. Madoff may speak if he wishes. Finally, I will hear from the government.

First the victims. I have received several hundred written statements from victims including the e-mails and letters submitted back in March. Every victim who made a timed request to speak will be permitted to speak today except in two instances. Two members of the same family asked to speak, and we will permit one person to speak on behalf of the family. Two victims have now withdrawn their request. Accordingly, we will hear from 9 victims today.

First we will hear from Mr. and Mrs. Ambrosino. The Ambrosinos can step up to the microphone. Go ahead. Mr. Ambrosino, go ahead. Come up to the microphone so everyone can hear you.

MR. AMBROSINO: Thank you, your Honor. My name is Dominic Ambrosino.

THE COURT: Sir, just keep your voice up.

MR. AMBROSINO: I thank the court for allowing me to speak today. As a retired New York City Correction Officer, I am very familiar with the inside of a courtroom. However, I never in my wildest dreams ever expected to be sitting in one as a victim of an indescribably heinous crime—

THE COURT: Mr. Ambrosino, slow down a touch so our Court Reporter can transcribe what you're saying.

MR. AMBROSINO: That dream came true on March 12th as I watched Bernie Madoff stand and be cuffed. However, the dream really started as a nightmare on December 11th. I can remember the exact second my wife told me the news. I immediately knew all the ramifications, but I don't think she did. The fallout from having your entire life savings drop right out from under your nose is truly like nothing you can ever describe. As [*sic*] first it was the obvious, and how will we pay our bills? How can someone do this to us?

We worked honestly and we worked so hard. This can't be real. We did nothing wrong.

I don't know if anyone other than another victim can explain what the less obvious effects are, how every decision directly and indirectly hinged on the fact that we had the security of our savings. When I was able to leave the job, we bought a motor home to travel the country. We took out a mortgage since it was better to keep our savings in Madoff. We sold the house my wife lived in for 27 years and also put all those profits—and they were high—into our Madoff account. We trusted that the saving and planning would see us through our retirement.

We had ideas of traveling the country. It all stopped abruptly on December 11th. As a result, we are left with no permanent house, a depreciating motor home, we are upside down on the loan and an income from my pension that is our life. This pension used to be perceived as spending money before December 11th, and now although it doesn't cover our monthly expenses, we rely on it fully. It is all we have.

I sustained a 52 percent hearing loss on my job, and I can't go back to my previous career so I have taken on a job this summer in Arizona as a construction project coordinator. The job will only last until August. Then I don't know what I am going to do.

My wife's foot was run over by a van while in New York City. There was a plea hearing in March. She had a job lined up before the trip. The expenses of the trip were given to us and we had to let it go since she was in a cast for eight weeks. She is now rehabilitating and still feels pain when she stands for long periods of time.

With that background as to who I am, I would like to share some of the specific problems Madoff's crime brought to us. My pension distribution, a one-time decision, were based on the fact that we had savings and security with Madoff. If I should die, my wife is left without my income or health insurance.

We sold our home in New York with the expectation that someday we would have the finances to purchase another one. We have no credit now and can't get a mortgage. We have been forced to take care of people's homes while they are traveling for the summer, as we used to do prior to December 11th.

We have through the generosity of friends been able to stay rent free on the RV lots of other people in the community. This will come to a screeching halt in October when the owners return for the winter season. We don't know where we'll go at that time. We don't have enough income from my pension to pay monthly rent.

The most devastating to us is we lost our freedom. We lost the ability to share our life every day as we explore the country every day. We lost the time to hold hands as we walked. As they say in the commercial, this is priceless.

In closing, I would like to say, Judge Chin, sentencing Bernard L. Madoff to the fullest extent will certainly not eliminate any of the issues I wrote about. It probably won't even gain me satisfaction. As the guard who used to be on the right side of the prison bars, I'll know what Mr. Madoff's experience will be and will know that he is in prison in much the same way he imprisoned us as well as others.

He took from us the freedom that we held so preciously close to our lives, the very thing I always valued and never took for granted. In a sense, I would like someone in the court today to tell me how long is my sentence.

Thank you very much.

THE COURT: Thank you. Next we'll hear from Mr. and Mrs. FitzMaurice.

MS. EBEL: No, Judge Chin. I am next.

THE COURT: I saw the gentleman standing up next and I thought you were Maureen Ebel.

MS. EBEL: Yes, I am. I am here with my brother, William Thomas McDonough.

THE COURT: All right.

MS. EBEL: My name is Maureen Ebel and I am a victim of Bernard L. Madoff.

I have lost all of my life's hard-earned savings. I have lost my life savings because of our government has failed me and thousands and thousands of other citizens. There are many levels of government complicity in this crime. The Securities and Exchange Commission, by its total incompetence and criminal negligence, has allowed a psychopath to steal from me and steal from the world.

I am a 61-year-old widow and I am now working full time. I have done many things to survive since December 11th, including selling a lot of my possessions and working three jobs at the same time. I have lost a home that my husband and I had owned for 25 years because of this theft.

I have lost my ability to care for myself in my old age. I have lost the ability to donate to charity, especially the Leukemia and Lymphoma Society. I have lost the ability to donate my time working for the charity as I had done in the past because now I must work full time in order to eat.

I have lost the ability to help future generations of my family get an education. I have lost the ability to help them with their housing needs. It pains me so much to remember my husband getting up in the middle of the night. He was a very fine physician. He would get up in the middle of the night year after year in all kinds of weather to go to the hospital to save someone's life in rain, ice and snow.

He would save someone's life so that Bernie Madoff could buy his wife another party rock. I have lost the ability to move around the world freely at this state in my life using the money my husband and I have worked so hard to earn. We had worked, saved and planned for our old age so that we could leave something behind and not be a burden when we became sick and old.

The emotional toll that this has taken on me has been devastating. I have had great pain and suffering at the hands of Bernie Madoff. My health deteriorated rapidly after December 11th. I could not eat or sleep. I was very agitated and hyperactive. I had all the signs and symptoms of someone undergoing great stress. I suffered rapid weight loss, rapid heart rate, sweating, insomnia and sometimes spells.

I had the horrible feeling that I had been pushed into the great black abyss, but I could not indulge these paralyzing feelings too long. I had work to do. While experiencing all these symptoms, I had to sell my home of 25 years, sell my car, sell my possessions and go to work full time. I accepted gifts of money from family and friends to pay for heat, electricity, gasoline and food.

I was the recipient of so many kindnesses and saw so much goodness in people. Goodness in people is something that you, Mr. Madoff, have been blind to your whole life, and that goodness is better than all the yachts and all the French homes in all the world put together.

Sadly, Mr. Madoff not only defrauded thousands of investors, he mastered the art of manipulating our government. FINRA and the Securities and Exchange Commission became his tools. They were willing to relax all regulations that would have uncovered his fraud. The justification for relaxing the regulations was to ease the burden on Wall Street firms, the very firm that bankrupted the world economy.

THE COURT: Ms. Ebel, this is not the time to criticize the agencies. That is not before me. What is before me is what sentence to impose, so if you would address that, please.

MS. EBEL: I will, Judge Chin.

Mr. Madoff, I have read you will be making a statement about your guilt and shame. I do not believe you. Judge Chin, Mr. Madoff should stay in jail until every person who enabled him to cause such a massive devastation is brought to justice. He should stay in jail until the families of every one of his victims are able to restore their financial stability. That could easily take 150 years. Thank you.

THE COURT: Thank you. Next we'll hear from Mr. and Mrs. FitzMaurice.

MR. FITZMAURICE: Thank you, Judge Chin, for allowing us to be heard in your courtroom today.

My wife and I here are today representing the thousands of Madoff victims. We have all suffered extensively as a result of his actions. It has been well chronicled that Madoff did not limit his treachery to a few. He stole from the rich, he stole from the poor and he stole from the in-between. He had no boundaries. He stole from individuals as well as charitable organizations of all types and denominations.

My wife and I are not millionaires. He has taken our entire life savings. We have not been overlooked just as many of his other victims. We have worked hard, long and hard for all of our lives to provide for our family and to be in a position to retire someday. I am now forced to work three jobs. My wife is working a full-time job only to make ends meet, to allow us to pay our mortgage and put food on the table.

We are 63 years' [*sic*] old. It will be no retirement for us in the next two or three years. There will be no trips to California to visit our one-year-old grandson. There will be no vacations of any type. Again we are too old to recoup the monies that he has taken from us. We can only work as long as our health will hold up and then we will have to sell our home and hope to survive on social security alone.

Madoff has shown no remorse. Please do not confuse his prepared statement as remorse. His crime was premeditated and calculated. He was attempting to scam investors only days before his arrest. If he had the opportunity, he would still be stealing from innocent investors. He has not truly cooperated with the authorities to recover the money that rightfully belongs to his investors, whom we are now known as victims.

He cheated his victims out of their money so that he and his wife Ruth and their two sons could live a life of luxury beyond belief. This life is normally reserved for royalty, not for common thieves.

Your Honor, we implore you to give him the maximum sentence at a maximum prison for this evil lowlife. This would be true justice. Minimum security prison would only allow Madoff too many freedoms that he does not deserve. He would be leading a life better than a lot of his victims. That is not true justice. His was a violent crime without the use of a tangible weapon.

His attorney will argue for a lenient sentence of up to twelve years. That is both insulting and another example of Madoff's arrogance. The scope of the devastation he has wreaked is unparalleled. It is impossible to compare his crime to any past criminal act. The pain he has inflicted will continue for many years. My life will never be the same. I am financially ruined and will worry every day about how I will take care of my wife.

Where will we be able to live? How will we pay our bills? How will we get medical insurance?

All of his victims worldwide will be waiting to see that true justice is served. True justice is a maximum sentence in a maximum security prison. I have a quotation from my wife, since only one of us could speak. She wants to say:

"I cry every day when I see the look of pain and despair in my husband's eyes. I cry for the life we once had before that monster took it away. Our two sons and daughter-in-law have rallied with constant love and support. You, on the other hand, Mr. Madoff, have two sons that despise you. Your wife, rightfully so, has been vilified and shunned by her friends in the community. You have left your children a legacy of shame. I have a marriage made in heaven. You have a marriage made in hell, and that is where you, Mr. Madoff, are going to return. May God spare you no mercy."

THE COURT: Thank you. Next we will hear from Carla Hirschhorn.

MS. HIRSCHIHORN: Good morning and thank you, your Honor, for allowing me to address you.

My husband and I write to you to explain the devastation caused by Bernard L. Madoff to our lives. Since 1992 we were invested with Bernard L. Madoff Investment Securities. We have never been rich people. We have worked throughout all our adult lives. Over the years my husband has worked hard to learn a trade as a glazer which afforded him the opportunity to start a small business. I have been a physical therapist and worked through to the day I was graduated from college in 1980. We have both diligently saved our hard-earned money to invest with Bernard Madoff over the years. We used our money to raise our children, purchase our home and put our savings in Bernard Madoff Securities.

Since December 11th, 2008 life has been a living hell. It feels like a nightmare that we can't wake up from. I am so thankful that my father died two years ago and was spared from having to live in his terminal condition without the money to provide him 24/7 health care which allowed him to die with dignity.

My father died and left my mother believing she would be able to live a safe and secure life with the money in her Bernard Madoff accounts. Now all she has to live on is a sparse social security check and a small pension which will last less than one year. She may not have enough money to maintain her home and living expenses.

It is our hope and in our prayers she does not become ill and require extraordinary means to sustain her. Our daughter who sits in this courtroom today to witness this horrific event is a junior at college and has worked two jobs since our Madoff accounts were stolen while going to school full time. The stress and worry about her family's financial situation and health of her parents has been devastating to her. We have no idea how we will continue to pay for college without it being a terrible financial burden and worry on all of us.

Immediately after hearing the news of the ponzi scheme, we filed papers for financial aid to sustain our daughter through college. We were informed we were not eligible for any grant money, that our only hope would be to take out loans. However, in this financial environment, without SIPIC insurance and with concern about claw-back litigation, we can't possibly take loans out to send our daughter to college. The turmoil caused by our financial devastation has caused us serious physical and emotional problems from which we need medical treatment.

Your Honor, please understand that we, the investors, have been punished by Madoff's crime. We were devastated by the SEC's failure to uncover Madoff's fraud and its continued stamp of approval behind Madoff over the decades of his crime. We have been abandoned by our elected officials which refuse to require the SEC to find income. We have been betrayed by SIPIC, which in order to save money, has invented a new definition of net equity to deprive us of the $500,000 of insurance which we were assured.

Please, your Honor, do not fail us. Please assure that Madoff is sentenced with the maximum possible time and he is required to serve his sentence in a maximum security prison. This is not a man who deserves a federal country club.

Respectfully, Carla Hirschhorn.

THE COURT: Thank you.

It is not up to me, by the way, where Mr. Madoff will be designated. A number of people have made that suggestion, but it is up to the Bureau of Prisons.

Next we'll hear from Sharon Lissauer.

MS. LISSAUER: My name is Sharon Lissauer. Thank you, your Honor, for letting me speak. I am very emotional, so please bear with me if I break down into tears. As everyone knows, this nightmare has begun six and a half months ago and yet it seems like a lifetime.

I keep on thinking I am going to wake up from it. It keeps on getting worse. My life and my future have been ruined. I was always so careful with my money, but I entrusted everything I had to Mr. Madoff, my whole life savings from modeling and the inheritance of my mom. She just died last year, and as soon as I got the money, because I just miss her and I trusted Mr. Madoff so much, I gave it all to him, but now I don't have my mom or the money.

I know I am not alone. I know he has ruined thousands of people's lives. In the March hearing he said that he was truly sorry, which I don't really believe, but even if it is a little bit true, then I am not asking him, I am begging him, if he has any money from the offshore accounts or his family has any money obtained from this horrible fraud, that they disgorge it and give it back to the victims so they can have a little bit of their lives back.

With respect to his sentencing, I used to think that it didn't matter if he got 150 years, what would that do for the victims? It wouldn't get their money back. But now upon reflection, I think he should spend his whole life in jail because of what he has done is just despicable. He has ruined so many people's lives. He killed my spirit and shattered my dreams. He destroyed my trust in people. He destroyed my life, and I have no other assets. I make very little money from modeling and he left me in a very difficult position to pay my bills and support myself. For the first time in my life I am very, very frightened of my future.

Thank you, your Honor.

THE COURT: Thank you.

Next we'll hear from Burt Ross. Mr. Ross.

MR. ROSS: Your honor, my name is Burt Ross and my wife Joan and I lost $5 million because of the criminal acts of Bernard Madoff. Not only have I lost the inheritance of my father who worked for his entire life so that his children and his children's children can leave [*sic*] a better life, I have lost our retirement accounts and funds in trust for our children.

The fact is though we are one of the fortunate ones because we still have a roof over our heads, food on our table, unlike so many others who have been forced to sell their homes, who have been forced to sell their homes and pick up the pieces of their lives.

Years ago I attended a Friends [*sic*] secondary school where we thought that in each person there was an inner light, that of God and everyone. For the life of me, as far as I have searched, I cannot find that inner light in Bernard Madoff.

What can we possibly say about Madoff, that he was a philanthropist, when the money he gave to charities he stole from the very same charities he ultimately devastated; that he was a good family man when he leaves his grandchildren a name that mortifies them, a name which they will live in infamy; that he is genuinely remorseful for his conduct when the statement he read in this very court was totally without emotion, when even after confessing he fought to keep assets away from those he hurt, when we all know his only regret was getting caught.

Can we say Madoff was a righteous Jew who served on the boards of Jewish institutions when he sank so low, when he sank so low as to steal from Elie Weisel, as if Weisel hasn't already suffered enough in his lifetime.

A righteous Jew, when in reality nobody has done more to reinforce the ugly stereotype that all we care about is money the fact is there are no people on this earth more charitable? But we will survive. We have survived worse than Madoff.

What Bernard L. Madoff did far transcends the loss of money. It involves his betrayal of the virtues people hold dearest—love, friendship, trust—and all so he can eat at the finest restaurants, stay at the most luxurious resorts, and travel on yachts and private jets. He has truly earned his reputation for being the most despised person to be in America today.

Several hundred years ago the Italian poet Dante in his "The Divine Comedy" recognized fraud as the worst of sins, the ultimate evil more than any other act contrary to God's greatest gift to mankind—love. In fact, he placed the perpetrators of fraud in the lowest depths of hell, even below those who had committed violent acts. ...

Please allow me to take a liberty now by speaking for many of those victims who because of frailty, privacy, distance, or other reasons are unable to bear witness today. We urge your Honor to commit Madoff to prison for the remainder of his natural life, and when he leaves this earth virtually unmourned, may Satan grow a fourth mouth where Bernard L. Madoff deserves to spend the rest of eternity.

Thank you.

THE COURT: Thank you. Next we'll hear from Michael Schwartz.

MR. SCHWARTZ: Can everyone hear me?

My name is Michael Schwartz. I am 33 years' [*sic*] old. It was my family's trust fund that helped fund the money for Bernard Madoff's organization. Since I was a teenager, I invested into what I thought was a forthright and legitimate investment firm. During this time I made sure I lived well within my means, nothing extravagant. I viewed my investment as a safety net in case I should hit hard times or perhaps face medical issues.

Unfortunately, several months ago, my job was regionalized, eliminated. I was handed a letter of recommendation and sent on my way. It didn't hit me until I got home that the company that you ran had already taken my life savings. At 33, I was wiped out.

I am one of the lucky ones by far. I have my health. I am young, I have great friends, got a loving wife. Unfortunately, the money you took from other members of my family wasn't a minor setback. It was quite a bit more. Your Honor, part of the trust fund wasn't set aside for a house in the Hamptons, a large yacht or box seat to the Mets. No, part of that money was set aside to take care of my twin brother who is mentally disabled, who at 33, he lives at home with my parents and will need care and supervision for the rest of his life.

In the final analysis, my family wants to remember that in addition to stealing from retirees, veterans, widows, Bernard Madoff stole from the disabled. Every time he cashed a check and paid for his family's decadent lifstyle, he killed dreams. My parents had a simple dream for my brother, a week at summer camp, someday being able to live in a good group home. Thanks to Bernard Madoff's greed, complete lack of ethics, that dream will be delayed.

At the end of the day my twin brother will be taken care of. My family is strong enough to weather this storm but, your Honor, I say this without any malice, Bernard Madoff should no longer be allowed back in society. I only hope that his prison sentence is long enough so that his jail cell becomes his coffin. Thank you.

THE COURT: Thank you.

We'll hear next from Miriam Siegman.

MS. SIEGMAN: I was born a few blocks from this courthouse. I still live here. On a cold winter's day just before my 65th birthday, the man sitting in front of me announced to the world that he had stolen everything I had. After that he refused to say another word to his victims. I am here today to bear witness for myself and others, silent victims.

The streets of my childhood felt safe. The streets I wander now feel threatening. The man sitting in this courtroom robbed me. In an instant his words and deeds beat me to near senselessness. He discarded me like road kill. Victims became the byproduct of his greed. We are what is left over, the remnants of stunning indifference and that of politicians and bureaucrats.

Six months have passed. I manage on food stamps. At the end of the month I sometimes scavage in dumpsters. I cannot afford new eyeglasses. I long to go to a concert, but I never do. Sometimes my heartbeats [*sic*] erratically for lack of medication when I cannot pay for it.

I shine my shoes each night, afraid they will wear out. My laundry is done by hand in the kitchen sink. I have collected empty cans and dragged them to the redemption centers.

I do this now. People ask how are you? My answer always is I'm fine, but it is not always true. I have lived with fear. It strikes me at all hours. I calculate again and again how long I can hold out.

It is only a matter of time. I will be unable to meet my own basic needs, food, shelter, medicine. I feel grief at no longer being able to help support my beloved sister. I feel shame and humiliation asking for help.

I also feel overwhelming sadness. I know that another human being did this to me and to all the victims, but I don't know why. What I do understand frightens me. The man who did this had deep contempt for his victims.

There are many victims including those we never hear from or see; union members, pipe-fitters, laborers, women who work in nursing homes, bricklayers, firemen, working people. One victim shot himself. The inquest informs us he was a highly decorated former soldier who could not face the shame of his ruin, his last words on a humanitarian mission in Afghanistan. By self-admission, this thief among us knew his victims were facing a kind of death at his hands, yet he continued to play with us as a cat would with a mouse.

What shall be the punishment for such a man? What sentence? Carry the burden we carry, feel his shame, humiliation and isolation as I do. Feel it each day wherever you are until life ends.

Face and acknowledge the murderous effects of your life's work. I long for the truth that might become of a trial and hope justice had placed a higher premium on truth and expediency. Forgiveness for now, it will have to come from someone other than me.

THE COURT: Thank you. Finally we'll hear from Sheryl Weinstein.

MS. WEINSTEIN: Hello, your Honor.

THE COURT: Good morning.

MS. WEINSTEIN: I was introduced to Bernard Madoff 21 years ago at a business meeting. At the time I was the chief financial officer of Hadassah, a charitable women's organization. I now view that day as perhaps the unluckiest day of my life because of the many events set into motion that would eventually have the most profound and devastating effect on me, my husband, my child, my parents, my in-laws and all those who depended upon us for their liveliness.

You have read and you appear from many of us, the old, the young, the healthy and infirm about the unimaginable extent of human tragedy and devastation. According to a Time Magazine article, there are over 3 million individuals worldwide who have been directly or indirectly affected. They, the press and the media, speak of us as being greedy and rich. Most of us are just ordinary working people, worker bees, as I like to refer to us.

My husband and I are now both in our 60's [*sic*] and have been married for 37 years. We have saved for most of our lives by living beneath our means in order to provide for our retirement. This past Thursday at 2:00 o'clock my husband and I sold our home of 20 years. People are always asking how much did we lose? My reply is that when you lose everything, it really doesn't matter because you have nothing left, and we have lost everything.

Many have told us we were lucky—I no longer know—to be able to sell in this depressed market although at a greatly reduced amount. We had to sell because four years ago we refinanced our mortgage and gave the excess cash to Bernie Madoff. There was very little left over after all was said and done at the closing.

It is difficult to describe how it feels due to circumstances outside of your control to be virtually forced out of your home, to leave unwillingly. Last Tuesday I walked out following the movers with a thought I would be back before the closing, but knowing in the back of my mind that I wouldn't.

My husband was the last to be in our home. He shared with me his hesitation of not wanting to leave, of wanting to remain, but realizing that staying was no longer an option. We chose not to go to the closing because it would have been too difficult and painful for either of us to be there. For months after December 11th I would wake in the dark hours of the night and early morning and to my horror realize that there was no calming, soothing words I could say to myself because it wasn't a dream. The monster who visited me was true, a reality. Those same thoughts would occur to me upon waking in the morning and during the day and a deep, heavy depression would surround me and not lift.

This went on for many months. I went on after bad dreams, virtually not unable to eat. The sight of food was making me feel sick, unable to escape the reality of my personal devastation. At times I could not even bear to be alone. I would ask my friends to either stay with me at the office even if there was very little work to do. It would prompt me to pick up the phone to call my husband to be reassured I was not alone.

This continued until March 12th when Madoff entered his plea of guilty. I began to speak out to the media, and the helpless and hopeless feelings began to retreat and I began to feel empowered. It came together for me while being interviewed by Katie Couric. She asked me wasn't I embarrassed being a CPA losing all my money? At that moment I realized and responded no, I am not embarrassed because I did not lose my money. My money was stolen from me.

Ms. Couric said to me you sound angry, and I said yes, you're right. When someone steals from you, you get angry. That was the beginning of my healing process.

I felt it was important for somebody who is personally acquainted with Madoff to speak. My family and I are not anonymous people to him. He knows my husband's name is Rob and my son's name is Eric. In fact, Eric worked for him one summer while in college many years ago. Eric would continue to call him over the years to ask for his advice and input. Eric entrusted him with his money that he worked and saved. A few months before all this happened Eric had spoken to him and thanked him for doing such a good job.

I would now like to have the opportunity to share with you my personal feelings about Madoff and to speak to his sentencing.

I remember when my son was perhaps a few weeks' [*sic*] old and I would watch him as he slept and he would whimper, not a cry of hunger, but a whimper. Even at a few weeks old there was something about his subconscious that could frighten him. It amazed me such a young child, an infant can have nightmares.

All of us from our earliest ages remember those times when the terror, the monsters and goblins would come visit us in those dark hours. Eventually we would be so frightened that we would awake sometimes calling out to our parents because of the fear.

It was calming to have our parents remind us it was only a dream. As we got older, we could wake ourselves and self-assure ourselves it was only a dream. That terror, that monster, that horror, that beast has a name to me, and it is Bernard L. Madoff. I will now attempt to explain to you the nature of this beast who I call Madoff.

He walks among us. He dresses like us. He drives and eats and drinks and speaks. Under the facade there is truly a beast. He is a beast that has stolen for his own needs the livelihoods, savings, lives, hopes and dreams and futures of others in total disregard. He has fed upon us to satisfy his own needs. No matter how much he takes and from whom he takes, he is never satisfied. He is an equal opportunity destroyer.

I felt it important for you to know in appearance, he would be just like everybody else and it is for this reason I am asking your Honor to keep him in a cage behind bars because he has lost the privilege of walking and being among us mortal human beings. He should not be given the opportunity to walk into our society again.

I would like to suggest that while any man, woman or child that has been affected by his heinous crime still walks this earth, Madoff the beast should not be free to walk among them. You should protect society from the likes of him. I have reread Madoff's March 12th statement to you. Certain quotes jumped out at me. His continuing self-serving references, and I quote, that his proprietary trading in the market making business managed by his brother and two sons was legitimate, profitable and successful in all respects, or that he felt, "compelled to satisfy my clients' expectations at any cost."

It sounds as if he is laying the blame on his clients' expectations and never admitting the truth he was stealing from these clients and the lives he ruined. If he was attempting to protect his family, he should not be given that opportunity because we, the victims, did not have the same opportunity to protect our families. Madoff the beast has stolen our ability to protect our loved ones away from us. He should have no opportunity to protect his family.

We, the victims, are greatly disappointed by those agencies that were set up to protect us. SIPIC has now redefined what we are entitled to. The IRS approved their office request to be a custodian of our IRSs [*sic*] and pension funds and the SEC appears to have looked the other way on numerous occasions. This is a human tragedy of historic proportions and we ask—no, we implore—that those whose agencies may have failed us in the past through acts of omissions, step up to the plate, fulfill their responsibilities. I thank your Honor for your indulgence and I feel comfortable you will make sure justice is served.

Thank you.

THE COURT: Thank you.

Thanks to all the victims who spoke today and to all those who wrote. I appreciate hearing your views.

Mr. Sorkin.

MR. SORKIN: Good morning, your Honor.

THE COURT: Good morning.

...

MR. SORKIN: Your Honor, I know I speak on behalf of all Mr. Madoff's counsel as well as Mr. Madoff who will speak. We cannot be unmoved by what we heard. There is no way that we cannot be insensitive to the victims' suffering.

This is a tragedy as some of the victims have said at every level. There is no doubt Mr. Madoff will speak. We represent a deeply flawed individual, be we represent, your Honor, a human being. We don't represent a statistic. We don't represent a number. We speak to the victims. We have heard what they've had to say and we can only imagine, your Honor, what we would have heard from others.

I say again, forgive me for being redundant, we represent a very flawed individual, an individual who appears before this court facing a sentence that is sufficient but not unreasonably necessary to carry out the mandate that this court has to carry out.

The magnificence of our legal system, your Honor, is that we do not seek an eye for an eye. To be sure, if it is any consolation to the victims, we have worked hopefully diligently with the U.S. Attorney's Office in an atmosphere of trying to recover assets. To that extent, your Honor, we have provided the government with what we believe to be the assets that Mr. Madoff has gathered over the years which the victims have referred to, and again if it is any consolation to them, to the extent that the government has left him and his family, his wife impoverished, we are just about there with respect to everything the government believes it can show in order to obtain the appropriate assets for forfeiture.

Vengeance is not the goal of punishment. Our system of justice, your Honor, has recognized that justice is and must always be blind and fair—not blind to the criminal acts that Mr. Madoff pleaded guilty to and certainly not blind to the suffering of the victims, but blind to the extent that it will achieve a sentence that has been set out over the years in the guidelines and the cases interpreting the guidelines, and the guidelines and the courts and the statutes, your Honor, do not speak of vengeance and revenge.

... For the government to ask for 150 years so that Mr. Madoff gets out of jail at the age of 221 because he is 71 now, he will face supervised release. By the same token, your Honor, it defies reason for the Probation Department to suggest that he be sentenced to 50 years in prison for the very same reasons.

I point out to the court, and forgive me, your Honor, for repeating what is in the letter we sent you most recently, that Mr. Madoff, as he pleaded to, as appears in the presentence report and appears in the information in which the government agrees, for most of the period of time that Mr. Madoff is alleged to have engaged in this ponzi scheme and, in fact, it was a ponzi scheme, it was money in and money out.

Most of the money went for redemptions. People who invested money were given back money. To be sure, it was fraud. To be sure, it was a ponzi scheme. To be sure, it was a crime, but nevertheless, your Honor, I point out, and in response respectfully to some of the victims, I think it is common knowledge in the industry that Mr. Madoff built up this firm on the proprietary trading side to the point in 1991, as the presentence report points out, the proprietary trading side which at the point of his arrest had approximately 200 employees separate and apart from the fraudulent advisory business, a hundred traders making markets and in 1991, your Honor, accounted for almost 10 percent of all transactions on the New York Stock Exchange.

Sufficient to provide revenue at the same time Mr. Madoff engaged in taking money in and taking money out, most of that money went for redemptions. As we point out in our letter of yesterday, and as the government notes, the loans, the commingling, and we do dispute this with the government, but I don't think it is a relevant issue, the commingling, the loans.

The loans, the commingling, commenced within the last eight to ten years. And as Mr. Madoff will say, things began to collapse. And then there was commingling with $250 million over the last eight or so years, of advisory money, as well as money in, money out of investments.

I think it's important to note, your Honor, again that Mr. Madoff stepped forward. He chose not to flee. He chose not to hide money. To the extent money is overseas, we are still actively engaged—we, his defense counsel—in assisting the government, at the request of the government, to obtain assets located overseas, as we speak, and we submitted that voluntarily, and we have been trying to help, with Mr. Madoff's authorization, permission, and blessing.

Mr. Madoff is 71 years old, your Honor. Based upon his health, his family history, his life expectancy, that is why we ask for a sentence of 12 years, just short, based upon the statistics that we have, of a life sentence.

We also said, if your Honor is inclined, your Honor obviously makes the decision, 15 to 20 years. So that if Mr. Madoff ever sees the light of day, in his 90s, impoverished and alone, he will have paid a terrible price. He expects, your Honor, to live out his years in prison.

Your Honor, as we noted in our letter to you, that the loss in this case is $13,226,000,000. What has not been heard publicly, your Honor, is the fact that over $1,276,000,000 is held by the SIPC trustee, and we have no control over how that money is disbursed. And I say this for the victims we have heard. Again, we have no control over what the SIPC trustee does with the money that he obtains, nor do we have any control over what the SEC will do, nor do we have any control as to how the government to whom we have forfeited all of the assets but a few, which the government and we have agreed were weighed against the risk of litigation, we have no control how that money is disbursed.

Additionally to the $1,276,000,000, the SIPC trustee has recovered $1,225,000,000, has sent demand letters to individuals for 735 million, and has commenced litigation to seek a clawback from some very large funds to obtain redemptions and interest payments in the amount of $10,100,000,000. It is our hope, your Honor, our sincerest hope, that all the money is collected, in an amount in excess of $13,226,000,000, that that will be provided to investors.

The frenzy, the media excitement, that Mr. Madoff engaged in a Ponzi scheme involving $65 billion and that he has ferreted money away, as far as we know, your Honor, that is simply not true, and it is not borne out by the government.

In closing, your Honor, there is no question that this case has taken an enormous toll, not only on Mr. Madoff and his family, but to the victims to be sure. But it has also taken a toll, your Honor, as Mr. Madoff will say, on the industry that he helped revolutionize, that he helped grow, and now has become the object of disrespect and abomination, and that is a tragedy as well.

We ask only, your Honor, that Mr. Madoff be given understanding and fairness, within the parameters of our legal system, and that the sentence that he be given be sufficient, but not greater than necessary, to carry out what this Court must carry out under the rules, statutes and guidelines.

Thank you, your Honor.

THE COURT: Thank you.

Mr. Madoff, if you would like to speak, now is the time.

THE DEFENDANT: Your Honor, I cannot offer you an excuse for my behavior. How do you excuse betraying thousands of investors who entrusted me with their life savings? How do you excuse deceiving 200 employees who have spent most of their working life working for me? How do you excuse lying to your brother and two sons who spent their whole adult life helping to build a successful and respectful business? How do you excuse lying and deceiving a wife who stood by you for 50 years, and still stands by you? And how do you excuse deceiving an industry that you spent a better part of your life trying to improve? There is no excuse for that, and I don't ask any forgiveness.

Although I may not have intended any harm, I did a great deal of harm. I believed when I started this problem, this crime, that it would be something I would be able to work my way out of, but that became impossible. As hard as I tried, the deeper I dug myself into a hole. I made a terrible mistake, but it wasn't the kind of mistake that I had made time and time again, which is a trading mistake. In my business, when you make a trading error, you're expected to make a trading error, it's accepted. My error was much more serious. I made an error of judgment. I refused to accept the fact, could not accept the fact, that for once in my life I failed. I couldn't admit that failure and that was a tragic mistake.

I am responsible for a great deal of suffering and pain. I understand that. I live in a tormented state now knowing all of the pain and suffering that I have created. I have left a legacy of shame, as some of my victims have pointed out, to my family and my grandchildren. That's something I will live with for the rest of my life.

People have accused me of being silent and not being sympathetic. That is not true. They have accused my wife of being silent and not being sympathetic. Nothing could be further from the truth. She cries herself to sleep every night knowing all of the pain and suffering I have caused, and I am tormented by that as well. She was advised to not speak publicly until after my sentencing by our attorneys, and she complied with that. Today she will make a statement about how she feels about my crimes. I ask you to listen to that. She is sincere and all I ask you is to listen to her.

Apologizing and saying I am sorry, that's not enough. Nothing I can say will correct the things that I have done. I feel terrible that an industry I spent my life trying to improve is being criticized terribly now, that regulators who I helped work with over the years are being criticized by what I have done. That is a horrible guilt to live with. There is nothing I can do that will make anyone feel better for the pain and suffering I caused them, but I will live with this pain, with this torment for the rest of my life.

I apologize to my victims. I will turn and face you. I am sorry. I know that doesn't help you.

Your Honor, thank you for listening to me.

THE COURT: Thank you.

Mr. Sorkin, did I understand Mr. Madoff to say that Mrs. Madoff wanted to speak?

MR. SORKIN: No, your Honor. Mrs. Madoff after the sentencing will be giving a statement. And I add what Mr. Madoff said about belaboring it, that she was advised by counsel to wait until after sentence.

THE COURT: I thought he was saying she wanted to speak. Thank you.

I will hear from the government.

MS. BARONI: This defendant carried out a fraud of unprecedented proportion over the course of more than a generation. For more than 20 years he stole ruthlessly and without remorse. Thousands of people placed their trust in him and he lied repeatedly to all of them. And as the Court heard from all of the victims, in their words and in the letters, he destroyed a lifetime of hard work of thousands of victims. And he used that victims' money to enrich himself and his family, with an opulent lifestyle, homes around the world, yachts, private jets, and tens of millions of dollars of loans to his family, loans of investors' money that has never been repaid.

The guideline sentence in this case, as your Honor knows, is 150 years and the government respectfully submits that a sentence of 150 years or a substantial term of imprisonment that will ensure that he spends the rest of his life in jail is appropriate in this case.

This was not a crime born of any financial distress or market pressures. It was a calculated, well orchestrated, long-term fraud, that this defendant carried out month after month, year after year, decade after decade. He created literally hundreds and hundreds of thousands of fake documents every year. Every time he told his clients that he was making trades for them he sent them trade confirmations filled with lies. At every month end he sent them account statements that were nothing but lies. And the defendant knew that his clients made critically important life decisions, as your Honor heard today, based on these lies. Decisions about their children's education, their retirement, how to care for elderly relatives, and how to provide for their families. He knew this, and he stole from them anyway.

In doing so, he drove charities, companies, pension plans and families to economic ruin. And even on the most dispassionate view of the evidence, the scale of the fraud, which is at a conservative estimate, your Honor, $13 billion, when you look at the duration of the fraud, which is more than 20 years, when you look at the fact that the defendant could have stopped this fraud and saved the victims' losses, all of these facts justify a guideline sentence of 150 years.

And to address briefly some of Mr. Sorkin's arguments, despite Mr. Sorkin's arguments, the defendant here deserves no leniency and certainly does not deserve a sentence of 12 years' imprisonment.

Mr. Sorkin tries to argue that the loss amount is actually going to be less than 13 billion because the trustee may recover some assets in clawback proceedings. As your Honor knows, that has nothing to do with the loss amount in this case. Further, the defendant shouldn't get any credit for anything the government or the trustee does after the fraud to recover money.

In asking for 12 years, your Honor, the defendant is asking you to impose a sentence that a defendant would receive in a garden variety fraud case in this district, a case with about $20 million of losses and far fewer victims. In imposing a 12 year sentence in this case, on the facts and circumstances here, would be profoundly unfair. Not only would it not reflect the seriousness and the scope of the defendant's crimes, but, also, it would not promote the goals of general deterrence going forward.

Mr. Sorkin's argument that the defendant should get some credit for coming forward and turning himself in is also entirely meritless. The defendant continued his fraud scheme until the very end, when he knew the scheme was days away from collapse, when he was almost out of money and when he was faced with redemption requests from clients that he knew he could not meet. And even at that point, rather than turning himself in, he tried to take the last of his victims' money. He prepared $173 million in checks that he planned to give to his family, his friends, and some preferred clients. It was his final effort to put his interests above those of his clients, and had the FBI not arrested him when they did, he might well have succeeded.

Your Honor, in sum, for running an investment advisory business that was a complete fraud, for betraying his clients for decades, and for repeatedly lying to regulators to cover up his fraud, for the staggering harm that he has inflicted on thousands of people, for all of these reasons and all of the reasons your Honor heard so eloquently from the victims, the government, respectfully requests that the Court sentence the defendant to 150 years in prison or a substantial term of imprisonment that ensures that he will spend the rest of his life in jail.

Thank you.

THE COURT: Thank you.

I take into account what I have read in the presentence report, the parties' sentencing submissions, and the e-mails and letters from victims. I take into account what I have heard today. I also consider the statutory factors as well as all the facts and circumstances in the case.

In his initial letter on behalf of Mr. Madoff, Mr. Sorkin argues that the unified tone of the victims' letters suggests a desire for mob vengeance. He also writes that Mr. Madoff seeks neither mercy nor sympathy, but justice and objectivity.

Despite all the emotion in the air, I do not agree with the suggestion that victims and others are seeking mob vengeance. The fact that many have sounded similar themes does not mean that they are acting together as a mob. I do agree that a just and proportionate sentence must be determined, objectively, and without hysteria or undue emotion.

Objectively speaking, the fraud here was staggering. It spanned more than 20 years. Mr. Madoff argues in his reply letter that the fraud did not begin until the 1990s. I guess it's more that the commingling did not begin until the 1990s, but it is clear that the fraud began earlier. And even if it is true that it only started in the 1990s, the fraud exceeded ten years, still an extraordinarily long period of time. The fraud reached thousands of victims.

As for the amount of the monetary loss, there appears to be some disagreement. Mr. Madoff disputes that the loss amount is $65 billion or even $13 billion. But Mr. Madoff has now acknowledged, however, that some $170 billion flowed into his business as a result of his fraudulent scheme. The presentence report uses a loss amount of $13 billion, but as I understand it, that number does not include the losses from moneys invested through the feeder funds. Mr. Madoff argues that the $13 billion amount should be reduced by the amounts that the SIPC trustee may be able to claw back, but that argument fails. Those clawbacks, if they happen, will result in others who suffered losses. Moreover, Mr. Madoff told his sons that there were $50 billion in losses. In any event, by any of these monetary measures, the fraud here is unprecedented.

...

Moreover, as many of the victims have pointed out, this is not just a matter of money. The breach of trust was massive.

Investors—individuals, charities, pension funds, institutional clients—were repeatedly lied to, as they were told their moneys would be invested in stocks when they were not. Clients were sent these millions of pages of account statements that the government just alluded to confirming trades that were never made, attesting to balances that did not exist. As the victims' letters and e-mails demonstrate, as the statements today demonstrate, investors made important life decisions based on these fictitious account statements—when to retire, how to care for elderly parents, whether to buy a car or sell a house, how to save for their children's college tuition. Charitable organizations and pension funds made important decisions based on false information about fictitious accounts. Mr. Madoff also repeatedly lied to the SEC and the regulators, in writing and in sworn testimony, by withholding material information, by creating false documents to cover up his scheme.

It is true that Mr. Madoff used much of the money to pay back investors who asked along the way to withdraw their accounts. But large sums were also taken by him, for his personal use and the use of his family, friends, and colleagues. For example, Mr. Madoff reported adjusted gross income of more than $250 million on his tax returns for the ten year period from 1998 through 2007. On numerous occasions, Mr. Madoff used his firm's bank accounts which contained customer funds to pay for his personal expenses and those of his family, including, for example, the purchase of a Manhattan apartment for a relative, the acquisition of two yachts, and the acquisition of four country club memberships at a cost of $950,000. Billions of dollars more were paid to individuals who generated investments for Mr. Madoff through these feeder funds.

Mr. Madoff argues a number of mitigating factors but they are less than compelling. It is true that he essentially turned himself in and confessed to the FBI. But the fact is that with the turn in the economy, he was not able to keep up with the requests of customers to withdraw their funds, and it is apparent that he knew that he was going to be caught soon. It is true that he consented to the entry of a $100 billion forfeiture order and has cooperated in transferring assets to the government for liquidation for the benefit of victims. But all of this was done only after he was arrested, and there is little that he could have done to fight the forfeiture of these assets. Moreover, the SIPC trustee has advised the Court Mr. Madoff has not been helpful, and I simply do not get the sense that Mr. Madoff has done all that he could or told all that he knows.

Mrs. Madoff has stipulated to the transfer of some $80 million dollars in assets to the government for the benefit of victims, but the record also shows that as it became clear that Mr. Madoff's scheme was unraveling, he made substantial loans to family members, he transferred some $15 million of firm funds into his wife's personal accounts, and he wrote out the checks that the government has just described.

I have taken into account the sentences imposed in other financial fraud cases in this district. But, frankly, none of these other cases is comparable to this case in terms of the scope, duration and enormity of the fraud, and the degree of the betrayal.

In terms of mitigating factors in a white-collar fraud case such as this, I would expect to see letters from family and friends and colleagues. But not a single letter has been submitted attesting to Mr. Madoff's good deeds or good character or civic or charitable activities. The absence of such support is telling.

We have heard much about a life expectancy analysis. Based on this analysis, Mr. Madoff has a life expectancy of 13 years, and he therefore asks for a sentence of 12 years or alternatively 15 to 20 years. If Mr. Sorkin's life expectancy analysis is correct, any sentence above 20 or 25 years would be largely, if not entirely, symbolic.

But the symbolism is important, for at least three reasons. First, retribution. One of the traditional notions of punishment is that an offender should be punished in proportion to his blameworthiness. Here, the message must be sent that Mr. Madoff's crimes were extraordinarily evil, and that this kind of irresponsible manipulation of the system is not merely a bloodless financial crime that takes place just on paper, but that it is instead, as we have heard, one that takes a staggering human toll. The symbolism is important because the message must be sent that in a society governed by the rule of law, Mr. Madoff will get what he deserves, and that he will be punished according to his moral culpability.

Second, deterrence. Another important goal of punishment is deterrence, and the symbolism is important here because the strongest possible message must be sent to those who would engage in similar conduct that they will be caught and that they will be punished to the fullest extent of the law.

Finally, the symbolism is also important for the victims. The victims include individuals from all walks of life. The victims include charities, both large and small, as well as academic institutions, pension funds, and other entities. Mr. Madoff's very personal betrayal struck at the rich and the not-so-rich, the elderly living on retirement funds and social security, middle class folks trying to put their kids through college, and ordinary people who worked hard to save their money and who thought they were investing it safely, for themselves and their families.

I received letters, and we have heard from for example, a retired forest worker, a corrections offices, an auto mechanic, a physical therapist, a retired New York City school secretary, who is now 86 years old and widowed, who must deal with the loss of her retirement funds. Their money is gone, leaving only a sense of betrayal.

I was particularly struck by one story that I read in the letters. A man invested his family's life savings with Mr. Madoff. Tragically, he died of a heart attack just two weeks later. The widow eventually went in to see Mr. Madoff. He put his arm around her, as she describes it, and in a kindly manner told her not to worry, the money is safe with me. And so not only did the widow leave the money with him, she eventually deposited more funds with him, her 401(k), her pension funds. Now, all the money is gone. She will have to sell her home, and she will not be able to keep her promise to help her granddaughter pay for college.

A substantial sentence will not give the victims back their retirement funds or the moneys they saved to send their children or grandchildren to college. It will not give them back their financial security or the freedom from financial worry. But more is at stake than money, as we have heard. The victims put their trust in Mr. Madoff. That trust was broken in a way that has left many—victims as well as others—doubting our financial institutions, our financial system, our government's ability to regulate and protect, and sadly, even themselves.

I do not agree that the victims are succumbing to the temptation of mob vengeance. Rather, they are doing what they are supposed to be doing—placing their trust in our system of justice. A substantial sentence, the knowledge that Mr. Madoff has been punished to the fullest extent of the law, may, in some small measure, help these victims in their healing process.

Mr. Madoff, please stand.

It is the judgment of this Court that the defendant, Bernard L. Madoff, shall be and hereby is sentenced to a term of imprisonment of 150 years, consisting of 20 years on each of Counts 1, 3, 4, 5, 6, and 10, 5 years on each of Counts 2, 8, 9, and 11, and 10 years on Count 7, all to run consecutively to each other. As a technical matter, the sentence must be expressed on the judgment in months. 150 years is equivalent to 1,800 months.

Although it is academic, for technical reasons, I must also impose supervised release. I impose a term of supervised release of 3 years on each count, all to run concurrently.

I will not impose a fine, as whatever assets Mr. Madoff has, as to whatever assets may be found, they shall be applied to restitution for the victims.

...

THE COURT: Mr. Madoff, please stand one more time.

Mr. Madoff, you have the right to appeal at least certain aspects of this judgment and conviction. If you wish to appeal, you must do so within ten days. If you cannot afford an attorney, the court will appoint one for you.

We are adjourned.

SCENARIO

Assume that you have been appointed by the Securities and Exchange Commission (SEC) to an advisory committee whose task is to make recommendations how the SEC can improve its detection of major investor frauds. The current economic and political situations are such that the SEC will not receive a significant increase of funds from Congress to hire more enforcement personnel.[1] What are some of the

1 Indeed, Congress evidently has not appropriated sufficient funds for the SEC to adequately undertake the agency's enhanced responsibilities mandated by the Dodd-Frank Act of 2010. See Hilzenath, *Budget Freeze Hampers Oversight, SEC Chair Says,* Wash. Post, Feb. 5, 2011, at A10; Holzer, *SEC Watchdog in a Plea for Cash,* Wall St. J., Feb. 11, at C6. Note that Section 922 of the Dodd-Frank Act provides that whistleblowers are entitled from ten percent to thirty percent of any penalties paid exceeding $1 million in SEC enforcement actions when the whistleblower provided original information that significantly contributed to the successful enforcement action. It remains to be seen whether this provision will induce whistleblowers to reveal frauds to the SEC, thereby helping the Commission to aptly enforce the securities laws.

key issues which should be explored to determine what recommendations are suitable?

CPSIA information can be obtained
at www.ICGtesting.com
Printed in the USA
LVHW101918090721
692312LV00003B/13

9 781609 277826